CHURCHILL'S
EMPIRE

Also by Richard Toye

LLOYD GEORGE AND CHURCHILL:
RIVALS FOR GREATNESS

RICHARD TOYE

CHURCHILL'S EMPIRE

*The World that Made Him
and the World He Made*

MACMILLAN

First published 2010 by Macmillan
an imprint of Pan Macmillan, a division of Macmillan Publishers Limited
Pan Macmillan, 20 New Wharf Road, London N1 9RR
Basingstoke and Oxford
Associated companies throughout the world
www.panmacmillan.com

ISBN 978-0-230-70384-1

A CIP catalogue record for this book is available from
the British Library.

Typeset by SetSystems Ltd, Saffron Walden, Essex
Printed in the UK by CPI Mackays, Chatham ME5 8TD

Although he didn't like to do so, Mr Churchill ended the stage of the British Empire. That was not his subjective will. He said that to President Roosevelt. But objectively he ended the British Empire.

Chou En Lai to Henry Kissinger, 20 October 1971.

Contents

PART THREE

LIQUIDATION

PROLOGUE

ON 10 DECEMBER 1954 a visitor from East Africa was waiting on a horsehair sofa in the hallway of 10 Downing Street. Suddenly, the small, frail figure of Winston Churchill appeared from behind a screen, said, 'Good afternoon, Mr Blundell,' and offered him a slightly stiffened hand to shake. The two men went together into the Cabinet Room. It was only three o'clock but Churchill – smoking his customary cigar – ordered them both a strong whisky and soda. As they sipped their drinks, their meeting, scheduled to take fifteen minutes, spilled out to last forty-five. The topic was the Mau Mau rebellion against British colonial rule in Kenya; and Michael Blundell, a prominent white settler with a somewhat spurious reputation as a liberal, was given an impassioned exposition of the Prime Minister's views.

Churchill began by recalling his own visit to the country in 1907. Then, he had found the Kikuyu group, from which most of the rebels were now drawn, to be 'a happy, naked and charming people'. He professed himself 'astonished at the change which had come over their minds'. He became animated over the problem of how settlers might be protected from attack, and he poured out a flood of ideas designed to defend farmers: trip-wires, bells and other early warning systems. But in his view the issue was not really a military one – the problem was to get to the rebels' minds. His eyes grew tearful as he told Blundell of the threat the situation posed to Britain's good name in the world. It was terrible that the country that was the home of culture, magnanimity and democracy should be using force to suppress Mau Mau. 'It's the power of a modern nation being used to kill savages. It's pretty terrible,' he declared. 'Savages, savages? Not savages. They're savages armed with ideas – much more difficult to deal with.'

Over and again he pressed on a reluctant Blundell the need for negotiation, arguing that the strength of the hold the Mau Mau had on the Kikuyu proved that the latter were not primitive, stupid and cowardly, as was often imagined. Rather, 'they were persons of considerable fibre and ability and steel, who could be brought to our side by just and wise treatment'. He offered an analogy with his own role in finding a solution for the problem of Ireland after World War I, when he had negotiated with the nationalist leader Michael Collins, once a hard-line terrorist opponent of the British. Churchill also deplored British brutality against the Kenyan rebels and the fact that so many of the local population were locked up in detention camps, before offering his views on race relations. He was old-fashioned, he said, and 'did not really think that black people were as capable or as efficient as white people'. All the same, 'If I meet a black man and he's a civilized educated fellow I have no feelings about him at all.' He showed some scepticism about the white settlers too, 'a highly individualistic and difficult people', although he put some of their attitude down to 'tension from the altitude' in the highland areas in which they lived. When Blundell asked him for a message of encouragement to pass on to them, he declined, but, as his visitor got up to leave, Churchill assured him that he was on the right path and had his support. Blundell wished him a slightly belated happy eightieth birthday, and the Prime Minister looked greatly touched. He was beginning to feel his age, he said. Then he revealed a secret that had been kept from the outside world: 'Hm. I've had two strokes. Most people don't know that, but it's a fact. I keep going.' Blundell deduced that this accounted for the stiffened handshake at the beginning. Churchill walked him to the exit of the room and then, when Blundell had gone about five steps into the hall, wished him goodbye and good luck.[1]

This conversation did not mark any great turning point in the history of Kenya. Churchill, just months from retirement, was no longer in a position to be a major influence on colonial policy. Nevertheless, it was highly revealing of his attitudes to race and Empire, touching numerous themes that had been present through-out his career. There were so many familiar hallmarks: the gift for a phrase ('savages armed with ideas'), the recollection of a happier, more innocent past, the emphasis on magnanimity and negotiating from strength. Also familiar was his unashamed belief in white

superiority, a conviction which, for him, however, did not lessen the
need to act humanely towards supposedly inferior races that might,
in their own way, be worthy of admiration. Recognizable as part of
this was his opinion that members of these races might earn equal
treatment, if not exactly warm acceptance, provided they reached
an approved cultural standard: a 'civilized educated' black man
would provoke 'no feelings' in him. Overall, the striking thing is the
complexity of his opinions. He emerges from Blundell's account of
the discussion as a holder of racist views but not as an imperial
diehard. He comes across in his plea for peace talks as a thoughtful
visionary, but also, in his description of the formerly 'happy, naked'
Kikuyu, as curiously naïve about the realities of imperialism. He
was prepared to question the conduct of a dirty colonial war, but
was in the end willing to assure its supporters of his backing.

Churchill's conversation with Blundell is a good starting point
for consideration of his lifelong involvement with the British Empire,
and the general attitudes to it from which his specific policies flowed.
In order to do this we need to contend with his reputation – or
reputations – on imperial issues. The popular image of him, which
draws in particular on his opposition to Indian independence in
the 1930s and 1940s, is of a last-ditcher for whom the integrity
of the Empire was paramount. Yet many of his contemporaries had
viewed him differently. As a youthful minister at the Colonial Office
in the Edwardian period, political antagonists had described him as
a Little Englander and a danger to the Empire. ('Little Englandism',
which today carries connotations of anti-European xenophobia, at
the time implied opposition to imperial expansion and to foreign
entanglements in general; it was often used as a term of abuse.) As
late as 1920, even the wild-eyed socialist MP James Maxton would
claim disapprovingly that 'the British Empire was approaching
complete disintegration' and that 'it was not going too far to say
that Mr Churchill had played a primary party in bringing about
that state of affairs'.[2] Such critics, it should be noted, were not
alleging that Churchill was actively hostile to the Empire, more that
it was not safe in his hands or that he was comparatively indifferent
to it. By the time of Churchill's final term in office, this view was
still maintained by a tenacious few. In 1953 the Conservative
politician Earl Winterton wrote to Leo Amery, one of Churchill's
former wartime colleagues, to congratulate him on the first volume

of his memoirs. He told him: 'I am particularly pleased that you have, whilst paying a tribute to Winston's great patriotism, stated, which is indubitably the case, that he has never been an imperialist in the sense that you and I are; we suffered from this point of view during the war, whilst we were in opposition after the war and are still suffering from it to-day.'[3]

Although similar opinions can be found in the historical literature, such contemporary opinions of Churchill need to be treated with some caution.[4] Those who accused him of not caring enough about the Empire often meant, underneath, that he did not happen to share their particular view of it. Nor is the conventional image completely misleading. Although during his post-1931 wilderness years Churchill publicly disclaimed the diehard label, it is clear that he came to revel in it. During the war, the topic of India frequently triggered such extreme reactions in him that he sometimes appeared not quite sane.[5] Nevertheless, this man who could be so disdainful of non-white peoples – 'I hate people with slit eyes & pig-tails' – also had another side to him.[6] In 1906, when criticizing the 'chronic bloodshed' caused by British punitive raids in West Africa, it was he who sarcastically wrote: 'the whole enterprise is liable to be misrepresented by persons unacquainted with Imperial terminology as the murdering of natives and stealing of their lands'.[7] As his talk with Blundell shows, this concern for the welfare of subject peoples stayed with him until the end of his career. In 1921, as Secretary of State for the Colonies, he stated that within the British Empire 'there should be no barrier of race, colour or creed which should prevent any man from reaching any station if he is fitted for it'. Yet he immediately qualified this by adding that 'such a principle has to be very carefully and gradually applied because intense local feelings are excited', which was in effect a way of saying that its implementation should be delayed indefinitely.[8] As one Indian politician put it the following year, when noting Churchill's seemingly inconsistent position on the controversial question of Asians in East Africa, it was 'a case, and a very strange case indeed', of the story of Dr Jekyll and Mr Hyde.[9]

Therefore, in order to understand the origins and impact of Churchill's imperialism, we do not need to overthrow the conventional picture so much as to understand how it arose. We also need to see why, during the second half of his career, it came to crowd

out the story in which he appeared as a conciliator and even as a
Radical. In order to do these things, we need a firm grasp of the
world in which he grew up and began to make his career at the end
of the nineteenth century. The British Empire at that time was in a
phase of rapid expansion, driven by multiple forces, from private
trading and missionary activity to international great-power rivalries.
At the time of Churchill's birth, in 1874, it was about to embark on
its most triumphant phase. In 1877, amid great controversy, Queen
Victoria was crowned 'Empress of India', in a symbolic adornment
of the longstanding British control of the subcontinent. During the
1880s, Britain took part in the 'scramble for Africa', a race between
European powers for colonies, acquiring Bechuanaland, Nigeria,
Somaliland, Zululand, Kenya, Rhodesia and (in 1890) Zanzibar.
This was by no means the end point of the growth of the Empire;
there were further acquisitions at the end of World War I and, if
enemy colonies conquered during World War II are taken into
account, it reached its maximum territorial extent only in 1945.[10]
At its zenith, around 500 million people, or about a quarter of the
world's population, were British subjects.

The very speed of the expansion, and the multiplicity of motives
behind it, helped ensure a great diversity in methods of rule.
Terminology shifted throughout the period of Churchill's lifetime –
for example 'Commonwealth' gradually replaced 'Empire', to his
considerable chagrin – but for the period of his political maturity
certain broad generalizations are possible. Loosely speaking, the
'dominions' were those territories such as Australia, New Zealand
and Canada which had achieved a substantial (and progressively
increasing) level of political autonomy.[11] During the interwar years
they gained the formal right to secede from the Empire if they
wished. The 'colonies', by contrast, were overseas possessions where
the Crown retained proprietorship. They might nonetheless be
'self-governing', which meant that the white settler elites had considerable control over local affairs. There were also other forms of
governance, including the League of Nations 'mandates' granted to
Britain after World War I, as for example in Palestine. India,
anomalously, was neither a dominion nor a colony, British rule
there being to a substantial extent based on cooperation with loyal
Indian princes.[12]

Such distinctions were probably lost on the majority of the

British population at the time.[13] This, however, does not necessarily constitute proof that the masses were indifferent to the Empire. Churchill, for one, believed that the imperial zeitgeist of his school-boy years had left 'a permanent imprint upon the national mind'.[14] As Churchill's headmaster at Harrow school put it in 1895:

> if the Elizabethan era marks the beginning, it is not less true that the Victorian era marks the consummation of the British Empire. The seventeenth century may be said to be the age of individual explorers, the eighteenth of commercial companies, the nineteenth of the State. [. . .] It is not the expansion of Empire, it is the spirit of Empire, which is the characteristic of the reign of Queen Victoria.[15]

This new spirit may have been largely restricted to elites; but then, Churchill was one of the elite.

The observation that this background was important is hardly original. When Jawaharlal Nehru (who was to become the first Prime Minister of independent India) remarked during World War II that Churchill had 'a Victorian mind' it served as a convenient way of saying that he was a reactionary.[16] Historians criticizing Churchill have often used similar shorthand.[17] Churchill's defenders also point to his Victorianism, but present it in a different way. For example his former private secretary John Colville, in a foreword to a new edition of *The River War*, Churchill's 1899 work on Kitchener's Sudan campaign, wrote the following.

> Churchill's imperialism, faithfully representing the feelings of his fellow-countrymen at this apogee of the British Empire, emerges clearly from this book: but it should be judged by the generally accepted standards prevailing at the end of the Victorian era and not by those in fashion today. [. . .] Churchill, for his part, was antagonised by Kitchener's ruthless treatment of the defeated Dervishes, whose courage he respected.[18]

Similarly, one sympathetic historian, seeking to explain Churchill's toleration of discrimination against black Africans, writes: 'Churchill was a Victorian by upbringing [. . .] and most Britons of his generation regarded black Africans as backward and relatively uncivilized.' But, he adds, 'Churchill's own outlook was more informed and relatively enlightened.'[19]

The defenders' pleas for contextualization are, on the surface, highly plausible. However, they are also problematic. References to 'generally accepted standards', and to the views of 'most Britons', do less than full justice to the range of opinion in Victorian Britain to which Churchill was exposed. Furthermore, we are being asked to believe two contradictory things simultaneously. On the one hand, it is suggested, the seemingly unpleasant aspects of his racial thinking can be excused on the grounds that he could not have been expected to escape from the mentality prevailing during his youth. On the other hand, we are told, he *did* escape it and is to be praised because he was actually unusually enlightened! We should not, in fact, use Churchill's Victorian background as an historical 'get out of jail free' card for him any more than we should use it as a blanket label of condemnation. In order to understand its true importance, it is necessary to appreciate that his Victorian heritage accounted for many of the apparently 'enlightened' elements of Churchill's thought as well as many of the 'reactionary' ones. At the same time, his attitudes in later life were not always a straight-forward extension of the ones he held earlier. He himself said that he 'had inclined more to the right as he got older', but there were some changes in his views that cannot be easily located on a left–right spectrum.[20] For example, although he showed much hostility to Islam in his early writings, this died away and was replaced during the interwar years with a near-fanatical hatred of Hinduism. In 1943 he remarked, 'I'm pro-Moslem – the only quality of the Hindus is that there's a lot of them and that is a vice'.[21]

This book aims at genuine explanation of these complex patterns, not tub-thumping or apologetics. Remarkable as it may seem, it is the first attempt to provide a comprehensive treatment of Churchill's relationship with the Empire within a single volume.[22] There have been some excellent short overviews, and numerous books dealing with particular countries, periods, themes and individuals, but no one has tackled the problem as a whole at volume length.[23] The task is indeed a daunting one, and it is not possible within the scope of this book to give an exhaustive treatment of every single imperial issue with which Churchill was involved. It is, however, feasible to investigate the key features of the most important episodes and questions. Furthermore, there is significant new evidence that can be brought to bear on many of them. For example, the unpublished

letters of Lady Lugard cast fresh light on the first controversial
months of Churchill's ministerial career, and the recently released
Cabinet Secretaries' notebooks (preserved for the post-1942 period)
increase our understanding of his involvement in episodes such as
the Mau Mau uprising.

The treasures of the archives should not, however, lead us to
neglect published sources, not least the many forgotten reviews of
Churchill's early books. These help us reconstruct the ideological
world in which Churchill was operating and improve our understanding of his arguments. They also remind us that, even if he
himself viewed his youthful imperial adventures simply as a shortcut
to a political career, they need to be considered more broadly.[24]
They were the means by which he established a reputation as the
premier 'public journalist of the Empire'.[25] As such, he did not
merely represent the Empire to the British people but affected the
way it was seen throughout the world. Churchill became a global
brand, inextricably mixed up with the image of the Empire, a
process that began in the 1890s and reached its culmination during
World War II. In one propaganda film shown in Africa, for
example, the war was portrayed as a jungle fight between a snake,
labelled 'Hitler', and its deadly enemy the mongoose, labelled
'Churchill'.[26] Not, of course, that the intended message always got
through: in the 1960s one Zambian woman obtained a devoted
religious following by playing an entirely worn-out record of one
of Churchill's wartime speeches on an ancient phonograph. She
persuaded the crowds that the incomprehensible rumbling was
'God's voice anointing her his emissary and commanding absolute
obeisance'.[27]

Therefore, this book does not adopt a purely biographical
approach but explores Churchill's career within the context of the
experiences and opinions of his contemporaries. It looks at attitudes
and ideas as well as events and policies; crucially, it also examines
the way in which Churchill was perceived and his messages understood not only in Britain but throughout the Empire. He must be
seen not only through his own words but also through the eyes of
his contemporaries. One such figure who recurs repeatedly in our
story is Leo Amery. It was said of him that had he been half a head
taller, and his speeches half an hour shorter, he could have been
Prime Minister.[28] As it was, he ended up – after some vicissitudes in

the two men's relations – as Churchill's Secretary of State for India in 1940–45. At the end of the war he was to suffer an appalling personal tragedy when his son was hanged for treason. For our purposes his career forms a useful counterpoint to that of Churchill. Moreover, for decades Amery maintained in his diary that Churchill was 'not really interested in the Empire'.[29] In fact, they both shared a strong commitment to the Empire, but that commitment took a very different form for each of them. Other figures that recur in these pages include the Canadian politician W. L. Mackenzie King and the South African J. C. Smuts as well, inescapably, as two key founders of modern India: M. K. Gandhi and Jawaharlal Nehru. Opinion of Churchill in the non-white parts of the Empire is a neglected area of study.[30] One insight that emerges from it is that colonial nationalist reactions to him were often far more subtle and nuanced than later criticisms from some individuals within the former Empire might lead one to expect.

Churchill's Empire – the picture he kept in his head and which he relayed in his speeches and writings – was a selective and sometimes superficial construct. This was in part because his direct experience of the Empire was incomplete. He saw much of Canada and the Middle East, and visited East Africa in 1907, but he did not return to India after the 1890s, or to South Africa after 1900, and never visited West Africa, Australia, New Zealand, or Britain's Far Eastern possessions.[31] Nevertheless, by the standards of most people at the time, his experience was wide indeed. This book relates how it interacted with other influences – intellectual, social and political – to shape the man that he became. It also shows how he in turn shaped, for good and ill, the world in which we live today.

Acknowledgements

While researching and writing this book I have accumulated many debts of gratitude. The first is to Jamie Wendell, who volunteered to act as a research assistant during the summer of 2007. His intelligence and capacity for hard work made him an ideal researcher, and the completion of the project was greatly speeded by his help. I am also grateful to my erstwhile colleagues at Homerton College, Cambridge, and my current ones at the University of Exeter. Both have been excellent places to work. I am glad as well to have had the assistance of numerous librarians and archivists, in particular Allen Packwood and his team at the Churchill Archives Centre, Cambridge. Quotations from the writings of Winston Churchill are reproduced with permission of Curtis Brown Ltd., London, on behalf of The Estate of Winston Churchill. Copyright Winston S. Churchill. A Leverhulme Research Fellowship in 2008–9 ensured that I could complete the book in a timely fashion.

Ahmed Abu-Zayed, David Anderson, Daniel Branch, Bruce Coleman, Michael Duffy, Andrew Thorpe and Stuart Ward all provided me with helpful information. Ronald Hyam, Stacey Hynd and Martin Thomas helped save me from error by reading the manuscript, in whole or in part. The guidance of all of them has been invaluable; any errors that remain are, of course, my own responsibility.

I am grateful too to my agent, Natasha Fairweather, and her assistants at A. P. Watt. Georgina Morley and Natasha Martin at Macmillan provided me with encouragement and thoughtful detailed guidance. Trevor Horwood made an excellent job of the copyediting.

My parents Janet and John Toye were, as ever, highly supportive throughout. So was my wife, Kristine, who read the entire manuscript with an eagle eye. It is to her and our sons Sven and Tristan that I dedicate this book.

PART ONE

RATIONALISM AND MACHINE GUNS

1

LEARNING TO THINK IMPERIALLY, 1874–1897

IN JUNE 1939 the MP and diarist Harold Nicolson attended a dinner at which Winston Churchill was the guest of honour. Also present was the celebrated American columnist Walter Lippmann. Lippmann told the assembled company that Joseph Kennedy, the appeasement-minded US ambassador to Britain, 'had informed him that war was inevitable' and that the British would 'be licked'. According to Nicolson, this reported defeatism prompted Churchill into 'a magnificent oration', during which he sat hunched, 'waving his whisky-and-soda to mark his periods, stubbing his cigar with the other hand'. He did not deny that the coming war would bring 'dire peril and fierce ordeals', but said that these would merely steel the British people and enhance their will for victory. He addressed Lippmann:

> Yet supposing (as I do not for one moment suppose) that Mr Kennedy were correct in his tragic utterance, then I for one would willingly lay down my life in combat, rather than, in fear of defeat, surrender to the menaces of these most sinister men. It will then be for you, for the Americans, to preserve and to maintain the great heritage of the English-speaking peoples. It will be for you to think imperially, which means to think always of something higher and more vast than one's own national interests.

Churchill reached a stirring peroration in which he envisaged the torch of liberty continuing to burn 'untarnished and (I trust and hope) undismayed'. And then, as Nicolson noted laconically, discussion moved to the topic of the giant panda.[1]

Churchill's injunction to the Americans to 'think imperially' was an echo of Joseph Chamberlain's injunction to the British people thirty-five years earlier.[2] Chamberlain made his remark during his crusade to integrate the British Empire as an economic bloc – a campaign that Churchill had opposed, to the point of leaving the Conservatives for the Liberals in order to combat it. He now gave his own construction of imperialism, which – doubtless with historic US anti-imperialism in mind – he defined simply as meaning to take responsibility in international affairs. That, though, was very different from his own past (and future) interpretations of the word. But where had his own ideas come from? His biographers, when they comment on such questions at all, tend to content themselves with generalizations such as 'Churchill absorbed the spirit of imperialism with the air he breathed',[3] or observe that he accepted contemporary ideas of Anglo-Saxon superiority 'unquestioningly'.[4] It is possible to discuss his early influences with a little more precision than this. This chapter will explore how it was that Winston Churchill learnt to think imperially, a story that is more complex than is often assumed.

I

Churchill's first public speech was made in defence of the Empire – the Empire Palace of Varieties in London's Leicester Square. It was November 1894. He was a cadet at the Royal Military College at Sandhurst and about to turn twenty. The theatre concerned was one of his favourite haunts, even though his beloved former nurse, Mrs Everest, had warned him against going there: 'it is too awful to think of, it can only lead to wickedness and everything bad'.[5] Morality campaigners shared her anxieties, and were now opposing the renewal of the Empire's music and dancing licence. They alleged that prostitutes solicited there, and that the dancing on stage 'was designed to excite impure thought and passion'.[6] Regarded by the young Churchill as detestable prudes, the puritans were particularly exercised by the theatre's Promenade, a space behind the dress circle in which men and women mingled freely and even drank alcohol. As a condition of renewing the licence, the London County Council insisted that no liquor be served in the auditorium, so the management erected canvas screens between the Promenade and the adjoining bars. The next Saturday, Churchill, on weekend leave, was there when the infuriated crowd 'rushed upon these flimsy barricades and tore them to pieces'.[7] Indeed, he afterwards boasted to his brother, 'It was I who led the rioters'.[8] He later recalled how, 'Mounting on the débris and indeed partially emerging from it, I addressed the tumultuous crowd.' He did not make worthy arguments about the traditions of British freedom but instead won the applause of the mob by appealing 'directly to sentiment and even passion'.[9] Then everyone spilled out into the night air, with the violent assistance of the theatre's 'chuckers out'.[10] But the riot was to no avail: the barricades were soon built again in brick.

Churchill's second speech, nearly three years later, was a rather more sober affair. It was to a Primrose League fête near Bath. The League was a national organization that aimed to marshal mass support for the Conservative Party. It was inclusive, insofar as working men (even if non-voters) and women could join, but also deeply hierarchical. (Churchill, who joined at the age of thirteen, achieved the rank of 'knight' two years later.)[11] As he reminded the Bath gathering, the League's mission was to teach the British people 'the splendour of their Empire, the nature of their Constitution, and the importance of their fleet'. His speech was notable as his first attempt to draw attention to himself politically, in the hope of finding a Tory seat in Parliament. In terms of the imperial sentiments he expressed, it is interesting for two reasons. First, Churchill was aware that many people believed that the Empire, in what was Queen Victoria's diamond jubilee year, had already reached its apogee, and from now on could only decline. Second, he radiated confidence (as his audience would surely have expected) that Britain's mission would continue unabated. To cheers from his audience, he declared: 'Do not believe these croakers but give the lie to their dismal croaking by showing by our actions that the vigour and vitality of our race is unimpaired and that our determination is to uphold the Empire that we have inherited from our fathers as Englishmen'. In his view, the British would 'continue to pursue that course marked out for us by an all-wise hand and carry out our mission of bearing peace, civilisation and good government to the uttermost ends of the earth'.[12]

Much had happened to Churchill in the interval between these two speeches. In January 1895 his father, Lord Randolph Churchill, died at the age of forty-five from a degenerative illness, possibly syphilis, his once-stellar political career having long since imploded. Then, having received an army commission – and following an adventurous trip to the United States and Cuba – the younger Churchill had been posted to India. There he had helped while away the tedium with an ambitious programme of self-education, trying to teach himself what he thought he had missed out on by not going to university. It is tempting to explain the contrast between the Leicester Square high-jinks and the high imperialism of the Bath meeting (which Churchill addressed while home on leave) as a symptom of these developments. In this interpretation, Churchill's new-found seriousness and direct experience of the Empire merged with a determination to vindicate his father's memory and at the same time achieve political fame in his own right. Conviction, reinforced by a wide reading of authors such as Edward Gibbon, dovetailed with a self-interested realization that a young man could draw attention to himself through daring exploits in the farther reaches of the British-ruled world. There is plenty of truth to be found in this view – which Churchill rather encouraged in his memoirs – but it is not the whole truth. Although he may not have been fully aware of it himself, Churchill's imperial conscious-ness began to form long before the autodidact phase of his early twenties.

As an adult, Churchill wrote that he had taken his politics 'almost unquestioningly' from his father.[13] This claim was perfectly sincere, but it cannot be accepted completely at face value, as an examination of Lord Randolph's thought and career will show. He was born in 1849, the third son of the seventh Duke of Marlbor-ough. He grew up to be an able but erratic youth, who could be genuinely charming but also witheringly scornful when (as often) he was displeased. He studied at Oxford University and was praised by his examiners for his knowledge of Gibbon's *Decline and Fall of the Roman Empire* – and Winston Churchill later read Gibbon in part because he had been told of its influence on Lord Randolph.[14] In 1873 Lord Randolph met and fell in love with Jennie Jerome, the nineteen-year-old daughter of a well-known New York businessman, but it took some time for the couple to overcome their parents' opposition to their marriage. The wedding eventually took place in April 1874, a few months after Lord Randolph had been elected as Conservative MP for Woodstock – a position he owed largely to his father's powerful local influence. A mere seven and a half months after the nuptials, Jennie gave birth to Winston Leonard Spencer-Churchill at Blenheim Palace, the spectacularly grand Marlborough family seat. The announcement in *The Times* claimed, perhaps not wholly plausibly, that the birth was premature.[15]

Lord Randolph applied himself more to high society than to the House of Commons, but he soon made a catastrophic social faux pas. His elder brother, the Marquis of Blandford, had an affair with Lady Aylesford while her husband was visiting India in 1875. Lord Aylesford wanted a divorce, which, if it went ahead, would drag Blandford's name into a public scandal. To avoid this, Lord Randolph pressed his friend the Prince of Wales to use his influence to halt the proceedings. Were this not done, he threatened to make public the Prince's own indiscreet letters to Lady Aylesford. The Prince was naturally outraged at this attempted blackmail, and Lord Randolph was ostracized from society as a result. A kind of exile followed when the Prime Minister, Benjamin Disraeli, offered his father the Lord-Lieutenancy of Ireland, and Lord Randolph went with him as his private secretary. Winston Churchill's first memory was of the Duke, his grandfather, unveiling a statue of the imperial hero, Lord Gough, in Dublin's Phoenix Park. The statue is no longer there, removed following the IRA's attempts to blow it up in the 1950s.

Ireland was already troubled by violence during Winston Churchill's childhood. Attempts at religious and educational reform by Gladstone's Liberals had failed to quell a nationalist upsurge driven by economic distress and a sharp sense of resentment at British rule. The armed revolutionaries of the Irish Republican Brotherhood, often referred to as the Fenians, were not of the political mainstream but they conjured a fearsome reputation. 'My nurse, Mrs Everest, was nervous about the Fenians', Churchill recalled. 'I gathered these were wicked people and there was no end to what they would do if they had their way.'[16] Later on, Gladstone was converted to the concept of Home Rule, under which control of Irish affairs would have been delegated from Westminster to Dublin. Lord Randolph, for his part, adopted a notoriously hard line against this plan. It would, he argued, plunge a knife into the heart of the British Empire. Moreover, the north of Ireland was dominated by Protestants, who feared subjection to the will of the

Catholic majority. 'Ulster will fight,' Lord Randolph declared at a crucial moment during the battles of the 1880s; 'Ulster will be right'.[17] Yet although Winston Churchill for some years shared his father's opposition to Home Rule, he was to prove much more flexible once he became a minister. Although protective of his father's memory, he did not adhere slavishly to his political positions.

In 1880 Disraeli was defeated at the general election and the Duke of Marlborough's time in Dublin came to an end. The social boycott of Lord Randolph had eased, and he began to make his mark as a Tory MP. He led a small group known as the 'Fourth Party', attacking Gladstone's Liberal government vigorously; he also fell out with the new leaders on account of his failure to toe the official party line. He became known as an advocate of 'Tory Democracy', a slogan Winston Churchill would adopt, although in Lord Randolph's hands it did not have much substance; some historians have accused him of inconsistency and opportunism. There was, however, something attractive in his very unpredictability, which extended to imperial issues, as the question of Egypt showed.

Egypt was part of the Ottoman Empire, ruled inefficiently by the Khedive, the Sultan's representative, and was massively indebted to European bondholders. In 1882 Britain intervened to put down a nationalist revolt and thus protect her investments. After the rebels were defeated by her forces at the Battle of Tel-el-Kebir in September, real power in Egypt was exercised by the British, although the Khedive still owed nominal allegiance to the Sultan. To some it seemed a dirty business. Wilfrid Scawen Blunt, poet, horse-breeder, womanizer and adventurer, was the anti-imperialist in chief. (He is best known for his later verse riposte to Rudyard Kipling: 'The White Man's Burden, Lord, is the burden of his cash'.)[18] A supporter of the Egyptian nationalists, he had returned from Cairo to put their case to Gladstone, but had been unable to forestall the British action. He came to believe that the Khedive had deliberately inspired a deadly riot that took place at Alexandria (and was then blamed on the nationalists) in order to draw the British in. Seeking help in drawing attention to his allegations, Blunt approached Lord Randolph, whom he recalled as a 'distinctly good-looking young man' with a 'certain distinction of manner' and a curling moustache that 'gave an aggressive tone to his countenance'.[19] Lord Randolph was persuaded of Blunt's case, and during 1883 publicly pressed the charge that the government was complicit in the actions of the Khedive, their 'puppet and ally'.[20] (He also described the execution of one nationalist officer, after a trial of doubtful fairness, as 'the grossest and vilest judicial murder that ever stained the annals of Oriental justice'.)[21] He may not have proven his accusations beyond all doubt, but he certainly made the government feel deeply uncomfortable. As Winston Churchill observed in his biography of his father, it was remarkable that, in officially rejecting the evidence he provided, 'the Government took no steps, by rebutting it in detail, to discredit their pertinacious assailant'.[22] Lord Randolph had undoubtedly demonstrated his unconventionality but he was no opponent of the Empire. He objected not to imperial rule per se, but to the halfway-house situation whereby the British propped up an unjust regime in Cairo. He declared that the government should either withdraw entirely or take total control: 'Let them take Egypt altogether if they liked, but let the country be under persons responsible to the English Government who would rid the country of its burdens and raise up the fellaheen from their present low state.'[23]

His chief concern was to find sticks with which to beat the government. The following year he lacerated ministers for their failure to go to the rescue of General Charles Gordon, Governor-General of the Sudan, who was under siege in Khartoum. The government eventually sent a relief mission, but too late. It arrived, in January 1885, two days after the city had fallen to the forces of the Mahdi ('The Expected One'), the charismatic Islamic leader who was determined to end Egyptian rule in his country. Gordon's brutal death by spearing at the hands of the Mahdi's warriors turned him into an imperial icon and helped seal the fate of Gladstone's government, which fell in June. In spite of Lord Randolph's tense relationship with his own party's leadership, he had won national popularity, bolstered by speeches in which he urged 'a policy of activity for the national welfare, combined with a zeal for Imperial security'.[24] Lord Salisbury, Prime Minister of the new minority Tory administration, could not fail to give him a Cabinet post, and appointed him Secretary of State for India.

His seven-month tenure at the India Office gave full play to the contradictions in his imperial attitudes. He had already made a long visit to India in advance of his appointment, and taken the trouble to meet a range of Indian intellectuals, politicians and journalists. Lala Baijnath, a lawyer, was 'greatly astonished at his intimate knowledge of Indian subjects as well as those discussed by the native papers'.[25] Nationalism was just beginning to flower in the country – the first Indian National Congress was held later in 1885 – and Lord Randolph appeared to be a polite and intelligent listener. He wrote to his mother: 'The natives are much pleased when one goes to their houses, for the officials out here hold themselves much too high and never seek any intercourse with the natives out of official lines; they are very foolish.'[26] He seemed genuinely to like the country (something that cannot be said of his son) and he won praise from papers such as the *Indian Spectator*, the *Bengalee* and the *Hindoo Patriot*.[27]

Back in England, and in office, Lord Randolph changed his tune. He had never doubted the benefits of British rule in India, even if – like many of its other supporters at the time – he admitted it to be 'purely despotic'.[28] (In a remark particularly admired by his son, he described the Raj as 'a sheet of oil spread out over the surface of, and keeping calm and quiet and unruffled by storms, an immense and profound ocean of humanity'.)[29] There was, however, the question of emphasis, and in language and policy he now showed himself a reactionary. The change was exemplified by his treatment of a delegation of Indians that came to Britain 'to advocate advanced native views of a Home Rule kind'.[30] At an interview arranged by Blunt, Churchill was charm itself, if politically noncommittal. 'Nothing could have exceeded the grace and kindliness with which Lord Randolph shook hands with us', recollected N. G. Chandavarkar. 'I do not wonder that they make a hero of him on Tory platforms.'[31] During that November's general election, however, the delegates lent support to John Bright, Lord Randolph's Liberal opponent in Central Birmingham, the constituency he was now fighting. He now mocked the 'ignorance and credulity' of the Indians, and added: 'what must be the desperation of the radical party when, in order to secure the return of Mr Bright, they had to bring down on the platform of that great Town Hall three Bengalee baboos'.[32] In the meantime Churchill had set in train the annexation of Upper Burma, which he clearly hoped would win him further Birmingham votes. The apparent liberality of the sentiments he had expressed in India had been replaced by military expansionism and cheap platform sneers.

Lord Randolph lost narrowly in Birmingham (although he easily found a new London seat) and the Tories lost the election as a whole. After Salisbury's government fell in January 1886, Gladstone became Prime Minister again, but his determination to press ahead with Home Rule in Ireland led to his defeat and split his party in two. At a further election in July the Liberals met with disaster, and were thereafter to be denied effective power for nearly twenty years. Lord Randolph, though, was to gain little in career terms from the new Tory hegemony. At first his star continued to rise. Salisbury appointed him – when he was still only thirty-seven – Chancellor of the Exchequer and Leader of the House of Commons. But his marriage was in difficulty (money worries may have contributed to this), he appeared ill, and he proved to be a mercurial, intemperate and ultimately impossible colleague. In December 1886, in an attempt to secure economy in naval spending, he offered his resignation. Greatly to his surprise, Salisbury accepted it. Lord Randolph never held office again. But his strangest imperial adventure was yet to come.

Within a few years, he was convinced that the Tory leaders meant to drive him out of the party: 'I am not yet however clear that being driven out of the party is equivalent to being driven out of public life.'[33] Indeed not. In February 1891 *The Times* reported that he had decided to visit South Africa; three months later the *Daily Graphic* announced that he had given its proprietors 'the exclusive right to publish a Series of Letters signed by himself, giving a detailed account of his experiences'.[34] He was to be paid the incredible sum of two thousand guineas for twenty letters. Owing to his and Jennie's wild extravagance, he needed the money; he hoped to further boost his fortunes through the gold-prospecting syndicate he had formed. The *Graphic* was certainly to get its money's worth, for once he arrived at Cape Town in May he began to generate spectacular and controversial copy. Almost everything he wrote – even his complaints about the catering onboard ship – generated heated debate at home. He attracted much criticism when he wrote that diamonds were mined in order to satisfy an 'essentially barbaric' feminine lust for personal adornment, and suggested that 'whatever may be the origin of man, woman is descended from an ape'.[35] His political pronouncements were startling too. He provocatively urged the British occupation of Portuguese territory on the Mozambique coast, following skirmishes between Portuguese soldiers and the forces of the British South Africa Company, at a time when the governments of Britain and Portugal were negotiating over the region. Perhaps most surprisingly, he endorsed the policy Gladstone had followed in South Africa in 1881. In that year, British defeat at the Battle of Majuba Hill had been followed by the restoration of the independent Boer republic of the Transvaal. (The Boers were Calvinists of mainly Dutch descent.) Many Conservatives had seen this as a pusillanimous imperial retreat, but Churchill now declared that the magnanimity of the peace settlement had allowed the British to escape 'a wretched and discreditable muddle, not without harm and damage, but probably in the best possible manner' given the circumstances.[36] In the future, the value of conciliating the Boers was not to be lost on Winston Churchill, although many factors weighed on him quite apart from his late father's opinions.

Lord Randolph's unexpected remarks about the Majuba episode did not prevent him being magnificently rude about the Boers themselves:

> The Boer farmer personifies useless idleness. [. . .] With the exception of the Bible, every word of which in its most literal interpretation he believes with fanatical credulity, he never opens a book, he never even reads a newspaper. His simple ignorance is unfathomable, and this in stolid composure he shares with his wife, his sons, his daughters, being proud that his children should grow up as ignorant, as uncultivated, as hopelessly unproductive as himself.[37]

Earlier, he had given a rather more positive impression of South Africa to Winston who, as a pupil at Harrow School, followed his progress avidly. A month into his tour Lord Randolph sent him an unusually affectionate letter. (He was by no means an attentive father, and when he wrote it was frequently to offer a reprimand.) 'I have been having a most agreeable travel in this very remarkable country', he wrote. 'I expect that when you are my age you will see S Africa to be the most populous and wealthy of all our colonies.'[38] Winston, for his part, informed Lord Randolph of the home press coverage, which he loyally denounced as 'exceedingly spiteful & vicious', and requested an antelope's head for his room.[39] 'I hear the horrid Boers are incensed with you', he told his father before going on to request some rare African stamps. 'It would have been much wiser, if you had waited till you came back before you "slanged the beggars".'[40]

To Lord Randolph's credit, his criticisms of the Boers included their treatment of black people. 'The Boer does not recognize that the native is in any degree raised above the level of the lower animals', he wrote, adding: 'His undying hatred for the English arises mainly from the fact that the English persist in according at least in theory equal rights to the coloured population as are enjoyed by whites.'[41] The 'at least in theory' was a very important reservation – and it should be noted that Lord Randolph did not hesitate to refer privately to 'niggers'[42] – but the willingness to pay lip service to equality shows that Victorian racial politics was rather more complex than is often assumed. Winston Churchill did not grow up in an atmosphere where straightforward and unqualified racism would invariably pass without challenge.

Lord Randolph's personal behaviour was highly eccentric. The degree to which this was a product of mental instability caused by illness is a moot point. His discourtesy to many of those he met on his journey could not but attract comment, and, when he travelled into Mashonaland, the mind-boggling extravagance of his expedition provoked the hilarity of the locals. (He took with him 103 oxen, a cow, 13 riding horses, 18 mules and a mare to run with them, 14 donkeys, 11 dogs, and 20 tons of food, ammunition and equipment.)[43] He seems to have been almost indifferent to the impression he was making, telling his mother that 'the carping and abuse of the Press' was due to jealousy of the amount he was being paid. Moreover, 'one must write the truth, and the truth is that the country is a disappointment and a failure'.[44] Lord Randolph's return to England was followed by a tragic mental and physical decline; his halting speeches became a horrible embarrassment. His friend Lord Rosebery famously observed, that 'He died by inches in public' and was 'the chief mourner at his own protracted funeral'.[45] In 1894 he started a world tour, which was cut short by a further collapse in his health. He died in London the following January.

His influence on Winston Churchill's world view in general, and on his imperialism in particular, is difficult to gauge. Lord Randolph never took his son, who so admired him, into his political confidence, so the latter's contemporary knowledge of his father's career was not much greater than any other observer's. 'When I became most closely acquainted with his thought and theme,' Winston later acknowledged, 'he was already dead.'[46] But the recently bereaved son threw himself into the study of his father's life, learning portions of his speeches by heart and even quoting them to acquaintances; one, made in patriotic opposition to the idea of a Channel tunnel, seemed to appeal to him specially.[47] In 1906 he published a massive and well-documented biography of Lord Randolph. By the time he finished it he had left the Conservative Party and was on the threshold of his ministerial career as a Liberal; he had abandoned the Tories after they had dropped their commitment to free trade, a highly controversial move that he thought would be economically damaging. With a combination of literary skill and judicious editing, he did his best in his book to iron out the inconsistencies in Lord Randolph's political journey and to play down facts that he himself found politically uncomfortable. For example, Winston, as a free trader, ignored evidence that Lord Randolph had done more than merely flirt with the protectionist 'Fair Trade' movement of the 1880s.[48] And, as Wilfrid Scawen Blunt noted at the time, 'there is nothing at all [in the book] about his father's more Indian liberal views'.[49]

It might have been expected, then, that Churchill would also seek to reinvent Lord Randolph as an unabashed imperialist, but interestingly he did not do so. The biography showed that Lord Randolph had at times adopted a 'Jingo' tone out of electoral expediency, and acknowledged that his attacks on Gladstone over Egypt had made some 'True Blue' Tories feel uneasy.[50] It even admitted that 'Lord Randolph Churchill was never what is nowadays called an Imperialist and always looked at home rather than abroad'.[51] Yet if Churchill recognized the limits to his father's imperialism – and if his own more powerful kind must therefore have owed much to other sources – we cannot discount Lord Randolph's influence entirely. Winston can hardly, for example, have overlooked an important lesson of the South African visit: that travelling to distant parts of the Empire and writing about them was an excellent way of gaining publicity and making money at the same time.

II

Not long before his death, Lord Randolph wrote to Winston of his certainty 'that if you cannot prevent yourself from leading the idle useless and unprofitable life you have had during your schooldays & later months, you will become a mere social wastrel one of the hundreds of the public school failures'.[52] Even allowing for Lord Randolph's considerable exaggeration of his son's idleness, the latter was certainly not a model pupil in most respects. This, taken together with the fact that he later felt the need to make good his educational deficit through self-instruction, might lead us to conclude that his formal schooling had little impact on him. The truth, however, was different. During his childhood, and during his time at Harrow School in particular, he was exposed to imperialist messages that would stay with him for decades.

This exposure began early, but it was not simply a question of formal indoctrination. As his parents were distant, even neglectful, they delegated his care to Mrs Everest, who became his childhood confidante. In *My Early Life* (1930) he recalled a visit made to her sister and her husband, a prison warder, on the Isle of Wight, when he was four. It was at the time of the Zulu War, and as he recollected, not without irony:

> There were pictures in the papers of the Zulus. They were black and naked, with spears called 'assegais' which they threw very cleverly. They killed a great many of our soldiers, but judging from the pictures, not nearly so many as our soldiers killed of them. I was very angry with the Zulus, and glad to hear they were being killed; and so was my friend, the old prison warder. After a while it seemed that they were all killed, because this particular war came to an end and there were no more pictures of Zulus in the papers and nobody worried any more about them.[53]

Historians of Empire rightly place much emphasis on the role such media images (and popular culture in general) played in inculcating the British people with the spirit of Empire, and also on that of schooling. How much effect this had on the masses is a matter of controversy. For many years scholars tended to argue that the populace was suffused with Empire sentiment, via sweeping propaganda ranging from children's literature to the music hall to imperial exhibitions.[54] More recently it has been argued that even when this propaganda reached the working classes they were often indifferent to it, and that popular feeling for the Empire erupted only rarely, for example during the Boer War.[55] There is little doubt, however, of the impact on the social elite. In Churchill's case, that impact can be traced with some certainty. There are, it is true, some gaps in our knowledge. We do not have detailed evidence of the curricula he followed at the preparatory schools he attended between the ages of seven and thirteen. Nevertheless, it seems probable that he was exposed, even if only obliquely, to some form of imperial education while he was there. (He would surely have become familiar with the world map – with the extensive 'pink bits' indicating British territory – that was an almost proverbial feature of the Victorian schoolroom.) The fact that he joined the Primrose League in 1887, and his eagerness to attend Queen Victoria's golden jubilee in the same year, suggests that he felt some degree of emotional attachment to Crown and Empire by the time he reached his teens.

We can be rather more precise about his subsequent years at Harrow. In later life he felt, to say the least, ambivalent about the time he spent there, but it undoubtedly made a profound impression on him. During World War II he told his private secretary John Colville that those days had been the unhappiest of his life. Nonetheless, Colville noted that the Prime Minister could still repeat the school songs by heart, and that, when he returned for a visit in December 1940, 'he made a brilliant impromptu speech to the school, saying how much Harrow Songs had meant to him, what an inspiration they had been at certain stages of his life, and pointing out that although Hitler claimed the Adolf Hitler Schools had shown their superiority to Eton, he had forgotten Harrow!'[56] (One of the songs that Churchill requested on this occasion was 'Giants', which includes a line paying tribute to 'the hero-race'.)[57] He certainly believed that Harrow and the other major public schools played an important imperial role, helping 'produce the type and

habit of mind which have played so indispensable a part in our
State and Empire', and providing its 'colonists and adventurers'.⁵⁸

During Churchill's time there, the headmaster, Revd J. E. C.
Welldon, was determined to create the imperial habit of mind in his
pupils. Born in 1854, Welldon had excelled at Cambridge University
and seemed to be destined for high things. Appointed to the
headmastership in 1885, he expressed the hope that 'the liberal
sentiments of Harrow people will make reform, so far as it is needed,
comparatively easy.'⁵⁹ 'Liberal' was a relative term; it did not mean
that Welldon was soft on his pupils. (He once remarked of the
'obstreperous, irresponsible' Churchill that 'he had birched him
more frequently than any other boy, but with little effect.')⁶⁰ He was
'an imposing figure' whose 'massive, towering form [. . .] expressed
authority incarnate'.⁶¹ He was also a confirmed imperial ideologue,
and this was reflected in his management of the school. In his
memoirs he recalled how an Egyptian pupil had appeared one
morning with two black eyes. Welldon made some inquiries, sent
for the boy who had inflicted them and demanded to know why he
had done it. The boy paused and then said apologetically, 'Please,
sir, he said something bad about the British race.' According to
Welldon, 'The only possible reply which I could make was: "That is
enough, my boy; you may go." '⁶²

If this makes Welldon sound like the comic caricature of a
Victorian headmaster, it was not the case that he simply despised
non-whites. He advised one pupil who joined the Indian Civil
Service on how to treat those over whom he exercised power: 'you
know how other Anglo-Indians treat them contemptuously; but
you must remember that the West owes to the East nearly all the
most precious part of its heritage, and then no native of India will
seem to you to be unworthy of your tender consideration'.⁶³ Such
attitudes were undoubtedly deeply patronizing, and a much later
letter demonstrates the assumptions underlying his imperialism. He
argued, 'it is clear to me that the British Government in India does
not and cannot ultimately rest upon the good-will of the people;
that the cry of equality among all citizens of the Empire is impracticable, because it would mean the subjection of the citizens of the
West to the far more numerous citizens of the East'.⁶⁴ The subjection of large numbers of Eastern citizens to small numbers of

Western ones was, by contrast, something that he evidently found wholly unproblematic. To him, the British race was the best in the world, because it was the one that had 'most succeeded in combining liberty with law, religion with freedom, [and] self-respect with respect for other races'.[65] In other words, the British capacity for racial tolerance was a fundamental part of British racial superiority!

Welldon was an admirer of the Cambridge historian J. R. Seeley's book *The Expansion of England* (1883), which he credited as both a cause and a symbol of Britain's new-found imperial spirit. (It is not clear if Churchill read Seeley's work himself, but he would certainly have encountered its central message, that Britain should consciously take charge of its imperial destiny.) Welldon believed that it was the duty of teachers to bring before their pupils 'the magnitude and dignity of the British Empire'; the history and geography of Empire were to be made into 'powerful educational instruments'.[66] Other masters at the school took their cue from Welldon.[67] The kind of imperial education that Welldon espoused had a significant impact on Churchill. He observed during his first parliamentary election campaign that the British people needed to be imperialistic 'because we shall thereby learn geography', a remark that may have been unconsciously revealing of this.[68] The school rewarded expressions of national and imperial pride by the boys. When Churchill wrote an essay describing an imaginary future invasion of Russia by Britain – illustrating 'the superiority of John Bull over the Russian Bear' – his English teacher was so impressed that he kept it.[69] After an outbreak of influenza swept across Europe in 1890, Churchill wrote a poem recounting the progress of the epidemic, and urging:

> God shield our Empire from the might
> Of war or famine, plague or blight
> And all the powers of Hell,
> And keep it ever in the hands
> Of those who fought 'gainst other lands
> Who fought & conquered well.[70]

For this he won a house prize.

The imperial content of the curriculum should not be overstated. One of Churchill's history notebooks, dealing with the eighteenth century, has survived. Aside from a brief reference to 'Colonial Causes' of the Seven Years War, the British Empire receives no mention.[71] But formal teaching was not all. Welldon made much of 'the festivals of the Empire' and tried to bring the pupils into contact 'with the leaders of imperial thought and action'.[72] This meant bringing lecturers to the school, including, in Churchill's time, Lord Wolesley, leader of the Canadian Red River expedition of 1870, and H. M. Stanley (of Dr Livingstone fame) who spoke on 'African Exploration'.[73] Churchill was particularly impressed by a talk given by G. R. Parkin, a well-known Canadian advocate of imperial federation – the idea that all parts of the Empire should be represented in the Parliament at Westminster. This was a notion that Lord Randolph considered 'moonshine'.[74] Although he did not become a profound enthusiast for it, Winston Churchill did argue as a young man that the colonies 'must be federated', and continued to make nods towards the idea into the 1920s.[75] Parkin's imagery made a vivid impression on him, and he could still remember it decades later. Parkin said that at the Battle of Trafalgar, Nelson had signalled to his fleet 'England expects that every man will do his duty'. He continued: 'if you take the steps that are necessary to bind together and hold together the great Empire to the Crown, and if at some future time danger and peril strikes at the heart and life of that Empire, then the signal will run, not along a line of battle ships but a line of nations'. Churchill, as he told Parkin when he met him after World War I, believed that the Empire's loyalty to Britain during that conflict was a vindication of this dream.[76]

There is a strong case to be made for Harrow's influence not only on Churchill but on a whole generation of politicians. Welldon counted 1923 as the school's *annus mirabilis*. Not only were the new Prime Minister, Stanley Baldwin, and many of his ministers Old Harrovians, but so was the Archbishop of Canterbury, 'to say nothing of three Harrovians among members of Parliament in the Labour Party'.[77] It is important to note, though, that the school did not produce a uniform stamp of mind, even amongst those of its students who became ardent imperialists and members of the same Tory cabinets. The point is proved by the example of Leo Amery, one of the ministers Welldon had in mind. A year older than Churchill, Amery was born in India, where his father was an official

in the forestry commission. (His mother, incidentally, was Jewish –
a point he concealed in his memoirs.)[78] When he was three, his
parents split up and he moved with his mother to Britain; he never
went back to India again. Amery had a strong interest in the Empire
even before arriving at the school. At the start of his first term, one
master, Mr Stogdon, asked the boys what they thought was the
most political event of the summer. There was general silence,
except from Amery who, to Stogdon's delight, replied 'the Nizam of
Hyderabad's offer to the Queen to supply money and troops in case
of trouble with Russia'.[79]

His first encounter with Churchill came at Harrow when the
latter deliberately pushed him into the swimming pool. On being
told that his victim was in the sixth-form, Churchill determined to
apologize, telling him, 'I mistook you for a Fourth Form boy. You
are so small.' This did not go down very well, but Churchill then
deftly placated Amery by telling him that Lord Randolph, who was
a great man, was also small.[80] Not only did Amery and Churchill
share many of the same influences, but their early careers had much
in common. Both had success as journalists before becoming Tory
MPs. Nevertheless, Amery's concept of imperialism was sharply
divergent from Churchill's. They were political antagonists during
Churchill's period in the Liberal Party after 1904; their differences
over imperial trade were symbolic of the ideological contrast between
them. They clashed repeatedly over policy, even when reunited as
members of Baldwin's Conservative Cabinet in 1924–9. In the 1930s
they both found themselves in the political wilderness as opponents
(in somewhat differing ways) of the policy of appeasement. After
1940, when Amery served as Churchill's Secretary of State for India,
they had serious disagreements once more, this time over the speed
of Indian political reform. Harrow had certainly made its impression
on both, but it did not turn out identikit imperialists.

Welldon's own career never lived up fully to its early promise.
In 1898 he was appointed Bishop of Calcutta, a post in which,
Churchill believed, he was not happy: 'The East without wife,
woman, sport, war, authority or friends seems to me a vy bad
bargain'.[81] For Welldon, the shortage of women was perhaps not a
great problem; he was unmarried, and his lifetime relationship with
his manservant was one of 'complete devotion'.[82] In India, however,
his determination to convert the population to Christianity led to

conflict with Lord Curzon, the Viceroy, who was more pragmatically inclined, and Welldon resigned in 1902 on grounds of ill health.[83] (Churchill also rejected Welldon's view, arguing that 'the Asiatic derives more real benefit from the perfect knowledge and practice of his own religion – albeit inferior – than from the imperfect and partial comprehension of Christianity.')[84] After his return to England he served as Dean of Manchester and then of Durham, and, before his death in 1937, he kept an eye on Churchill's career. In 1923 Welldon observed that Churchill had 'shown more of the public school spirit' than some other leading politicians, but he disapproved of his decision to publish confidential wartime documents in his book *The World Crisis*, noting, 'It is now taken as an axiom that everything must be told [. . .] without much or any regard to the danger of creating a false impression or of conveying information in a rather unpatriotic spirit.'[85] And when Churchill campaigned against greater self-government for India, Welldon came down firmly on the other side. In 1935 he wrote to the wife of Sir Samuel Hoare, Secretary of State for India (who was also an Harrovian), praising his Government of India Bill, which Churchill so vigorously opposed. 'If he [Hoare] can effect, as I hope he may, what will be a practically pacific revolution in the constitutional history of India, he will live in history as one of the principal benefactors, not of India only, but of the British Empire.'[86] In other words, although Churchill's imperial attitudes are often explained with reference to his Victorian background, other Victorians who contributed to and shared that background were frequently able to take different (and sometimes more liberal) approaches. Jawaharlal Nehru, who attended Harrow in the Edwardian period, testified that the school's atmosphere was in fact far from stifling. In 1950 he and Churchill attended a dinner for Old Harrovians at Westminster. One of the organizers recalled:

> Winston had once during the troubles in India put Nehru under arrest for a time, but we felt sure that this would not be allowed to rankle, nor did it. The toast to Nehru was proposed by Winston in the felicitous manner of which only he was capable. Nehru replied and referred to his time at Harrow. He said he left Harrow with a feeling of regret. He could not say why he had this feeling. He had thought about it since and had come to the conclusion that he had learnt something at Harrow

that served him well in later life: that, before you make a decision, always bear in mind that there are two sides to every question.[87]

Churchill, then, was not merely a sponge, absorbing the propaganda of his schoolmasters without question. His imperialism, already strong by the time he entered Sandhurst, was to receive a further unique imprint from his own direct experience, and from the books that, sensing the gaps in his education, he anxiously sought out.

III

After Harrow, Churchill went to Sandhurst, his father having decided he was not bright enough for the Bar. Here too imperial messages were in evidence: the inside of the Royal Memorial Chapel was decorated with plaques commemorating graduates killed fighting in Empire and other campaigns.[88] Churchill worked hard although, as he later recalled, he and his fellow cadets believed there was little chance of them ever making practical use of their training. It seemed a shame that – as they believed – the era of war between 'civilized' countries had ended. Fortunately, though, there were still 'savages and barbarous peoples' such as the Afghans, the Zulus and the Sudanese Dervishes. 'Some of these might, if they were well-disposed, "put up a show" some day.'[89] Although he sometimes used racist epithets,[90] Churchill was prepared to deal with individuals on equal terms if they were 'civilized', which in practice meant rich and well educated or, in the case of one Afghan officer with whom he and some friends dined, good at billiards. ('Everyone likes him,' he told his mother.[91]) Meanwhile, Churchill continued to absorb the imperial culture of the day. His love of the music hall, as shown by his Empire Theatre escapade, might not appear important at first sight, but patriotism and imperialism were staples of this form of entertainment. Dance pageants such as 'Our Empire' and songs like 'It's the English-Speaking Race against the World' were typical.[92] Although he was later dismissive of the slogans of the 'pothouse Music Hall' and of the 'cheap Imperialist productions' of the popular press (though he thought the latter did some good amongst the 'vulgar' classes),[93] he clearly enjoyed the music hall atmosphere enough to defend it against the puritans, and it is hard to believe that he was altogether indifferent to the ideological messages that it conveyed.

Having completed his training, Churchill joined the Fourth Hussars, a cavalry regiment, in February 1895, less than a month after Lord Randolph's death. He determined to make the most of his generous leave entitlement before the regiment shipped to India and so, the following winter, he and a friend travelled to Cuba via New York. They had chosen this destination because they wanted to get a taste of war at first-hand: the island was in the throes of rebellion against Spanish rule. It was also a chance for Churchill to earn a little bit of money and fame, by contracting to provide articles on the conflict to the *Daily Graphic*. He accompanied the Spanish forces as they tried to hunt down the insurgents and, on his twenty-first birthday, heard shots fired in anger for the first time. His initial sympathy for the rebels dwindled as he began to see how pained the Spanish were at the prospect of losing their treasured colonial possession; his discovery that they had similar feelings to the British in this respect came as a rather uncomfortable surprise.[94] He told the *Graphic*'s readers that Spanish administration was corrupt to the point that made rebellion inevitable and justifiable, but the rebels themselves were mere brigands, and Cuban autonomy was not a practical possibility.[95] He made no suggestion that imperial rule per se – rather than the specifically Spanish version of it – was at fault. Indeed, he wrote to Bourke Cockran, a prominent Democrat politician whom he had met in New York, that he hoped the US would not force Spain to disgorge Cuba – unless America itself was prepared to take on the responsibility of governing her. Cockran's reply has not survived, but apparently he found that idea unpalatable, preferring that the Cubans should rule themselves.[96] This was an early hint of the difference in British and American attitudes to Empire and national independence movements that would take on such importance during the most crucial phase of Churchill's career.

Churchill's regiment shipped out to India in September 1896. One book he read by way of preparation was *Twenty-One Days in India* by George Aberigh-Mackay. This 'brilliant though little-known writer', as Churchill later described him, had been Principal of Rajkumar College, Indore.[97] Originally published in serial form in the *Bombay Gazette* in 1880, the year before the author's death at thirty-three, the book was subtitled *The Tour of Sir Ali Baba K.C.B.*, and formed a satirical look at a range of Indian and Anglo-Indian 'types'. These ranged from the 'Great Ornamental' Viceroy, 'absolutely and necessarily withdrawn from all knowledge of India', to the 'Bengali Baboo', 'Full of inappropriate words and phrases'.[98] Churchill was advised to read the book by a family friend in the Indian Civil Service. In 1942 he in turn sent a copy to William Phillips, who was about to go to Delhi as President Roosevelt's personal representative. He acknowledged that the world Aberigh-Mackay described had long since passed; nevertheless, there were 'serious things beneath the surface of this old book' which gave 'a sweeping glance at a vast, marvellous scene'.[99] At some point during his time in India Churchill read Sir George Chesney's *Indian Polity*, which argued that 'the state of anarchy and universal strife throughout the land, which was replaced by the peace everywhere established under British rule, must have been attended with a degree of suffering which far outweighs the defects inseparable from a rule by foreigners'.[100] Such arguments, which were to be echoed by Churchill in the 1930s, were the commonplaces of the time.

Churchill's views of what to expect from India would already have been conditioned by his boyhood reading. At school he had read standard juvenile literature such as *Every Boy's Annual*, which contained military adventure stories of the kind often credited with helping instil an imperial mentality in Victorian youth.[101] Churchill's own adventures would in turn be held up as a model for later generations. Hastings Ismay, his key military aide during World War II, recalled how, as a young soldier, he had aimed to emulate his future boss's early career.[102] In the 1950s, Churchill's life was serialized in strip-cartoon form in the *Eagle*, a weekly publication intended as a wholesome alternative to the prevalent American 'horror comics'.[103]

Churchill was also a fan of two of the most classic imperialist writers. As a teenager, he begged a meeting with H. Rider Haggard, who afterwards sent him a copy of his novel *Allan Quatermain*.[104] He was a great admirer of Rudyard Kipling's writing too (although, as with Haggard, he did not think all of his books were of equal quality), as were many of his fellow soldiers in India. He noted that, when fighting on the North-West Frontier in 1897, he often heard one of Kipling's poems, 'Arithmetic on the Frontier', quoted.[105] In

1899, Kipling caught pneumonia, and it seemed he might die. Churchill thought this would be a 'terrible loss to the English speaking world'.[106] Kipling actually lived for almost another four decades, but, although they met on a number of occasions, he never reciprocated Churchill's respect for him. During the latter's period as a Liberal Kipling remarked of him that 'it is impossible to cure a political prostitute from whoring'.[107] After the 1922 general election he gloated over Churchill's loss of his seat.[108] Churchill was aware of this hostility, but claimed, in his public tribute after Kipling's death in 1937, that their joint opposition to Indian self-government had ended their estrangement.[109] This was at best only partially true. Kipling was actually not as hard line on India as Churchill was, and wrote in 1935, 'The only point at which, I personally, would draw the line in present politics, would be in following Mr W. Churchill.'[110] Churchill was a man who 'very many praise but dam-few follow'.[111] However, this is no reason to doubt the sincerity of Churchill's own claims to have been influenced by Kipling. As he put it in his eulogy, 'Although in my political actions I was often fiercely opposed to him, yet there was never a moment when I did not feel the surge of his appeal upon the great verities of our race and State.' He also claimed on this occasion that, even if Britain's Indian Empire should cease to exist, Kipling's works would 'remain to prove that while we were there we did our best for all'.[112]

Churchill's own first impressions of the Indian scene were favourable. The regiment was stationed at Bangalore, where the climate was good, with cool nights, mornings and evenings providing relief from the heat of the day. The officers were not given quarters, but instead were provided with a lodging allowance, so Churchill and two friends shared an impressive white and pink bungalow set in an extensive garden. Each of them had the services of a 'Butler' (Churchill put the term in quotation marks), a First Dressing Boy, a Second Dressing Boy, and a groom for every horse or pony they owned. In addition, the household shared two gardeners, three water carriers, four washer-men and one watchman.[113] This all had to be paid for, of course, and officers' salaries and allowances were grossly inadequate in relation to the manner in which they were expected to live – a manner which served its own purpose of impressing the local population. Churchill was paid around £300 a year, including an allowance for keeping two horses, supplemented by £500 a year from his mother.[114] The combined total was no negligible sum – it was roughly equivalent to £46,000 in 2009 prices. But Lord Randolph had not died rich, and neither Winston nor Lady Randolph was good at managing finance, so money was a constant bone of contention between them. Even a life of massive privilege can have its irritations.

Life in Bangalore was comfortable, if boring. The regiment was on parade by six o'clock in the morning, but drills and other military duties were complete by half-past ten. After that it was too hot to do anything much until five, which was the hour for playing polo. Churchill was an enthusiast for the game, which was lucky for him as there were so few other ways of passing the time. Of ancient Indo-Persian origin, the sport had been adopted and standardized by the British, many of whom saw this process as evidence of the benefits of imperial rule. One sports writer suggested, for example, that 'the order-loving and disciplined minds of the Westerns have organised a game which was a wild helter-skelter into a careful, scientific and military sport. These things are an allegory, and the polo of East and West may to the careful observer give a suggestion why in war and government the West ever prevails.'[115] The game appealed to upper-class Indians for rather different reasons. Dangerous and highly expensive (a point not lost on the cash-strapped Churchill), it was a way for princes – in the absence of war – to demonstrate their personal courage and elite status.[116] Polo competitions also provided a rare opportunity for Indians and Englishmen to meet on something like equal terms. In his first book, *The Story of the Malakand Field Force*, Churchill recognized this, arguing that the game had improved relations between British officers and the princes, and should therefore be counted as 'an Imperial factor'. He did not think it likely that Indian army officers would ever serve on an equal footing with British ones, 'but if it should ever come to pass, the way will have been prepared on the polo ground'.[117]

Churchill excelled as a member of the regimental team, which, within six weeks of the Fourth Hussars' arrival in India, had won the prestigious Golconda Cup at Hyderabad. But polo could not be everything, and Churchill was understandably eager to broaden his horizons. Even before leaving England he had started to seek out the books that would give him the intellectual polish he felt he lacked as a consequence of his 'purely technical' education.[118] Now, he launched into his reading programme with alacrity, starting with Gibbon. It was certainly not the case that everything he read had some explicit imperial theme. Undoubtedly, though, his thinking about empire was profoundly affected by much of what he absorbed in the long, hot afternoons between duty and polo.

It has been claimed that 'Churchill supported the British Empire largely for Gibbonian reasons'. Whereas Gibbon, while despising ancient Rome's political despotism, believed that its empire brought concrete benefits to the ruled, Churchill thought that Britain had achieved a double advantage by spreading such benefits in combination with liberty.[119] Certainly, Churchill repeatedly referenced Gibbon throughout his career, and many similarities can be traced in terms of thinking as well as literary style. Yet this influence should not be blown out of proportion, and needs to be considered alongside that of other authors. After Gibbon, Churchill tackled Thomas Babington Macaulay's *History of England*, and also his essays. As with Gibbon, the style had an effect on his own, and he was to quote him at some significant points in the future. Notably, he picked up on a remark in Macaulay's essay on Warren Hastings describing the iniquities of eighteenth-century British rule in India. Macaulay referred to 'the most frightful of all spectacles, the strength of civilisation without its mercy'.[120] Churchill deployed this same imagery in *The Story of the Malakand Field Force*, although he used it to describe not British abuses but rather what happened when tribesmen got hold of modern weapons.[121] During the Commons debate in 1920 on the notorious Amritsar massacre – when, at a time of nationalist disturbances, British forces shot into a crowd of unarmed Indians – he used it in the original sense, to deplore the killing of defenceless civilians.[122] This did not mean that he, any more than Macaulay, entertained doubts about the fundamental virtues of British rule. Rather, he was making the claim that that rule did not depend exclusively on physical force, and that it was incumbent upon the rulers, given their vast military superiority over the indigenous population, to exercise restraint. The subject peoples of the Empire were to rely for their welfare, then, on the elevated moral qualities of their conquerors.

A far more obscure yet nonetheless important influence was Winwood Reade's book *The Martyrdom of Man*, which was recommended to Churchill by his commanding officer, Colonel John

Brabazon. This has been described as 'a classic of Victorian atheism' which left Churchill with a 'sombre vision of a godless universe'.[123] In fact, Reade was not an atheist (although his arguments were sufficiently shocking that contemporaries understood him to be one) but merely an anti-Christian. He argued that 'God is so great that he does not deign to have personal relations with us human atoms that are called men'.[124] Furthermore, his world view could actually be described as one of wild, unabashed optimism about the possibilities of human progress. Reade, an explorer and failed novelist, published his epic work in 1872, three years before his death at the age of thirty-six, his health having broken down after a third and final visit to Africa. Although the book met much hostility, it continued to sell in significant numbers. (Amongst those it influenced was H. G. Wells, another author Churchill admired greatly.)[125] Churchill, in his memoirs, focused on the blow Reade dealt to his religious beliefs; although initially shocked by what he read, he found Reade's message confirmed by Gibbon's secular viewpoint and by the works of W. E. H. Lecky, who believed that old superstitions would die away as the spirit of rationalism grew.[126] (He also emphasized that his resulting anti-religious phase was short-lived, although in reality his belief in conventional Christianity never recovered.)[127] Equally important, arguably, was Reade's impact on his thinking about Empire and human development.[128]

The book's message needs to be understood in the context of an intellectual atmosphere much influenced by Charles Darwin (with whom Reade had corresponded). It was common to apply Darwinian insights not only to the social competition between individuals but also to that between nations. It was widely believed that – as Joseph Chamberlain was to put it later – the day of the small nations had passed, and that of empires had arrived. In order to survive in a predatory world, states needed to expand in order to maximize their populations and natural resources.[129] The first part of *The Martyrdom of Man* consisted of a reckless romp through thousands of years of world history, leading to the conclusion that war had acted as 'the chief agent of civilisation' in the ancient world.[130] The book went on to suggest that the world's major religions (including Islam) had, at certain times and places, served a useful social function, stamping out the more primitive beliefs of barbarous peoples. They would, however, die away as man became more perfect and acquired a true religion that would harmonize with his intellect. This progress would be driven by suffering, mental as well as physical, which was what Reade meant by 'the martyrdom of man'. Such suffering was inherently undesirable and yet was also, paradoxically, the motor of beneficent change. He even argued that the slave trade, 'though cruel and atrocious in itself' had 'like most wars, been of service to mankind'.[131] Not only had it created for slave-owners the leisure essential to the cultural achievements of the ancient world but also, more recently, awareness of its cruelties had stimulated the moral improvement of the Anglo-Saxon peoples as they strove towards its abolition. Reade's attitude to race was equally complex (or convoluted). He criticized 'pride of colour and prejudice of race' while remaining agnostic on the question of whether 'negroes are equal in average capacity to the white man'.[132] Africans could, in his view, be induced to want things that they did not positively need, and, thus equipped with the same incentives to work as whites had, be brought within the ambit of civilization. But if need be European governments should compel them to labour both for their own good and for the sake of progress: 'Children are ruled and schooled by force, and it is not an empty metaphor to say that savages are children.'[133] We may see an echo of this in Churchill's later (much more mildly stated) conviction that Africans, even with their basic needs satisfied, had no right to remain idle. They would benefit from having their wants multiplied and, like everyone else, were 'bound to go forward and take an honest share in the general work of the world'. He too saw Africans (or at least the Kikuyu) as educable, if brutish, children, albeit he could certainly have absorbed this point of view from many other sources in addition to Reade.[134] We might even locate in *The Martyrdom of Man* the origin of a famous Churchillian trope. Reade cited an eighteenth-century MP's condemnation of a slave-ship: 'never was so much suffering condensed into so small a space'.[135]

From Reade's perspective, Empire and progress went hand in hand. The uneducated populations of the world would never begin to advance until their property was secure and they enjoyed the rights of man, 'and these they will never obtain except by means of European conquest'. Such security, he argued, had been brought by the British to the population of India. He criticized the 'sickly school of politicians who declare that all countries belong to their inhabitants, and that to take them is a crime'. But in Asia, the masses of the people were in fact slaves to their rulers, he claimed. 'The conquest of Asia by European Powers is therefore in reality emancipation [. . .] Thus war will, for long years yet to come, be required to prepare the way for freedom and progress in the East'.[136] It seems that Churchill's cheerful vision of war as the engine of social improvement – which he maintained into the 1940s[137] – was heavily influenced by Reade. On the eve of his first election campaign he told the Midland Conservative Club of his lack of enthusiasm for the then ongoing Hague peace conference. 'It was only one more instance of the reaction against the spirit of competition', he said. 'Destroy the rivalry of men and nations, and all that made for the betterment and progress of the world would be destroyed'. Decay and degeneration would follow, he argued; the 'clear blue ocean of national passion' was preferable to the 'stagnant pool of international agreement'. This speech, however, revealed him to be much more of a British (or at least white) chauvinist than Reade was. 'He [Churchill] cared little for the improvement of the human race', reported the *Birmingham Daily Post*. 'The supremacy of our own race was good enough for him'.[138]

In India, Churchill continued his feats of reading. He sought out Adam Smith's *Wealth of Nations*, Plato's *Republic*, and the memoirs of the Duc de Saint Simon, amongst others.[139] He secured copies of the *Annual Register* from the 1870s and wrote his own comments on the debates they recorded. He gave his views, for example, on the Indian famine of 1873–4, claiming that the Viceroy had been right to refuse demands that he prohibit grain exports. In Churchill's opinion, a food shortage did not justify interfering with the free market in such a way. He also expressed approval of the contentious Royal Titles Act that had made Queen Victoria Empress of India. The 'natives of India', he argued, would be 'impressed by the Imperial'. The whole question, he suggested, was trivial, 'except from an Indian aspect. In India these things count.'[140] Throughout his career, Churchill argued that the Crown was fundamental to the Empire, serving as the mystical link which held it together, in spite of the weakness of its formal constitutional apparatus. This was, perhaps, a way of reconciling his strong emotional attachment to the monarchy with his recognition that it had little formal power. (Such that it had withered further during the course of his lifetime.)

These early comments, however, should alert us to the fact that there was an instrumental, even cynical, aspect to his championship of titles and ceremony. If the pomp associated with the Crown could be used to impress 'the natives', then so too, as the years went on, could it be used as a rhetorical fig-leaf to disguise the increasingly naked decline of British power.

This was also the time when Churchill began to write. He later recalled that one of his first, unpublished efforts was an attack upon an article by George Bernard Shaw 'which he had written disparaging and deriding the British Army in some minor war'.[141] By April 1897 Churchill had decided that, although he was 'a Liberal in all but name', his opposition to Home Rule precluded him standing for the party at an election. He would therefore adopt Lord Randolph's slogan of 'Tory Democracy', campaigning for reform at home and imperialism abroad. Britain should remain aloof from European politics, he believed, and the colonies should contribute more to the motherland's defence. 'East of Suez Democratic reins are impossible', he wrote. 'India must be governed on old principles.'[142]

Were these old principles really so satisfactory? Almost as soon as he arrived, Churchill was writing home about the bubonic plague that threatened Bombay, and the shortage of rain that threatened drought, famine and accompanying riots.[143] The blame for these disasters should not perhaps have been laid exclusively at the door of the British administration – Britain did in fact make an effort to help by sending large quantities of vegetable seed.[144] Nevertheless, they should surely have stimulated more concern than they did. Churchill's attitude to the local population was probably typical of Anglo-Indian opinion – his indifference, verging on callousness, alternated with occasional twinges of concern. In March 1898 he observed in a letter to his younger brother Jack that the plague was 'going on merrily' with four hundred people a day dying in Bombay alone. 'The population however is superabundant.'[145] At the end of the year the plague came to Bangalore and so rather closer to home. Two of Churchill's grooms were carried off, as were the wife and mother of the bearer who had accompanied him to the North-West Frontier. Sixty people were dying a day but, as Churchill wrote with a hint of disgust, 'nobody cares a rap & you never hear a word about it'.[146] Soon, the epidemic began to subside, and he said little more about the subject himself. Earlier, he had visited Hyderabad with Pamela Plowden, his first love, to whom he had recently been introduced during a polo tournament. They had to travel into the city on an elephant, because Europeans would be spat at if they walked in the streets, 'which provokes retaliation leading to riots'.[147] Such signs of Indian discontent did not disturb his initial sense that England was fulfilling her 'high mission' to rule over the 'primitive but agreeable' local population in an entirely benevolent way.[148] The prevailing racial attitudes of the British in India certainly rubbed off on him. 'When you learn to think of a race as inferior beings it is difficult to get rid of that way of thinking', he acknowledged in the 1950s; 'when I was a subaltern the Indian did not seem to me equal to the white man'.[149]

In the spring of 1897 Churchill returned home on leave. It was while he was there that he made his speech to the Bath Primrose League on the 'splendour' of the Empire. (Naturally, he did not share with his audience the fact that he found the particular part of the Empire to which he had been sent tedious rather than splendid.) His early imperial education was not yet finished. Not only was the formative experience of his military campaigning across the Empire still to come, but he was keenly aware that his knowledge even of India was woefully incomplete. As he complained to his mother, he had no access, as a mere subaltern, to people of influence and expertise; and he had no time for the 'despicable' Indian press (from which he could perhaps have learnt more than he chose to).[150] Nevertheless, it is clear that he had learnt to think imperially – not merely in the sense of having a sentimental attachment to the Empire, but in having developed his own rationale for it. His world view, as articulated to the Tories of Bath, was pretty orthodox; Winwood Reade had convinced him that Christianity might be false, but not that it was 'wise or expedient to say so'.[151] One might say, then, that he had reached an apparently conventional viewpoint by a somewhat unconventional route. Primed by his Harrow education and the imperial culture of the time, his encounter with heterodoxy led him to view international relations as an evolutionary battle, but never to question the idea that Britain, because of its inherent superiority, would be able to win that struggle. Ultimately, he thought, such a victory would be for the good of the world as a whole, but in practical (and electioneering) terms the welfare of the rest of the world was low on his list of priorities. The notion that thinking imperially meant thinking always of 'something higher and more vast than one's own national interests' was one that at this stage remained alien to him.

IV

Churchill freely conceded that he was a 'child of the Victorian era'.[152] In the interwar period and beyond, though, the term 'Victorian' had become practically a term of abuse, the equivalent, when the Empire was discussed, of 'reactionary'. The surprising thing is that his Victorian background was used against him not just by political progressives, but by imperialists within the Conservative Party who were themselves of a similar vintage to Churchill. In 1929, when Baldwin (b. 1867) pondered making Churchill Secretary of State for India, the Viceroy, Lord Irwin (b. 1881), advised him not. Irwin suggested that Churchill held antediluvian opinions, writing that he 'has always been a much more vigorous Imperialist in the 1890–1900 sense of the word than you and me'.[153] A later Viceroy, Lord Wavell (b. 1883), remarked that Churchill 'has still at heart his cavalry subaltern's idea of India; just as his military tactics are inclined to date from the Boer War'.[154] Leo Amery (b. 1873) believed, for his part, that 'the key to Winston is to realise that he is a Mid Victorian, steeped in the politics of his father's period, and unable ever to get the modern point of view'.[155] Even Churchill's doctor, Lord Moran (b. 1882), had a view. He wrote of Churchill's attitude to the Chinese: 'Winston thinks only of the colour of their skin; it is when he talks of India or China that you remember he is a Victorian.'[156]

Describing Churchill's attitudes as 'Victorian' may in part have been a convenient way for those who opposed him to stress the contrasting 'modernity' of their own imperial views. Or perhaps Churchill did to some extent suffer a genuine case of arrested development. Either way, we can see the limitations of the suggestion that Churchill's later opinions were the inevitable product of a Victorian upbringing per se. And, whether or not it is right to criticize his views on issues such as race, it can scarcely be considered *anachronistic* to do so, when his own contemporaries did not hold back themselves. By the time he had reached the threshold of his public career, he had absorbed a particular version of imperialism, but not one that was universally held. No homogeneous view of Empire existed in late-Victorian Britain; there was in fact vibrant debate, not about the Empire's inherent validity, but about how its interests could best be pursued. Churchill's first real military excursion, on the Indian frontier in 1897, led to his wholehearted launch into this field of controversy.

2

JOLLY LITTLE WARS AGAINST
BARBAROUS PEOPLES, 1897–1899

In 1929 Churchill took up the honorific position of Chancellor of Bristol University. In a speech to the students he reflected on his own lack of a university education and remembered how his military training had led him instead to a period of adventure. He recalled how at that time Britain had fought 'a lot of jolly little wars against barbarous peoples' and how he himself had gone 'scurrying about the world from one exciting scene to another'.[1] If this sounds like a parody of Victorian imperial adventurism, it is more than possible that Churchill was intentionally sending himself up. He was certainly capable of humour at his own expense; the persistently ironical tone of *My Early Life*, for example, is part of what gives the book its charm. But if it would be unfair to dismiss that book as merely a sequence of thrilling scenes – a charge more easily levelled against treatments such the 1972 film *Young Winston* – it is nonetheless true that the picture it paints of the Empire is romantic and depoliticized. Churchill's failure to give his readers a full sense of his role in fin-de-siècle imperial debates may have been a wise commercial decision in the gloomy circumstances of 1930; yet without an understanding of that context, his 'scurrying' phase is reduced to not much more than the 'jolly little wars' of his own caricature. Churchill may have been courageous as a soldier, but when he combined that role with that of journalist, he was by no means always the candid scourge of authority that legend depicts.

I

On the very day in 1897 that Churchill made his first political speech at Bath, there was a rising of Pathan tribesmen in the Swat

Valley on the North-West Frontier of India. The news was reported in Britain two days later. After two years of quiet, the garrison at Malakand had suddenly been attacked at the behest of a local religious leader called Sadullah, dubbed the 'Mad Mullah' by the British, who was intent on raising jihad. The attack was repulsed, but it quickly transpired that the whole valley was up in arms. In the view of *The Times* the episode was simply an example of what was to be expected in the early years of occupation of new territories. 'It is absolutely necessary to show the tribesmen without delay that we can bring an overwhelming force to act against them even in the fastnesses of their own mountains, and to teach them that treachery and insurrection will be sharply and swiftly punished', the paper claimed. 'That is a lesson which we have been obliged to teach savage peoples very often in many parts of the world'. If this was done then in due course the 'wild and fanatic' tribesmen would 'subside into loyal soldiers, peaceful husbandmen, and industrious traders'.[2]

That view, however, was far from unanimously held. Colonel H. B. Hanna, a veteran of the 1857 mutiny and author of several books on Indian questions, wrote to *The Times* to express his scepticism about the so-called 'forward policy'. That policy involved trying to bring independent tribal territories on the frontier under British control. It was not based merely on an altruistic desire to civilize the tribesmen; rather, it was aimed at countering the influence of Russia and the potential threat she posed to India. Hanna argued, though, that that threat was not nearly as severe as the policy's proponents claimed, and that the policy itself was provoking the tribesmen.[3] Plenty of other correspondents criticized his views, but Hanna was no lone voice. Liberal politicians denounced the government's folly, which, they suggested, was putting the Indian Empire at risk.[4] Even the arch-imperialist *Daily Mail* was to describe the idea of turning the tribesmen into British subjects as a dangerous and expensive fallacy. 'As long as they are friendly, the caterans of the hills form a frontier garrison very formidable to the invader. [. . .] Interference exasperates them and changes them from virtual allies into uncompromising foes.'[5] The proudly independent Afghans naturally wanted to repel the British from their borders – which remained ill-defined – and to stave off a repeat of earlier invasions.

In his published writings at the time, Churchill – like many of his contemporaries[6] – blamed the rising on Islamic fanaticism. In this view, the ignorant and credulous tribespeople were seduced by the wave of religious emotion for which Sadullah was the conduit and which had been fomented with help from Kabul.[7] Because fanatics were not amenable to common sense, and because their actions threatened the safety of the Empire, they had to be crushed.[8] Interestingly, when he wrote about the episode in *My Early Life*, he dismissed the religious explanation, and suggested that the outbreak could be explained 'on quite ordinary grounds'.[9] The chief of these was the presence of British troops in lands the local people considered their own. Indeed, even at the time Churchill conceded in private that the cause of the war was the forward policy itself and that it would never have taken place had the British not retained the outpost of Chitral after a previous uprising in 1895.[10]

As soon as he learnt of the rising, Churchill cut short his leave and headed back to India. A year earlier, in England, he had met Major-General Sir Bindon Blood, the man now appointed to lead the Malakand Field Force to put down the trouble. He had extracted from Blood – who had led the Chitral relief expedition – the promise that, should he ever again command a force on the frontier, he would allow Churchill to be a part of it. Churchill cabled the general to remind him of this, but to his great frustration received no reply until he was actually back in India. Blood then told Churchill that he had no places on his personal staff, but 'I should advise your coming to me as a press correspondent, and when you are here I shall put you on the strength at the first opportunity.'[11] Churchill headed for the front straight away. In line with Blood's plan, he got himself accredited to the London *Daily Telegraph* and to the *Pioneer*, an Allahabad paper on which Rudyard Kipling had cut his teeth as a young journalist.

On the face it, the idea that a serving soldier might alternate his regular job with that of journalist, at the direct instigation of the top brass, might seem a little odd. (Churchill carried on writing for the papers even after Blood made him his orderly officer.) But he was not receiving a unique favour. The same thing had already been done for Viscount Fincastle, who acted as correspondent for *The Times* and then joined the Guides Cavalry after another officer was killed. Fincastle went on to win the Victoria Cross for his conspicuous bravery in action. Churchill felt some rivalry with him and rushed out his own book on the conflict in order that Fincastle would not beat him to it. Both men were, in fact, 'embedded correspondents', for whom the pen and sword (or revolver) were interchangeable. It was through the work of such journalists – who were subject to strict military control even if they were civilians – that tales of war were communicated to the public at home. The army's approach to them was ambivalent. Many commanders regarded correspondents as a nuisance with the potential to report inconvenient facts; many of the frustrations of Churchill's early career are a testament to this. Others, however – and Blood was a case in point – recognized their possible utility as a means of communicating the army's point of view to the British people. As Lord Wolseley, the army's commander-in-chief, once explained, generals could make use of correspondents' thirst for information 'by spreading fake news among the gentlemen of the Press' as a means to deceive the enemy.[12] There is no evidence that what Churchill wrote was subject to direct manipulation, but he was certainly induced to see things from the perspective of the commanders. (By contrast he did not hold back from criticism of the Viceroy's government based at Simla.) Although he was disquieted by some of the horrors he saw during the campaign, he appreciated that the unspoken terms of Blood's offer required discretion. He wrote to his grandmother, for example, of the appalling effects that the expanding 'dum-dum' bullets used by the British had on the human body: 'The picture is a terrible one, and naturally it has a side to which one does not allude in print,'[13] although he later defended their use as being no more likely to cause suffering than ordinary bullets.[14] (Later still, when the Boers used them against the British in South Africa, it was a different story again.)[15] Well might an article in the *Fortnightly Review* ask, 'Can We Rely on Our War News?'[16]

Churchill's journey to the frontier began with a rail trip from Bangalore. Told by the ticket clerk that the distance was 2,027 miles, he gleefully contemplated the revulsion he thought Little Englanders would feel at this vastness of British territory.[17] He broke his travel at Rawalpindi and, after dinner, paid a visit to the sergeants' mess, where a sing-song was in progress. The best song, in Churchill's view, ran:

> Great White Mother, far across the sea,
> Ruler of the Empire may she ever be.
> Long may she reign, glorious and free,
> In the Great White Motherland.[18]

Suitably inspired by these lofty sentiments he continued on his way to Nowshera, the Malakand Field Force's base of operations. From then on, in the extreme heat, he had to travel an uncomfortable fifty miles in a horse-drawn tonga to the Malakand Pass. He had to wait several days in the British camp before seeing any action, but when it came it was dramatic.

On 16 September he took part in a punitive raid in the Mamund Valley. As the British forces moved into the valley they saw many tribesmen seated in lines on the terraced hillsides, their rifles upright beside them. As the British got nearer, bullets started to fly, but the skirmish did neither side much harm. Sikh infantrymen moved upwards to occupy a village (Indians formed the bulk of the British armed forces in India). The enemy seemed to have disappeared; but when the British began to retire homewards the tribesmen suddenly attacked. Churchill's newspaper account of the action was somewhat veiled, but he admitted to his mother that the retreat had been 'an awful rout' in which the wounded had been horribly mutilated by 'these wild beasts' of tribesmen. He himself fired forty rifle rounds and hit, he thought, four men. He also – with some thought of being noticed for his bravery – helped drag away a wounded Indian soldier, although the process hurt the man so much that the sepoy decided he preferred to stagger down unaided.[19] More than one in ten of those on the British side were killed or wounded in the encounter.[20]

In the wake of this humiliating battle, Blood ordered that the valley be laid waste. Churchill recalled: 'We proceeded systematically, village by village, and we destroyed the houses, filled up the wells, blew down the towers, cut down the shady trees, burned the crops and broke the reservoirs in punitive devastation.'[21] Privately he was shocked at the kind of warfare that was taking place – not only at the brutality of the tribesmen but also at the British refusal to take prisoners, wounded or otherwise.[22] On one occasion he saw Sikh troops burn a wounded man alive.[23] Publicly, though, he defended the destruction: 'Of course, it is cruel and barbarous, as is everything else in war, but it is only an unphilosophic mind that will hold it legitimate to take a man's life, and illegitimate to destroy his property.' (This was a false distinction: destroying crops and villages inevitably meant that many tribespeople would die of cold or starvation.) He argued that domestic critics of the policy, who worried about the effects on non-combatants, were deluded to think that any such people existed. In fact, he suggested, all the (male) inhabitants were combatants from childhood onwards, and all the houses were fortified, so that meaningful discrimination was impossible. The good sense of the British people would, he felt, lead them to agree with these sound and pragmatic conclusions as soon as the necessary information was put in front of them.[24] 'I have not soiled my hands with any dirty work', he told his mother, 'though I recognise the necessity of some things.'[25]

Churchill's attitude to the men he was fighting was predictably negative. In his despatches he described the rebellious Pathans as 'vermin', although he did also concede that they were brave and warlike.[26] After operations had ended he had the chance to write about them in a more reflective way, and in doing so he granted that there were occasional moments when lovers of the picturesque might feel some sympathy with their hopes and fears. Nevertheless, he believed that the Pathans were disposed to treachery and violence by virtue of their 'strong aboriginal propensity to kill'. That propensity was compounded by their religion, which in Churchill's eyes was responsible for stimulating 'a wild and merciless fanaticism'. The tribes were dirty, ignorant, superstitious and degraded, he claimed. They loved plunder and had an incomprehensible code of honour. Their state of mental development, he suggested, was such that civilized people would not know whether to laugh or cry. He did not believe, though, that they were condemned to degradation purely by virtue of their ethnicity. After all, those tribesmen who had earlier come over to the British side proved themselves highly useful. To him, the Afridi and Pathan companies of the Guides Infantry were like 'a well-trained pack of hounds. Their cries, their movements, and their natures are similar.' Although he viewed these soldiers as dirty, lazy spendthrifts (in contrast to the hygienic, thrifty Sikhs), he defended them against charges of untrustworthiness.[27] Churchill's opinions may strike the modern reader as patronizing and Islamophobic, but it is important not to romanticize the tribesmen, or to suggest that Churchill's views were completely antediluvian. His strictures on the tribes' treatment of women, for example, were by no means unfounded. However, his bald assertion 'Civilisation is face to face with militant Mohammedanism' greatly exaggerated the threat that the Empire faced.[28]

II

Throughout the fighting Churchill did his best to impress his superiors through conspicuous bravery (or recklessness). When the firing started he carried on riding his pony while others dived for cover – but only, as he told Lady Randolph, when there was a chance that someone might notice.[29] He did not get the medal he longed for, and had to be content with a mention in despatches for having 'made himself useful at a critical moment' during the action of 16 September.[30] When the fighting in the Mamund Valley came to an end he was obliged to return to his regiment and the old routine. By late October, barely seven weeks after he had left, he was back in Bangalore. He was already bent on writing *The Story of the Malakand Field Force*, which would bring his name before a wider public and help get him into politics. (He had been annoyed that his *Daily Telegraph* letters had been published anonymously.) His manuscript was completed by the end of the year, with the assistance David Konar, a clerk of around his own age, who recalled him as quiet but hard working.[31] On the part of the original manuscript that survives there is a telling amendment made by Churchill: 'the prestige of the dominant race enables them to ~~keep up appearances before~~ maintain their superiority over the native troops'.[32] In his rush to beat Fincastle into print, Churchill sacrificed the chance to check the proofs himself and entrusted them to his uncle, Moreton Frewen, known as 'The Mortal Ruin' because of the permanently catastrophic state of his finances. The result was an embarrassing series of errors that detracted from the book's genuine literary virtues. The *Athenaeum* said it resembled 'a volume by Disraëli revised by a mad printer's reader'.[33] It remains one of Churchill's most misunderstood works, but when read in conjunction with his original despatches and his private letters it yields important insights into his early imperial thought.

Many scholars have suggested that the book revealed Churchill as an outspoken critic of the government's frontier policy.[34] 'Winston was not timid about criticizing British policy', we are told. 'What was the point of extending the British presence into the inaccessible North-West Frontier?' he asked. 'The tribesmen were best left alone.'[35] He is said to have viewed the forward policy 'with great scepticism'.[36] Another writer argues, 'Churchill opposed the extension of the imperial frontier on both financial and moral grounds.'[37] Others show signs of confusion. For example, the official biographer claims that Churchill thought the whole Malakand expedition was a mistake while simultaneously suggesting that he favoured annexation of the borderlands.[38] Yet another writer argues that Churchill favoured an expansionary policy, albeit 'not without regrets'.[39]

So what was Churchill really arguing? In the preface to the book, he disclaimed any intention to write a party pamphlet on an imperial issue. He had no case to make, he claimed, against any policy or person; he had merely recorded the facts.[40] This was disingenuous. As the *United Service Gazette* observed, there was an obvious disparity between Churchill's promise of neutrality and his actual performance.[41] In spite of his protestations, he had a clear policy agenda in favour of the forward policy. We can see this by tracing in detail the way in which his thinking about the frontier had evolved.

He first addressed the question even while the fighting was still going on, in a despatch of 21 September 1897. Using a line of reasoning that he was to deploy consistently, he suggested that although it was not hard to find arguments against the forward policy, it was doubtful that it had ever been possible to avoid that policy. The forward movement was now, he said, 'beyond recall'. Retreat was impossible, and 'the more rapid the advance the sooner will the troubles of a transition stage be over'. He argued for the (very ambitious) frontier Gilgit–Chitral–Jellabad–Kandahar.[42] At first his mother declined to forward this despatch to the *Daily Telegraph*; she appears to have thought it would get her son into difficulties with his superiors.[43] Churchill assured her that it was not the case: 'Far from getting me into trouble it expresses what is essentially the military view.' He pointed out that his views were in line with those of Sir George White, the Commander-in-Chief in India.[44] Churchill was absolutely right about this. White's term was about to end, and at his farewell dinner he argued that 'civilization and barbarism' could not coexist peaceably. 'We hear a great deal of abuse of the "forward" policy, but look back on the history of the world and you will see that, by fate's inexorable decree, civilization must advance and savagery recede.'[45] In the light of this it is unsurprising that Churchill's article, when published, did not cause him any problems with the army hierarchy. In the final letter of the series, written on 16 October, Churchill argued that the gains from trade in the newly pacified valleys would never repay the cost of the military expenditure, but that it was impossible to retreat. He also remarked that 'morally, it is unfortunate for the tribesmen that our spheres of influence clash with their spheres of existence'.[46] When he reproduced this observation in his book, the *United Service Gazette* commented that it was not a bad epigram, 'though to our duller comprehension it would seem as if the moral misfortune did not attach to the tribesmen'.[47]

In private, Churchill was more ambivalent. Back in Bangalore in October, he wrote to his mother that although the initiators of the forward policy bore responsibility for the war, they may in fact have found it impossible to act otherwise.

> At any rate now we are started we can't go back and must go on. And the sooner the better. Financially it is ruinous. Morally it is wicked. Militarily it is an open question, and politically it is a blunder. But we can't pull up now. Annexation is the word which the B.P. [British Public] will have ultimately to swallow, and the sooner they do it, the sooner things will begin to mend.

He added that Britain would eventually have to absorb territory right up to the frontier with Russia.[48]

Several days later he sent Lady Randolph a tribeswoman's amulet, and commented sarcastically that although it was neither valuable nor pretty it was at least 'a tangible result of the "Forward Policy"'. He had found it in a village which had cost the British seventy casualties to take, and he thus found it 'a bitter comment on the wild and wasteful course upon which we are now embarked'.[49] He told another relative that the forward policy was 'an awful business'.[50] However, he appears to have objected not to expansion and annexation per se but rather to the methods by which it was being pursued. And even his dislike of those methods does not appear to have dented his belief that, having been started, the policy should be continued. That was to be the keynote of his argument in the final chapter of *The Story of the Malakand Field Force*, which he called 'The Riddle of the Frontier'.

Churchill, it is true, made some efforts to hedge his bets. He emphasized that he was proceeding in a spirit of cautious inquiry, and that his conclusions were only a guess. He acknowledged that there were plenty of plausible arguments against the forward policy. As in his original despatches, he made no attempt to deny one of the strongest of these – that it cost more money than it could possibly generate in return. However, he believed that, as he put it elsewhere in the book, 'Imperialism and economics clash as often as honesty and self-interest'; that is to say, the policy should not be rejected on grounds of expense alone.[51] And he suggested that it was fruitless to argue over whether it had been right to begin it. 'We have crossed the Rubicon', he claimed. It was necessary to find a defensible frontier: 'The old line has been left, and between that line and an advanced line continuous with Afghan territory, and south of which all shall be reduced to law and order, there does not appear to be any prospect of a peaceful and permanent settlement.' This did not mean that he favoured a policy of 'full steam ahead', as he put it. He ridiculed the idea of a field force operating non-stop in the frontier valleys until they had been rendered as pacific as Hyde Park, an exercise for which Britain lacked both the money and the troops. He preferred instead the system in force prior to the uprising – that is one 'of gradual advance, of political intrigue among the tribes, of subsidies and small expeditions'. This, it should be noted, was an argument about means and not about ends. Churchill *did* criticize both the government of India and that of Britain, not for their advocacy of the forward policy, but rather for their failure to advocate it openly. 'They know they cannot turn back. They fully intend to go on. Yet they fear to admit the situation, to frankly lay their case before the country, and trust to the good sense and courage of an ancient democracy.'[52] The authorities were thus reproached not with excessive ardour but with unnecessary timidity – a criticism which, although it cannot have been entirely welcome, was hardly deeply wounding in the circumstances.

Contemporaries were quite able to recognize the drift of his

argument. Although some reviewers took his claim not to be offering a political tract at face value,[53] many others saw through it.
In fact, he makes it abundantly clear that he is a strong partisan of
the most forward "Forward Policy"', observed the *United Service
Gazette*.[54] The *Pall Mall Gazette* likewise noted that 'he plunges for
the Forward Policy'.[55] The *Review of Reviews* found that Churchill's
political views were 'not new, being simply a repetition of the stock
arguments of the advocates of the Forward School'.[56] Some reviewers expressed approval of Churchill's stance; others were scornful of
his extensive territorial ambitions. The Liberal *Daily News* suggested
that Churchill was in favour of Britain occupying the whole of
Afghanistan, as far as its border with Russia. It sneered, 'If the
Forwards mean to annex Jellalabad and Candahar, why they may
just as well finish the job by annexing the city of Cabul and all
Afghanistan up to and beyond Herat, and shake hands (or exchange
shots) with the Russian outposts.'[57] Of the British papers, only the
Scotsman's reviewer seemed in any doubt about what the book was
arguing, and even he succeeded in puzzling through the policy
implications in the end: 'he [Churchill] seems, if we understand
him aright [. . .] to criticise unfavourably the Forward Policy. But
then he is still more severe upon the alternative policy, of standing
still, and upon its advocates; and he holds that having committed
ourselves to the course of garrisoning the passes and defending
Afghanistan against aggression, we are bound on all accounts to
go through with it.'[58] One can almost hear the mental cogs turning. The *Times of India*, for its part, offered general applause for
Churchill's views on the frontier issue as well as for his defence of
village-burning. It ventured that although such practices might invite
condemnation if employed in the course of 'ordinary international
warfare', civilized standards sometimes required 'considerable qualification' in the special conditions of the North-West Frontier.[59]
Churchill visited the paper's editor and thanked him with a smile:
'That's the very first time any newspaper has ever published a
leading article about me, *but it won't be the last!*'[60]

Almost as if he desired to erase any remaining ambiguity,
Churchill followed up his book with an article on 'The Ethics of
Frontier Policy'. In it, he repeated the now-familiar argument that
it was impossible either to turn back or to stand still, and revealed
the ultimate scope of his ambitions for expansion. 'The weary march

of civilization lies onward', he wrote portentously. 'We must follow it till the Afghan border is reached and thence beyond, until ultimately India is divided from Russia only by a line of painted signposts'. (The *Daily News* was proved right.) He also said explicitly that his own ideas did not differ fundamentally from the forward policy, and that the government's attitude was to be applauded.[61] In sending a copy of the piece to a friend, he noted that he had adopted a 'circuitous insidious but none the less effective method of defending the Forward Policy'.[62] His defence of it was not really all that subtle; he may have convinced himself he was carrying an argumentative rapier, but somewhere along the line he had exchanged it for a blunderbuss. His admission that he had tried to be 'insidious', though, is compelling evidence that we should take the reservations in his arguments for the forward policy – which appear to have misled many historians – with a generous pinch of salt.

Given Churchill's views on the frontier question, it is hardly surprising that *The Story of the Malakand Field Force* found favour with Lord Salisbury, who asked to see Churchill when the latter returned to England briefly in the summer of 1898. According to Churchill's later recollection, the Prime Minister praised both the book's subject matter and its style.[63] Doubtless, Salisbury would not have shown such interest if it had been unreadable, but neither would he have done so had he perceived it as an attack on his own policy. Indeed, not long before the book came out, he had made a speech in the House of Lords in which he used a very similar argument to that deployed by Churchill. He opposed, he said, 'a military forward policy' and yet he argued that a forward policy, secured by other means, was 'inevitable'. The march of civilization could not be stopped.[64] (As a matter of fact the incoming Viceroy, Lord Curzon, successfully abandoned the forward policy, which proves that it was not inevitable at all.) Churchill, then, was no Young Turk daringly challenging received orthodoxy; rather, he was defending Establishment wisdom against the attacks of the heretics. In 1888, Salisbury had described small imperial wars as 'merely the surf that marks the edge of the advancing wave of civilisation'.[65] Churchill had chosen this remark as an epigraph – which was a useful method of currying favour and signifying the book's ideological agenda at the same time.[66]

III

Churchill's enforced return to his regiment after Malakand irritated him. He was eager to see more action and, even before he had completed his book, he was agitating for a place on another expedition. The tribesmen of the mountainous Tirah region – between the Khanki Valley and the Khyber Pass – had exploited the opportunity created by the Malakand rising to stage a rebellion of their own. General Sir William Lockhart was given command of an expeditionary force of 40,000 men to suppress what was the most serious anti-British outbreak since the 1857 mutiny. Lord George Hamilton, the Secretary of State for India, talked boldly of transforming the 'wild tribesmen' into loyal subjects, just as the Scottish rebels of the eighteenth century had been transformed into the Highland regiments now fighting them.[67] Those soldiers were incredibly brave, but nonetheless incurred heavy losses, provoking Liberal criticism of the sacrifice of men and money.[68] Having made substantial advances, the troops retired for the winter; but as one commander later admitted, what was 'politely called an evacuation [. . .] was really a "get away" of the worst type'.[69] In January 1898 – although still hankering to see the fighting himself – Churchill told Lady Randolph that the whole expedition had been a mistake. Regular troops, which made an ideal target for guerrilla fighters, could not 'catch or kill an impalpable cloud of skirmishers'. Lacking the means to subdue the tribesmen, it was wrong to make the attempt.[70] Yet if these remarks appeared to signal a change in his thinking about the frontier question, that change was to be short lived.

In March 1898 Churchill's efforts to get to the front – which had included a fruitless visit to Calcutta to lobby the authorities – paid off at last. Colonel Ian Hamilton, who had befriended him on his journey to England the previous year, made efforts to smooth his way. Clever, courageous and charming – 'brilliant and chivalrous', as Churchill put it – Hamilton had repeatedly showed his fearlessness in battle in Afghanistan and elsewhere. He was severely wounded during the first Boer War (1881) and was afterwards left with a withered hand. In 1891 became the youngest colonel in the British army.[71] In Churchill he clearly recognized a kindred spirit, someone who would go out and look for action rather than sit and wait for instructions. Churchill, while at a polo tournament in Meerut (only one and a half days' rail journey from the front), now begged Hamilton by telegram to arrange an interview for him with General Lockhart. Accounts conflict as to whether Hamilton actually succeeded in fixing this, but he at any rate advised Churchill to take the risk of going to see the general in Peshawar. Churchill did so, even though, unless his application for a position on the force was accepted, he would not be able to get back to Bangalore before his leave expired.[72] At this point, another man came into the picture. This was Captain Aylmer Haldane, Lockhart's aide-de-camp, who, like Hamilton, was to play a significant role in Churchill's future career.

Haldane was a dozen years older than Churchill and, prior to his service with the Tirah field force, had seen action in Waziristan and with the Chitral relief force. On 5 March he was at the bungalow headquarters of William Nicholson, the field force's Chief of Staff, when Churchill arrived, and was delegated to find out what he wanted. Haldane had already heard of Churchill, and was immediately impressed by him. 'He struck me almost at first sight as cut out on a vastly different pattern from any officer of his years I had so far met', he recalled.[73] He persuaded Nicholson to accept him onto the staff. Churchill wrote: 'I have never met this man before and I am at a loss to know why he should have espoused my cause – with so strange an earnestness.' His first impression was that Haldane was intelligent, brave, ambitious and conscientious, and with extraordinary influence over Nicholson, albeit he was very unpopular.[74] Although he soon decided that his new friend was not quite as clever as he first thought – and at times found him overbearing and irritating – the two got on 'capitally'. Haldane confessed to Churchill that he was unhappily married.[75] Churchill, for his part, told Haldane that he aimed to go into politics, and talked to him of books (including H. G. Wells, Winwood Reade and Gibbon). 'As we trudged along the dusty roads near Peshawar he would quote snatches from Rudyard Kipling', Haldane remembered.[76]

By this time the field force's activities were more or less at an end. Churchill did see some fighting – Ian Hamilton, another latecomer to the expedition, recalled seeing him 'enjoying himself amongst the bullets' in the Bara Valley.[77] His chief service, though, was as a propagandist. As Hamilton acknowledged in his memoirs, under the terms of the peace deal that Nicholson patched up, the tribesmen 'surrendered some thousands of their rifles, most of them captured or stolen from us, and were [. . .] given umpteen heavy bags of silver to induce them to go on pretending they had been defeated'.[78] Churchill, though, was to drop his previous private criticisms and to describe the outcome much more optimistically. Haldane's influence may have been important here. 'So far as I could I took care to ensure that he [Churchill] should meet those whose views on frontier policy I had imbibed from my seniors and which seemed to be sound', the older man recalled; 'and he several times discussed with Colonel Warbuton [one of the force's political officers] the recent troubles on the border and their bearing on future problems'.[79] As Churchill put it later, Haldane's inside descriptions of the operations 'showed me that much went on of which I and the general public were unconscious'.[80] Or to put it another way, he was given the army's 'spin'.

Churchill showed his usefulness when Haldane revealed to him that Nicholson had been incensed by an article in the *Fortnightly Review* criticizing the conduct of the campaign.[81] The general had been so stung, in fact, that he had written a reply, signed it 'Chief of the Staff', and sent it to the *Fortnightly*. Churchill realized that this was undignified, if not improper, and successfully urged that Nicholson should withdraw the piece from publication.[82] Probably as a direct result of this incident, Churchill wrote his own article. Styled as a private letter to a Conservative MP – an artifice which can have fooled few – it was published in *The Times*. He did not make any effort to rebut criticisms of the campaign in detail, but instead dismissed them as gossip generated by 'stragglers' who had rushed home early. He denied that the results had been disappointing: 'The business has been finished and yet while the army receives the humble submission of the most ferocious savages in Asia, we are assailed by the taunts and reproaches of our countrymen at home.' At one point, though, he seemed to give the game away. He told the touching story of Private James Clow, who was accidentally shot by one of his fellow-soldiers with a dum-dum bullet and had to have his leg amputated. Invalided home, Clow and others of the wounded were visited by the Queen, and he told her he thought he had been hit by a Martini bullet (which might have been fired by a tribesman).

Churchill saluted Clow's well-meaning disingenuity: 'This poor man – penniless & a cripple, because he thought the truth might "give away" the regiment to which he belonged, had concocted this fiction' in order to save its honour.[83] But as the Liberal *Westminster Gazette* pointed out, Churchill clearly believed that if Clow was entitled to deceive the Queen to spare his regiment, then he, Churchill, was also entitled to deceive the public so as to shield the army. 'We are not criticising this ingenious "concocter of fiction", James Clow, but the eulogy he gets is a sufficient revelation of what Mr Churchill's "accepted creed" in these matters is. Mr Churchill may not be deceiving us – but how can we be in the least sure that he is not a second Clow?'[84]

IV

After the Tirah campaign, Churchill determined to make his way to the Sudan, where the British reconquest was entering its climactic phase. After the death of General Gordon at Khartoum in 1885, British and Egyptian forces had withdrawn from the country. The Mahdi died just a few months after his victory. Under his nominated successor, the Khalifa 'Abdallahi, the Mahdist state established its writ with a fair degree of success. It had a tolerable postal service, a taxation system that aspired towards fairness, and its own currency. In Omdurman, the new capital, the Khalifa made some efforts at slum clearance.[85] All this belied the idea that the Mahdists – usually referred to by the British as 'Dervishes' – were merely savages. A similar point struck Churchill when he at last found his way into the Khalifa's abandoned house, with its bathroom served by hot and cold water. Its owner, he thought, 'must have possessed civilised qualities', as he was clearly a man who understood life's decencies.[86] Nonetheless, the state was a tyranny, and suffered from corruption. Confiscation was used as a weapon against internal enemies, but the more it was deployed the more those enemies multiplied. The Khalifa's power base weakened. Jihad, the state's guiding force and motivational principle, generated diminishing returns as the population wearied of war. There was, moreover, the type of legislation that is familiar in Islamist states today. Women were to be veiled outside the home, and those who disobeyed were beaten; those who ventured into the market place could be punished with one hundred lashes.[87] The escaped European captives who acted as anti-Mahdist propagandists may have exaggerated the horrors of the regime – as Churchill for one appreciated – but they had plenty of material with which to work.[88]

Neither dislike for the regime nor the desire for revenge for Gordon's death was enough in itself to provoke the British into action. But in 1896 the Italian army was heavily defeated by the Abyssinians at the Battle of Adowa. The Cabinet agreed to help the Italians by relieving Mahdist pressure on their garrison at Kassala. The resulting British–Egyptian advance was to turn into an unstoppable juggernaut of reconquest. This satisfied several impulses at once: Lord Salisbury's hatred of the 'false religion' of Islam, the public's desire to avenge Gordon, the government's wish to frustrate other great powers in the region, and its urge to control the upper reaches of the Nile in the interests of Egypt's economy and in turn its bondholders.[89] It should not be assumed, however, that support for the reconquest was unanimous. Some Liberals felt that it had not been properly thought through, and warned that Britain risked overtaxing her strength.[90]

The man in charge was H. H. Kitchener, the Commander-in-Chief (or 'Sirdar') of the Egyptian army. He spoke Arabic and he knew the ground, having served in Sudan as an intelligence officer with the doomed Gordon Relief Expedition. His most remarkable achievement of the campaign was his construction of a railway across the desert, cutting journey times to a fraction of what had been possible by steamer or camel and ending the seasonal dependence on the level of the Nile. Churchill observed in a masterly chapter of *The River War* that mere flesh and blood could scarcely hope to prevail against this magnificent combination of planning and machinery. 'Fighting the Dervish was primarily a matter of transport', he wrote. 'The Khalifa was conquered on the railway.'[91] Kitchener gained a reputation as 'the man who has cut out his human heart and made himself a machine to retake Khartum'.[92] He was also autocratic, highly secretive and did not, as a rule, care much for correspondents.

After the British victory at Atbara in April 1898, the fall of the Mahdist regime was all but assured. The question for Churchill was whether he could get to the Sudan in time to see the endgame.

After Tirah he headed to England on leave, which was when he had the meeting with Salisbury mentioned above. He prevailed upon the Prime Minister, and as many others as he could (including the Prince of Wales), to persuade Kitchener to accept his attachment. He was, in fact, only one of a long list of supplicants; the Queen's grandson Prince Christian Victor of Schleswig-Holstein, for instance, was another.[93] Yet in this instance the Sirdar would not bend. He was probably suspicious of Churchill's intention to write about the campaign. Only a last-minute vacancy in the 21st Lancers – which was not part of the Egyptian army and therefore came under the authority of the War Office rather than the Sirdar – enabled Churchill to join in time for the final phase. His bitterness against Kitchener was considerable.

Churchill again contracted to write for the press – this time for the *Morning Post*. He was, in fact, one of a whole pack of journalists; Kitchener had earlier tried and failed to limit coverage to that of Reuters.[94] One of the correspondents was G. W. Steevens of the *Daily Mail*, described by H. L. Mencken as 'the greatest newspaper reporter who ever lived';[95] by Churchill as 'the most brilliant man in journalism I have ever met';[96] and by Kitchener (who plagiarized his reports for his own despatches) as a 'genius'.[97] Pale and thin but also witty and cheerful, he held strong Social Darwinist views and was a brilliant propagandist of Empire; Churchill was especially impressed by his article 'From the New Gibbon', a pastiche which warned against the decadence that might lead to the downfall of the British Empire.[98] Steevens was soon to boost Churchill's career with an article that dubbed him 'the youngest man in Europe'. He shrewdly observed that his new friend had qualities that could make him 'almost at will, a great popular leader, a great journalist, or the founder of a great advertising business'.[99] He and Churchill were often compared to one another, although the latter was undoubtedly the superior writer.[100] After Steevens's death of fever during the Boer War, Churchill repaid his compliments: 'Modest yet proud, wise as well as witty, cynical but above all things sincere, he combined the characters of a charming companion and a good comrade.'[101] Another colleague in the Sudan was Hubert Howard of *The Times*, who was to survive the Battle of Omdurman only to be hit by 'a friendly shell' later the same day. It struck Churchill as strange that the experienced Howard should be killed and he himself escape unscathed; but, as he vaingloriously remarked to his mother, who could say that that result should not be better for the Empire?[102]

V

The Battle of Omdurman – or Karari, as it is known locally – took place on 2 September 1898. The Mahdists chose to fight outside the city, and to attack in daylight. Against the amassed British weaponry they stood no chance; surviving veterans interviewed in the 1970s spoke unaffectedly of their quest for martyrdom.[103] The Mahdists were to suffer, by one estimate, 11,000 dead and 16,000 wounded.[104] British-Egyptian losses were trivial in comparison – 48 killed and 428 wounded.[105] From their point of view the only thing that went seriously wrong during the battle was the famous charge of the 21st Lancers, in which Churchill was caught up. At 8.40 a.m. the Lancers received orders to harass the enemy, who by this time had already suffered heavy losses, and to try and prevent them retreating to Omdurman. As they advanced they came under fire from a group of what appeared to be only a few hundred Mahdists. The Lancers' colonel – who was clearly out for glory come what may – ordered the troops to turn and charge directly at them. However, they discovered too late that a further great mass of enemy soldiers were concealed in a dry watercourse for which they were directly headed. The Lancers plunged in, and in the next two minutes five officers and sixty-five men out of a total strength of 310 were killed or wounded, as were about 120 horses. Churchill described vividly how the mutual butchery seemed to pass in silence; the scene seemed to flicker like a cinematograph picture.[106] He had previously expressed his 'keen aboriginal desire to kill several of these odious dervishes', and he now got his wish.[107] His estimates of his personal tally were to vary, but he was certain he shot at least three.[108] He reached the far side unscathed, but was frustrated that the regiment did not turn about and do it all over again. Although this would have been 'magnificent' rather than 'practical', he told his mother, 'another fifty or sixty casualties would have made the performance historic – & have made us all proud of our race & blood'.[109]

The charge was instantly commemorated as an act of imperial

heroism, but Kitchener was displeased at the needless loss of life.[110] Steevens – not a man quick to allege military incompetence – condemned it as a 'gross blunder'. 'For cavalry to charge unbroken infantry, of unknown strength, over unknown ground, within a mile of their own advancing infantry, was as grave a tactical crime as cavalry could possibly commit', he argued.[111] Churchill, though, claimed that the charge – even though it had little impact on the actual outcome of the battle – 'was of perhaps as great value to the Empire as the victory itself'. This was because the courage of the soldiers would reassure British patriots that the Empire was not suffering degeneration or decay, and that 'the blood of the race' continued to circulate with health and vigour.[112]

Such views might suggest that Churchill's ideas had developed little since his North-West Frontier experiences. He continued often (if not invariably) to use the word 'savages' to refer to the Sudanese – although in one despatch he restrainedly struck out the word 'filthy' that had originally preceded it.[113] He continued to view Islam as being 'as dangerous in a man as hydrophobia in a dog', and blamed it for stifling economic development – although he did acknowledge that it gave its believers bravery in death.[114] Nevertheless, he came to admire the courage of the Sudanese warriors; furthermore, the aftermath of the battle made a profound impression on him. The horrors that he saw may help explain the relatively nuanced (if sometimes conflicting) opinions that he was to express over the coming months. He never questioned that the war had been necessary, yet he did criticize certain aspects of its conduct and showed some appreciation of the Mahdists' motives. The contradictions in his behaviour may well be accounted for by his mixed emotions – on the one hand, unstinted faith in the British Empire; on the other, first-hand knowledge of the cruelties it could sometimes inflict. The picture was further complicated by his feelings of resentment towards Kitchener.

Of course, he had seen barbarities committed by the British side in India, but the sheer scale of the killing at Omdurman was new to him. Three days after the battle he toured the site with the Marquess of Tullibardine, who was serving with the Egyptian cavalry, and he described the scene in an extraordinary despatch of 10 September. The dead Sudanese were strewn across the ground, sometimes two or three deep. In one place more than four hundred bodies were packed into a hundred square yards. The corpses were of monstrous appearance, bloated to huge proportions by the sun. Churchill and Tullibardine cautiously approached the remaining wounded, and distributed what water they had. They saw a man with only one foot who had crawled a mile since the battle but who was still two miles from the river. Another man had reached the Nile only to die at its edge. Churchill wrote, in what has become a famous passage:

> there was nothing *dulce et decorum* about the Dervish dead. Nothing of the dignity of unconquerable manhood. All was filthy corruption. Yet these were as brave men as ever walked the earth. The conviction was borne in on me that their claim beyond the grave in respect of a valiant death was as good as that which any of our countrymen could make. The thought may not be original. It may happily be untrue. It was certainly most unwelcome.[115]

Expressions of respect for the enemy dead were indeed quite conventional – 'the Dervishes were superb', wrote Steevens[116] – but that is not to say that Churchill's sentiments were less than heartfelt. He even wrote of how his sense of victory faded to be replaced by a 'mournful feeling of disgust'. Yet he ended his despatch on an optimistic note, perhaps comforted by Winwood Reade's vision of warfare rendering itself redundant once it had fulfilled its social function. The 'terrible machinery of scientific war' had completed its work, Churchill wrote. He looked forward to a time long in the future when the plain of Omdurman would be converted through irrigation to a 'fertile garden' supporting a great metropolis, and the battle itself would be but dimly remembered.[117] In this analysis, even the filthy corruption of the defeated dead did not detract from the war's ultimate civilizing purpose.

VI

After the Sudanese war, Churchill went back to India briefly. But in the spring of 1899 he left the army – not least because writing and journalism were more profitable, and because in England he could pursue politics – and he never returned to India again. By this stage he had embarked on *The River War* (and he also completed a novel, *Savrola*). This book illustrates Churchill's growing intellectual maturity; and yet, other statements made around the time he was writing it are suggestive of some internal conflict on his part.

Churchill had been upset by two aspects of the battle's aftermath: the maltreatment of the Sudanese wounded and the of desecration of the Mahdi's tomb. He underwent several twists and turns of opinion in respect to both issues. In a letter to Ian Hamilton of 16 September 1898 he called the treatment of the wounded 'disgraceful', and reported that his private remarks on these lines had been repeated to an angry Kitchener.[118] Furthermore, his account of the battle's aftermath – quoted above – provided fuel for critics of the campaign. In October the editor of *Concord* magazine wrote to the *Westminster Gazette*, describing the battle as a 'massacre' and citing in support 'Lieutenant Churchill's account of how the enemy was "destroyed, not conquered by machinery", and of the terrible scenes on the battlefield afterwards'. However, Churchill did not like the construction placed on his account and wrote a reply. He declined to discuss 'the legitimacy of the practice of killing the wounded' but denied there had been 'unnecessary bloodthirstiness'.[119]

Churchill then changed his tune again. Ernest Bennett, the *Gazette*'s war correspondent, had written a book in which he alleged that 'in many cases wounded Dervishes, unarmed and helpless, were butchered from sheer wantonness and lust of bloodshed'.[120] He reiterated these charges in the *Contemporary Review* in January 1899, and also turned his fire on Churchill. Bennett poured scorn on one of his *Morning Post* articles, in which Churchill argued, 'The laws of war do not admit the right of a beaten enemy to quarter.'[121] Bennett wrote that this 'truly remarkable utterance' was 'absolutely at variance' with the laws of war; it was 'monstrous' to assert 'that quarter need not be given to the vanquished'.[122] Perhaps Churchill's conscience was stung by this, as he now told his cousin that he was determined to reveal the truth, even at the risk of an outcry.[123] He told his mother that he had read Bennett's article, without mentioning that he himself had been attacked in it. 'It is vy clever & as far as my experience goes absolutely correct', he wrote. 'I am going to avoid details of all kinds on this subject and shall merely say that "the victory at Omdurman" was disgraced by the inhuman slaughter of the wounded and that Kitchener is responsible for this.'[124]

In the book itself, published in November, Churchill claimed that unarmed wounded had been killed and that Kitchener could have done more to make it clear he did not desire this. It is worth noting that Churchill blamed the atrocities chiefly on non-white troops, plenty of whom had been recently assimilated from the ranks of the enemy.[125] (Some years later, though, he recalled that he had seen British troops 'spearing the wounded and leaning with their whole weight on their lances'.)[126] Yet even these fairly modest criticisms were silently withdrawn when a new condensed edition of the book was published in 1902. It was a similar tale with the Mahdi's tomb episode. Churchill witnessed the Commons debate on the issue, and later recalled his sympathy with the Liberal attacks.[127] But in June, on the eve of his first election campaign, he said that Kitchener's critics had blown things out of proportion, and that the Sirdar himself had not been directly responsible for 'the barbarity which was perpetrated' and was in fact sheltering his subordinates.[128] In response, Wilfrid Scawen Blunt wrote to the *Daily News* arguing that Kitchener was 'the sole culprit';[129] perhaps it was on account of this that Churchill said in *The River War* that the tomb had been profaned 'By Sir H. Kitchener's orders'. If the Sudanese still venerated the Mahdi, the book argued, then 'to destroy what was sacred and holy to them was a wicked act'.[130] But again, the criticisms were cut out of the later edition.

Churchill's alternating attitudes may be explained partly by the ambivalence of his own feelings.[131] He struggled to reconcile the demands of his conscience with those of political conformity. He originally submitted the passages on Kitchener to Lord Salisbury, to whom he dedicated the book, offering to delete them if the Prime Minister disapproved. Salisbury was happy to accept the dedication without any excisions being made – which suggests that he did not think Churchill had gone beyond the bounds of fair comment.[132] (After all, even the Queen disapproved of the destruction of the tomb.)[133] Nor did the book's publication provoke the storm of criticism that Churchill had anticipated. The *Daily Telegraph*, it is true, was not the only paper to feel that the criticisms of Kitchener were an 'obvious and serious blot' on the book (which it thought otherwise admirable). The *World* thought the volumes revealed Churchill's belief that he could have run the campaign better than Kitchener.[134] The harshest review of all, by F. I. Maxse in the *National Review*, strongly deprecated the attacks on the Sirdar, alleged serial errors of fact and claimed that Churchill had played up the role of British soldiers at the expense of their Egyptian and Sudanese comrades.[135] Luckily for Churchill, though, Maxse's piece did not come out until 1900, by which time he had achieved hero status in the Boer War and the negative publicity found no purchase. Many of the other reviewers did not comment on the Kitchener aspect at all. At least one positively approved of his 'blistering castigation' of the Sirdar.[136] In other words, although his statements were surely unusual for someone seeking a Conservative parliamentary seat, they did not, for most commentators, stray outside the limits of acceptable discourse. Perhaps, though, Churchill became aware of his own public inconsistencies as his passions about the issues faded. If so, the need to shorten the book for the one-volume republication may have provided a useful excuse to exclude problematic material.[137]

This puzzle should not distract us from other, equally interesting elements of the book. There is a very striking passage near the beginning in which he reflects on the disparity between the noble aspirations of imperialists and the sordid realities that arose when attempts were made to put them into practice: 'The inevitable gap between conquest and dominion becomes filled with the figures of the greedy trader, the inopportune missionary, the ambitious soldier, and the lying speculator, who disquiet the minds of the conquered and excite the sordid appetites of the conquerors.' His way of reconciling himself to this problem was simply to assert that, nonetheless, the desire to conquer was an innate and healthy part of the human condition.[138] Such reflections, together with Churchill's sensitive portrayals of General Gordon and even of the Mahdi, show that he was not content merely to churn out the standard imperial propaganda. Again, some reviewers approved.[139] Churchill rejected the idea – and here was a contrast with his writings on the frontier revolt – that the original Mahdist rebellion had simply been a product of fanaticism. In his opinion, the Sudanese had had legitimate grievances against Egyptian rule. He also denied that the reconquest had been fought either to avenge Gordon – a popular view – or to 'chastise the wickedness of the Dervishes'. Rather, its justification was simple: 'Certain savage men had invaded the Egyptian territories, had killed their inhabitants and their guardians, and had possessed themselves of the land. In due course it became convenient, as well as desirable, to expel these intruders and reoccupy these territories.'[140] This explanation begged a number of questions – were the Egyptians themselves not intruders in the Sudan? – but it was seen at the time as refreshingly lacking in cant.[141]

Churchill's description of his hopes for the future of the Sudan is revealing of his conception of the link between empire, race and economic development. He suggested that after the war, as the population of the country gradually recovered, pressure on land and the local inhabitants' demand for the products of civilization would bring the less fertile areas into cultivation. As a result, the condition of the people would gradually improve and they would – over a very extensive period – experience biological and cultural evolution. Their 'type and intelligence' would improve and their ideals and morality would become purer and less degraded. (Churchill confessed himself unable to explain why they should be obliged to toil and not stay 'contented, if degraded'; but he argued that proof that there was no such obligation would amount to 'a very good case for universal suicide'.)[142] The book thus married the belief that non-white races were *currently* inferior with the conviction that they had the potential to advance in the future and deserved guidance, in the form of British rule, towards that end. Admittedly, it would not be easy to attract to the Sudan the kind of men who could give that guidance. Churchill conceded that a proportion of British officers were adherents of 'what is known as "the damned nigger" theory'. But, he claimed, this view almost always disappeared as soon as the officers realized that their honour was dependent on the condition of the people under their control being satisfactory.[143] Empire, therefore, helped improve the rulers as well as the ruled. Defenders of Churchill's racial attitudes correctly point out that throughout his career he often spoke up for the welfare of indigenous peoples. His humanitarianism did not imply a belief in racial equality, though, but rather accompanied a conviction that 'degraded' races were susceptible to improvement over the very long run.

Success in the Sudan helped the government recover ground it had lost over the Indian frontier uprisings. The unequivocal military victory reminded people of Gladstone's humiliation over Gordon's death, and divided the opposition. The Liberals split between those such as John Morley, who were sceptical of what they saw as a policy of indefinite imperial expansion, and those such as Sir Edward Grey, who held that the expedition had been necessary. At the same time the government sent a clear message to the other great powers. It dramatically faced down France, who had sent a force to Fashoda on the Upper Nile to lay claim to a vast tract of territory; for a time, until France retreated, it seemed that war might break out. (Churchill described the French actions as a 'vile intrigue'.)[144] All this generated British self-confidence – what Churchill called the 'Imperial spark'.[145] If the Sudan had impressed on him some of the darker aspects of Empire, it had not shaken his fundamental faith in its civilizing mission. He remained optimistically certain – as he had put it in *The Story of the Malakand Field Force* – that the credulity and fanaticism of indigenous peoples could be driven from the earth 'under the combined influences of Rationalism and machine guns'.[146] But Britain's next war, in South Africa, was to demonstrate that imperial optimism could easily verge into hubris.

3

A CONVENIENT WAY OF SEEING
THE EMPIRE, 1899–1901

ON-BOARD ship after his landmark conference with Roosevelt and Stalin at Yalta in February 1945, Churchill fell to reminiscing about the Boer War, as he often did when he was in a good mood. 'That was before war degenerated', he said. 'It was great fun galloping about.'[1] At the close of a world war in which millions had been killed, such nostalgia for the supposedly more 'sporting' warfare of times past was understandable, but it did not do justice to the brutal realities of the South African conflict. At the time, moreover, Churchill had approached that war, not only with the spirit of adventure, but with a strong sense of political commitment as well. The war not only cemented his reputation as an Empire journalist,[2] it was also a formative ideological moment for him, as his initial hostility to the rebellious Boers was much tempered by his experience as their temporary captive. Of course, the boyish nature of his initial enthusiasm for the war should not be underplayed. In the autumn of 1899, as Britain and the Boer republics headed for the precipice, he wrote to Lord Curzon that he was heading to cover the likely conflict as correspondent of the *Morning Post*. He observed: 'It is a convenient way of seeing the Empire and perhaps a memorable war, without any personal expense.'[3]

I

The war had been a long time in the making. The 1881 British defeat at Majuba Hill – in which the Boers of the Transvaal won back their autonomy – had been viewed by many as a national humiliation. The uneasy peace that followed was broken in 1895 by the so-called Jameson Raid – a pathetically botched attempt to stir up a rebellion by British settlers (known as 'Outlanders' or 'Uitlanders') in the Transvaal. In later years, Churchill came to see the raid as a 'fountain of ill', but admitted that, at twenty-one, he had been all for it.[4] His sense of frustration at its failure was reflected in an article he wrote in its aftermath called 'Our Account with the Boers', which has never been published in full. He portrayed the Boers as an intractable people, stubbornly opposed to the progress of mankind. One part of his indictment of them was their maltreatment of the African population. He placed much more emphasis, however, on the position of the Uitlanders. They, having moved to the Transvaal in growing numbers in pursuit of its gold wealth, were denied full political rights; the Boer government understandably feared that to grant them would be a step towards British domination. Churchill, interestingly, did not rage against the oppression of the Uitlanders; he claimed that in due course they would inevitably gain direction of the Transvaal government, regardless of what Britain did. 'But if they obtain that power without British aid, they will owe no debt to the Empire, and they will bear it no loyalty.' In that case they would lose their British identity, and seize the leadership of an 'African United States', to which the British-dominated Cape Colony would be 'at best but a Canada'. Britain's power and prestige would thus be weakened, unless it was *seen to act* in the interests of its fellow-countrymen. '*Imperial* aid must redress the wrongs of the Outlanders', he wrote; '*Imperial* troops must curb the insolence of the Boers' (emphasis added). Sooner or later, he concluded, whether in 'a righteous cause or a picked quarrel', Britain would have to fight.[5] In May 1899, in a speech in Cardiff, he suggested that a military solution would be no worse than removing an aching tooth: there would be 'a wrench, a little blood' and the pain would be over. There was, he said, 'a limit to our patience, and the end was not far off'.[6] Such remarks certainly cast doubt on his claim, made during the 1900 general election, that he had 'nearly' been 'a peace-at-any price man up to the time of the declaration of the war'.[7]

By the summer of 1899, the British seemed ready to pick a fight. Uitlander grievances formed the pretext for much self-righteous posturing by Salisbury's government, while the Boers remained intransigent. The build-up to war provided the backdrop to Churchill's first election campaign. In June, soon after his final return from India, he was selected to fight a by-election at Oldham.

This was a two-member constituency, previously represented by two Tories, of whom one had died and one retired. Churchill's fellow Conservative candidate was James Mawdsley, a prominent local trade unionist. It was an implausible pairing, but it allowed the correspondent of the *Yorkshire Post* to claim that Conservatism and the workers were walking hand-in-hand in the persons of the 'Imperialistic' Churchill and the 'democratic' Mawdsley.[8] The staunchly Tory *Oldham Daily Standard* gave a fulsome account of how, at one of their meetings, they asked to be allowed 'to work for the expansion of our glorious Empire [. . .] and to devote the talent that heaven has given them for the benefit of humanity'.[9] The Liberal *Oldham Evening Chronicle*, by contrast, poured scorn on Churchill's credentials. 'He has scampered across the Soudan with the Kitchener campaign and returned with a consuming desire to enter Parliament', it scoffed. 'This experience might have qualified him as member for the Nile division of the Soudan, but it is hardly a reason why he should come and ask Oldham electors to make a member of Parliament of him.'[10] One of the Liberal candidates, Walter Runciman, criticized Churchill for his 'swashbucklering' habits. He smartly replied that the Lancashire Fusiliers had fought at Omdurman. 'They would hardly like their member [of Parliament] to welcome home a Lancashire regiment by saying they had been "swashbucklering" about the world.'[11]

This first Churchillian electoral battle has been imperfectly understood by historians. It is often discussed as though it was dominated by religion – doubtless because it was this aspect that a rueful Churchill emphasized in his memoirs.[12] During the campaign he was persuaded by his supporters to declare his opposition to the government's Clerical Tithes Bill, which was unpopular with local Nonconformist voters. As he quickly realized, such opportunism did him no great favours either with the voters or with his party's leaders. At least as important, though, were imperial questions.[13] Churchill declared that the Empire was no 'weary titan' but emphasized that if Britain was to keep it 'we must have an Imperial stock'. This required a free, well-fed and well-educated population: 'That is why we are in favour of social reform.' (The Tory commitment to social reform was genuine, but rather limited in practical terms.) 'The Radicals would have no Empire at all', he claimed. 'We would have one, and let all share the glory.'[14] Yet in spite of his attempts to paint his opponents as Little Englanders, this was no straight-forward contest between pro- and anti-imperialists. Rather, the two sides both supported imperialism but interpreted it in different ways. Alfred Emmott, Runciman's running-mate, denied Churchill's accu-sation: 'as Liberals they were anxious to preserve the Empire intact, and hand it down to future generations'. Churchill, he claimed, was enamoured of the glories of war – an accusation made throughout his career – whereas 'The interests of the men of Oldham and of this empire were summed up in the one word "Peace." '[15]

Debate was not conducted only in terms of generalities. Imperial questions intersected with local ones. Oldham was at the heart of Lancashire's textile industry, for which India was the main market. In 1894, the Liberal government had reluctantly allowed the Government of India to impose a 5 per cent duty on cotton goods in order to raise much-needed revenue. Lancashire opinion was outraged at the threat to its interests, and two years later the new Tory government secured a reduction to $3^1/_2$ per cent.[16] Yet even the reduced rate rankled, hence the question put to Churchill at one public meeting asking whether he would be prepared to vote for the total abolition of such duties. He did not commit himself firmly, but he did remark that 'if he was a representative of Oldham, and was called upon to decide whether Oldham or Bombay should suffer, his opinion was [. . .] that Bombay was very likely to go to the wall'.[17] The Radicals, he claimed, were by contrast 'prepared to sacrifice the welfare of Lancashire to the welfare of India'.[18] The theme of India's alleged exploitation of England was to crop up again in later years. In 1943 the Viceroy, Lord Wavell, wrote mockingly of how, during discussions of Britain's war debts to India, 'Winston drew [a] harrowing picture of British workmen in rags struggling to pay rich Indian mill-owners'.[19]

The dynamics of the campaign were also affected by South African developments. Early on, Churchill declared that Britain faced no threats either at home or abroad: 'India is loyal, Ireland tranquil, and never were the relations of the country with foreign powers more excellent'.[20] There was no mention of the Boers, even though he had raised the issue in his Cardiff speech the previous month. The very next day, though, Joseph Chamberlain, the Colo-nial Secretary, warned publicly that the situation in the Transvaal constituted a 'menace to British interests'.[21] Although he was not yet ready to issue an ultimatum, his speech made it clear that the British line was hardening, and that war was a real possibility if the Boers did not back down.[22] 'Directly Mr Churchill had promised Oldham the peace and prosperity of Imperialism Mr Chamberlain announced the possibility of a Transvaal war,' the Liberal *Manchester Guardian* commented sarcastically.[23] Churchill adapted his line to meet the new developments. He now argued that with the eyes of Pretoria concentrated on England, defeat of the Tories in Oldham might encourage the Transvaal regime 'to think that the Government were not supported by the great masses in England, and it might lead them to bring on war'. For this reason, the voters should back the Conservatives 'on Imperial grounds'.[24]

In fact, both Liberals were elected. This was probably nothing more than a normal mid-term anti-government swing. Churchill was not downhearted by his defeat, for which he believed superior Liberal organization was partly to blame. In a valedictory speech at the local Conservative Club, he compared the Tory struggle without a fully organized system of electoral machinery to that of the Sudanese against Kitchener's army at Omdurman.[25] In the aftermath of the campaign, as the South African situation became more acute, he stepped up his rhetoric against the Boers. At a Tory fête at Blenheim in August, he predicted that war was bound to break out eventually, but he was 'not so sure that that was such a very terrible prospect'. England, he said, was a very great power, and the Boers were 'a miserably small people'. How long, he asked, was 'the peace of the country and the Empire to be disturbed by a party of filibustering Boers'?[26] His desire for conflict was soon met. In October, while the British were preparing for a showdown, the Transvaal government handed them a propaganda coup by issuing an ultimatum of its own, demanding the withdrawal of troops on the borders and the cancelling of reinforcements. As these demands were impossible, war came quickly, the Orange Free State throwing in its lot with the Transvaal. By 14 October – two days after the first shots were fired – Churchill was on-board ship, a commission from the *Morning Post* under his belt, heading for the Cape. In *My Early Life* he satirized his own complacency about the military prospects, which at the time was widely shared.[27] 'I thought it very sporting of the Boers to take on the whole British Empire,' he recalled, 'and I felt quite glad they were not defenceless and had put themselves in the wrong by making preparations.'[28]

Within days of landing, he realized that things were not as simple as he had thought, as the Boers proved themselves to be formidable opponents. They invaded Cape Colony and besieged Kimberley and Mafeking. They also invaded the British colony of Natal and surrounded Ladysmith (Churchill's fellow correspondent G. W. Steevens was to die during the siege). They were equipped with modern weaponry, including smokeless powder and quick-firing artillery; British preparations and methods were exposed as embarrassingly inadequate.[29] 'It is astonishing how we have under-rated these people', Churchill wrote privately.[30] Publicly, he blamed the lack of preparedness on Liberals at home – the efforts of the 'Peace Party', he claimed, had delayed the despatch of vital rein-forcements.[31] Heading for Durban by steamer, he found some relief from the gloom, falling into rhapsodies about the future possibilities of the development of South Africa. Here, finally, was a land where white men could rule and prosper, he felt. 'As yet only the indolent Kaffir enjoys its bounty, and, according to the antiquated philos-ophy of Liberalism, it is to such that it should for ever belong.'[32]

From Durban he travelled on to the small township of Estcourt, where he found Aylmer Haldane (his friend from Tirah days) and Leo Amery (his former schoolmate who was now a correspondent with *The Times*). There he fretted for a few days, seeking oppor-tunities for action. On the night of 14 November Churchill and Amery accepted Haldane's invitation to join a reconnaissance mission towards Ladysmith the next day aboard an armoured train.[33] (Churchill had already taken part in one such mission, which had been uneventful.) When he and Amery, who shared a tent, were called at 5.30 a.m., the latter was convinced the train would not depart on time so stayed in bed. In fact, it left promptly and Churchill only just caught it, setting off on a journey that would end in his capture and imprisonment. Years later, during a discussion of early rising, Amery took the episode as proof that the early worm is likely to get caught. Churchill responded: 'If I had not been early, I should not have been caught. But if I had not been caught, I could not have escaped, and my imprisonment and escape provided me with materials for lectures and a book which brought me enough money to get into Parliament in 1900 – ten years before you!'[34]

The armoured train was practically useless as a military tool. The enemy received audible warning of its progress, it provided an all-too-visible target for fire, and its way could be easily blocked. Churchill was well aware of its defects, yet he was reckless. The train got as far as the station at Frere, where Haldane reported back to HQ by telegraph, but instead of waiting for a reply – which would have told him to stay put as the Boers had the previous night been sighted at Chieveley, twelve miles further on – he allowed the train to move onwards. Haldane later admitted that he himself was to blame, but had been carried away by the audacity of his 'impetuous young friend Churchill'.[35] After reaching Chieveley the train turned back – and ran into a trap. It came under fire from Boer forces on a hillside – 'Keep cool, men', said Churchill, adding, 'This will be interesting for my paper'[36] – and increased its speed accordingly. Rounding a downhill bend at pace, it smashed into a pile of rocks with which the Boers had obstructed the line. As deadly artillery fire rained down on the derailed trucks, Churchill bravely rallied the defenders and helped clear the line so that the engine, which was still moveable, could escape. This accomplished, and with the engine heading for home carrying the wounded, he went to round up stragglers and was promptly caught by the Boers. As he was led away under escort he told Haldane, who had also been captured, 'that what had taken place, though it had caused the temporary loss of his post as war correspondent, would help considerably in opening the door for him to enter the House of Commons'.[37]

II

After two days of marching, the captives were taken on to Pretoria, the Transvaal capital, by train. During the journey Churchill fell into a discussion about the war with one of his guards, H. G. Spaarwater. At one point the conversation turned to the issue of the way that black people were treated in Cape Colony in contrast to the Boer Republics. Scholars of the war have long recognized that the conflict had a major impact on the four-fifths of the region's population who were not white.[38] Many of them were simply victims, being caught up in sieges against their will – those trapped in Mafeking were forced to make do with horse-food while whites received decent rations[39] – but plenty took more active roles. For example, after overcoming resistance from the British authorities, Mohandas K. Gandhi led an ambulance corps comprising 1,100 Indians.[40] (Both he and Churchill would be present at the Battle of Spion Kop, although they did not meet.) Tens of thousands of black and 'Coloured' (mixed race) individuals became involved as auxiliaries and combatants on both sides. Non-whites who fought against the Boers risked instant execution if caught. By May 1902 at least 115,000 black people who had got in the way of British sweeping-up operations were incarcerated in concentration camps, and of these at least 14,000 died.[41] Churchill himself was aware of the role of non-white combatants, and was 'conscious of a feeling of irritation that Kaffirs should be allowed to fire on white men'.[42] Yet in time he abandoned the idea that the conflict should remain 'a white man's war', and became willing to countenance the use of Indian troops.[43] One would be hard pressed to detect the significance of the non-white dimension of the war, though, from the scholarship on Churchill. That in turn reflects the fact that comments on it in Churchill's own speeches and writings were few and far between. (When he discussed 'the two valiant, strong races' in South Africa he was referring to the British and the Dutch.)[44] Churchill's published account of the talk with Spaarwater, then, is unusual in its sustained discussion of 'the native question', and it is this which lends it particular interest.

According to Churchill, the issue of race came up when he predicted to his guard that the Boer Republics would one day enjoy freedom, under the British flag. Spaarwater responded: 'No, no, old chappie, we don't want your flag; we want to be left alone. We are free, you are not free.' Churchill asked what he meant, bringing the response: 'Well, is it right that a dirty Kaffir should walk on the pavement – without a pass too? That's what they do in your British Colonies. Brother! Equal! Ugh! Free! Not a bit. We know how to treat Kaffirs.' Reflecting on this, Churchill determined that he had exposed the genuine root of Boer hostility to British rule. Episodes such as the Jameson Raid had merely fostered that hostility, he thought, but its true origin lay in 'the abiding fear and hatred of the movement that seeks to place the native on a level with the white man'. British administration, he claimed, was linked in the Boer mind with 'violent social revolution' in which blacks would be declared equal with whites and given the same political rights. Churchill went on to develop an amusing skit, pointing up the oddities of the position of the British 'pro-Boers', in which he imagined Spaarwater conducting John Morley toward Pretoria as an honoured guest. As the Liberal pro-Boer and the actual Boer discuss the war they agree on everything, denouncing both imperialism and capitalism, until Spaarwater reveals his racial prejudices: 'And after that no more agreement: but argument growing keener and keener; gulf widening every moment.'[45]

This intriguing passage, first published in the *Morning Post*, has generally been interpreted as a sign of Churchill's relatively enlightened attitude to race.[46] When Churchill's collected despatches were printed in book form in 1900, several reviewers commented on it favourably. The *Spectator*, for example, approved of Churchill's 'moralising', and commended him for illuminating the Boers' abhorrent racial views.[47] The *Pall Mall Gazette* agreed that the Boers' 'black filth' attitude was 'the secret of so much'.[48] Churchill's friend Violet Bonham Carter (the daughter of the Liberal Imperialist H. H. Asquith) later wrote that the passage proved that 'even in those days the racial issue was the main bone of contention between the Boers and ourselves'.[49] However, Churchill's words were sometimes read more cynically by contemporaries. 'The philanthropic motives of the greedy invader are extolled [by Churchill]', sneered the Irish nationalist *Freeman's Journal*. 'Among the latest found motives for the war is a burning desire to secure equal rights for the poor Kaffir, who is ten times worse treated by the philanthropic capitalists in the [*sic*] Rhodesia than by the Boers in the Transvaal.'[50] The claim that black people were worse off under British than Boer rule was implausible, but we may indeed subject Churchill's arguments to some critical probing.

We need to be clear about what he was actually saying. Certainly, he was concerned about the welfare of the Africans, and, as he stated a little later, he believed that the British had gained from their 'kindly and humane' policy whereas Boer cruelty had rebounded on the perpetrators.[51] Yet, as his earlier comments on 'the indolent Kaffir' suggest, Churchill was by no means a believer in racial equality. In the crucial passage he was not advocating the 'social revolution' that full equality would involve. Note his statement that 'British government is associated *in the Boer farmer's mind* with violent social revolution' (emphasis added). He was in fact mocking the racially paranoid Boers for their misplaced belief that British rule would bring such a revolution about. (Equality in the British territories was recognized in theory but serially violated in practice.)[52] He may even have been hinting – although this was not how it struck contemporaries – that the liberal-inspired 'movement that seeks to place the native on a level with the white man' was indirectly to blame for the war because it had stoked up Boer anxieties. Churchill undoubtedly believed that the humane treatment of Africans was important but this did not imply that Europeans would have to sacrifice their dominant position. And his belief that the British already provided such treatment was in itself staggeringly complacent.

Moreover, far from being strikingly radical, Churchill's position was little removed from that of the British government. As the war opened, Chamberlain denounced the treatment of the non-white population of the Transvaal as 'brutal', 'disgraceful' and 'unworthy'.[53] However, the Treaty of Vereeniging that brought it to a close guaranteed that the question of extending the franchise to non-whites would be left to the Boers to decide after they achieved the promised self-rule under British sovereignty. This, of course, disposed of any notion that the war had been fought in the interests of racial equality: the British authorities paid lip service to the idea, but in the end they prioritized appeasing the Boers in order to end the war as soon as possible. In their view it was unfortunate if, having been granted self-government, the local white rulers of British territories maltreated other races, but only a limited amount could be done about it. 'We have got in some cases to put up with those things', said Churchill regretfully as a Liberal minister in 1906.[54]

Churchill's disapproval of Boer racial attitudes was not sufficiently strong to undermine his growing respect for his captors. 'The Boers were the most humane people where white men were concerned', he recalled in *My Early Life*. Their treatment of 'Kaffirs' notwithstanding, they were 'the most good-hearted enemy' against which he had ever fought.[55] According to Haldane, the 'plain-speaking, ignorant'

Boers with whom Churchill argued vociferously about the war, 'somewhat shook his faith, and certainly gained his sympathy'.[56] This did not mean that his belief in the justice of the war was dented. Rather, it reinforced his existing belief that the Boers should be treated magnanimously in defeat. (Before the war he had written that the military blow against the Transvaal 'must be stunning; afterwards we may be generous'.)[57] Imprisoned along with around sixty British officers in the States Model School in Pretoria, he wrote a letter to his American friend Bourke Cockran in which he explained why he did not support the Boers. 'Perhaps I do sympathise with their love of freedom and pride of race', he said, but added that to him British imperial self-preservation seemed to involve 'a bigger principle' than either of these things.[58] (He thus elevated realpolitik into a principle.) Churchill wanted to send telegrams to the *Morning Post*, raising the suspicions of the Boers. J. W. B. Gunning, a camp administrator, believed that one of his draft messages was intended to encourage Britain to send more troops. 'This he showed clearly during a[n] excited stupid conversation with me yesterday evening', Gunning reported, adding, 'I don't trust that little man'.[59] Permission to send that telegram was refused.[60]

Even though Churchill's sympathy towards his captors gradually increased, his determination to get out of their hands was not in any way diminished. After his attempts to persuade the authorities to release him as a non-combatant failed – his efforts to defend the armoured train had called that status into question – he determined to break free. Several aspects of his escape on 12 December have caused controversy, but not on the whole deservedly. One of the most significant allegations is that, having originally made a plan with Haldane and another prisoner, he impetuously slipped over the wall without waiting for his colleagues, jeopardizing the other men's chances of escape. After years of brooding, Haldane – who himself escaped later by another method – concluded, 'Had Churchill only possessed the moral courage to admit that, in the excitement of the moment, he saw a chance of escape and could not resist the temptation to take advantage of it, not realizing that it would compromise the escape of his companions, all would have been well.'[61] In other words, the brunt of Haldane's criticism was directed not at Churchill's behaviour at the time of the escape, but rather at his subsequent somewhat self-righteous efforts at self-justification. A perhaps more serious charge was levelled in the *Manchester Guardian* a few weeks after the British capture of Pretoria in June 1900. A journalist reported: 'I gather from private letters written by one of the released officers that considerable resentment was felt at Mr Winston Churchill's publication of the full details of his escape, as thereby others among the imprisoned officers who had hoped to avail themselves of the same means of escape were prevented from doing so by reason of the extra precautions taken.'[62] Doubtless some new precautions would have been taken anyway, and it is impossible to say whether or not publication did harm anyone else's chances. Nevertheless, it was surely a little foolhardy, and yet for some reason this particular criticism never achieved the wide currency that others did.

Once he was over the wall, Churchill accomplished the next phase of his escape by hopping onto a moving goods train. He jumped off before dawn, in order to find a hiding-place until dark fell again. The next night, however, there were no trains. Churchill stumbled on on foot and at last found refuge at a colliery that, luckily for him, was managed by a Britisher, John Howard. With the assistance of Howard and other sympathizers, Churchill hid down the mine for a few days before boarding a train for Lourenço Marques in Portuguese East Africa, where he identified himself to the British Consul. 'I am very weak but I am free', he wrote in a telegram to the *Morning Post*. 'I have lost many pounds in weight but I am lighter in heart.'[63] He then headed to Durban by steamer, where he arrived two days before Christmas and was greeted as a hero by the crowds. His escapade provided British loyalists with a point of light in the aftermath of 'Black Week' which had seen major Boer victories at Stormberg, Magersfontein and Colenso. In a pair of impromptu speeches he warned, 'We are in the midst of a fierce struggle with [a] vast military power' which was 'resolved at all costs to gratify its reckless ambition by beating the British out of South Africa'. He promised, though, 'With the determination of a great Empire surrounded by colonies of unprecedented loyalty we shall carry our policy to a successful conclusion'.[64] 'I was received as if I had won a great victory', he later recalled, adding: 'Youth seeks Adventure. Journalism requires Advertisement. Certainly I had found both. I became for the time quite famous.'[65]

III

Churchill was by no means sanguine about the progress of the war, and revealed to journalists the Boers' conviction that they would drive the British into the sea.[66] In a telegram to the *Morning Post* he warned that one Boer fighter, in the right conditions, was equal to three to five regular British soldiers. He claimed presciently that 250,000 more men were needed, arguing that South Africa was 'well worth the cost in blood and money'. Calling for more volunteers, he asked sarcastically, 'Are the gentlemen of England all fox-hunting?'[67] His family, for its part, undoubtedly did its bit. He himself secured a temporary commission in the South African Light Horse but was allowed nonetheless to continue acting as a correspondent. His brother Jack received a commission in the same regiment and when he was wounded in February 1900 he was one of the first patients of the hospital ship *Maine*, the nursing team of which Lady Randolph was managing. She had recently caused more than a few eyebrows to be raised by becoming engaged to George Cornwallis-West, an officer in the Scots Guards who was only a couple of weeks older than Churchill. Cornwallis-West had already been serving in the war but had to return home in the *Maine* after contracting enteric fever; his marriage to Lady Randolph, which subsequently broke down, took place in July.[68] Later, Churchill was joined by his cousin, the ninth Duke of Marlborough, known as 'Sunny'. Meanwhile Churchill's aunt, Lady Sarah Wilson (Lord Randolph's sister) was acting as a correspondent for the *Daily Mail*.

Churchill owed permission to revive his dual soldier–journalist role to General Sir Redvers Buller, the commander of operations in Natal. After the Sudan War – not least with Churchill's own activities in mind – the War Office had forbidden combatants to act as correspondents and vice versa, but he was granted a unique dispensation from the new rule. Churchill's position, of course, made it difficult for him to publicly attack Buller's inept conduct. In private he was scathing, writing that were he to begin to criticize Buller he would never stop. Yet given that there was no plausible figure to take the General's place, he argued, he had to be backed for all he was worth, 'which at this moment is very little'.[69] So, when Buller's ponderous attempts to relieve Ladysmith met a major setback at the end of January at the Battle of Spion Kop – British troops captured this key summit only to beat an ignominious retreat – Churchill insisted the defeat was not a catastrophe. Rather it was 'simply a bloody action, in which was effected a lodgement in the enemy's entrenchments that proved untenable'.[70] (A few months later, back in England, he admitted it had in fact been a disaster.)[71] At the time, Churchill did maintain a reputation as an outspoken figure, which was by no means wholly unjustified. One officer of his acquaintance noted: 'He is an awfully good little chap, & will undoubtedly make his mark, but not I think a very big one, as he has little power of self restraint – if he is thirsty he *must* drink – if he has nothing to talk about, he still *must* talk – the same with his writing.'[72] All the same, some other journalists were at times prepared to go further than Churchill did. In April one of *The Times*'s correspondents (possibly Leo Amery) wrote, 'Our generals, regimental officers, and soldiers are all brave, none braver, but it is useless to shirk the fact that the majority of them are stupid.'[73] This, commented *Reynolds's Newspaper*, 'out-Churchills Mr Winston Churchill'; indeed, Churchill himself was critical of such attacks.[74]

Churchill did ruffle some feathers himself, however, as a long-forgotten episode demonstrates. At the end of February, Ladysmith was relieved at last. Churchill gave a dramatic description of the British column's ride towards the town, and of how a 'score of tattered men' came running from the trenches and rifle pits to meet it, some crying, some cheering, all pale and thin.[75] The next evening Sir George White, who had led the defence against the siege, granted him an interview. White had been much criticized for allowing his men to be trapped in Ladysmith in the first place. 'He spoke with some bitterness of the attacks which had been made on him in the newspapers, and of the attempts of the War Office to supersede him, attempts which Sir Redvers Buller had prevented', noted Churchill.[76] This appeared to reveal an intrigue against a man now regarded in Britain – if not amongst his colleagues – as an authentic imperial hero. It was claimed that the War Office had tried to make White a scapegoat for its own blunders.[77] White described Churchill's report as 'mischievous' – he appears to have thought he had been having a private conversation – but he pointedly refused to repudiate the comments ascribed to him.[78] Perhaps realizing he had been indiscreet, Churchill edited out the phrase about the War Office when his despatches were published in his *London to Ladysmith, via Pretoria*.[79]

The fighting in Natal now died down as the Boers retreated, and Churchill tried to get moved to a more eventful theatre. While awaiting permission for a transfer, he developed his opinions on how the Boers should be treated after the war. After his escape he had emphasized that his new-found respect for the 'manly virtues' of the Boers did not at all reduce his belief in the necessity of fighting them, which was essential for the sake of *British* manhood.[80] However, in contrast to the prevailing opinion, he did not favour revenge against the enemy once they had been defeated. In late March he outlined his views in a telegram to the *Morning Post* and a letter to the *Natal Witness*. The pursuit of an 'eye for an eye' attitude would lead to the war being prolonged into a lengthy guerrilla phase, he argued. 'Peace and happiness can only come to South Africa through the fusion and concord of the Dutch and British races, who must forever live side by side under the supremacy of Britain.'[81] He had genuinely gone out on a limb here. Although the *Manchester Guardian* praised his 'rare logic and commonsense', his views were predictably unpopular with British colonists in South Africa.[82] The war correspondent of the *Chronicle* wrote sardonically of how the 'apparition of a real member of the aristocracy like Mr Winston Churchill advocating clemency has startled them out of their wits'.[83] The *Freeman's Journal* claimed, improbably, that Churchill's comments had put his life at risk.[84] 'Winston is being severely criticised about his Peaceful telegrams – and everyone here in Natal is going against his views', wrote his brother in a letter to Lady Randolph. 'They say that even if you are going to treat these Boers well after their surrender, this is not the time to say so.'[85] The latter point would also be impressed upon Churchill by Sir Alfred Milner, the British High Commissioner, as they lunched together below Table Mountain a few months later. But Milner was sympathetic to Churchill's views and he won, if only for the time being, the younger man's loyalty.

At last, Churchill secured permission to join the army headed by Lord Roberts, the Commander-in-Chief, as it moved into the Boer territories. In his friend Ian Hamilton he at last found a general whose conduct of operations he could truly admire, a point he emphasized by calling his second book of despatches *Ian Hamilton's*

March. Churchill was present at the relief of Pretoria in June and a few days later showed 'conspicuous gallantry' (Hamilton's words) at Diamond Hill. He climbed to within a short distance of the enemy and then signalled to Hamilton that the summit could be rushed.[86] In spite of the run of victories, the Boers were as yet far from defeated; the guerrilla phase that Churchill had anticipated was about to begin. He himself, in expectation of a general election, gave up his army commission and returned to Britain in July. On coming ashore at Southampton, his first concern was to establish whether the fearsome Christiaan De Wet, Commandant General of the Orange Free State, had yet been captured. Informed that he had not, Churchill showed chagrin but not surprise. 'De Wet is an eel', he remarked.[87]

IV

A few days after landing he travelled to Oldham, where he received a rapturous reception from the townspeople, and, although the election had not yet been formally announced, he was once more adopted as a Tory candidate. (His running-mate this time was to be C. B. Crisp, a stockbroker.) Speaking at the town's Empire Theatre, on a stage decorated with Union Jacks, he reflected on the 'stirring succession of violent events' in South Africa which had moved the country 'as nothing had moved it for a great number of years'. Volunteer recruitment after Black Week had provided proof that the 'gentlemen of England' did not shirk their duty. The war, he predicted, would be over within months: 'He did not wish to be sanguine, or he would like to say a week [. . .] but he would rather keep within the limits of absolute certainty.' He claimed that when he had first gone to the Cape he had hoped that the Boers could be given back their independence after the war – if so he had not said so at the time – but said he had now reached the conclusion that they could not be allowed 'a Republic the size of a shilling'. Such a thing would endanger British authority in South Africa, and the Boer territories must therefore be absorbed into the Empire. He also eulogized Milner: were he to be removed from his present position as High Commissioner it would be 'a serious national loss'.[88]

A few weeks after this Churchill sent a letter to Milner which shows that he was not quite as confident as some of his public words suggested. He advised him that the British public were 'rather worried at the wearisome prolongation of the war'. Although Churchill did not share the widespread 'hard view of the Boer, as a creature unfit to live', he also believed that it would be 'useless and even mischievous to say anything now that could lessen the hostility and contempt with which the Boer is regarded'. That was because an angry public opinion would be needed to sustain the war effort: 'You will want all the fire to carry you up the steep gradient.' He feared, however, that there was a remarkable amount 'of pent up feeling, Liberalism, sentimentality, humanitarianism, chivalry' that was threatening to burst free. This, he explained, was what accounted for his public support for the harsh anti-guerrilla tactics that the British were now employing:

> The ordinary safety valves of public expression and free speech are screwed down. Someday there will be an explosion, so that your steam engine had better get to the end of its journey as soon as possible, otherwise it may, when the machinery breaks, slip backwards down the hill.
>
> It is because I fear that contingency that I try my best to justify all these farm burnings and other measures of severity. We must top the rise before the Power is withdrawn.

With a combination of sycophancy and self-confidence, he told Milner: 'I have neither influence nor power, but I can reach a wide public, and if there be anything you want said – without saying it yourself – and my political conscience approves it, I should be proud to be your servant.' He could, he said, 'draw an audience of 4000 people in any big town'.[89] Milner reciprocated Churchill's approval – he read his letter with 'appreciation and a great measure of agreement' – but within a few years the relationship between them would sour.[90]

It should be emphasized again that Churchill was not a completely slavish follower of the government line. In a speech in August in Plymouth, he launched a scathing attack on the War Office. During the past few years it had, he said, 'neglected every one of the lessons which it ought to have deduced from the military progress of the Continent'. After he concluded his detailed indictment – subsequently quoted in a Liberal leaflet – a heckler called out, 'And all this while you had a Conservative Government in power.' According to one report, 'Mr Churchill was quite disconcerted by the cutting words, and is declared to have found it necessary to make a pause to recover himself.'[91] During the subsequent election he did not retract his criticisms, but he did downplay them.[92] Thus although his departures from Conservative orthodoxy were not insignificant, they were limited. The Boers should be treated decently after the war, he thought, but in the meantime it was justifiable to burn their farms, as 'repressive measures were necessary' in order to bring them into submission.[93] The War Office might be susceptible of improvement, but the war effort as a whole had been the 'Pride of the Empire and the astonishment of the world'.[94]

Churchill's role in the election campaign itself, which began in September, has received relatively little attention.[95] The promises of 'Tory Democracy' had not been forgotten entirely – his election address spoke in favour of old-age pensions – and religion again reared its head, this time with Churchill denouncing ritualism in the Church of England, a topic about which, given the unconventional nature of his religious views, it is hard to believe he really cared much.[96] Predictably, though, the war dominated debate in Oldham, as it did throughout the country.[97] In spite of his hero status and the overall weakness of the Liberal Party, Churchill could not expect a walkover; the battle was hard fought. His opponents – Emmott and Runciman again – were Liberal Imperialist supporters of the war and could not be attacked as pro-Boers. On the other hand, it was not too hard to ridicule their position. The voters would have to choose, Churchill said, between two Conservative candidates and two Liberal candidates who agreed with the Conservatives: 'It will be like choosing between turtle and mock-turtle!' His Liberal opponents did not dispute the justice of the war, merely alleging that it had been mismanaged; but Churchill scorned the notion that a Liberal government 'supported by the Peace Party' would be 'skilled in the management of bloody wars'.[98]

Nevertheless, Churchill did not have everything his own way. The *Oldham Evening Chronicle*, attempting to wrest discussion back towards domestic questions, devoted an editorial to his turtle soup metaphor and claimed that it was apt. This was because the government's 'turtle policy' benefited the wealthy at the expense of the poor: 'During the last five years the rich man's plate has been handed up many times and has always returned filled with turtle.'[99]

And when Churchill denounced Gladstone's 'shameful' surrender to the Boers in 1881, the *Leeds Mercury* quoted Lord Randolph who, of course, had eventually come to approve the settlement. 'Mr Winston Churchill is entitled to manufacture what political capital he can out of Majuba Hill; but he ought not to forget that in sneering at Mr Gladstone's South African policy he is also sneering at the deliberate judgement of his own father, who was once the idol of the Tory party.'[100] Such attacks may not have done Churchill much harm – few Oldham voters would have read the *Leeds Mercury* anyway – but they do remind us that not everyone was dazzled by his reputation. Indeed, when polling day came in Oldham (on 1 October) the result was very tight. As can be seen from the figures below, the combined Liberal vote was 203 greater than the Tory total; Churchill owed his victorious second place to the way votes were distributed among the candidates.

Emmott (Liberal)	12,947 (elected)
Churchill (Unionist)	12,931 (elected)
Runciman (Liberal)	12,709
Crisp (Unionist)	12,522

The national result was a massive Tory victory, albeit with a reduction in the party's majority as compared with 1895. As was then customary, polling extended over a number of weeks, and so Churchill, whose result had been declared early, was able to campaign on behalf of other Tories throughout the country. His tour turned into a kind of 'triumphal progress' through key seats selected by the party managers.[101] The *Glasgow Herald* described him (not disapprovingly) as playing the role of 'an itinerant juvenile Gladstone'.[102] He was astute enough to realize, though, that the wave of Conservative popularity might not last for ever. He wrote privately: 'I think this election – fought by the Liberals as a soldiers battle, without a plan or leaders, or enthusiasm has shown so far the strength not the weakness of Liberalism in the country.'[103]

V

MPs did not receive a salary, so Churchill needed to earn money to carry him through the years ahead. As soon as the election was over, then, he embarked on a lucrative lecture tour describing his experiences in South Africa. In this way, the Empire would come to his financial rescue. He was now transformed into an imperial educator of the kind who had impressed him in his youth – appropriately, his first effort was made at Harrow School.[104] Equipped with a magic lantern – the Victorian equivalent of PowerPoint – he often used a geography teacher's flourish: 'This is a map of South Africa. Take a good look at it, it belongs to us.' (This evoked loud applause.)[105] One of the most dramatic accounts of one of his lectures is of his appearance in Leeds:

> A vivid description of the awful night and day on Spion Kop and a triumphant eulogy of the superb genius of Lord Roberts, and a hearty and repeated acknowledgement of the courage and tenacity of Sir Redvers Buller, were the conspicuous features of the lecture, spiced, as it was, with allusions to the 'far-famed plainness of the Dutch frau' or contemptuous references to the ill-equipped critics of our 'stupid officers', and ending on a really solemn note – the realisation, with something like a feeling of awe, and almost of sadness, of the extinction of separate nationalities, but at the same time the expression of a confident belief that the bravery and skill of such men as De Wet and [General Piet] Joubert might in the future be among the supports of a united South Africa.[106]

The audience, in other words, received not only entertainment but also a clear didactic message: the Boers were to be absorbed into the Empire not merely territorially but spiritually, as their sense of a separate national identity was extinguished.

The American leg of his tour was less successful both financially – owing to an incompetent and grasping promoter – and in terms of its reception. There was significant pro-Boer feeling in the USA, much of it coming from the Dutch and Irish populations. Bourke Cockran, Churchill's Irish-born politician friend, thought the war to be 'the greatest violation of justice attempted by any civilized nation since the partition of Poland'.[107] (The men's personal relationship was not affected by this political difference.) The ambivalent response to Churchill was nicely captured when the author Mark Twain introduced him to a fashionable audience at the Waldorf-Astoria in New York on the anniversary of his escape from prison.

Churchill, Twain said, 'knew all about war and nothing about peace'. Twain added that he himself disapproved of the war in South Africa, 'and he thought England sinned when she interfered with the Boers, as the United States is sinning in meddling in the affairs of the Filipinos. England and America were kin in almost everything; now they are kin in sin.' But in spite of his Boer sympathies, he generously welcomed Churchill (himself half American) as 'a blend of America and England which makes a perfect match'.[108] Churchill recalled that, when he argued with Twain in private conversation, he was forced back to the refuge of 'My country right or wrong'. 'When the poor country is fighting for its life, I agree', rejoined Twain, 'But this was not your case.'[109] It was with some relief that Churchill arrived in Canada just before Christmas. 'Thank God, we are once more on British soil', he said as he stepped off the train in Montreal.[110] His reception in the country was much warmer than the one he had had in America. He also met, for the first time, the future Canadian Prime Minister W. L. Mackenzie King. The fastidious King later claimed privately that on this occasion he found Churchill at his hotel drinking champagne at eleven o'clock in the morning.[111]

He subsequently returned to the US, where, on 9 January 1901, at the University of Ann Arbor, he again received an unfriendly reception from anti-imperialists. That same evening he confided his thoughts on world politics to a student journalist, in an interview that was not published in full until after his death. The influence of Winwood Reade was still apparent: 'I believe that as civilized nations become more powerful they will get more ruthless, and the time will come when the world will impatiently bear the existence of great barbaric nations who may at any time arm themselves and menace civilized nations. [. . .] The Aryan stock is bound to triumph.'[112]

On 2 February 1901, the day of Queen Victoria's funeral, he boarded ship for England. The stage was now set for his House of Commons debut. He had warned Milner a few weeks before that 'Everyone is sorely vexed and worried by the continuance of the war', and that the forthcoming parliamentary debates would be 'bitter'. He proposed a temporary armistice and negotiation.[113] Public concern was growing about British tactics, which were soon to be labelled by Sir Henry Campbell-Bannerman as 'methods of barbarism'. In *My Early Life* Churchill acknowledged that the guerrilla phase of the war had led to 'shocking evils'. He wrote that, in order to cope with surprise assaults by a non-uniformed enemy, the British army cleared entire districts and herded the population into concentration camps, but the Boers cut railway lines, causing supply problems. 'Disease broke out and several thousands of women and children died. The policy of burning farms whose owners had broken their oath [of neutrality], far from quelling the fighting Boers, only rendered them desperate.'[114] He gave no clue, though, that he himself had publicly justified farm burnings and concentration camps at the time. His maiden speech, on 18 February, made some efforts in this direction, in the context of a general defence of government policy in South Africa. He spoke immediately after the radical Liberal pro-Boer MP David Lloyd George, who made a speech condemning the 'infamy which is perpetrated in the name of Great Britain in Africa'.[115] Churchill did not answer Lloyd George's arguments in detail, not least because, having learnt his own speech by heart, his ability to improvise was limited. He said, though, 'that as compared with other wars, especially those in which a civil population took part, this war in South Africa has been on the whole carried on with unusual humanity and generosity'.[116] A few months later he stated his belief that the concentration camps, if imperfect, involved 'the *minimum* of suffering to the unfortunate people for whom we have made ourselves responsible'.[117]

As usual though, there were complex undercurrents. He had not lost his respect for the manly qualities of the Boers. In a famous passage in his maiden speech, he scorned the 'verbal sympathy' the enemy had received from Liberal MPs, unmatched by practical support. 'If I were a Boer fighting in the field – and if I were a Boer I hope I should be fighting in the field – I would not allow myself to be taken in by any message of sympathy, not even if it were signed by a hundred hon. Members.'[118] The apparent admission that the Boers were motivated by a legitimate patriotism drew him some criticism. Chamberlain, sitting on the Treasury bench, muttered 'That's the way to throw away seats!'[119] Even more telling was a letter Churchill sent to Milner in March. He wrote of 'this miserable war, unfortunate and ill-omened in its beginning, inglorious in its course, cruel and hideous in its conclusion'. He had, he said, 'hated these latter stages with their barbarous features – questionable even according to the bloody precedents of 1870, certainly most horrible'. (But he had cited the Franco-Prussian War himself in his maiden speech, pointing out that Paris had been shelled and reduced to starvation, and arguing that British forces should not be restrained from following such precedents!) He was still 'absolutely determined' to take away the Boers' independence, but could not 'face the idea of their being economically and socially ruined too'.[120] Doubtless he would have justified the discrepancy between his public claim, that the conflict was conducted with 'unusual humanity', and his private one, that it had 'barbarous features', with the need to maintain public backing for what he still saw, fundamentally, as a just war. During its concluding phase (the Treaty of Vereeniging was signed in May 1902), he combined newly outspoken criticism of the government's handling of the military situation with the conviction that a supreme effort could bring about a victory that would 'combine the peace of Africa with the honour of Britain'.[121]

As Churchill set out on his parliamentary career, then, his position was uncomfortable. Prior to the outbreak of war he had taken a conventional Conservative position and, in spite of his growing concerns in private, had largely sustained that in public through to his first months in the Commons. Nevertheless, his experiences of the war did make him sceptical of the way it was conducted in practice, and also greatly increased his respect for the Boers. Hence his (somewhat intermittent) criticisms of the War Office and also his calls for a magnanimous approach towards the enemy. He did at times appear opportunistic. After his embarrassment with the heckler at Plymouth he toned down his attacks on the War Office during his election campaign – when he ridiculed Liberal charges of muddle – only to revive his concerns later. In October 1901 Sir Edward Grey observed that 'criticisms had ably been pressed home of late by Mr Winston Churchill, but what a satire his speeches were upon the last election at Oldham'.[122] However, as his comments to Milner make clear, he felt a genuine dilemma about what he should say in public, given the need (in his view) to sustain patriotic sentiment at home as a precondition for victory. And although he may not have been the ruthless apostle of truth that legend favours, he did, to his credit, take the political risk of expressing his concerns when, in the dying months of the war, he felt that a dangerous public apathy was taking hold. Finally, we should not rush to conclude that his multiple twists and turns were the product of calculation, cynical or otherwise. To a fair degree they were the product of sheer inexperience and even of uncertainty. We can see a hint of his problems in his response to questions about the alleged inefficiency of the army after one of his Canadian lectures. His first response was to claim that its organization in South Africa was 'perfect', but he then paused before remarking that there were many reforms to be made and that he was pledged to his constituents to that effect.[123] We can see here his instinctive 'My country right or wrong' attitude warring with his (in this case legitimate) intolerance of established methods and his (perhaps not always sufficiently developed) awareness of the hostages to fortune that he had already given. If he did not always achieve a perfect balance it is perhaps worth recalling that, at the time he entered Parliament, he was only twenty-six.

At the same time we may note that the war in South Africa had been ideologically disconcerting for him. The experience of fighting fellow white colonialists seems to have presented a greater challenge to his world view than battling the brave but alien-seeming tribesmen of the North-West Frontier or the warriors of the Sudan.[124] The collapse of his contempt for the Boers under the pressure of reality did not imply any weakening of his faith in the Empire, but it did introduce new paradoxes. In particular, his increasing sympathy for their aspiration to freedom – provided that that freedom was exercised *within the Empire* – meant that the welfare of the black majority was put to one side. This did not mean that Churchill did not care about that issue, merely that he did not at this time care enough about it to prioritize it or indeed to say much of meaning about it at all. In this of course he was hardly unique, and his jibes at the inconsistencies of the pro-Boers were not without their point, but the absence was significant. In a speech made shortly after he became an MP he spoke of how the Boer War was 'the people's war' and also 'the Empire's war'. He said he knew from his visit to Canada – and he believed it also true of Australia – that 'the people, by their effective participation in this memorable struggle, had been able to feel, down to the poorest farmer in the most distant province, that they belonged to the Empire and that, in a certain sense, the British Empire belonged to them'.[125] Yet it seems very unlikely either that many non-white colonial subjects of the Empire felt this profound sense of participation or ownership, or indeed that Churchill was even referring to them. If the implication of his words was that the British Empire required the moral sanction of its people, then he could only realistically claim it had that sanction on a highly restricted view of who 'the people' were. In other words, his narrow angle of vision regarding race helped him claim a democratic basis for his broader arguments for imperialism. For a young politician hoping to exploit his own imperial background in a new era of mass politics, this was, indeed, a convenient way of seeing the Empire.

PART TWO

DIVIDE ET IMPERA!

4

THAT WILD WINSTON,
1901–1908

DURING THE first months of 1906 Churchill made himself highly unpopular, not only with political opponents but also with important sections of opinion within the Empire. As a new minister in Sir Henry Campbell-Bannerman's Liberal government, he was an obvious target for those on the Conservative side, from which he had 'ratted' two years earlier. The attacks of Joseph Chamberlain and other Unionists, who alleged that he was more concerned with party politics than with Empire, were therefore par for the course. Yet the criticisms of Churchill came from all sides. Ramsay MacDonald, secretary of the newly emergent Labour Party, accused him of tactlessness in his efforts to exert control over local colonial governments' treatment of their non-white populations. 'I do not think I am an over-cautious man, or that my sympathies with oppressed black and yellow men in South Africa are niggardly', MacDonald wrote. 'But I am bound to say that, unless the Cabinet muzzle Mr Winston Churchill, they will bring themselves into a disastrous conflict with the Colonies.'[1] The right-wing *Morning Post*, Churchill's former employer, applauded MacDonald's remarks and claimed that the new minister had become 'a national danger'.[2] And at a Colonial Institute dinner in London the very mention of Churchill's name 'evoked hisses and ironical exclamations',[3] a reaction which *The Times* blamed on his apparent pursuit of 'mere party purposes' in place of efforts to secure 'the confidence of those bearing the heat and burden in far-off lands for the benefit of the whole Empire'.[4] The central issue of controversy was South Africa; and when the *Times of Natal* denounced Churchill's imperial policy as 'rotten and vicious' it was representative of the response of the British press there.[5] Lord Selborne, who had replaced Milner as High Commissioner, was driven almost to apoplexy by Churchill's behaviour:

'Winston keeps up a very friendly correspondence with me, but the only fixed purpose I can detect in his policy is that of keeping well with the extreme radicals. They are a crowd! of dangerous lunatics I say! the Empire cannot survive much of them.'[6] Although Churchill was still talked of, even in distant parts of the Empire, as a future Prime Minister, it was far from the happiest of starts to a ministerial career.[7]

I

How, then, had Churchill made the switch from ardent Tory imperialist in 1900 to Liberal *enfant terrible* and alleged menace to British interests? Had he really changed his ideological spots, or was he a victim of misrepresentation? The answers to these questions take us back to the unhappy closing phases of the Boer War and its political aftermath. There were some signs, even before the war, that he did not regard the Conservative Party as his natural political home. In 1897 he told his mother that he was a Liberal at heart and that, were it not for the party's commitment to Irish Home Rule, 'to which I will never consent', he would join it.[8] Yet, since he subsequently fought two vigorous Tory campaigns and then joined a Liberal Party which had *not* abandoned Home Rule – although in fairness it had put the issue on the back burner – we should perhaps not take these remarks too seriously. The indications are that, on election to Parliament, he intended to be 'an independent Conservative' who would not, rebel as he might, be drawn from his 'true allegiance' to the Tories 'by any fulsome flattery or self-interested compliments which may come from the Radical side'.[9] This position, however, was to prove unsustainable.

Churchill seemed to aspire to recreate the 'Fourth Party', the group of parliamentary guerrillas that had formed a springboard for his father's career. He banded together with a few other like-minded young Tories, including Lord Hugh Cecil, a son of Lord Salisbury; the group became known as the Hooligans or 'Hughligans'. Churchill explicitly took up Lord Randolph's mantle – the cause of economy – in his first big act of rebellion, his attack on the army reform scheme introduced by the Secretary of State for War, St John Brodrick. Brodrick wanted to expand the army to comprise six corps. Three of these would form a potential expeditionary force (presaging a greater commitment to involvement in European warfare) and three were to be kept for home defence.[10] Churchill was pledged to reform of the army but not to its growth, and in May 1901 he attacked Brodrick in the Commons, quoting Lord Randolph's 1886 resignation letter which warned of the dangers of excess military spending. One army corps, the younger Churchill argued, was 'quite enough to fight savages' whereas three were not enough 'even to begin to fight Europeans'. In case of war in Europe, he put his faith in the navy's capacity to defend Britain until such time as land forces could be made ready; the Admiralty was the only department 'strong enough to insure the British Empire'.[11] Clearly riled, Brodrick hit back, offering up the hope that Churchill would in time 'look back with regret to the day when he came down to the House to preach Imperialism, without being willing to bear the burdens of Imperialism, and when the hereditary qualities he possesses of eloquence and courage may be tempered also by discarding the hereditary desire to run Imperialism on the cheap'.[12] Churchill was by no means the only Conservative to oppose Brodrick. Leo Amery, with whom Churchill was in touch over the question, was another notable critic, and in 1903 he published influential *Times* articles which were broadly in line with Churchill's arguments.[13] Such criticism contributed to the overall failure of Brodrick's plans. But although Churchill was not a lone voice amongst Tories, his calls for retrenchment brought him closer to mainstream Liberal opinion. At the same time they raised suspicions on his own side that, having used 'his graphic pen to excite a spirit of militarism', he was making a U-turn in order to ride the changing tide of public opinion. His opportunism, it was thought, made him a true son of his father.[14]

By 1902 he had ceased to regard the Conservative Party as his long-term political home. He briefly put his hopes in the Liberal Imperialist Lord Rosebery, who had been a failure as Prime Minister in 1894–5, but who continued to hold an almost mystical sway over his supporters. When Rosebery appeared to hold out the prospect that he might emerge from retirement, Churchill commented that the 'muddy waters of the Opposition' were getting clearer, and 'The slime, the sewage, and other Radical impurities are sinking slowly to the bottom, the clearer waters of Liberalism

[are] rising steadily to the top'.[15] He tried to persuade Rosebery that he should head 'a central coalition', together with Sir Michael Hicks Beach, the former Tory Chancellor. He noted: 'The one real difficulty I have to encounter is the suspicion that I am moved by mere restless ambition: & if some definite issue – such as Tariff – were to arise – that difficulty would disappear.'[16] Rosebery was to prove as elusive as ever and did not commit himself. However, Churchill's desire that trade policy should emerge as an issue was to be fulfilled, and it was to provide him with his opportunity, even if not in exactly the form that he had sought. The idea of a centre party was to prove a mirage, but the grand upheavals of the next few years enabled him to find a new home with the Liberals.

It was the Colonial Secretary, Joseph Chamberlain, who was to shake the political kaleidoscope. In 1902 Arthur Balfour had succeeded Salisbury as Conservative Prime Minister. At sixty-six, Chamberlain must have known that he himself was unlikely ever to lead a government, not least because he was not universally trusted within the Tory Party, of which, as a Liberal Unionist, he was an ally rather than a member. Nevertheless, he was determined to leave his mark on the Empire. In May 1903 he gave a speech in Birmingham, his great power base, in which he argued for a system of imperial tariff preference; that is to say Empire countries would treat each other's products more favourably than they did foreign goods. In his view, this was an essential means to consolidate the Empire 'which can only be maintained by relations of interest as well as sentiment', and which should, indeed, be 'self-sustaining and self-sufficient, able to maintain itself against the competition of all its rivals'.[17] The speech blew apart the broad free-trade consensus that had dominated British politics for decades. Tariff reform raised the unpopular prospect of tariffs on staple imports, which the Liberals quickly labelled 'food taxes'. The controversy was bitter. As Chamberlain's comments show, the argument was not just about economics. It was a debate about international power, and about the fundamental nature, even the very soul, of the British Empire.

Churchill's immediate response to Chamberlain's démarche was sceptical. The Unionists should follow a policy of imperialism, he declared, 'but not one of one-sided Imperialism'.[18] However, his support for free trade was not of the knee-jerk variety. A year earlier, he had written privately that although his instinct was against an imperial customs union, he wanted to see the arguments for it 'set out in black and white; for after all it is primarily a matter of profit and loss'. It might, he thought, be in Britain's interests to give Empire countries tariff concessions 'in return for some substantial accession of military strength – such as is undoubtedly in their power to confer'.[19] He seems to have had his free-trade instincts confirmed by a book by Leo Chiozza Money, a radical journalist and future Liberal MP, in which it was argued that Britain could not afford to give preference to colonial goods, as her colonies simply could not produce enough food and raw materials to supply her in sufficient quantities.[20] It took some months for his views to harden fully, but in November 1903, two months after Chamberlain had resigned from the Cabinet to pursue his campaign in the country, Churchill pulled out the stops in a speech made on Chamberlain's home turf. The view of Empire he laid out was in clear contrast to the materialism of the tariff reformers. Drawing on his own experience, he ridiculed the idea that the loyalty of the Canadians and the Australians, who had given vital help during the Boer War, would melt away for ever unless it were purchased by a trifling preference on their exports.

> I have seen enough in peace and war of the frontiers of our Empire to know that the British dominion all over the world could not endure for a year, perhaps not for a month, if it was founded upon a material basis. The strength and splendour of our authority is derived not from physical forces, but from moral ascendancy, liberty, justice, English tolerance, and English honesty.[21]

He developed this theme further in the years that followed. In a key speech at the 1907 Colonial Conference, he expanded on his view that the Empire was a family and not a syndicate. There was no anti-colonial party in Britain, he noted, but forcing the House of Commons to consider each year, through its regulation of preferential tariffs, the narrow 'profit-and-loss account' of Britain's relations with her dependencies and Dominions, would be guaranteed to create one. Furthermore, any meaningful system of preference would involve taxing food imports. (This was because the Empire countries mainly produced food and raw materials, and so Britain could not give their exports *preferential* treatment unless she put tariffs on non-Empire goods of the same class.) And the 'imposition of duties upon the necessaries of life and of industry' would cause popular resentment, breeding amongst the poor 'a deep feeling of sullen hatred of the Colonies, and of Colonial affairs'. It followed that preferential tariffs *'even if economically desirable,* would prove an element of strain and discord in the structure and system of the British Empire' (emphasis added).[22] They would, as he later put it, make the Empire odious to the British working people.[23] These arguments point forcefully to the lesson that the electorate, when it rejected imperial preference in the Liberal landslide of 1906, was not, as is sometimes asserted, showing its indifference to the Empire as a whole. Rather, it was rejecting one particular concept of it. Likewise, when critics such as Amery (an ardent Chamberlainite) later bemoaned Churchill's supposed Little Englandism, they were in fact denying the legitimacy of his actual imperial vision. It is worth noting, though, that Churchill seemed to think that the non-material ties of affection that in his view bound the Empire together could be damaged remarkably easily by material concerns such as higher food prices.

II

Churchill was far from the sole 'Imperialist Free Trader' in the Conservative Party, but the opponents of Chamberlain were increasingly beleaguered.[24] Churchill himself ran into trouble with his constituency party. In November 1903 he was refused a hearing at one of the Oldham Conservative Clubs, a hard comedown for one who had so recently been 'the demi-god of the local Tories'.[25] The following January, the Oldham Conservative Association passed a resolution declaring its lack of confidence in him. By this time, with no sign that a centre party would emerge, he had already decided to join the reunited and invigorated Liberals. On 31 May 1904 he formally crossed the floor of the House of Commons, having already been chosen as Liberal candidate for North-West Manchester at the next election. The process of adaptation was assisted by the fact that his new colleagues had put their differences over the Boer War behind them, but it was not without its challenges. Although the Liberal Party as a whole was by no means anti-imperialist, there

were Radicals within its ranks who were sceptical about British
expansion and who were often critical of the way that the Empire
was run in practice. As a junior minister in the Colonial Office,
responsible for defending its activities in the House of Commons,
Churchill would have to take some account of the humanitarian
(some would have said sentimental) preoccupations of Liberal backbenchers. One cannot say, however, that his imperial discourse
underwent any dramatic shift as a result of his switch of parties.
This was because he already belonged to a centre-ground consensus
about the Empire in British politics, of which prominent Liberals
such as Sir Edward Grey and H. H. Asquith were a part, and from
which it could plausibly be claimed that the Tories, under Chamberlain's inspiration, were moving away.

So Churchill's alliance with the Liberals, although undeniably
helpful to his career, was no mere marriage of convenience. Aside
from the crucial issue of trade, there was a growing congruence
between his ideas and those of so-called New Liberals sympathetic
to greater state involvement in social welfare. His interest in social
reform was longstanding, and had been stimulated in part by
imperial concerns. In *The Story of the Malakand Field Force* he had
decried the state's failure to take adequate care of discharged
wounded soldiers.[26] In 1901 he was shocked by the revelations in
Seebohm Rowntree's famous study of poverty in York. In an unpublished review of the book he wrote, with no small tinge of irony:

> Let it be granted that nations exist and peoples labour to
> produce armies with which they conquer other nations, and the
> nation best qualified to do this is of course the most highly
> civilised and the most deserving of honour. But supposing the
> common people shall be so stunted and deformed in body as to
> be unfit to fill the ranks the army corps may lack. And thus –
> strange as it may seem, eccentric almost incredible to write –
> our Imperial reputation is actually involved in their condition.[27]

He wrote privately at this time that he could 'see little glory in
an Empire which can rule the waves and is unable to flush its
sewers'.[28] The Conservative Party was not innately hostile to social
reform, but it had failed to deliver much of substance.[29] Churchill
did not have a clear set of plans – as late as the election of 1906 he
argued for voluntary as opposed to state action to help the poor –

but then neither, at this stage, did the Liberal Party.[30] To ask if he was motivated by compassion, or by concern for the health of the Empire, is to miss the point. He was motivated by both these things; in his mind there was no tension between targeting help at the less well off for altruistic reasons and using social reform to increase 'National Efficiency', as the current slogan had it. From Churchill's perspective, a strong Empire would itself benefit the working class, and a healthy working class would strengthen the Empire.

The Tory government staggered on, racked by its divisions over trade, until Balfour at last resigned in December 1905. Sir Henry Campbell-Bannerman was called upon to form a new Liberal administration. Churchill did not get a Cabinet post, but was offered a junior ministerial role as Financial Secretary to the Treasury. Rather than accept this, he held out successfully for a job at the Colonial Office. As this was considered a less senior position, it seems clear that he was seriously committed to tackling imperial issues at this time. He may also have hoped that with the new Colonial Secretary, the Earl of Elgin, sitting in the House of Lords, his own position in the Commons would allow him the kind of dominance on colonial questions previously achieved by Chamberlain; but if so it was wishful thinking.[31] The congratulations rolled in, including from J. E. C. Welldon, his old headmaster, but not everyone was pleased.[32] W. L. Mackenzie King (now the top official in the Canadian Ministry of Labour) wrote in his diary that it was 'a bad & dangerous appointment from [the] imperial point of view'.[33] Of more immediate significance was the reaction in South Africa, where the view of the Cape Colony press was that Churchill had only a scanty knowledge of the opinions, aspirations and difficulties of the colonies.[34]

Elgin, the departmental boss, was later described by Edward Marsh, Churchill's new private secretary, as 'a rugged old thane of antique virtue and simplicity'.[35] He was in fact only fifty-six, although his manner may have seemed to belie this. The grandson of the better known Seventh Earl, of Elgin Marbles fame, he has deservedly been rescued by a leading scholar from the condescension of posterity; his personal reticence and unwillingness to defend himself against critics disguised his considerable administrative (if not political) ability.[36] From 1894 to 1899 he achieved a generally sound record as Viceroy of India. He was not a notable enthusiast for the forward policy; at the time of the frontier wars, Churchill wrote that he was a member of 'that party in the State which has clung passionately, vainly, and often unwisely to a policy of peace and retrenchment'. But the younger man did not doubt his future chief's earnestness.[37] Marsh's description of their relationship is telling, if a little guarded. Churchill, he wrote, regarded Elgin 'with impatient respect, recognizing his four-square stability and his canniness, but desiderating initiative and dash. What Elgin thought of Winston was his own secret, but I imagine that their qualified esteem was mutual.'[38]

In March 1906 Flora Lugard, the formidable wife of Sir Frederick, High Commissioner of Northern Nigeria, wrote of 'how Lord Elgin is keeping that wild Winston in check within the office'.[39] Harry Verney, one of Elgin's private secretaries, later recalled one of the ways in which this was achieved. There were two main doors to Elgin's office, one from the private secretaries' room and one from the corridor. Churchill wanted constant access to Elgin and liked to barge in on him without warning from the corridor entrance. Elgin wanted him curbed and, without confronting him directly, gave instructions that he was only to enter via the anteroom. In Verney's recollection, 'Churchill's room was on the floor below Lord Elgin's, and as soon as Churchill had set off to invade his Chief, Marsh telephoned me and all hands were summoned to block the way from the passage and persuade a surprised Under Secretary that the only access was through our room if and when the Secretary of State was disengaged. It worked.'[40] In such ways the two ministers avoided serious acrimony. This, in the face of Churchill's opinionated hyperactivity, was no small tribute to Elgin's tact. But there was an underlying uneasiness. Churchill repeatedly thanked Elgin for his indulgence and for what he had learnt from him about the conduct of official business; Elgin felt some admiration for this 'curious and impulsive creature', yet often found his subordinate's behaviour profoundly trying.[41] 'Qualified esteem' was just about right.

The advent of the new government triggered a general election, held in January and February 1906. While battle raged on the hustings, Churchill and Elgin had to start dealing straight away with Colonial Office problems that were themselves controversial. The key issue for them was South Africa and, immediately, the question of the workers from China who had been imported into the Transvaal in order to meet the labour shortage there. Many Liberals attacked this as 'Chinese Slavery'. On the one hand, there was genuine concern about the pay and conditions of the indentured labourers on the Rand, and on the other there was an appeal to baser instincts: the fear that Chinese workers were taking white men's jobs. There was also a generalized hostility to the capitalist mine-owners who benefited from the system. Yet that system could not be ended merely by the stroke of a pen. Nearly fifteen thousand new Chinese were due to arrive in South Africa under contracts agreed before the Tories fell from office, and to halt their arrival might involve the government in expensive compensation claims. At the risk of alienating Radical MPs, the Cabinet took the pragmatic decision to allow these workers to come.[42]

Churchill claimed to 'hate Chinese Labour as much as I honour the Flag'.[43] Aware of its complexities, though, he did not make this a central issue in his own election campaign in Manchester. After-wards, Chamberlain was forced to withdraw the false allegation that gangs of Liberals dressed up as Chinamen had paraded through the streets of the constituency 'accompanied by an agent got up as a slave-driver'.[44] Churchill did refer in public to 'the battle of white labour against the whole force of the capitalist interest in South Africa', but the slogans used on his posters were innocuous: 'Churchill and Free Trade', 'Cheap Food', and 'A United Empire'.[45] His election address promised that the government would 'restrict' the system of Chinese Labour and 'put down its abuses' but – on Elgin's advice – he did not make any firm pledge to end it.[46]

He won the seat by a substantial margin, part of a crushing Liberal victory nationwide. In February, during one of Churchill's early appearances at the despatch box, he made it clear that, undesirable as the current state of affairs might be, the government would not take instant action to deport the Chinese. To laughter, he declared that as the labourers had entered their contracts voluntarily and for a limited period, and were paid wages they found adequate, the system could not 'in the opinion of His Majesty's Government be classified as slavery in the extreme accep-tance of the word without some risk of terminological inexactitude'.[47] The *Liverpool Daily Courier* printed a cartoon of Churchill hoisting himself into the Colonial Office with the aid of a Chinaman's pigtail. The legend ran: 'Mr Winston Churchill's autobiography will describe the thrilling story of how he climbed into office with the aid of his patent terminological inexactitude.'[48] Such anger was understandable, given the language that had been used by other Liberals, but it was unfair to Churchill personally. During the election he had made clear to the voters that the conditions of the Chinese, although 'servile and improper', did not constitute slavery.[49]

That episode is well known; but it was small beer compared to the (now strangely forgotten) row that broke out the following month. By this time the government had arrived at a moderate policy. It had decided not to end the existing labour contracts, although no more would be issued; to modify the rules so as to prevent abuses; to repatriate all Chinese workers who wished to go home; and to allow the Transvaal itself, once it had gained self-government, to decide whether the system should continue into the future. This last point was subject to the proviso that the government in London would, if necessary, exercise its right to veto any legislation that a future Transvaal parliament might pass regarding Chinese labour, and Churchill made this clear in the Commons in February.[50] During a debate in March, he was stung by Chamberlain into repeating the point in a more provocative way. No matter how well a proposal from the Transvaal was supported by public opinion there, he said, the home government would not shrink from vetoing anything that offended the principles of liberty and decency.[51]

Traditionally, the use of the Crown's right of veto of colonial governments' decisions was restricted to matters affecting the rights of British subjects elsewhere or Britain's relations with foreign powers. It now seemed as though Churchill was claiming a general right to interfere in the business of any self-governing colony that offended Liberal ministers' sense of right and wrong. South African shares fell on the Stock Exchange, which Churchill unconvincingly tried to blame on 'the lugubrious and pessimistic orations' of Balfour and Chamberlain.[52] British South Africans were outraged by the speech. 'The Cabinet must not forget it is dealing with its own flesh and blood', declared the *Rand Mail*: 'We will not forgo the birthright of freedom we have inherited.' Another South African paper, the *Star*, thought the speech 'a gratuitous insult to every self-governing colony'. There was even discussion of 'cutting the painter' tying

South Africa to the motherland, although no paper openly advocated this.[53] One New Zealand paper claimed that Churchill's
'deplorable indiscretion' had 'aroused a keen resentment far beyond
the limits of South Africa'.[54]

In Britain, the *Pall Mall Gazette* derisively labelled Churchill 'The
Blenheim Pup'.[55] Chamberlain said – with considerable chutzpah,
given that he was an ex-Liberal himself – that Churchill's speech
was 'inconsistent with declared Liberal principles'. By these he
meant the ideal of self-government, but he might better have said
that Liberal principles were inconsistent.[56] For Churchill had come
up hard against a central dilemma of Liberal colonial policy. One
could intervene to protect the indigenous population (and non-
natives such as the Chinese) and thus stand accused of stripping
white minorities of their hereditary freedoms. Or one could do
nothing, which would lead to charges at home of permitting abuses
under the British flag. Churchill had a very clear sense that the
more opportunistic of his opponents would adopt and adapt these
alternative lines of attack exactly as they saw fit.[57] Within the
Empire, he won some support from Liberal opinion. The *Toronto
Daily Star* ridiculed the idea that colonial self-government as a whole
was in danger, and pointed out that the South African colonies were
a special case. 'If they were treated as Canada or Australia is
treated, they would complain loudly of neglect, and it would be said
that the "Little Englanders'" Government was neglecting Imperial
interests.'[58]

A week later, in a much better-known incident, Churchill
provoked further upset. It had been revealed that Lord Milner,
during his now-expired term as High Commissioner for South
Africa, had sanctioned the unlawful flogging of Chinese workers. A
Liberal backbencher, William Byles, moved a motion deploring
Milner's conduct. From the government's point of view it was
unhelpful to stir up bad feeling against a widely admired figure,
especially given that 'our excitable British friends' in South Africa
would resent the criticism. So with the consent of his colleagues
Churchill moved an amendment, condemning the flogging but
deprecating the censure of individuals in the interests of peace and
reconciliation.[59] But even though the amendment was carried, the
attempt to smooth things over misfired. His speech, which in
rehearsal had seemed full of generosity of spirit towards the now-

eclipsed Milner, came across in performance, Edward Marsh recalled, as the 'taunting [of] a discredited statesman with the evil days on which he had fallen'.[60] It also went down badly with the British South Africans, both as a slight on Milner (whose racial views were at any rate thought by them to be dangerously progressive) and as an interference with 'the native problem', which the local whites felt was theirs alone to deal with.[61] The *Cape Times*, observing that a few years earlier Churchill had shared Milner's ideas, described the speech as nauseous, hypocritical and unprincipled.[62] Churchill, however, defended himself, telling Selborne that 'no other course but the one adopted by me, would have prevented Lord Milner from being censured formally by the House of Commons. We interfered to parry the blow – & did parry it, much to the disgust of many of our own supporters.'[63]

South African affairs continued to go wrong. A Zulu rebellion had recently broken out in the British colony of Natal, and at the end of March 1906 the Colonial Office was informed that twelve rebels had been convicted of murder and sentenced to death by court martial. In response, perhaps at Churchill's instance, a telegram was sent requesting the executions be delayed pending the receipt of further information.[64] The colonists were soon 'boiling with indignation' at a move they saw as endangering the white population.[65] The Natal government resigned, although the resignations were quickly rescinded when the Colonial Office backed down, allowing the sentences to be carried out. In the Commons, Churchill denied there had been any U-turn, stressing that the request for information had been perfectly proper and that this had not implied criticism of the Natal authorities or any intention to veto their decision.[66] The executions, of course, provoked the anger of Radicals, which demonstrated the government's difficulty in satisfying opinion in the Empire and on its own backbenches at the same time. Churchill's mood was inevitably affected. In May, Lady Lugard reported, 'He seemed irritable, ill, and out of spirits – and very much oppressed by the questions which he had to answer in the House of Commons.'[67]

Over the next few months the rebellion was put down with the loss of around 3,500 African lives. One of the rebel leaders, Bambatha, was killed in battle and when his body was found his head was cut off for the purposes of identification. When questions were asked in Parliament, Churchill was on a sticky wicket, and fell back on the question-begging claim that what had been done was not 'half so discreditable to civilization' as Kitchener's treatment of the Mahdi's body in 1898.[68] He was, in fact, consistently infuriated by the behaviour of the Natal government and made serious efforts to improve the welfare of Zulu prisoners. In 1907 he wrote a striking minute condemning 'the disgusting butchery of natives' which to him demonstrated 'the kind of tyranny against which these unfortunate Zulus have been struggling'.[69] Elgin was less inclined to intervention than Churchill, which reflected both the older man's innate caution and his perhaps more realistic appreciation of the powers of the Colonial Office, which were in practice quite limited. It was hard to control territories thousands of miles away using telegrams or written despatches; it was easy for those on the spot to use their supposedly superior knowledge of local conditions as an excuse for circumventing the wishes of Whitehall. Deferring to such knowledge was at any rate a standard tenet of imperial administration. As the battle over the execution of the twelve rebels showed, it was easier to put up with the criticism of a few Radicals at home than it was to hold British colonial governments to account. The Radicals were at any rate to be appeased by the successful (albeit rather drawn-out) ending of Chinese labour. By the time he was campaigning for re-election in 1908, Churchill was able to boast of 'how the yellow plague had been stayed and the coolies sent home' by the government of which he was a member.[70]

The outcome of the controversy over the Natal executions seemed to show that the Liberals had no intention of systematically overriding the judgement of local administrations. Further reassurance was given to the colonists in April 1906 when Churchill told the Commons that the government had decided to move ahead swiftly with full self-government in the Transvaal and the Orange River Colony (ORC – the former Orange Free State). Although he talked much of reconciliation between the races – British and Boer, that is – he emphasized that the government was committed to the maintenance of British supremacy in South Africa and that it did not intend that future constitutional arrangements should undermine this.[71] This seemingly unexceptional statement came as quite a revelation to the jittery British South Africans. The Mayor of Johannesburg said that 'with the exercise of a little charity the name of Mr Churchill might yet be favourably received in South Africa'.[72] A corner had been turned. Churchill was now careful to make soothing noises about the need for Britain to have good relations 'with the great self-governing Colonies', and this helped win over opinion in Australia and New Zealand too.[73] In June the *Transvaal Leader* noted with satisfaction how 'Three months ago the extremists were applauding Mr Churchill to the echo; now he and his chief are regarded as foes to Liberalism'.[74] Chamberlain was quick to ridicule the change in Churchill's attitude. 'In the early days of this government he did more than anybody else to produce a Radical millennium', he claimed in a speech made shortly before a major stroke removed him from active politics. 'He came into office like a bull entering a china shop. Now he roars as gently as any sucking dove.'[75]

III

At the same time as Churchill was dealing with the Chinese labour problem and with the sensitivities of the British in South Africa, he was thinking about the question of future constitutional arrangements in the Transvaal and the ORC. All these issues were intimately related. From the first, Churchill believed that it was necessary to grant full self-government fast, and in this he was in line with the thinking of his senior colleagues. The Tories had been a planning to grant the Transvaal so-called 'representative government', a kind of halfway house in which a (partly nominated) Executive Council would not be responsible to the elected legislature. Liberal ministers quickly determined to abandon this scheme and proceed directly to 'responsible government', with the executive accountable to the assembly. This was judged necessary in part to appease South African opinion, both British and Boer. Moreover, granting responsible government would mean offloading the charge of some awkward issues from London to Pretoria. As Churchill put it in an early memorandum on the issue, the representative government solution would mean giving much power to the locals; even so, ministers in Westminster would not be able to escape accountability in the House of Commons for what the Transvaal government actually did. Given the known proclivities of the South Africans, 'Many things will be done of which we disapprove, which we shall be powerless to prevent, but which we shall be forced to defend, to the intense dissatisfaction of our supporters.'[76] There was an obvious attraction to a solution which would put the responsibility for tricky questions such as the (at this point still unresolved) Chinese labour problem at arm's length from the Colonial Office.

Ministers' discussions on how to move forward coincided with the arrival of J. C. Smuts in London in January 1906 on a mission for the Boer Het Volk party. At the age of thirty-five – four years older than Churchill – Smuts was already established as a major figure in South African and imperial politics and would remain so until his death in 1950. He was a hugely talented but also puzzling, ambivalent and almost sphinx-like figure. A formidable general with a Cambridge education, he carried the New Testament in Greek and Kant's *Critique of Pure Reason* with him while on campaign during the Boer War. He came to count English Quaker feminists amongst his closest friends.[77] After his initial faith in the British (and Cecil Rhodes in particular) was destroyed by the Jameson raid, he had fought vociferously against them; yet he then played a key role in the peace settlement, hoping for Boer–British solidarity in the face of threats to white supremacy. (In 1906, Churchill hoped to exploit such racial fears for imperial purposes. He believed that '"the black peril"' would act as a 'unifying force, drawing the two white races together [. . .] and leading them to turn gratefully to the military power of the Crown'.)[78] Smuts's subsequent career seemed to prove that such reconciliation was not merely an idle dream. He served in Lloyd George's War Cabinet during World War I and provided crucial advice to Churchill during World War II, 'the only man who has any influence with the P.M.', according to Lord Moran.[79] Yet his emergence as a great imperial statesman came at the cost of distrust from more extreme Afrikaner nationalists at home.

Racial issues were, of course, to be fundamental to South African politics far beyond the Edwardian period; Smuts's attitude towards them was intriguing. This is not because his paranoid fears of the majority population's 'immemorial barbarism and animal savagery' were unusual in a Boer leader. Rather it is because even in spite of them one cannot entirely escape a sense that he was uncomfortably aware of the defects of his own attitude and record.[80] Despite his failure throughout his career ever to do anything meaningful on behalf of the rights of Africans, at the end of World War II he drafted the preamble to the UN Charter, which affirms faith in 'fundamental human rights, in the dignity and worth of the human person, [and] in the equal rights of men and women'.[81] Not long after this, Francis Williams, press secretary to Labour Prime Minister Clement Attlee, met him at a reception in London. Williams, fully aware of the contrast between 'Smuts, the political philosopher' and 'Smuts, the Prime Minister of South Africa', offered some 'rather empty compliments' about the speech he had made earlier that day. Williams recalled:

> He looked at me with the steady open-air stare which was one of his characteristics and said, 'I know what you young liberals think when you hear me talking like that. You say: Why doesn't he do better by the Africans in his own country instead of talking to us about human rights? Well, my friend, some day you'll appreciate what an avalanche I've been holding back.'[82]

This should count as Smuts's apologia, and it contained an obvious element of truth. In 1948, after Smuts's election defeat at the hands of the Nationalist Party, the profound existing racial discriminations were made yet more severe with the advent of the apartheid system. It is genuinely tragic though, that such a generally intelligent and courageous individual consistently chose to accommodate the racial anxieties he shared with his fellow whites rather than to confront or transcend them. Even Churchill criticized him for this, observing privately in 1944 that, 'while Smuts was a great Liberal, when it came to the negro question, he would just cut it off from all the rest of his Liberal views'.[83]

During Smuts's 1906 mission, however, 'the negro question' lay somewhat in the background. His primary aims were to secure responsible government for the Transvaal and to ensure that the franchise was drawn up as far as possible in the Boers' favour. He feared that his people might 'continue the victims of that Jewish-Jingo gang' but hoped that the Liberal government would grant 'justice'.[84] Yet although he was to establish a warm relationship with Churchill in later years, it is clear that at the beginning he had little confidence in either him or (probably) in Elgin. He had considerably more faith in Campbell-Bannerman; the Prime Minister had, after all, denounced the harsh treatment of the Boers during the war. At a one-to-one meeting with 'C-B' at 10 Downing Street on

7 February, Smuts made an emotive statement of the Boer case. He
came to believe that his impact had been decisive. In fact, ministers
had already made up their minds to grant responsible government
quite independently, although he may have had some influence on
the actual manner in which they proceeded, helping to ensure that
the breach with Tory policy was made as overt as possible. If he
was allowed to persuade himself that his influence had been critical
then it was perhaps he, rather than the British, who was won over.[85]
But this did not lead to any outpouring of affection for Churchill.
On the latter's early ministerial trials Smuts commented: 'I see our
friend Winston is occupying the stage under the full limelight and
that his pity for the Chinese-flogging Milner is no less Olympian
than for the benighted radical who thought the Chinese indentures
partook of the nature of slavery'.[86]

Increasingly aware that the government, not least thanks to him,
was making itself unpopular in South Africa, Churchill was anxious
to settle things quickly. Uncertainty about the future would contribute to the British population's distrust of the home government, and
would drive British voters away from the Transvaal, thus undermining the prospects of future British control. If the uncertainty was not
ended, the British and the Boers might even join together 'in
common repudiation' of the imperial government – a variant of the
nightmare scenario he had feared after the Jameson Raid.[87] By the
end of July the government had drawn up detailed plans for a new
constitution for the Transvaal (the ORC constitution was finalized a
few months later). Announcing the details to the Commons,
Churchill ended his speech with a stirring though unfruitful appeal
to the Opposition to support it. 'With all our majority we can only
make it the gift of a Party', he said; 'they can make it the gift of
England.'[88]

A striking though wholly predictable feature of the Transvaal
constitution was the restriction of the franchise to whites. Churchill
– whose views were fully in line with those of his colleagues – had
already made clear in February that he was sensitive to the colonists'
anxieties about the 'ever-swelling sea of dark humanity' by which
they were surrounded. At the same time he had stated the government's commitment to the principle of 'equal rights of civilised men
irrespective of colour'.[89] This salutary-sounding sentiment, which
echoed Cecil Rhodes, carried with it much baggage. Similar slogans

had been used in Cape Colony in the 1890s as a justification for the
disenfranchisement of as many Africans as could be managed; being
'civilised' in that context meant meeting a significant property
qualification and being able to fill in a form in Dutch or English.[90]
To his credit, Churchill criticized the fact that the principle had
previously been applied in a very nominal way.[91] It must be
appreciated, though, that when Churchill spoke up for it himself he
was not advocating full racial equality. Rather he promised only
that the government would do what was in its power to 'encourage'
a 'careful, patient discrimination between the different classes of
coloured men'. (By way of context, it should be remembered that
the parliamentary franchise in Britain did not yet extend to all
classes of men, let alone to women, although there was no prohibi-
tion on the basis of race.) The possible implication of this seemed to
be that some British Indians might be deserving of the vote, but
there was no definite commitment to actually obtain it for them.
Churchill believed that Britain's hands were to a great extent tied
by Treaty of Vereeniging and, moreover, he clearly expected that
'the African aboriginal, for whom civilisation has no charms' would
be excluded from the franchise.[92]

At this point, though, things were not yet settled, and there was
in fact some lobbying from non-whites in South Africa. In June
Abdullah Abdurahman, a Cape Malay doctor trained in Glasgow
who was president of the nascent African Political Organisation, wrote
to Churchill from Cape Town, enclosing a petition addressed to the
King. It argued that non-African 'Coloured' British subjects who
had emigrated to the Transvaal and the ORC, and their descendants, were not 'natives' under the terms of Vereeniging. Therefore
it would be wrong to deny them the franchise, especially given that
several thousand of them had previously enjoyed voting rights in
Cape Colony.[93] (This was Milner's interpretation too.) Abdurahman
also led a deputation to Elgin in London, but the protests were to
no avail.[94] The ministers and officials were at one with the recent
committee of inquiry, which had concluded that, as white South
Africans took 'natives' to include all non-whites, it was politically
impossible to proceed on the basis of a more legalistic interpretation.
Hence Churchill's defence of this aspect of the constitution in the
Commons: 'I am not going to plunge into the argument as to what
"native" means or as to its legal or technical character [. . .] it is

undoubted that the Boers would regard it as a breach of that treaty, if the franchise were in the first instance extended to any persons who are not white men'. He expressed some 'regret' at this situation, as did Elgin in the Lords, but in Churchill's case at least it was of the mild rather than the tortured variety.[95] It must be admitted that the difficulties of any other course of action would have been severe, and yet one cannot fail to understand Abdurahman's sense that his people had been betrayed. In his Presidential Address to the African People's Organisation, he launched a coruscating attack on the British record. Whereas Churchill had likened the ORC to a model republic, Abdurahman said, 'it was far from that as Hell from Heaven [. . .] The best thing Mr Churchill could do was to draw a veil over this black page of South African administration.' The Coloured people had been told that the resolution of the injustices they faced depended on British victory in the Boer War, he said: 'Mr Chamberlain promised the franchise clearly and plainly in the name of the Imperial Government.' But after exploiting their grievances the British had cast them aside.[96]

IV

In November 1906, following in the footsteps of Smuts and Abdurahman, Mohandas K. Gandhi arrived in London.[97] He already knew the city well. Born in Western India in 1869 into a privileged Hindu family, he had been sent to Britain as a young man to study law. His three years in Britain made a profound impression. Late-Victorian London was a cosmopolitan place; it was not too difficult for him to find vegetarian restaurants. He became a member of the Vegetarian Society's committee and made friends with a number of fringe religious thinkers. It was, in fact, his contacts with Eastern-influenced British esotericism that stimulated his serious interest in Hinduism, his understanding of which was unorthodox.[98] He was not the first or last Indian student to find his return home a rude shock: accustomed to being treated on an equal basis in the free atmosphere of London, he found the attitude of the British sahibs insulting. Things were worse still when he arrived in South Africa in 1893 on a business mission. On the way to Pretoria he was ejected from his railway compartment, in spite of having a first-class ticket, because a white passenger refused to sit with an Indian. Rather than tolerate such treatment he spent most of the next two decades in South Africa fighting for the Indian community's rights. His wartime ambulance work was motivated by the conviction – in spite of his sympathy for the Boer desire for independence – that it was his duty as a British citizen to help defend the British Empire. As he recalled in his memoirs, 'I held then that India could achieve her complete emancipation only within and through the British Empire.'[99]

It was a new threat to the rights of Indians in the Transvaal that now brought Gandhi to London together with a Muslim colleague, H. O. Ally. This threat was the so-called 'Black Ordinance', proposed by the existing Crown Colony government, which would shut out new Indian immigration to the Transvaal and force Asians already living there to register themselves on pain of expulsion from the territory. These measures were a sop to Boer opinion; Smuts had spoken of eradicating the 'Asiatic cancer', and Louis Botha, the leader of his party, intended to 'drive the coolies out of the country'.[100] Gandhi and Ally arrived at pivotal moment, shortly before the new constitution came into effect; they hoped for London's veto of the Ordinance. For his part, Churchill hoped that, if the Colonial Office could delay action sufficiently, responsibility for the controversial measure could be passed to the incoming elected Transvaal government. 'The new parliament may shoulder the burden', he minuted. 'Why should we? Dawdle or disallow – preferably the former.'[101]

On 8 November Gandhi and Ally met with Elgin, who was not completely unsympathetic but gave them no indication of his decision.[102] The Secretary of State had recently received a petition signed by 437 Indians in South Africa denying that Gandhi had any authority to speak for them, and he gave the startled delegates a hint of this.[103] (Churchill was clearly informed as he subsequently gave details of the petition in a House of Commons answer.)[104] A few days later, having obtained more information, Gandhi and Ally responded with the claim – which Colonial Office officials seemed to accept – that the signatures had been obtained under false pretences. Gandhi also suggested that William Godfrey, one of the petition's organizers, was ' "touched" in the head'.[105] Gandhi and Ally were not granted their request for a further interview with

Elgin in order to put things straight, but at the end of the month they did see Churchill, who was still inclined to 'dawdle' with regard to the Ordinance.[106] This meeting was significant as the sole occasion on which Gandhi and Churchill met. The only record was made by Gandhi:

> We met Mr Winston Churchill at the time fixed by him. He spoke nicely. He asked both of us whether we were not afraid of responsible government in case the Ordinance were refused assent. What if a worse act were to be passed by the new Government? We replied that we could not imagine an act worse than the present Ordinance, and that we had asked for refusal of assent leaving the future to take care of itself.

After Churchill promised to think about it, Ally emphasized his own loyalty to the British, telling him that he had been present at Durban Point to welcome him after his escape from Boer captivity. 'And it was with the same Mr Churchill that he now pleaded for redress on behalf of the Indian community.' At this, Churchill 'smiled, patted Mr Ally on the back, and said that he would do all he could'. Gandhi noted: 'This answer added to our hopes.'[107]

Churchill seems to have made a generally good impression on Gandhi. In 1935 the latter remarked to a friend that he had 'got a good recollection of Mr Churchill when he was in the Colonial Office and somehow or other since then I have held the opinion that I can always rely on his sympathy and goodwill'.[108] This was a remarkably sunny comment, given the differences that the two had had in the meantime. Churchill, for his part, never made any reference to the meeting, and we cannot know for certain that it made any lasting impact on him. It may not have been insignificant for the future, though, that Gandhi had already been portrayed to him, via the apparently spurious petition, as a professional agitator who did not really speak for those he claimed to represent.

In the short term Gandhi and Ally's mission appeared successful. When their boat stopped at Madeira on the way back to Africa, they received cablegrams telling them that Elgin had refused assent to the Ordinance.[109] But it was not much of a victory. Contrary to British expectations, at the Transvaal election of February 1907 the Het Volk party under Botha secured a majority. Hardly had it taken office than it passed a new law, practically identical to the rejected

Ordinance. In May Churchill announced that the Colonial Office declined to intervene.[110] His attitude seemed to be one of resignation.[111] Gandhi now fought the Transvaal government with his new weapon of satyagraha, or non-violent resistance, which he would later use to such effect in India itself. In response to Churchill's declaration that the people of South Africa had the freedom to make whatever laws they wished to in respect of Asiatic immigration and the treatment of non-whites, he observed that 'the local governments in South Africa will be able to attack the Indian community with impunity'. He added: 'The only weapon with which to ward off the attack is our resolution on gaol-going.'[112] In January 1908, having refused to register with the authorities as the law required, he was sent to prison for the first time. It fell to Smuts, as the Transvaal's Colonial Secretary, to negotiate with him to reach a compromise solution whereby Indians would register voluntarily. Gandhi came to believe that Smuts had reneged on a promise to repeal the law in exchange for this concession; the situation reached a kind of stalemate in the years before Gandhi's return to India in 1914. As for Churchill, at the time of Gandhi's jailing, he cabled High Commissioner Selborne: 'Please tell Botha I am going to support his Government most strongly on the Indian question and that I thoroughly understand the views of white South Africa.'[113]

After his bruising first months in office, Churchill increasingly emphasized the continuity between his and Elgin's policies and those implemented earlier by the Conservatives: 'The rotation of the crops, he urged, was highly beneficial to the soil, and the Liberal party were but garnering the fruits of their predecessors.'[114] We need not conclude, though, that Churchill's period at the Colonial Office saw him shifting from Radicalism to reaction (which were at any rate not simple categories). His bullishness about the Empire's long-term prospects never wavered. In 1906 he rebuked an official who had predicted it would not last another hundred years: 'such pessimism is unworthy of the C.O.'.[115] But in spite of the strength of his commitment, others continued to regard him as reckless. Towards the end of Churchill's tenure Selborne was still fulminating at his 'mad and wicked' speeches in the Commons, 'goading at the British'. In fury, he wrote: 'I see Winston veering round to a position in which he will say the whole Boer war was iniquitous!'[116] On the face of it, Churchill's positions sometimes seemed contradictory.

Almost simultaneously with his reassurance to Botha that he understood the concerns of white South Africans, Churchill wrote a Colonial Office minute condemning British punitive raids against the rebellious Kisii tribe in East Africa: 'It looks like a butchery [. . .] Surely it cannot be necessary to go on killing these defenceless people on such an enormous scale.'[117] In Churchill's mind, however, there was no inconsistency. He never questioned his belief in white racial superiority, but this did not mean that he felt that people of other races were undeserving of consideration, and if he discerned ill-treatment he could become genuinely angry (a feeling perhaps accentuated by the prospect of awkward questions in the House of Commons). In other words, he did not perceive that there was any necessary conflict between racial inequality and humanitarianism. The phrase 'equal rights for all civilized men' summed up his attitude effectively because – resting on a racially determined concept of 'civilization' – it squared his belief in equality before the law with an acceptance that in practice some racial groups were 'more equal' than others.

V

As the example of the Kisii revolt shows, Churchill's activities at the Colonial Office extended far beyond South Africa. The diverse issues he dealt with included policy in West Africa, Newfoundland's fishing dispute with the USA, and even such minutiae as petitions for reinstatement by dismissed employees of the Ceylon government railways. Disconcertingly for Elgin, he showed an obsessive interest in the latter, being much concerned with the rights of the underdog.[118] With regard to Nigeria, he even demonstrated that he was prepared to consider scaling back the Empire, in order better to secure its overall future. In May 1906 Lady Lugard wrote to her husband that his pioneering work in the country appeared to be under threat. She had had long talks with Churchill at Blenheim and he had, she said, been 'talking rank little Englandism'. She lamented to Lugard that:

> He repeated all the foolish things you have ever heard about having gone too fast and added to them the extreme radical

rubbish about holding innocent peoples tight in the grip of a military despotism. To abolish the Waff [the West African Frontier Force], to give up the greater part of Nigeria 'which is much too big for us to hold', put an end to the whole system of punitive expeditions and to be content with the peaceful administration of one small corner of the whole were the principal suggestions which he had to make.[119]

Elgin, although he shared Churchill's dislike of punitive raids, was not prepared to entertain his radical suggestion of a partial withdrawal.[120] Churchill did not press the point, but it is clear that, at this stage of his career, he remained open-minded and flexible to a significant degree.

From Churchill's point of view, the main events of 1907 were the Colonial Conference in the spring and his tour of Africa in the autumn. He was well aware that the conference would be a mere 'business meeting which cannot arrive at any positive decision', as there was no chance that a Liberal government would grant trade preferences to the colonies, which was the chief demand of the visiting Empire politicians.[121] Anticipating the hostility of Alfred Deakin, the pro-tariff reform Australian Prime Minister, he nagged Elgin to invite the premiers of the individual Australian States. For this he offered the rationale '*Divide et impera!*' – the state premiers would counterbalance Deakin's influence, he thought – but his arguments for divide and rule were to no avail.[122] Churchill's most notable contribution to the conference itself was 'a rasping & injudicious speech full of highsounding phrases', in which he developed his established theme that imperial preference would threaten the concord of the Empire.[123] Asquith and Lloyd George were more soothing in their negatives, and in the end the visiting dignitaries were appeased with some small-scale concessions on inter-imperial transport and communications.

Such occasions gave Churchill the chance to thrust himself into the limelight; his African journey was another opportunity to earn publicity and (by writing about his adventures) money. Naturally, this produced satirical comment. *Punch* published spoof despatches in which the running gag, based on a genuine Reuters telegram, was Churchill's failure to bag any lions. He was said to have been interrogated by 'Twysta, Chief of the Pozas, a very intelligent tribe', who asked who ruled England in Churchill's absence and when did he intend to give Lord Elgin an old-age pension.[124] (A topical joke, this: state pensions were introduced in Britain the following year.) The *Crown*, a short-lived publication, printed a similar set of 'Unofficial Despatches' in cartoon form. In one frame, African tribesmen, in typical racist caricature, form a deputation demanding 'free fetishes' and 'fatter missionaries'. In another, the radical Labour MP Keir Hardie is seen springing naked out of the bush, greeting Churchill, who is dressed in African tribal costume, as 'My long lost black brother'.[125]

Churchill was away from Britain between September 1907 and January 1908. This prolonged absence was possible because there was no autumn session of Parliament that year – a testament to the comparatively relaxed (albeit even then steadily increasing) pace of government in those days. Before reaching Africa he visited the British dependencies of Malta and Cyprus, where he engaged in detailed discussion of local affairs. This was a sign of things to come. Elgin later complained that the tour had originally been intended as 'a purely sporting and private expedition – & I really don't know how it drifted into so essentially an official progress'. Churchill began to spew forth missives making proposals which Elgin thought hopelessly impractical.[126] An early example was a letter from Cyprus to Sir Francis Hopwood, Permanent Secretary at the Colonial Office. Churchill argued that the island's majority population's aspirations to unity with Greece – 'Enosis' – might be countered through ambitious schemes of economic development. Churchill expressed concern for the island's minority Muslim population, 'who have always behaved so well to us & to whom we have given so many pledges', but also looked forward to a time 'when the Moslem minority has been more or less painlessly submerged or extinguished', presumably through intermarriage and cultural assimilation.[127] From Cyprus he travelled to Aden and then Somaliland, where he spent several days, before sailing to Mombasa in the East African Protectorate (later the Crown Colony of Kenya). He journeyed onwards to Uganda and thence to Cairo via Sudan. In Uganda, in the absence of train or steamboat, he went on safari; his party of ten was accompanied by between three and four hundred African porters. Edward Marsh, who was himself writing about the trip for the *Manchester Guardian*, reported these arrangements to a friend, observing that 'one can't help feeling that it is a great personal convenience to belong to a dominant race'.[128] A subsequent American visitor claimed that it was possible to trace Churchill's route by the empty champagne and beer bottles he had left by the side of the trail.[129]

In addition to letters and memoranda, he also produced articles for *Strand* magazine (later published in book form as *My African Journey*) for which he was paid handsomely. H. Hesketh Bell, the Governor of Uganda, recorded that Churchill kept him awake one night by dictating to a clerk while he was in the bath.[130] The time spent on politics and journalism did not mean that sport was neglected altogether. Churchill reported to his mother that in one day's hunting he killed '1 zebra, 1 wildebeeste, 2 hartebeeste, 1 gazelle, [and] 1 bustard (a giant bird)'. A couple of days later he helped kill two rhinos; and a lion *was* bagged, although not by him.[131] He addressed gatherings of African leaders who were clad in traditional attire. According to the Governor of Kenya's official report:

> To all these assemblies of chiefs short suitable speeches were delivered, thanking them for the welcome he had accorded him, impressing upon them the advantage of working and developing their lands, and the benefits they would receive by contact with white men from whom they would learn many arts of which they were ignorant, and assuring them of the pleasure with which he had heard that they had settled down quietly under the aegis of the Government, and of the fact that the lands which had been allotted to them would be theirs for ever, to be enjoyed by them and their children's children so long as they lived at amity with the Government.[132]

These promises about security of land tenure were doubtless well meant but they were, as time would show, completely worthless. Over the years, and with the collusion of the authorities, the settlers were to use unfair means to dispossess Africans wherever they could. The resultant land hunger would be a major cause of the Mau Mau rebellion in the 1950s.

The evidence permits us to catch only the barest glimpses of the impression that Churchill made on ordinary Africans, mediated through the eyes of the whites. According to a woman settler in

Uganda, writing in the *Daily Graphic*, 'One of my "boys" wanted to know if this white man is the King's brother. I explained by saying that he was a big chief. He replied: "He must be a Saza chief," which means the chief of a whole county.'[133] Hesketh Bell, introducing Churchill to a gathering of chiefs at Kampala, tried to give a simple explanation of the position of the Colonial Under-Secretary in relation to the King and the Empire. The young Bagandan who translated simplified things further, saying that Churchill was the 'toto' of one of the King's servants. According to Bell, 'The amusing part of this matter is that, in Uganda, a *toto* is the small black urchin which a cook or other servant pays to help him in his job and who is usually remunerated by pickings from the master's table.'[134]

The views of the settlers themselves can be traced much more easily. For these people, oppressed by the heat and perhaps bored and frustrated with colonial life, Churchill's visit was a big event. According to the *Star of East Africa*, 'Practically all European Nairobi' turned out to meet him at the station, 'from the lordly official strutting it proudly in his uniform' to the humble worker. They felt that his arrival might signify 'the beginning of a new epoch', presumably hoping that the London government would now take a greater interest in their doings and welfare.[135] He met deputations tirelessly even though he thought many of their complaints trivial; he blamed their vexatiousness partly on the recent influx of 'a vy low class of S. African'.[136] But although he seems to have won the settlers over at the personal level, many of them were deeply suspicious of the Liberal government, with its element 'which always sticks up for the "poor native"', and wondered if he could have real influence over its doings.[137] The *Star of East Africa* declared that 'Mr Churchill has to be considered – and with sympathetic insight it may be divined that he considers himself – as an able, energetic statesman struggling with a fate too strong for him.'[138] He had clearly succeeded, without saying very much that was concrete, in conveying a sense that he understood the settlers' aspirations. This was a notable contrast with his reputation in South Africa.

Churchill had to contend with racial questions that were just as toxic in East Africa as in the Transvaal. He encountered the well-established demand for Kenya to become 'a white man's country'. He was prepared to pay lip-service to the desirability of this 'respectable and impressive policy' but he did not hide his scepticism about its practicality.[139] It should be noted that – as Churchill was surely aware – that the idea was not to be taken absolutely literally, in the sense of demand for the complete expulsion of non-whites. The tiny settler population clearly did not intend to do without African labour.[140] The slogan was in large part motivated by resentment against the substantial and entrepreneurial British Indian population, and the settlers did their best to claim that an end to further non-white immigration was in the Africans' own best interests.[141] 'We are strongly of the opinion that the people of our own Race and the African should progress hand in hand [. . .] and that the Asiatic should have no place in the country whatsoever', declared one settler petition presented to Churchill.[142] At the same time, they made no efforts to disguise their desire to control all the best land themselves. In particular, they wanted the temperate highlands of Kenya to be reserved for their own use, something Elgin had in practice granted in 1906 using a classic obfuscatory formula: 'It would not be in accordance with the policy of H.M.G. to exclude any class of H.M. subjects from holding land in any part of a British protectorate, but that in view of the comparatively limited area in the Protectorate suitable for European colonization, a reasonable discretion will be exercised in dealing with applications for land on the part of natives of India and other non-Europeans.'[143] Naturally, this provoked a reaction from the Indians. Churchill – according to one anonymous contributor to the *Manchester Dispatch*, who claimed to have accompanied him throughout much of his tour – experienced 'a decided embarrassment' in dealing with delegations of Indians concerned about their future and prospects. He offered them only generalized assurances, but his soothing words were enough to make the whites worry about the 'traditional curse' of Whitehall interference with colour problems.[144]

In fact, his own conviction (expressed the previous year in connection with South Africa) was that 'the practice of allowing European, Asiatic, and native families to live side by side in mixed communities is fraught with many evils'.[145] It is unsurprising, then, that in *My African Journey* he endorsed the general reservation of the highlands to the whites – in spite of his doubt that Europeans could live at such high altitudes for more than fifteen or twenty years without suffering 'degeneration'. But – and this won him the praise of the Liberal *Daily Chronicle* – he did not support the 'squeezing out' of Indians from East Africa as a whole. Rather, he thought that they should be encouraged to settle 'in the enormous regions of tropical fertility' to which they were 'naturally adapted'.[146] One reviewer summarized the book's message approvingly: 'Mr Churchill, with long vision, foresees Africa partitioned off both racially and economically – a peaceful, self-sufficing, equal division of labor and of material. But before that millennium is reached there must be an endless succession of particular stages calling for every quality of tact and sympathy in the ruling race.'[147]

Although he favoured the settler viewpoint in regard to the highlands, Churchill felt no great sympathy for the settlers themselves. A few years later, he wrote, 'Although they are only a few thousand, they firmly believe they are entitled to monopolise the whole fortunes of East Africa and to be the sole beneficiaries of the resources of the country and to the work and contributions of the Imperial Government.' They were 'a very troublesome crowd' who needed to be dealt with firmly.[148] For this reason he opposed giving self-government to the whites of the East Africa Protectorate: there could be no question of handing over millions of Africans 'to the control of the first few thousand white men who happen to arrive in the country'. He believed that the British imperial officials, in contrast to the potentially exploitative colonists, were disinterested and praiseworthy.[149] This was particularly evident in his comments on Uganda: 'A class of rulers is provided by an outside power as remote from, and in all that constitutes fitness to direct, as superior to the Baganda as Mr Wells's Martians would have been to us.'[150] It was more than a little ironic that Churchill should have used this illustration, not only because the Martians in *The War of the Worlds* (1898) are utterly malevolent, but also because they ultimately fail in their war of conquest due to their poor adaptation to local conditions.

Such remarks help make *My African Journey* appear, on the face of it, a rather perplexing text. It can be mined by Churchill's supporters for quotations which appear to show his concern for the welfare of Africans and by his critics for evidence of his racism. In the first category is his ironical comment at the expense of the settlers:

> 'The natives,' says the planter, 'evince a great reluctance to work, especially to work regularly.' 'They must be made to

work,' say others. 'Made to work for whom?' we innocently ask. 'For us, of course,' is the ready answer; 'what did you think we meant?'[151]

In the second category was his description of 'the life and lot of the African aboriginal – secure in his abyss of contented degradation' and his view of the Africans as childlike.[152] In reality, both sets of sentiments were part of a complex of beliefs in which the Africans were undoubtedly seen as inferior *but as capable of improvement*; it was thus the duty of the imperial government to facilitate this by protecting them from the rapacious self-interest of the white settlers. The ambivalence of Churchill's attitude was nicely captured by the following comment:

> No one can travel even for a little while among the Kikuyu tribes without acquiring a liking for these light-hearted, tractable, if brutish children, or without feeling that they are capable of being instructed and raised from their present degradation. [. . .] Their care imposes a grave, and I think an inalienable, responsibility upon the British Government.[153]

Overall, his outlook was an optimistic one. He was particularly encouraged – as he said in a speech at the National Liberal Club on his return – by the large numbers of 'clothed, cultivated, educated natives' in Uganda, who had converted to Christianity and abandoned polygamy. In his view this evidence went a long way 'to vindicate the ideal which the negrophile has so often held up before the British public, and which in other places has so often been disappointed'; and it also prompted some praise, rather unusual for him, of missionary activity.[154] Furthermore, his concern for African welfare – and his appreciation of the possible benefits to the British economy – spurred him towards grandiose visions of economic development. Envisaging a huge dam across the Ripon Falls at the north end of Lake Victoria he wrote, 'It is possible that nowhere else in the world could so enormous a mass of water be held up by so little masonry.'[155] At the end of 1908, the right-wing *Observer* reviewed his book under the headline 'Mr Churchill – Imperialist!' It found in his suggestions 'the real spirit of constructive statesmanship which convinces us once more that Mr Churchill's natural place was with the party he has left'.[156] This should not be taken as

an indication that Churchill was drifting ideologically back towards
the Tories, but rather as evidence that the rhetoric of imperial
developmentalism could play well across the political spectrum.
The Liberal *Daily News* perceived that, with his emphasis on the role
of the state, Churchill was offering 'a different sort of Imperialism'
to that favoured by Conservatives. 'He will have nothing to do with
the speculator-capitalist, he has no wish to leave the future of this
beautiful country to the tender mercies of the casual empire-builder.
[. . .] One cannot but contrast his philosophical suggestions with
the vague chimeras which have bewildered the followers of Mr
Chamberlain.'[157]

VI

Churchill was now entering the most left-wing phase of his career.
Just before Christmas 1907, while travelling down the Nile, he wrote
to J. A. Spender, editor of the *Westminster Gazette*, about domestic
economic and social issues. The British people, he argued, were
increasingly turning their minds to such questions. 'Minimum standards of wages and comfort, insurance in some effective form or
other against sickness, unemployment, old age, these are the questions and the only questions on which politics is going to turn in the
future. Woe to Liberalism, if they slip through its fingers.' These
thoughts, he added, were 'the fruit of my Central African reflections'.[158] When he spoke at the National Liberal Club in January he
made the link between Empire and social reform explicit, as he had
done in the past: 'If the British people will have a great Empire, if
any ray of true glory is to fall upon it, they will need an imperial
race to support the burden. They will never erect that great fabric
upon the shoulders of stunted millions crowded together in the
slums of cities, trampled in the slush of streets.'[159] In April 1908
Asquith replaced the terminally sick Campbell-Bannerman as Prime
Minister. He gave Churchill the opportunity to turn his thinking on
welfare into practical action by appointing him President of the
Board of Trade with a seat in the Cabinet. The *Cape Times* said that
South Africa could congratulate itself upon the fact that he had not
been made Colonial Secretary; the *Cape Argus* expressed relief at his
removal from the Colonial Office and pleasure at the appointment

of Earl Crewe as Colonial Secretary.[160] It was Elgin who emerged the loser from these changes. Relieved of his post by Asquith in a rather peremptory fashion – 'even a housemaid gets a better warning', complained the victim – he retired embittered to his estate and took no further part in politics.[161] He hinted to his successor that Churchill's flamboyant behaviour over the past two and a half years had undermined him (Elgin) with his colleagues.[162]

Examining Churchill's tenure at the Colonial Office as a whole we can see that it illustrates many of the paradoxes and complexities of his attitudes to Empire. It shows that he was not dedicated to the expansion of territory regardless of circumstance. One of the main practical consequences of his African trip was an effort to cut back British commitments in the disturbed Somaliland protectorate, which he described as 'one vast undulating waste-land of stony scrubby wilderness producing nothing but a scattered swarm of human hornets'.[163] (He referred to his policy of moving troops to the coast not as 'evacuation' but as 'concentration' because 'it sounds better'.)[164] Nor can he be accused of pandering to the racist sentiments of white colonialists at all costs. He was eager, for instance, to extract reforms to improve the position of Africans as a quid pro quo for assisting the Natal government with its political difficulties.[165] Yet although he was undoubtedly sincere in his intention that all races should be treated with justice, that notion was perfectly consistent in his mind with the concept of white supremacy. For him, there was a duty incumbent on the superior British race to safeguard and improve lesser ones. That, indeed, was part of the justification for imperial rule. In 1909 he told Wilfrid Scawen Blunt that the Empire brought no advantage to Britain and was 'a lot of bother'. After these uncharacteristic words, he went on to express something much closer to his normal sentiments: 'The only thing one can say for it is that it is justified if it is undertaken in an altruistic spirit for the good of the subject races.' Blunt responded, 'Yes, but where do we find the altruism?'[166] It was a good question. Churchill, Elgin and men like them could provide some of it, when political expediency and their own racial assumptions did not get in the way. But all too often the interests of the 'subject races' were sacrificed in the face of pressures from intransigent local whites. London's reserves of altruism were real, yet in the end they were insufficient to service an entire empire.

5

THE FATE OF AN EMPIRE,
1908–1922

IN JANUARY 1922, Churchill was the chief guest at a Kenya Colony and Uganda dinner held at the Hotel Victoria in London. During World War I his career had met with near catastrophe, but he had fought hard to salvage his reputation. He was now back at the Colonial Office, where he had started his ministerial career, this time as Colonial Secretary himself. In his speech at the dinner Churchill dealt with some of the unfinished business from the years that he had served under Lord Elgin. He began with some general remarks in which he stressed that colonial officials should combine firmness with sensitivity to the feelings of indigenous populations. Careful understanding of their viewpoint was better, he suggested, than the impractical application of enlightenment theories. Indeed, 'The democratic principles of Europe are by no means suited to the development of Asiatic and African people.' He then went on to talk about East Africa and referred to Elgin's 1906 commitment to the white settlers: 'We consider we are pledged by undertakings given in the past to reserve the highlands of East Africa exclusively for European settlers, and we do not intend to depart from that pledge.' All future Indian immigration to East Africa was to be strictly regulated.[1] The Secretary of State for India and the Viceroy, neither of whom had been consulted, were furious.[2] The remarks caused a storm in India, where it was said that Churchill had 'libelled the people of this country'.[3] Not only did his remarks seem to contradict a resolution of the previous year's imperial conference recognizing Indians citizens as equal citizens of the Empire but, moderate politicians suggested, Churchill was playing into the hands of Gandhi and the extremists. One member of the Legislative Council – a largely toothless body, but one which gave some Indians a political voice – quoted at length from a book describing the economic achievements of Asians in East Africa and the role that Indian capital had played in financing some white settlers there. He then revealed, to prolonged laughter, that the writer was none other than Winston Churchill and that the book was *My African Journey*.[4]

The episode was a revealing one, not least in terms of how Churchill was perceived. During the Edwardian period he had, of course, been seen as an imperialist, but not in the sense of being a diehard or a reactionary. (Many right-wingers had thought of him, for a brief time at least, as a dangerous Radical.) Although he had not been immune to criticism from figures such as Gandhi and Abdurahman, they had never suggested that his views were specially or uniquely unpleasant or old-fashioned. Yet now, in the early 1920s, he began to cement a reputation as someone who, from the progressive point of view, was both backward and ill informed. He appeared also to be out of step with many of his own colleagues. One possible explanation for this might be that Churchill had got stuck in a pre-1914 imperial mindset, whereas other people had moved on. This might convince on some issues, such as his negative attitude to Indian nationalism, even if his denunciation of the 'frightfulness' of the 1919 Amritsar massacre might seem to belie his reactionary image.[5] Elsewhere, though, the picture is more complicated. For example, rather than standing still on the question of Indian immigration to East Africa, he had actually moved to the right. Yet over Ireland he appeared flexible. Moreover, he had not returned to the imperial expansionism represented by his support for the forward policy in the 1890s, as can be seen from his scepticism about the new Middle Eastern territories that Britain acquired during the war. 'I know it will be found very hard to relinquish the satisfaction of those dreams of conquest and aggrandisement which are gratified by the retention of Palestine and Mesopotamia', he wrote in 1919. 'As a matter of fact we have far more territory in the British Empire than we shall be able to develop for many generations.'[6]

I

In order to understand the shifts in Churchill's thought, as well as his seeming inconsistencies, it is necessary to review his actions from his first entry to the Cabinet in 1908 to the collapse of Lloyd

George's coalition government at the end of 1922. These were dramatic years in his personal life. A few months after he became President of the Board of Trade he married the beautiful and elegant Clementine Hozier, whom he drove to distraction through his financial extravagance but who remained fiercely loyal to him nonetheless. They had five children – Diana, Randolph, Sarah, Marigold, and Mary – although Marigold died in 1921 at the age of two following a throat infection. They were also dramatic years politically, as the Liberal ascendancy was broken by the Great War, paving the way for the realignment of the party system. Taking over the Board of Trade was a breakthrough for Churchill in more ways than one. It was not just another step up on the ladder of success. So far, the Empire, in one form or another, had formed the backdrop to his political rise, from his military adventures, via debates about free trade, to the Colonial Office itself. Now, he had his first home portfolio, and this required him to redefine himself politically.

Churchill was to a great extent drawn away from direct imperial responsibilities and did not return to them until after World War I. Although references to the Empire still cropped up in his rhetoric with some regularity, he made no efforts to resist this shift to home affairs, which was in fact to his advantage. His Cabinet colleague David Lloyd George had made skilful use of his Welsh background during his early phase at Westminster but had in the end broken free from it to achieve stature as a truly national British politician. Churchill's progress was almost the obverse of this. He had required the Empire as a springboard into politics, but now needed to transcend an exclusive association with it if his career as a domestic politician was to thrive fully. For the next dozen years he did engage with important imperial issues but in a more episodic way than formerly. Nevertheless, his capacity to stir up trouble had not deserted him, and his eventual return to the Colonial Office was to see him preside over decisions, notably on the Middle East, that are controversial even today. The period as a whole was marked, moreover, by a darkening of his imperial vision, as British power was faced with a succession of monumental challenges. In 1909 – in contrast to his earlier ridicule of the 'croakers' who spoke of decline – he talked of the possible collapse of the Empire if social evils at home were not addressed.[7] In 1922 he warned that 'the whole accumulated greatness of Britain' was at risk.[8]

Lloyd George, promoted to be Chancellor of the Exchequer, had been Churchill's predecessor as President of the Board of Trade. Following such a dynamic minister was a tough act, but Churchill pulled it off, although he alienated some colleagues who deplored his disruptive influence in Cabinet.[9] His social reform achievements were impressive. He introduced legislation to enforce minimum wages in the 'sweated' trades and to create labour exchanges to help the workless find jobs. He also devised plans (in collaboration with Lloyd George) for state-sponsored National Insurance to protect workers against unemployment and sickness. Since the start of his public life his concern with social welfare had been entangled with fears that the effects of poverty could damage the Empire and its reputation. In *My African Journey* he quoted a settler as saying, 'It would destroy the respect of the native for the white man, if he saw what miserable people we have got at home.'[10] In 1909 Lloyd George introduced a radical budget which drastically increased the scope of taxation in order to help fund welfare commitments and to meet the cost of naval competition with Germany. This provoked an epic battle between the government and the Conservative-dominated House of Lords which – after two Liberal general election victories during 1910 – ended with the curtailment of the Lords' rights to block legislation. In one of his speeches defending the budget, notable for its threat to 'smash to pieces' the Lords' veto, Churchill spoke of his anxiety at the coexistence 'of extreme wealth and of extreme want'. The greatest peril to the British Empire and the British people, he suggested, did not lie in Europe, India, or the colonies. Rather it lay in domestic social evils, including economic insecurity and the 'physical degeneration' consequent on poverty. The danger was 'here in our midst, close at home, close at hand, in the vast growing cities of England and Scotland, and in the dwindling and cramped villages of our denuded countryside. It is there you will find the seeds of Imperial ruin and national decay.'[11] And when he spoke at a meeting in support of a well-known charity, Dr Barnardo's Homes for children, he 'said in the case of the young they should be moved not only by compassion, but by the instinct of national self-preservation'.[12]

We might wonder if such phrases were mere rhetorical flourishes to help justify reforms that Churchill favoured for other, non-imperial reasons. We should not discount the possibility that he entertained genuine altruistic feelings towards the poor, aside from his fears about the impact that squalor and degradation might have on the Empire. (At the same time, it is well worth noting that social legislation was a potential way for the government to outflank the Conservatives and the nascent Labour Party, and for Churchill himself to win popularity in the dawning age of mass politics.) Churchill, however, would probably have rejected the very idea of a distinction between altruism and imperialism, which for him were two sides of the same coin. In his view the Empire itself was good for the British people, morally as well as materially. Strengthening its sinews via social reform was in this analysis entirely compatible with a compassionate response to the problems of those he called 'the left-out millions'.[13] There was, however, a sinister aspect to the problem. In 1910, the Prime Minister moved Churchill to the Home Office, where he took a strong interest, shared by many other contemporaries, in the pseudo-science of eugenics. He believed that the mentally and physically defective should be sterilized, in part for national-imperial reasons. He told Asquith: 'I am convinced that the multiplication of the Feeble-Minded, which is proceeding now at an artificial rate, unchecked by any of the old restraints of nature, and actually fostered by civilised conditions, is a very terrible danger to the race.'[14]

It was only when he was appointed First Lord of the Admiralty in the autumn of 1911 that the Empire again came close to the forefront of Churchill's activities. The following year Wilfrid Scawen Blunt observed in his diary that Churchill's new connection with the Navy had 'turned his mind back into an ultra Imperialist groove'.[15] Nevertheless, a number of contemporaries questioned Churchill's commitment to imperial defence cooperation during his Admiralty years – one political opponent accused him of gambling with the fate of the Empire[16] – and some naval historians have also criticized him for this. Central to the issues at stake was the so-called 'fleet unit' concept, developed in response to the scare of 1909 provoked by German naval expansion. The Dominions had not previously had their own navies, and were reliant on the British fleet for protection. The Admiralty's new proposal was that the

Dominions should fund fleet units, on a uniform pattern, which would be independent during peacetime but which would be subject to imperial control if war broke out. The Canadians were lukewarm about the plan and no help was forthcoming from South Africa, but Australia and New Zealand were cooperative. The key point about the new fleet was that it should stay in the Pacific permanently regardless of developments elsewhere. When still Home Secretary in 1910–11, however, Churchill resisted the idea that ships paid for by the Dominions should be despatched to the Pacific. He demanded that they be retained in the North Sea instead.[17]

His order of priorities remained the same when he took over the Admiralty himself. Prior to his move he had championed the cause of naval economy, but early in 1912 Germany promulgated a new naval law that compelled him to abandon any such thoughts. Even before he learnt the full extent of the German plans, though, he was insisting on the return of all possible ships from Australian waters and the retention of New Zealand's sole Dreadnought-class ship in the vicinity of Britain.[18] In a letter to Lewis Harcourt, the Colonial Secretary, he attacked the fleet unit scheme and declared that the 'whole principle of local Navies is, of course, thoroughly vicious'.[19] However, in public he expressed quite opposite views. In May 1912 he predicted that, given the increasing need for the British fleet in home waters, the main naval development of the next ten years would be 'the growth of effective naval forces in the great Dominions overseas'. These were to be under full Dominion control in peacetime. This would allow 'the true division of labour between the Mother Country and her daughter States, which is that we should maintain sea supremacy against all comers at the decisive point, and that they should guard and patrol all the rest of the British Empire'.[20] G. R. Parkin, the imperial educationalist who had inspired Churchill in his youth, stated his approval, and the response from the Dominions was generally favourable.[21] Soon afterwards the *Sydney Morning Herald* declared, 'One of the most hopeful signs of the times is the success with which Mr Churchill has grouped the whole nation, indeed, the whole Empire behind his naval policy.'[22]

Yet that apparent unity was on the basis of a policy with which Churchill did not actually agree. He was, of course, genuinely eager for the Dominions to make a financial contribution, but he wanted Britain to retain of control any ships they might contribute. In the

summer Robert Borden, the recently elected Conservative Prime
Minister of Canada, arrived in London for consultations. A convinced imperialist, he was committed to a Canadian 'emergency
contribution' to Empire naval defence, provided that a crisis really
did exist.[23] This was excellent news for Churchill, who had to
contend both with Liberal supporters of economy and with Tories
who alleged that the government was neglecting Britain's defences.
However, the idea of Canada giving ships to the British rather than
creating its own section of an imperial navy concept was disconcerting to the Australians, because it seemed to be at odds with the fleet
unit idea, which they were already trying to put into effect.[24]
Churchill gave Borden the required assurance that the situation was
severe enough to require 'special measures' by Canada in the
immediate future; the precise nature of these was not made public
until after Borden had returned to his own country and consulted
his colleagues.[25]

At the end of the year Borden announced plans to pay for three
dreadnoughts, the future maintenance costs of which would fall
on the British Treasury. This thrust him into a political storm, as
Canadian opinion was deeply divided. Quebecois nationalists wanted
to contribute nothing to imperial defence. The opposition Liberals
were sceptical that an emergency really existed while preferring, if
money was to be spent, that it should be used to develop a Canadian
navy. Borden's scheme was denounced as 'a policy of tribute'.[26]
Churchill's name was also dragged into the debate. The *Ottawa Free
Press*, observing the shift from his earlier endorsement of local naval
units, described him as 'a really clever political acrobat' and suggested he was trying to 'drag the Dominions into the maelstrom of
barbaric jingoism with which Europe is afflicted'.[27] W. L. Mackenzie
King, who had lost his parliamentary seat in the Liberal defeat the
year before, made a speech casting doubt on the idea that an
emergency existed. He quoted Churchill himself as saying that there
was no need for panic or alarm.[28] Building the ships themselves in
Canada would have helped appease opinion there, but Churchill
presented Borden with arguments that this was impractical, given
the ill-developed state of the Canadian shipbuilding industry.[29]
When the correspondence was made public, it was claimed that
Churchill was branding Canadians as incapable of manufacturing.
'He thinks we are all lumbermen or Red Indians', declared one

MP.[30] Another said that whereas Lord North (Prime Minister of England at the time of the US War of Independence) had lost Britain her American colonies, 'conceivably Mr Winston Churchill's latest naval memorandum might lose to the Empire Canada and Australia. The people of Canada were disinclined to bow down before an Admiralty Lord.'[31]

In March 1913, when Churchill presented the Admiralty's annual spending plans, he proposed a new 'imperial squadron' to include any ships that Canada might provide. This would be based at Gibraltar, from which it would 'cruise freely about the British Empire, visiting the various Dominions and showing itself ready to operate at any threatened point at Home or abroad'.[32] This appeared to be a strong commitment to imperial defence, and Borden considered it an 'inspiring proposal'.[33] But to many in Australia and New Zealand, Churchill's assurance that the squadron could beat any equivalent European force to any point in the Empire seemed to be beside the point. They were not afraid of any European force; rather, in spite of the Anglo-Japanese treaty of 1902, they were afraid of Japan. (There was often an unpleasant element to these fears: the following year Churchill's friend Ian Hamilton spoke in Auckland of the dangers posed by the 'hardworking, rice-eating, parsimonious "yellow" races'.)[34] The Wellington *Evening Post* suggested that Churchill had drifted into 'forgetfulness of the Pacific'.[35] Furthermore, the imperial squadron idea marked a clear if unstated rejection of the fleet unit concept. However, the new plan died in turn when Borden's naval programme, which got through the Canadian House of Commons on the basis of a reduced majority, was emphatically rejected by the Liberal-dominated Senate. Borden did not risk a general election on the issue.[36]

'Unfortunately', declared *The Times* not long before the outbreak of World War I, 'the disposition of our naval authorities, from Mr Churchill downwards, has been rather to dismiss with an impatient wave of the hand the fears of Australia and New Zealand than to reassure them by making more than adequate provision for their safety.'[37] One historian has commented, 'Churchill, who during much of his career gloried in the strength and gifts of the British Empire, was as first lord so bent on the defense of the British Isles that he was indifferent to the obligations of imperial co-operation, one of the abiding sources of the empire's strength.'[38] It is certainly true that he was high-handed, failing to fulfil the pledges made by his predecessor in 1909: the Australians acquired the ships for their fleet unit only to find that the British did not live up to the spirit of the bargain. (Churchill blithely dismissed Australian concerns, but there was outrage in Canberra.)[39] It is also true that Churchill's primary focus was on the defence of Britain. It is by no means clear, though, that this judgement was strategically unsound. In 1914–18 the main fleet operations were largely restricted to the North Sea, and the abandonment of the fleet unit plan led to no great cataclysm. (Even had it been implemented the Admiralty could still have disposed of the ships as it wished during wartime.) Nevertheless, these pre-war developments do lend some weight to the argument that for Churchill it was England, and not the wider Empire, that was 'the starting point and the ultimate object of policy'.[40] They also had a wider significance. To quote the Wellington *Evening Post* again: 'It becomes increasingly clear that if we do not ourselves attend to what is primarily our own business, we cannot expect our friends on the other side of the world to do it for us.'[41] This was a lesson that the Australasians would have to learn again, rather painfully, during World War II.

The rejection of the Borden plan increased the pressure on Churchill at a time when he was casting around for ways to alleviate Britain's financial burden. At the very end of 1913 Borden informed him that he would not try again to push the proposals through the Senate, claiming that 'Imperial interests will be materially prejudiced by renewed rejection'.[42] This came at a bad moment for Churchill, who was by now battling with Lloyd George over his large-scale spending plans for 1914. The Chancellor's demands for economy were backed by a number of other ministers as well as by the Liberal press. C. P. Scott, editor of the *Manchester Guardian*, was one who believed that the 'great change for the better in our relations with Germany' had rendered the expenditure unnecessary.[43] For a time, it looked as though either Churchill or Lloyd George might have to resign, but in the end the former got the bulk of what he wanted in return for some symbolic concessions. Churchill emerged from the fight politically strengthened, and it might have been thought, given his known enthusiasm for all things military, that the outbreak of war in August would have bolstered his position further.

Yet in fact his career was to plunge into free fall within the space of months.

II

The assassination of the Archduke Franz Ferdinand in Sarajevo in June 1914 triggered an ultimatum from Austria-Hungary to Serbia that soon resulted in world war. From his position at the Admiralty, Churchill, enthusiastic for the conflict, seemed poised to profit from it politically by enhancing his reputation as a man of action. This was not to be: the implosion of his political hopes was forever to be associated with the fiasco of Gallipoli.

The origins of the disaster were complex. On the Western Front, the rival armies quickly fought each other to a stalemate. By the start of 1915, British politicians and officials, Churchill included, had begun to look for ways to break the deadlock. The plan that emerged was for an attempt to drive a naval force through the Dardanelles – the narrow stretch of water that separates Asia from Europe – and thus, it was hoped, knock Turkey out of the war. It was not originally Churchill's idea, nor, by any means, did he bear sole responsibility for the decision to put it into action. But he could not, in the end, evade the blame. In spite of his misgivings about the idea of a purely naval assault – and the initial failure to deploy the army on land in support was indeed a catastrophic error – he gave it the go-ahead. In March the naval action met severe setbacks and was suspended; it was decided, after all, to deploy troops on the Gallipoli peninsula (on the eastern side of the straits). They were to be commanded by Ian Hamilton, still in fine form at the age of sixty-two, but perhaps overconfident in the face of tough odds. When the landings did at last take place, on 25 April, they were botched. The French and British forces failed to displace the outnumbered Turks, and by the end of the first day they had barely established themselves on the fringes of the peninsula. Nor was there any major breakthrough over the next weeks, although Churchill heaped praise on 'the brilliant and memorable achievement of the Australian and New Zealand troops at the Dardanelles'.[44] The soldiers of the Australia and New Zealand Army Corps – the

ANZACs – were brave but poorly trained. Throughout the course of the campaign, the combined British forces suffered 36,000 dead or missing and the French around 11,000.[45] Although it is the appalling ANZAC losses that dominate the popular memory, the sufferings of the rest, including Indian and Gurkha troops and men from the French Empire, should not be forgotten either.

The failure at Gallipoli – which was not yet apparent to the public – was not the immediate cause of Churchill's downfall. In mid-May, Admiral Lord Fisher, the First Sea Lord, suddenly resigned after falling out with Churchill over the question of naval reinforcements for the Dardanelles. It was the aged and highly eccentric Fisher who was unreasonable, but the crisis destroyed confidence in Churchill's administration of the Admiralty. Indeed, Churchill himself had insisted on recalling Fisher from retirement in 1914. Asquith was simultaneously faced with press revelations about the shortage of shells faced by the army on the Western Front. The combination of pressures forced him to act to defuse Opposition criticism by forming a coalition government. For the Conservatives, an essential condition of joining was that Churchill be moved. When Asquith made clear to Churchill that he was to leave the Admiralty, he asked if he would prefer to stay in the government in a different post or to take a military command in France. At this point, Lloyd George came into the room and said, 'Why do you not send him to the Colonial Office? There is great work to be done there.' Churchill demurred, and we may deduce that he saw the job, in wartime, as a political backwater, and that he thought he could hold out for something better.[46] Within days, though, he was reduced to pleading with the Prime Minister for 'any office – the lowest if you like – that you care to offer me'.[47] In the end he was given a junior Cabinet role as Chancellor of the Duchy of Lancaster, a position lacking defined departmental responsibilities. He vented his anger by denouncing Lloyd George, whom he felt had not done enough to protect his position, but the latter denied this. He swore that he had 'done all he possibly could – has proposed & supported Winston for Colonies, India [Office], & Viceroyalty of India all in turn and has loyally stood by him'.[48] In terms of perceptions of Churchill at this time, it is telling that, even some years after he had moved on from the Colonial Office, Lloyd George's proposed roles for him were all related to the Empire. Churchill's own failure to show any interest in these suggestions may indicate that he was reluctant to be pigeonholed in this way.

Yet even if so, his public rhetoric retained a strong imperial dimension. In a major speech in his Dundee constituency in June he said that the Allies were only a few miles from victory at the Dardanelles, 'a victory such as the war had not yet seen'. He spoke boldly and optimistically of the Empire's role in the war:

> The loyalty of our Dominions and Colonies vindicates our civ-ilization, and the hate of our enemies proves the effectiveness of our warfare. (Cheers.) [. . .] See Australia and New Zealand smiting down in the last and finest crusade the combined bar-barism of Prussia and Turkey. (Cheers.) General Louis Botha holding South Africa for the King. (Cheers.) See Canada defend-ing to the death the last few miles of shattered Belgium. Look further, and, across the smoke and carnage of the immense battlefield, look forward to the vision of a united British Empire on the calm background of a liberated Europe.[49]

If the speech was read by any of the soldiers at Gallipoli it may have rung rather hollow. The journalist H. W. Nevinson, who arrived there in July, found 'depression and loss of heart, bitter criticism of G.H.Q. [General Headquarters], and savage rage against Mr Winston Churchill, who "ought to be publicly hanged" for having suggested the campaign'.[50] In private, Churchill admit-ted some culpability. When Wilfrid Scawen Blunt visited him in August he found him painting – a new hobby which helped alleviate his gloom. 'There is more blood than paint upon these hands', Churchill said, at the same time making 'a queer little tragic gesture pointing to his hands which he had smeared with his colours'.[51] Two years later Blunt recorded that 'Winston said I had been right when I told him Providence had punished him for his wickedness and performed a miracle by enabling the Turks to defeat the whole power of the British Empire by sea and land.'[52]

In the autumn of 1915 the true state of affairs at Gallipoli started to filter back to the British and Empire publics. In September the London representative of the Sydney *Sun* wrote that Churchill, in his predictions of victory, had been 'talking hot air. The ferment of his own imagination betrayed him into gross and inexcusable exaggeration.'[53] In October, as the extent of the failure became clear, Hamilton was recalled from his command; he never again saw active service, although he lived on until 1947. In November Churchill discovered that he himself was to be excluded from the government's new War Committee. As he would now have no part to play in the higher direction of the war, he determined to resign. Amongst the gleeful comments in the German press was the suggestion that the King reward his services by making him Earl of Gallipoli.[54] A few days after his resignation statement the Cabinet decided to withdraw British forces there. There was a final irony: after all the disasters, the evacuation, completed in January 1916, was carried out brilliantly.

What was Churchill to do next? At first he sought the command of the British forces battling the Germans in East Africa.[55] When this idea came to nothing he joined the army in France, crossing the Channel on 18 November. He soon acclimatized himself to trench warfare, showing himself 'very keen and very enthusiastic' in spite of the cold, the dirt, the discomfort, and the unpalatable rations.[56] Soon he was appointed to the command of a battalion which in January 1916 took up position at Ploegsteert ('Plug Street'), in Belgium. He acquitted himself well, winning the respect of his men, but he was soon hankering to return to politics. After he visited London briefly on leave, Lloyd George noted: 'He is anxious to come back. Sick of the trenches. He ought never to have gone there.'[57] Churchill hoped that the Cabinet's divisions over conscription would facilitate his emergence as a leading critic of the government, but Asquith, as so often, avoided a major split through adroit manoeuvring. Although the opportunity Churchill hoped for did not arise, he decided to go back to Westminster anyhow, leaving his battalion for the last time in May.

Asquith, in spite of his short-term astuteness in political tactics, was facing growing concern about deficiencies in the conduct of the war. At the end of 1916 the long-suppressed tensions erupted into a first-rate crisis. This resulted in Lloyd George's emergence as Prime Minister of a new coalition, at the cost of a fatal schism in the Liberal Party between his followers and Asquith's. Churchill had hoped, even expected, to be in the new government; but his hopes were dashed owing to Tory opposition. Over the next months right-wing hostility to Churchill did not die away – the *Sunday Times* declared that his appointment to the Cabinet would be 'a grave danger to the Administration and to the Empire as a whole' – but Lloyd George's political strength was growing.[58] In March 1917 J. C. Smuts arrived in Britain to represent South Africa at the Imperial War Conference, having previously held the command in East Africa that had been denied to Churchill. Smuts's transition from Boer rebel to British imperial statesman was now complete. He became such a trusted adviser to the government that, in June, he was elevated to the Imperial War Cabinet. Shortly before that he wrote to Lloyd George advising him to ignore the (highly vocal) critics and give Churchill a job as head of the Air Board: 'In spite of the strong party opposition to this appointment, I think you will do the country a real service by appointing a man of his calibre to this department'. Smuts – who had clearly overcome the scepticism he had himself felt in 1906 – also met with Churchill and urged him to accept the post if it was offered to him.[59] In July, Lloyd George did give Churchill a job, as Minister of Munitions, albeit without a seat in the War Cabinet. There were howls of Tory protest, but they died down without causing much damage. Smuts wrote to Churchill with some wise, tactfully phrased advice about the importance of not making enemies amongst his colleagues: 'Now that you are well in the saddle [. . .] you must not ride too far ahead of your more slow-going friends.'[60] Churchill's aunt, Lady Cornelia Wimborne, was rather more direct: 'My advice is stick to munitions & don't try and run the Govt!'[61]

Although Churchill was never exactly an easy colleague, it must be said that he largely took the point on board. When introduced to his new officials by his predecessor, Christopher Addison, he tackled their suspicions of him head on. He stood for a moment surveying their distrustful faces. 'Gentlemen,' he said, 'Dr Addison has said that whatever the Minister of Munitions may do he can never be popular. In that respect at least I start from scratch.'[62] This unexpected self-deprecation quickly won the civil servants over, and during the next year and a half he built on this, proving himself an effective minister. Because he was focused on the technical task of turning out supplies of weapons and ammunition, he had little opportunity to influence grand questions of national or imperial policy. His public speeches did, however, give him the opportunity to discourse on the issue of Britain's future place in a world that had been thrown into upheaval by catastrophic war. The entry of the United States into the conflict in 1917 was a factor likely to have profound consequences for the British Empire. Before the war, in the kind of language that others had also used, Churchill had predicted the future 'unity of the English-speaking races'.[63] Now he stressed that the longer that Britain and America fought together in a common cause, the more closely would 'these two branches of the Anglo-Saxon world' be drawn together; this, he claimed, was the logical climax of all previous English history. The resulting 'comradeship and reconciliation' of the USA with Britain, Canada, Australia and New Zealand was to form 'the mainstay of the future world when the war is over'.[64] This can be read both as an attempt to reconcile his audience to the realities of growing US power and as an implicit acknowledgement that the British Empire could not long survive in the absence of America's blessing. In the years ahead – especially from the 1930s onwards – he often deployed the concept of 'the unity of the English-speaking peoples', to American audiences as well as British ones, in the hope of securing that survival by winning them over to this ambitious geopolitical project.

III

After the armistice in November 1918, Lloyd George called an immediate general election. The result was a massive victory for the coalition. Lloyd George now gave Churchill the job of Secretary of State for War and Air. It was no easy posting. During the war Britain had conquered new territories, notably in the Middle East, that would have to be absorbed into the Empire. At the same time there was continuing nationalist ferment in Ireland, and in India there were the first mass protests against the Raj. In Egypt, too, there was a major revolt against British rule. Thus, Britain's worldwide military capacity was stretched to the limit just when pressure was emerging at home to reduce spending and when conscripted troops were demanding rapid demobilization. The Bolshevik triumph in Russia fuelled fears of revolution at home in Britain, which, although exaggerated, were given credence by major outbreaks of industrial unrest. It was the Bolshevik threat, in particular, that obsessed Churchill, and the question of British involvement in the Russian civil war dominated much of his period at the War

Office. In April 1919 Lloyd George described him privately as 'a dangerous man' who had 'Bolshevism on the brain'.[65] Lloyd George himself had no love for the Bolsheviks but, together with the majority of the Cabinet, was not prepared to make an unlimited commitment in support of the opposing, counter-revolutionary 'White' forces. Churchill did not share the essentially pragmatic viewpoint of his colleagues on this issue as, in his eyes, they failed to recognize the severity of the issues at stake. He claimed that Lenin, Sinn Féin (the Irish republican party) and the Indian and Egyptian extremists were all linked in a joint effort to overthrow the Empire. 'It is becoming increasingly clear that all these factions are in touch with one another, and that they are acting in concert', he declared in a speech in 1920. 'In fact there is developing a world-wide conspiracy against our country, designed to deprive us of our place in the world and to rob us of the fruits of victory.'[66]

Churchill was himself capable of pragmatism, however, as his involvement with the Irish question was to demonstrate. Up until his entry into government in 1905, he had been an instinctive opponent of Home Rule. At the point that he became a minister it had been dormant as an issue for some time, but looked set to re-emerge; Churchill feared that if it did so it would put a great many people, himself included, 'in an awful hole'.[67] From 1910 onwards, when John Redmond's moderate nationalist Irish Parliamentary Party held the balance of power in the House of Commons, the government was obliged to offer Home Rule as the price of its support. This provoked Unionist rage, but Churchill argued that the achievement of an Irish settlement would be 'a boon and a blessing' to the Empire and 'a masterstroke of imperial policy'. He drew comparisons with the settlement that had been made with the Boers, and argued that a solution would increase trust between the self-governing Dominions and the motherland.[68] Redmond reciprocated by saying that with the advent of Home Rule 'every Irishman on the habitable globe will become a loyal citizen of and a loyal friend to the Empire'.[69]

Ireland was, of course, an imperial question unlike any other, insofar as the country was represented directly at Westminster. This enhanced the intensity and bitterness of the debate. When Andrew Bonar Law, the new leader of the Conservative Party, spoke in support of the rebellious anti-Home Rule Protestants of Ulster, Churchill suggested Law's arguments for non-compliance with the government's will could be used to justify 'every lawless or disruptive movement in any part of the Empire'.[70] Churchill wrote to Redmond, 'I do not believe there is any real feeling against Home Rule in the Tory Party apart from the Ulster question, but they hate the Government, are bitterly desirous of turning it out, and see in the resistance of Ulster an extra parliamentary force which they will not hesitate to use to the full.'[71] Recognizing this, he and Lloyd George were amongst the first ministers to see that the Protestant-dominated northern counties might have to be excluded from the operation of the Home Rule Bill. Churchill's notorious speech of March 1914 was widely seen by Unionists as an attempt to coerce Ulster into acceptance of Home Rule under threat of state violence. In fact, he was arguing that Ulster did deserve special treatment, in the form of the six-year exclusion from Home Rule that the government was now offering. In his view that offer removed all possible excuse for rebellion, which, he emphasized, would be met firmly. But, in the febrile atmosphere of the times, it is hardly surprising that his language was seen as provocative. He insisted that 'there are things worse than bloodshed, even on extreme scale. An eclipse of the central Government of the British Empire would be worse.'[72] He seemed to think that extremity of language would wake the populace up to the enormities of the situation and thus facilitate an accord between the two sides. Around this time he commented privately: 'Public opinion had got to have a shock. [. . .] "A little red-blood had got to flow" & then public opinion would wake up & then—!'[73]

Churchill's tendency – whether he was dealing with nationalist or loyalist opinion – was to veer between the language of coercion and that of conciliation. This remained true over the following years. After the outbreak of war, Home Rule was put onto the statute book but with its operation suspended for the duration. The resulting nationalist frustration contributed to the Easter Rising of 1916, which was brutally suppressed by the British. (Churchill was out of office at the time and so was not implicated in the Cabinet's misjudgements.) These events sounded the death knell of constitutionalist Redmondite nationalism and triggered the emergence of Sinn Féin as a major political force. In 1918 the party won 73 out of the 105 Irish seats, but its MPs declined to attend Westminster and established an alternative, illegal parliament (the Dáil Éireann) instead. In January 1919 the murder of two men of the Royal Irish

Constabulary (RIC) triggered the cut-throat and deadly Anglo-Irish War, or War of Independence. As War Secretary, Churchill put his faith in the RIC's reserve force, the 'Black and Tans', which was responsible for indiscriminate shootings and burnings in reprisal for attacks by the Irish Republican Army (IRA). Churchill knew this – he may have been reminded of his experiences on the North-West Frontier of India – but he defended Black and Tan officers as 'loyal and gallant'.[74] He was confident of victory, asserting in a speech in October 1920 that the IRA's terrorist tactics would not change the history of the British Empire: 'We are going to break up this murder gang.'[75]

That confidence, which was shared by most of Churchill's colleagues, including Lloyd George, was soon eroded. The enemy's guerrilla tactics could not be overcome, even by theoretically over-whelming force, and reprisals simply increased the local population's resentment of the British. In July 1921, a few months after moving to the Colonial Office, Churchill privately 'acknowledged the failure of the policy of force'.[76] However, the Irish rebel leaders were also tiring of the war, and they now agreed a truce. In due course they agreed to negotiate on 'how the association of Ireland with the community of nations known as the British Empire can best be reconciled with Irish national aspirations'.[77] This was a euphemistic way of addressing the ultimate point of division between the two sides. Although the British were prepared to offer Ireland de facto independence they were insistent that this would be on the basis of Dominion status within the Empire. For Sinn Féin only full, formal independence would do.[78]

Churchill was assigned to the ministerial team of the negotiators on the British side, although his centrality to the talks should not be overstated. One of the leading figures on the Irish side was Michael Collins, a young, dashing impresario of terror who had played a key role in Bloody Sunday – the murder of twelve British officers on 21 November 1920. Collins's impressions of Churchill were not positive, as his contemporary notes reveal: 'Outlook: political gain, nothing else. [. . .] Inclined to be bombastic. Full of ex-officer jingo or similar outlook. Don't actually trust him.'[79] Subsequently, rela-tions between the two warmed up, albeit not perhaps to the extent depicted in the more romantic interpretations, but it is at any rate important not to focus on the personalities of the 'great men' involved to the exclusion of the issues at stake. The eight weeks of the negotiations were to lead to the creation of an Irish Free State, but there were major stumbling blocks on the way. The first of these was the right of the six counties comprising 'Northern Ireland' to opt out of Home Rule – a right that was exercised immediately – and the British demand that MPs in the new Southern parliament swear allegiance to the Crown. The former problem, the question of partition, may have been the more substantive, but the oath of loyalty was an emotive issue that struck at the heart of national identity. Churchill was present on 5 December 1921 when Lloyd George presented the Irish delegates with an ultimatum: either sign the treaty as it stood, partition and the oath of allegiance included, or face a renewal of the war. One of the Irish delegates, Erskine Childers, wrote that his 'chief recollection of these inexpressibly miserable hours' was of Churchill in evening dress walking up and down 'with his loping stoop and long strides and a huge cigar like a bowsprit'.[80] After some hours of hesitation, the Irish signed, with heavy hearts. Collins remarked that in doing so he was signing his own death warrant.[81]

In his Commons defence of the treaty, Churchill maintained his imperial theme: 'Every Colonial statesman will feel that if this succeeds, his task in his Dominion of bringing people closer and closer into the confederation of the British Empire will be eased and facilitated.'[82] This kind of rhetoric was useful in the difficult task of selling the agreement to the government's Conservative supporters. Yet the more Churchill and Lloyd George emphasized that a free Ireland would be tightly bound into the Empire, the more doubts were raised in Irish minds about whether such an Ireland would be free at all. This was seen during the debates about the treaty in the Dáil. Eamon De Valera, the Dáil's President, had agreed to the negotiations but had stayed away from them himself; he now repudiated the outcome. He demanded, 'does this assembly think the Irish people have changed so much within the past year or two that they now want to get into the British Empire after seven centuries of fighting?'[83] Constance Markievicz, aristocrat and veteran of the Easter Rising, declared that she 'would sooner die than give a declaration of fidelity to King George or the British Empire'. (Given that she had been sentenced to death for her part in the Rising – and then reprieved because she was a woman – these words carried some conviction.) She argued that 'if we pledge ourselves to this oath we pledge our allegiance to this thing, whether you call it Empire or Commonwealth of Nations, that is treading down the people of Egypt and of India. [...] And mind you, England wants peace in Ireland to bring her troops over to India and Egypt.'[84] Collins, by contrast, argued that the treaty gave Ireland scope to increase its freedom in the future. He pointed out that it defined Ireland as having the same constitutional status of Canada, Australia, New Zealand, and South Africa, which had real solid independence. 'Judged by that touchstone, the relations between Ireland and Britain will have a certainty of freedom and equality which cannot be interfered with.' As for those who quoted Lloyd George and Churchill's interpretations of the document, 'I say the quotation of those people is what marks the slave mind.'[85]

In January 1922, in a fraught atmosphere, the Dáil approved the treaty by 64 votes to 57. But De Valera and his supporters were not prepared to live with the result, and in June the country descended into civil war. Although the pro-treaty forces won within a year, Collins's prediction as to his own fate was proved correct. In August he was killed in an ambush by anti-treaty republicans. Not long before, he had sent a message to Churchill thanking him for the support he had given to the fledging Free State government: 'Tell Winston we could never have done anything without him.'[86] Arguably, however, Churchill was not completely even-handed in his dealings with the governments of North and South. He privately assured the Northern loyalists that 'Ulster would come out top' from the deliberations of the Boundary Commission, which was established under the Treaty to review the demarcation of the border.[87] This was a sound prediction, for when the Commission drew up its report in 1925 it recommended only trivial changes, frustrating Free State hopes of major gains of territory; in fact its plans proved so controversial that its report was not published, the two governments agreeing to ratify the existing border unchanged.

De Valera was able to portray the Irish government's acceptance of this as a sell-out, and by 1932 he had mounted a remarkable political comeback, as Prime Minister at the head of a new party, Fianna Fáil. The following year his government passed the Constitution (Removal of Oath) Act. This, ironically, proved Collins's point that the treaty had created the conditions for increasing Irish freedom in the long run. It also seemed to falsify Churchill's hopes of reconciling 'the spirit of the Irish nation to the British Empire'.[88] In spite of Churchill's contempt for De Valera, which Ireland's neutrality in World War II only increased, he sometimes talked about the possibility of Irish reunification.[89] As he put it in June 1940, weeks after becoming Prime Minister, 'I could never be a party to the coercion of Ulster to join the Southern counties: but I am much in favour of their being persuaded. The key to this is de Valera showing some loyalty to Crown & Empire.'[90] This shows that Churchill was not very serious about the possibility of a United Ireland because, as he well knew, 'Dev' was about as likely to show enthusiasm for the Empire as he was to grow wings and fly.

IV

Churchill's involvement with Ireland had, of course, straddled his War Office and Colonial Office periods; but why had the Prime Minister moved him to the colonies at all? It was not because of any positive enthusiasm on Churchill's part. Lloyd George proposed the move to him on 1 January 1921 but it was a few days before he accepted. 'I am afraid this venture is going to break me', he said despondently.[91] Sir Henry Wilson, the Chief of the Imperial General Staff, noted: 'Winston told me he took the Colonies because he would not have lasted much longer in the WO owing to differences with LG.'[92] It may well be that Lloyd George also felt that a switch would help reduce the tension that had arisen between them over Russia. He was almost certainly influenced too by the interest that Churchill had lately been taking in Middle Eastern affairs, with a view to reducing military expenditure there. Clementine Churchill tried to reassure her husband that she thought his new post 'the best office just now'. With a hint of wry humour she added: 'if you are able to "feature" the Empire once more it will make all English people happy, at peace with each other (more or less) & able to resume our lofty but unconscious contempt of the Foreigner'.[93] Yet Churchill felt he deserved higher things. When, shortly after his appointment, the position of Chancellor of the Exchequer became free, he was furious not to be given the job. Leo Amery, who himself served as a junior minister at the Colonial Office in

1. Winston Churchill
as a boy in 1889.

2. & 3. Winston's father,
Lord Randolph
Churchill. In 1891 he
made a highly publicised
visit to South Africa.
His eccentric behaviour
during his travels there
was widely mocked,
as in this *Punch* satire.

"GRANDOLPH AD LEONES."

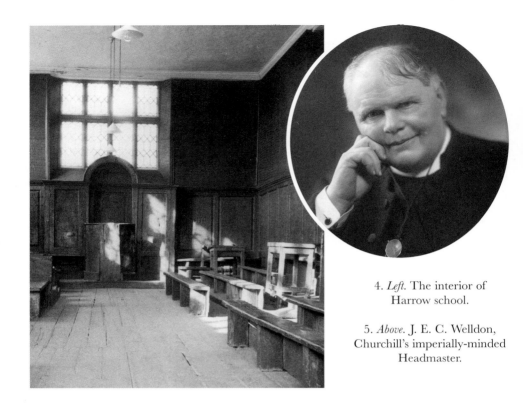

4. *Left.* The interior of Harrow school.

5. *Above.* J. E. C. Welldon, Churchill's imperially-minded Headmaster.

6. Lieutenant Churchill in India, 1896. Decades later he acknowledged that at this time he had seen Indians as 'a race as inferior beings'.

7. Churchill during the Boer War. He served as both a war correspondent and as a soldier; his escape from Boer captivity led him to be celebrated as an imperial hero.

8. Churchill during the Edwardian period, when he moved from the Conservatives to the Liberals over the issue of Free Trade.

9. Boer War scene: a man being flogged by the British for stealing bread.

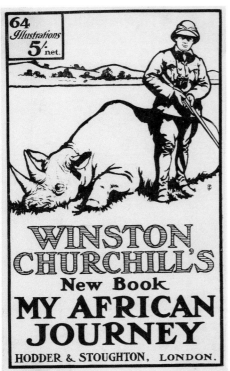

64 Illustrations
5/- net.

WINSTON CHURCHILL'S
New Book
MY AFRICAN JOURNEY
HODDER & STOUGHTON, LONDON.

10. Lord Elgin was Churchill's ministerial boss at the Colonial Office where the latter began his political career. Elgin complained that Churchill's 1907 African trip turned from a private expedition into 'an official progress'.

11. Churchill with Clementine Hozier at the time of their engagement.

12. M. K. Gandhi around the time of his sole meeting with Churchill, which took place in 1906. The occasion was amicable but after World War I Churchill said privately that Gandhi should be 'trampled on by an enormous elephant' because of his campaign against British rule in India.

13. South African prime minister (1919–24; 1939–48), J. C. Smuts, was a sceptic turned admirer of Churchill. Smuts himself cast off his rebellious past to become one of the greatest imperial statesmen of the age.

14. Lord Elgin pictured in 1890, fifteen years before he worked with Churchill at the Colonial Office.

15. Anti-Home Rulers attack Churchill's car in Belfast in 1912. Churchill argued that Home Rule would strengthen the Empire, a claim endorsed at the time by the Irish nationalist leader John Redmond.

16. Churchill pictured with Gertrude Bell, T. E. Lawrence and others in 1921, during his period as Colonial Secretary. Both advised him on the future of the Middle East.

17. The 1921 Cairo conference. Churchill has received too much of the blame for the failings of British Middle Eastern policy at this time, which left a legacy into the twenty-first century.

TALES OF THE DOMINIONS.

18. Secretary of State for the Colonies, Leo Amery, attempts to beguile Lord Birkenhead
(Secretary of State for India), Churchill and Prime Minister Stanley Baldwin with
his visions of Empire in this cartoon of February 1928.

19. Grappling with Gandhi-ism: Churchill addresses the Indian Empire Society
in December 1930. His campaign against greater self-government for India led him
into the political wilderness.

1919–21, believed that 'except for Ireland and Iraq' Churchill 'largely neglected the work' of his department.[94] There were, however, other exceptions too. Churchill took considerable interest, for example, in the introduction of responsible government in Southern Rhodesia. When this was under discussion, the white settlers were granted a referendum on the possibility of joining the territory to South Africa. Smuts blamed his friend for the fact that they rejected this option, although in reality Churchill would probably have been pleased to see them accept and thus to operate as a counterweight to Afrikaner influence within the Union.[95]

Churchill insisted, as a condition of accepting Lloyd George's offer, on being allowed to create a new Middle East Department within the Colonial Office. Lord Curzon, the Foreign Secretary, thought Churchill was trying to usurp his prerogatives. 'He wants to grab everything into his new Dept, and to be a sort of Asiatic Foreign Secretary', Curzon told his wife.[96] One of Churchill's first recruits was T. E. Lawrence, better known as Lawrence of Arabia. Born in 1888, Lawrence took a First in Modern History at Oxford before taking part in archaeological digs in Syria in the years before the war. 'I don't think anyone who tasted the East as I have would give it up half-way, for a seat at high table and a chair in the Bodleian', he wrote.[97] In 1914 he took on a military intelligence role for the British in Cairo, paving the way for his involvement in the Arab Revolt that broke out two years later. He led contingents of tribesmen in daring attacks against Turkish forces, and immortalized his experiences in *The Seven Pillars of Wisdom*, first published privately in 1926. Crucially, Lawrence believed that Arab national aspirations and the defeat of Ottoman power could be harmonized with British interests and the outfoxing of the rival French. When Churchill first met him in 1919 he was unimpressed, but his opinion changed when he saw him again at the Paris Peace Conference a few weeks later. Lawrence was wearing Arab dress. 'From amid the flowing draperies his noble features, his perfectly-chiselled lips and flashing eyes loaded with fire and comprehension shone forth', Churchill recalled in typically romantic style. 'He looked what he was, one of Nature's greatest princes.'[98]

Lawrence was one of Churchill's major advisers at the seminal Cairo conference of March 1921, the series of discussions amongst British officials held to determine the future map of the Middle East.

Another was the archaeologist and traveller Gertrude Bell, also a believer in Arab self-rule – under British guidance. She was one of the key subordinates of Sir Percy Cox, High Commissioner of Mesopotamia (soon to be renamed Iraq), who played a leading role at the Cairo talks. Although some other officials complained that Churchill did not take the time needed to brief himself, she was impressed with Churchill's conduct of the conference, writing that he 'was admirable, most ready to meet everyone half way and masterly alike in guiding a big meeting and in conducting the small political committees into which we broke up'.[99] Lawrence too praised his 'imagination and courage' and thought him 'so considerate as sometimes to seem more like a senior partner than a master'.[100] A factor making for this harmony was the fact that Churchill's policy position was closely in line with that of the officials on the spot. As Bell put it, 'Not the least favourable circumstance was that Sir Percy and I, coming out with a definite programme, found when we came to open our packets that it coincided exactly with that which the S.[ecretary] of S.[tate] had brought with him.'[101] This is worth remembering, given that Churchill's 'crucial role [. . .] in giving birth to the Middle East we live with today' has been subject to so much criticism.[102] The typical indictment is that 'By lumping together [in Iraq] populations that had nothing in common under an alien ruler, Churchill guaranteed eight decades of instability'.[103] Yet Churchill did not just wade in and impose his own opinions. Doubtless aware of his lack of specialist knowledge, he deferred to the expertise available, even when this involved overriding his own instincts. For example, both he and Lawrence were sympathetic to the idea of an independent Kurdish state, and majority opinion at Cairo was actually in favour of this. Over the following months, however, Cox used his position as 'the man on the spot' to negate this decision, and Churchill acquiesced.[104] With the benefit of hindsight, the decisions taken at Cairo certainly appear flawed in important respects, but the failures were collective (as Churchill's critics in fact tend to acknowledge). Nonetheless, Churchill's conspicuous desire to act as impresario, indulging his 'roving propensities' by going out to the Middle East himself, may have helped attract the retrospective blame onto his own head.[105]

The purpose of the conference was to sort out the aftermath of Britain's conquests in the region during the war. Its occupation of

Mesopotamia had led to it being granted the League of Nations mandate (a form of protectorate) for the country at the 1919 Peace Conference. Early in 1920 General Aylmer Haldane, Churchill's ex-prison mate from Boer War days, was appointed to command the British troops there. A few days before he departed he reported to the War Office, 'where Mr Churchill harangued me for twenty minutes on the necessity for making drastic reductions in the garrison of Mesopotamia, the cost of which, he said, was becoming intolerable to British taxpayers'.[106] In May, hopes of economy were sandbagged by a major anti-British rebellion that persisted for several months. In an unsent letter to Lloyd George in August, Churchill wrote of his frustration that 'we should be compelled to go on pouring armies and treasure into these thankless deserts'.[107] He hoped to reduce spending by using air power rather than ground troops. As part of this scheme – for which he eventually won acceptance – he suggested 'experimental work on gas bombs, especially mustard gas, which would inflict punishment on recalcitrant natives without inflicting grave injury upon them'.[108] These remarks have gained notoriety, even though Churchill was clearly talking about non-lethal gas. Just as horrifying, if not more so, were the casualties inflicted by machine guns and bombing. After a particularly appalling episode the following year, Churchill wrote, 'To fire wilfully on women and children taking refuge in a lake is a disgraceful act', but, beyond complaining, he took no action.[109] Not long before his move from the War Office, and with the rebellion suppressed, Churchill circulated to the Cabinet a memorandum by the Director of Military Operations. This suggested withdrawal from the provinces of Baghdad and Mosul in the spring and the retention thereafter of the southern part of the country only.[110] When the Cabinet rejected this idea, he defended the status quo in the House of Commons, portraying the idea of withdrawal as a policy of 'scuttle'.[111]

It is clear, therefore, that Churchill did not believe in holding on to territory for the sake of it and at any price. His actions at Cairo were the product of pragmatism not diehardism. One of the key decisions taken there was to install Lawrence's friend the Emir Feisal as ruler of the new Kingdom of Iraq. In a blow to Zionists, Feisal's brother Abdullah was put in charge of neighbouring Transjordan, which was now divided from the rest of Palestine. All of this was high-handed, certainly, and there was an element of black comedy in the efforts taken to make it look as though Feisal was the Iraqi people's choice. The government claimed to be neutral yet arrested and deported a rival candidate.[112] The aim of the whole strategy was to minimize the British commitment through indirect rule by a government amenable to British guidance. Lawrence, for one, saw this as a 'liberal' policy based on national self-determination rather than domination. Noble as this might sound in theory, the policy caused problems for the British – Feisal soon started showing dangerous signs of mental independence. In September 1922, as Churchill's frustration increased, he wrote to Lloyd George: 'At present we are paying eight millions a year for the privilege of living on an ungrateful volcano out of which we are in no circumstances to get anything worth having.'[113] During that year's general election he downplayed his role in forming policy for Palestine and Mesopotamia.[114]

The British position in the Middle East was much complicated by the competing promises to Arabs and Jews made by the Allies during the war. The most famous of these was the Balfour Declaration of 1917, which stated the British government's support for the creation of a Jewish 'national home' in Palestine. It was there that Churchill travelled at the conclusion of the Cairo conference, in the company of Sir Herbert Samuel, who as High Commissioner in Jerusalem was responsible for administering the British mandate. His train journey was chronicled by Maxwell Henry Coote of the RAF, who was acting as Churchill's aide-de-camp for the duration of his trip. 'After lunch we stopped at Gaza where Winston had a most tremendous reception of a howling mob all shouting in unison "Cheers for the Minister" and also for Great Britain but their chief cry over which they waxed quite frenzied was "Down with the Jew", "cut their throats" and such like "anti-Zionist" cries', Coote noted. 'Winston and Herbert Samuel also were quite delighted with their reception not the least understanding what was being said.'[115] A few days later Churchill visited the site of the planned new Hebrew University in Jerusalem. According to Coote, 'He made a tremendously pro-Zionist speech which rather surprised me although I suppose he had to [be seen as] as upholding the Government (Balfour) policy. It seems curious though when one knows he is really not in sympathy with the Zionist cause.'[116]

Churchill's attitude was indeed ambivalent. In 1919 he had mused that Britain could return both Palestine and Mesopotamia to Turkish control, and spoke scathingly of 'the Jews, whom we are pledged to introduce into Palestine and who take it for granted that the local population will be cleared out to suit their convenience'.[117] It would not be correct, though, to describe him as an anti-Zionist. In a notorious newspaper article of 1920 he distinguished between praiseworthy 'National Jews', loyal to the countries in which they lived, and the 'sinister confederacy' of 'International Jews' whom he claimed were largely responsible for the Bolshevik revolution. In this analysis Zionism offered a 'third sphere to the political conceptions of the Jewish race', and Churchill predicted that, 'if, as may well happen, there should be created in our own lifetime by the banks of the Jordan a Jewish State under the protection of the British Crown [. . .] an event would have occurred in the history of the world which would, from every point of view, be beneficial, and would be especially in harmony with the truest interests of the British Empire'.[118] His belief that Zionism would help combat the Bolshevik conspiracy was not greatly dissimilar to the views of Lloyd George and Balfour, both of whom believed that international Jewry was highly influential and its support worth cultivating.[119] Meeting with a Palestinian Arab delegation in Jerusalem, Churchill rejected its concerns, which were couched in anti-Semitic language. He airily assured them that Zionism would be 'good for the world, good for the Jews, good for the British Empire, but also good for the Arabs who dwell in Palestine'. He emphasized that the existing form of British rule would continue for many years: 'Step by step we shall develop representative institutions leading to full selfgovernment, but our children's children will have passed away before that is completed.'[120] Lloyd George, in private, was more explicit. During a meeting with the prominent Zionist leader Chaim Weizmann in July 1921 he said to Churchill: 'You mustn't give representative government to Palestine.'[121] Given the relative sizes of the Arab and Jewish populations, to have done so before much greater Jewish immigration took place would have been a catastrophe for Zionist hopes.

In 1922 Churchill presented a White Paper to the House of Commons laying out the government's policy on Palestine, a document which, having been preoccupied with Ireland and domestic politics over the previous winter, he had played little part in writing. Drawn up in the aftermath of Arab disturbances, it was an attempt to soothe both sides by correcting their supposedly misguided 'apprehensions' about British intentions. The commitment to the Balfour Declaration was reaffirmed. However, it was not contemplated 'that Palestine as a whole should be converted into a Jewish National Home', but merely 'that such a Home should be founded *in Palestine*'. On the one hand it was stated that the Jewish people were in Palestine 'as of right and not on sufferance'; on the other hand Zionist hopes that the land would become 'as Jewish as England is English' were said to be impracticable. The Jewish community was to be allowed to increase its numbers by immigration, yet this was not to be so great in volume as to exceed the country's economic capacity to absorb new arrivals.[122]

The White Paper left many questions unanswered – the formula on immigration, for example, was evidently vague – but the Zionists swallowed it reluctantly.[123] More encouraging from their point of view was the government's defence of the controversial concession granted to Pinhas Rutenberg, a Jewish entrepreneur, for the exclusive production of electricity in Palestine. In the House of Commons, Churchill strongly defended both the Rutenberg concession and the Zionist role in the development of Palestine in general. His remarks were reminiscent of his insistence in *My African Journey* that indigenous populations had no right to remain idle, even if contented in their inactivity:

> Left to themselves, the Arabs of Palestine would not in a thousand years have taken effective steps towards the irrigation and electrification of Palestine. They would have been quite content to dwell – a handful of philosophic people – in the wasted sun-scorched plains, letting the waters of the Jordan continue to flow unbridled and unharnessed into the Dead Sea.[124]

Later, in the 1930s, he declared during the course of an argument about Palestine 'that the Arabs were barbaric hordes who ate little but camels' dung'.[125] Nevertheless, attempts to portray Churchill as a lifelong, ardent Zionist fail to convince, even though Zionists themselves often praised him for their own purposes.[126] Churchill supported Zionism only insofar as it was compatible with

British power, and over the coming years the aspiration for Jewish statehood was to conflict increasingly with imperial rule.

If, in some moods, Churchill was willing to advocate withdrawal from Mesopotamia and Palestine, this was in part because of his awareness that staying there might have consequences for the rest of the Empire. In the post-war years he frequently spoke of Britain's position 'as the greatest Mahommedan Power'.[127] In 1920 the Muslim population of the Empire was 87 million, including 70 million in India and 13 million in Egypt.[128] He believed that a policy hostile to the defeated Turks, and the retention of the former Ottoman territories, could alienate these people. In other words, he criticized 'dreams of conquest and aggrandisement' in the Middle East precisely because he wanted to avoid dissipating British power elsewhere.[129]

V

If his approach to 'new enlargements' was, like his treatment of Ireland, relatively pragmatic, his view of the established non-white territories of the Empire was less so. Egyptian, Indian and African issues prompted strong emotional responses in him. In 1919 an uprising broke out in Egypt after the British tried to clamp down on the nationalist Wafd party. At this point the Colonial Secretary was Lord Milner. He had bounced back from the difficult aftermath of his South African years to take office under Lloyd George during the war, and now led a commission to investigate the discontent. Its report, published in February 1921, recommended the abolition of the British protectorate (which had been established formally in 1914) and the granting of internal self-government to Egypt under a constitutional monarchy. Churchill fought against these proposals every step of the way and annoyed Curzon – who was himself uneasy about the policy – through his public pronouncements. Just before the Milner report came out, for example, Churchill spoke of his hope that in the future both Ireland and Egypt would unfold their destinies 'peacefully and prosperously within the elastic circle of the British Empire'.[130] This raised the hackles of the nationalists in Cairo, who did not wish Egypt to be part of the Empire at all but instead demanded full independence.[131] In spite of Churchill's 'difficult and insolent' behaviour the Milner plan was implemented in 1922.[132] Not long beforehand Curzon complained that 'the Jingoes in the Cabinet, of whom the strongest are the PM and Winston, want to concede nothing and to stamp out rebellion in Egypt by fire and sword'.[133] To a high-minded imperialist like Curzon, nothing was more debased and insincere than vulgar, pseudo-patriotic 'Jingoism'. Churchill, who deplored Jingoism too, would have recognized the insult.

Churchill's public attitude to the concurrent disturbances in India to some extent contradicted his growing reputation as a diehard. The troubles arose because of the Government of India's extension of wartime measures to suppress sedition, including drastic restrictions on freedom of expression. Since his return to India at the outbreak of war Gandhi had made no direct challenge to British rule, but in early 1919 he launched a campaign of satyagraha directed at the new law. To his distress, the campaign turned violent. Trains were derailed, telegraph wires cut, buildings burnt and property plundered. A number of Europeans were killed. This – as many British conservatives liked to emphasize – was the context for General Reginald Dyer's decision to order his soldiers to shoot at an unarmed mob in Amritsar, the administrative capital of Punjab. Trapped within the Jallianwallah Bagh, a walled area near the Golden Temple, the crowd had little chance to escape. The official inquiry into the massacre led by Lord Hunter found that 1,650 rounds were fired and estimated that 379 people were killed. It is probable that around three times that many were wounded.[134] In the aftermath, as peace was restored to the city, Dyer issued the so-called 'crawling order': Indians passing along a narrow lane where a female missionary had been attacked were to be forced to do so on their hands and knees. A few days after the massacre Gandhi called off his campaign, confessing to a 'Himalayan miscalculation' in having launched it before his supporters were spiritually ready for the practice of non-violence.[135]

In Britain, opinion on Dyer was bitterly divided between those who saw him as a monster and those who thought him the saviour of the Raj. The Secretary of State for India, Edwin Montagu, was one of those who were horrified. Five years younger than Churchill, he was first elected to Parliament in the sweeping Liberal victory of 1906, and his career flourished under Asquith. Asquith himself, however, mocked his protégé as 'the Assyrian' – a slighting reference to Montagu's Jewishness – in the stream of passionate letters that he poured out to his young confidante Venetia Stanley. In a further twist, Montagu married Stanley in 1915: '*this* breaks my heart', the Prime Minister told her when he learnt of the engagement.[136] Montagu lost office when Asquith fell in 1916, but was given a new job by Lloyd George shortly afterwards. His promotion to the India Office a few months later was as unpopular with Tories as Churchill's simultaneous appointment to the Ministry of Munitions. He was a self-tormented individual whose private comments (not least about Churchill) often had an air of cynicism, but his interest in India was genuine and longstanding. In August 1917 he made an official declaration that the country should move towards 'responsible government', which implied an eventual move to Dominion status.[137] The so-called Montagu–Chelmsford reforms that followed after the war were a severely limited but nonetheless significant step on the road to Indians taking charge of their own affairs. After Amritsar, Montagu attempted without success to stiffen the Hunter report's criticisms of those responsible.[138] When the report was debated in the Commons on 8 July 1920 he faced the impossible job of squaring his own convictions with the need to appease Dyer's powerful supporters in Parliament. The previous day Churchill had told the House of the Army Council's decision that Dyer, who had been removed from employment in India by the Commander-in-Chief, would not be offered a post elsewhere. (This meant that he would be placed on half pay but his status and rank would not be affected.) In response to this announcement there were passionate cries of 'Why?' and 'Shame'.[139]

Montagu opened the debate in an electric atmosphere, with Dyer himself looking down from the gallery on to the packed benches. Although Montagu's own commitment to the Empire was profound, his speech was not calculated to soothe the diehards. Although he paid lip service to Dyer's 'gallant' personal record, he denounced his attempt to use the shootings to teach 'a moral lesson' to the whole Punjab as 'a doctrine of terrorism'. He denounced the outrages that had taken place after the massacre, and demanded: 'Are you going to keep your hold upon India by terrorism, racial humiliation and subordination, and frightfulness, or are you going to rest it upon the goodwill, and the growing goodwill, of the people of your Indian Empire? I believe that to be the whole question at issue.'[140] He persevered courageously as the mood became angrier and angrier. Some MPs seemed ready to hit him for his effrontery, and there was an undoubted anti-Semitic element in the response.[141] 'A Jew, a foreigner, rounding on an Englishman and throwing him to the wolves – that was the feeling', noted Austen Chamberlain, who was soon to become leader of the Conservatives himself.[142]

After Montagu sat down, things continued to go badly for the government until Churchill rose to speak. He proceeded, with great skill, to extract the government's chestnuts from the fire. He first gave the House time to simmer down by delivering a long, dry exposition of the technicalities of how the conduct of military officers could be dealt with. He then turned to the merits of the case, about which he was unequivocal. The massacre, he claimed, was an episode 'without precedent or parallel in the modern history of the British Empire'. He conceded that British officers who had to decide whether or not to open fire in such circumstances were in a difficult situation. However, Churchill made clear that it was the job of such officers to weigh up the situation appropriately. ' "I was confronted," says General Dyer, "by a revolutionary army." What is the chief characteristic of an army? Surely it is that it is armed. This crowd was unarmed. These are simple tests which it is not too much to expect officers in these difficult situations to apply.'

He went on to restate, in essence, the argument made by Montagu, albeit in a rather more emollient way:

> There is surely one general prohibition which we can make. I mean a prohibition against what is called 'frightfulness'. What I mean by frightfulness is the inflicting of great slaughter or massacre upon a particular crowd of people, with the intention of terrorising not merely the rest of the crowd, but the whole district or the whole country.

Furthermore, he said, the claim that the massacre had 'saved India' was not credible. Indeed, 'Our reign in India or anywhere else has never stood on the basis of physical force alone, and it would be fatal to the British Empire if we were to try to base ourselves only upon it.' Finally Churchill offered what he said was his personal opinion. This was that Dyer deserved not merely the loss of employment but to be subjected to 'a distinct disciplinary act, namely, his being placed compulsorily on the retired list'. Churchill had in fact battled for this with the Army Council and lost; its military members sympathized with Dyer. He now said that such a solution was not really possible, given that Dyer's actions had in effect been condoned subsequently by a succession of his superiors. Therefore he invited the House to endorse the Army Council's 'moderate and considered' decision to deny Dyer future employment without formally disciplining him.[143] The speech as a whole was utterly masterful. It emphasized that the massacre was horrible but also made the claim that it was unique.[144] It criticized Dyer's conduct severely, while at the same time stressing that he was not actually going to be punished. The effect was to calm the House, and although many MPs rebelled against the government, the hostile amendment put down by Dyer's supporters was defeated.

Churchill, with no little skill, had distanced himself clearly from the position held by the diehards even while he assuaged their wrath. Yet his speech still received some criticism in Punjab itself. The *Tribune*, a newspaper published in Lahore, offered some trenchant comments:

What does Mr Churchill mean by describing the Jallianwalla Bagh incident as a 'monstrous event standing out in sinister isolation' . . . The Jallianwalla Bagh incident stands on exactly the same footing as the shooting at most of the other places. Whom were the crowd attacking at the Upper Mall, for instance, or at the railway bridge at Amritsar itself until the crowd was fired upon? And is it not the case that in both these cases as well as almost all other places the crowd was unarmed? Lastly, if, as Mr Churchill said, frightfulness is not admissible in any form, can it be denied that the Jallianwalla Bagh massacre was not an isolated instance of frightfulness in the dark days of April and May, when frightfulness was more the rule than the exception.[145]

A recent commentator has written that the Amritsar speech was Churchill's finest hour 'from a moral point of view'.[146] One could equally say it was one of his finest hours from the point of view of parliamentary politics. During the episode he showed a tactical skill which belied his bull-in-a-china-shop reputation. The moral heroics were Montagu's – and they led directly to political failure.

Montagu did survive in office for the time being, although his position was much weakened. Nevertheless he stuck to his principles, as his position on the issue of Indians in East Africa demonstrates. This became a point of tension with Churchill once the latter had moved to the Colonial Office. The white settlers in Kenya were becoming increasingly militant in the face of Indian demands for an end to commercial and residential segregation, admission to the franchise on the same terms as whites and the right to buy land in the highlands.[147] In the face of Montagu's support for equitable treatment, Churchill – in his own eyes – did his best to be helpful. 'At the present time I am inclined to think that I cannot meet you fully in regard to franchise and representation', he wrote in May 1921. 'I hope to be able to meet you in regard to segregation by substituting for invidious segregation on race lines, a very strict system of sanitary, social and building regulations which will in fact ensure that the only Indians who will live in the white quarters will be those who are really suited by their mode of living for residence amid a European community.' Regarding the highlands, 'I fear that a virtual pledge has already been given to the white settlers.'[148] After an unsatisfactory meeting in June, Montagu disputed this final point in a long and heartfelt letter. He could not help it, he said, if Europeans refused to sell land to Indians; nor did he object to sanitary regulations so stringent 'that no Indian who does not live completely in European fashion can live in the Uplands'. Yet he would continue to protest 'so long as there is upon the statute book a regulation which differentiates between European and Indian subjects of the King'.[149]

Some weeks later, Churchill met with an Indian delegation. He told it that its demands, if granted, would lead eventually to 'the leadership of the country in [*sic*] the Indians, with the white man underneath'. However, an exchange with one of the delegates, S. S. Varma, revealed certain shared assumptions:

MR CHURCHILL: Broadly speaking, would you subscribe to
    Mr Rhodes' formula – Equal Rights for Civilised Men?
MR VARMA: I say exactly in those words, for civilised men,
    even including Indians.

MR CHURCHILL: Certainly, if the individual becomes civilised
and lives in a civilised way, in a civilised house, and
observes civilised behaviour in his goings on, and in his
family life, and he is also educated sufficiently – that
principle seems to be a very valuable principle, and it is very
practical too. It is absurd to go and give the naked savages
of the Kikuyu and the Kavirondo equal electoral rights,
although they are human beings – you cannot do that.
MR VARMA: No.[150]

There was no overall meeting of minds, of course, and
Churchill's patience eventually wore thin. 'The Indians in East
Africa are mainly of a very low class of coolies, and the idea that
they should be put on an equality with the Europeans is revolting to
every white man throughout British Africa', he told Montagu in
October.[151] In his reply, Montagu spoke of his despair at Churchill's
attitude, whose remark about coolies might, he said, 'have been
written by an European settler of a most fanatical type'.[152]

For their part, the whites feared that Churchill would not
safeguard their interests sufficiently, and sent a delegation to Britain
to press their case.[153] While they were in London, Churchill made
his controversial speech at the Kenya Colony and Uganda dinner,
in which he declared that the government looked forward to Kenya
becoming 'a characteristically and distinctively British colony' and
promised that the highlands would be reserved for the whites.[154]
Montagu was enraged at his failure to consult him or the Cabinet.
(Churchill claimed to have been speaking in line with the advice of
his officials.) In another long letter he said that he supported the
principle of 'equal rights for all civilised men' that Churchill had
invoked in the speech. However, 'what distresses me is that you
seem to think that the existing residents in the country can only
mean the European residents. Under every rule of equal rights for
all civilised men, the term must mean the residents in the country
regardless of race.'[155] Churchill was unbending, and told fellow
ministers that the demands of Indians in East Africa were unreasonable and that the whites might rebel if there was any repudiation of
his statement at the dinner.[156] The settlers, indeed, took a slightly
dim view of Churchill, and were underwhelmed by his promises.[157]
The *East African Standard* portrayed him as a beguiling post-prandial

speaker who revelled in 'the loftier regions of Imperialism', but who failed afterwards to give substance to his eloquence. Although he was supposedly committed to full white self-government, his real masters, it claimed, were radical anti-imperialists such as the Labour MP Josiah Wedgwood. The settlers had somehow 'to free Mr Churchill from the tyranny in which he is at present bound'.[158]

Just a few weeks later Montagu committed an extraordinary indiscretion by publishing a telegram revealing the Government of India's critical views on Lloyd George's anti-Turkish foreign policy. He was forced to resign for having breached the doctrine of collective Cabinet responsibility. In a speech to his constituents justifying his conduct, he pointed out that Churchill's Kenya speech, which had had 'a most terrible effect in India', had been made without consulting the Cabinet at all. 'Where was collective responsibility there?'[159] *The Times*'s correspondent in Delhi reported that 'Indian politicians undoubtedly feel that if Mr Montagu goes, Mr Churchill must go; otherwise there is no justice in the Cabinet'.[160] The difference, of course, was that Montagu had launched a direct political assault on the Prime Minister without having the allies he needed to back him up. He had in effect committed political suicide. He lost his seat at the general election of November that year; broken-hearted and embittered, he died just two years later, at the age of forty-five, from a combination of arteriosclerosis and septicaemia.

Yet Montagu's downfall was not the end of the India Office concern with the welfare of the Kenyan Indians, nor did Churchill's speech mark the final triumph of the settler attitude. Churchill allowed his under-secretary of state, Edward Wood, to hammer out an agreement with Earl Winterton, a junior minister at the India Office. The Wood–Winterton agreement conceded the settlers' demands on the highlands, but not on voting, immigration or segregation.[161] When the terms were revealed to the settlers later in 1922 they were widely seen as a breach of the promises made by Churchill at the start of the year. There was anger too at his recall of the pro-settler Governor of Kenya, Sir Edward Northey.[162] 'The old Bostonian spirit is abroad and must be taken very seriously', wrote one observer of the mood in Nairobi. 'The terms laid down by Mr Churchill in September will have to be very greatly modified or there will be civil war.'[163] The settlers began planning an insurrection. However, the Lloyd George coalition fell before it could come to fruition, and the new Conservative government succeeded in patching together a compromise the following year.[164]

The settlers were, of course, very difficult people to satisfy. Churchill had already alienated them in 1921 by acting to restrict (although not abolish) the existing system of forced labour in Kenya.[165] This issue demonstrated both his good intentions and their limits. On the one hand, it seemed to belie his growing public image as an imperialist reactionary. British officials had been battling the settlers over the question, and one of them hailed Churchill's decision as the 'Emancipation act for which the administration fought long and persistently'.[166] But it was not always implemented on the ground. In the spring of 1922, Harry Thuku, a young Kikuyu activist, came across a group of young girls and women being made to cut reeds. 'Well,' he told one of the African policemen in charge, 'whoever told you to force these women to do this forced labour is acting illegally. Don't you know that forced labour of this sort has been stopped by the order of Winston Churchill in the Colonial Office?' The police agreed to let the women go, but the authorities were displeased and ordered Thuku's arrest.[167] When an angry crowd surrounded the police station in which he was held the police opened fire and around twenty people were killed.[168] In Churchill's view, no blame attached to the police or officials for this outcome, and he approved Thuku's exile to the city of Kismayu, where he remained until 1930.[169] There was no trial, and the official account made no mention of the immediate cause of the arrest, which was justified on the basis of Thuku's other allegedly seditious activities.[170] It was more than a little ironic that Thuku's attempt to secure the implementation of Churchill's own policy should lead to a situation where Churchill himself considered him a danger to the peace of the colony.

VI

Throughout 1922 the troubles of the coalition deepened. Many Conservative MPs disliked their own leaders' acquiescence in the Irish settlement, and public revelations about Lloyd George's practice of selling political honours did the government's reputation no good. It was the perceived recklessness of its foreign policy, however, that was the immediate cause of its downfall. In September Turkish nationalist troops under Mustafa Kemal routed Greek troops and occupied the port of Smyrna, in Asia Minor, which had been allocated to Greece under the 1920 Treaty of Sèvres. Kemal's advance seemed to pose a direct threat to British troops at Chanak, on the Asian side of the Dardanelles. On 15 September the Cabinet took a clear decision to defend, by force if need be, the neutral 'Zone of the Straits'. Churchill was deputed to draw up a telegram to be sent to each of the Dominions informing them of this and seeking their support. Lloyd George approved his draft, and the messages were sent out late the same evening. On the 16th the two men worked together on a press communiqué, declaring it to be the duty of the wartime Allies to defend 'the deep-water line between Europe and Asia against a violent and hostile Turkish aggression'.[171] This was a tactless error, because the story became public before the Dominions had been able to digest what was being asked of them. Australia and New Zealand quickly indicated their readiness to act if required, although Australian Prime Minister W. M. Hughes was privately furious at the turn of events, believing that the behaviour of the British 'savoured of sharp practice'.[172] The response from South Africa was equivocal. Smuts, Prime Minister of the Union since 1919, was up-country when the cable arrived. By the time he got back the crisis had receded somewhat, and the government could therefore claim that there was no longer a need for active South African intervention.[173] (Smuts later sent a supportive message direct to Churchill.)[174] In Canada, there was major controversy. Mackenzie King, who had become Prime Minister at the previous year's general election, saw the telegram – which he heard about first from a journalist – as an attempt to bounce the Dominions into war. 'I confess it annoyed me', he wrote in his diary. 'It is drafted designedly to play the imperial game, to test out centralization vs. autonomy as regards [E]uropean wars.'[175] Following another 'very startling message' from Churchill a few weeks later, Mackenzie King wrote: 'It is a serious business having matters in [the] hand of a man like Churchill – the fate of an Empire!'[176]

Mackenzie King did not voice his criticisms openly, but played for time by referring the matter to the Canadian Parliament, which was not in session. Press criticism, though, was vociferous. 'Winston

Churchill, being colonial secretary, is overlord of Mesopotamia', observed the *Toronto Daily Star*. 'He can't divorce the idea that he is also overlord of Australia and Canada, South Africa and New Zealand – the one statesman to whom continents are bailiwicks.'[177] In the event, war was averted: the commander of the Allied forces in Turkey held back from delivering to the Kemalists a provocative ultimatum which had been drawn up by the Cabinet. Kemal decided not to attack and agreed to negotiate. In public, Churchill claimed this as a victory for the stance that he and his colleagues had taken. 'General Smuts, the great Liberal statesman of South Africa, has vindicated the action which we took', he declared. 'Australia and New Zealand have stood at our side.'[178] Unsurprisingly, he made no mention of Hughes's private anger; nor did he refer to Canada. The Chanak episode made Mackenzie King determined to resist what he saw as British attempts to centralize control of the Empire, and at the following year's imperial conference he successfully pressed for recognition of Dominion autonomy in important spheres such as the making of treaties. Not for the last time, an attempt by Churchill to strengthen Empire ties had the unintended consequence of weakening them instead.

The prospect of war had caused alarm in Britain as well as in the Dominions. On 7 October *The Times* published a letter from Andrew Bonar Law in which he argued, 'We cannot alone act as the policeman of the world'.[179] This was a signal that Law – who had stood down as Conservative leader the previous year because of illness, but whose health was now improved – was prepared to give an independent lead to Conservatives in a way that Austen Chamberlain, the party's official leader and a supporter of the coalition, would not. On 19 October Tory MPs, meeting at the Carlton Club, voted heavily to withdraw support from the coalition. As a result, Lloyd George resigned and Law became both leader of the Conservative Party and Prime Minister. At the vital moment – not that he could have affected the result – Churchill was struck down by appendicitis. He had an operation, and later recalled that 'in the morning when I recovered consciousness I learned that the Lloyd George Government had resigned, and that I had lost not only my appendix but my office as Secretary of State for the Dominions and Colonies'.[180] (Lloyd George joked that, although ill in bed, Churchill was 'busily drafting political programmes'.)[181] The general election that followed was a landslide for the Tories. Churchill, fighting once more as a Lloyd George Liberal, lost his seat to an independent Prohibitionist candidate. The Tory victory was widely welcomed in South Africa and Australia.[182] In Canada, Mackenzie King – himself a Liberal – had thought it would be 'a good thing for England' to get rid of Lloyd George, Churchill and their colleagues.[183] *The Times* reported that amongst Indians in Delhi the news of Edwin Montagu's defeat was 'more than compensated' for by the return of Ramsay MacDonald as a Labour MP and by the defeat of Churchill.[184]

Churchill's personal unpopularity within the Empire should not be exaggerated. If, for example, Australians and New Zealanders had borne him a terrible grudge about Gallipoli, it is doubtful that he would have been invited to speak at an ANZAC day lunch in London in 1921.[185] Some influential figures such as Smuts were friendly towards him and were prepared to give him the benefit of the doubt in a crisis. It is also clear that some of the criticisms made of him were excessive. The Chanak telegram and communiqué were undoubtedly misjudged, but Mackenzie King's belief that 'Lloyd George, Churchill and others were out to play an Imperialist game to help the Coalition politically' was unfair.[186] There had been no deliberate conspiracy. Furthermore, we may note that the reasons Churchill was distrusted varied considerably from country to country and group to group. If Indians disliked his speech on Kenya, then the white settlers disliked his failure, as they saw it, to deliver on its promises. In general, though, he was increasingly thought of as a diehard. Gandhi, for instance, said that he understood 'only the gospel of force'.[187] Churchill courted this reputation to some extent – with his interventions on Egypt, for example – but it did disguise the complexities of his attitudes.

Nevertheless, it is notable that, by the time of his fall from office, no one was criticizing his views on Empire as being too radical in the left-wing sense (even if East African settlers thought that he was too responsive to left-wing demands). This was in marked contrast to his first Colonial Office period. In the public mind, he had become increasingly associated with a domineering and allegedly old-fashioned form of imperialism. Ironically, even as he acquired this image, he was doing his best to break free from the constraints imposed by his ministerial remit. In 1921 Curzon complained about his interference in foreign affairs, and asked how Churchill would feel if he, Curzon, made public interventions on Colonial Office questions without consulting him. Churchill replied that 'there is no comparison between these vital foreign matters wh[ich] affect the whole future of the world and the mere departmental topics with the Colonial Office is concerned'.[188] The idea that Churchill was not really interested in imperial affairs would be absurd; yet, as the following years would show, the Empire was just one part of the canvas on which he wished to splash his paint.

6

DIEHARD, 1922–1939

AT THE end of 1923 Churchill published a swingeing attack on
H. G. Wells's views on imperialism in the pages of the *Empire Review*.
This was in response to an article by Wells in the previous issue of
the same journal, which argued that the British Empire should
eventually be merged into a system of world federal government,
acting in the meantime as a 'trustee' for this as-yet-unborn global
organization.[1] Churchill, although he praised the 'imagination and
foresight' of Wells's science-fiction writings, poured scorn upon this
political vision. Wells, he suggested, was an unrealistic dreamer. 'We
see him airily discarding, or melting down, all those props and
guard rails on which the population of this crowded and precari-
ously conditioned island have been accustomed to rely', Churchill
declared. 'We can almost hear him smacking his lips at every
symptom or upheaval in India or in Africa.' He ridiculed Wells's
world federation proposal: 'In this sublime conception the British
inheritance accumulated by the thrift and effort of so many centuries
would be liquidated and generously shared with all nations.'[2] Wells
replied in turn that Churchill's talk of thrift, effort and 'inheritance'
was cant. He, Wells, was merely pointing out the obvious, he said:
the Empire in its current form was unstable and bound to undergo
major changes in the future. He then put the boot in at the personal
level. He described Churchill as his friend, but added: 'There are
times when the evil spirit comes upon him and when I can think of
him only as a very intractable little boy, a mischievous, dangerous
little boy, a knee-worthy little boy. Only by thinking of him in that
way can one go on liking him.'[3]

The spat should not, perhaps, be taken too seriously; indeed, it
was somewhat prefabricated. Churchill and his friend Brendan
Bracken had themselves prevailed upon Wells to write his initial
article, which was on a topic he would probably not have chosen
himself, in order to help revive the *Empire Review*.[4] Nevertheless, the

episode was telling. To begin with, it showed how far Churchill had moved politically since his promotion to the Cabinet in 1908. At that point Wells, praising his 'fair and statesmanlike utterances', had urged socialists to vote for him, and Churchill had been happy to accept the endorsement.[5] Secondly, Churchill's use of the word 'liquidated' saw him rehearsing for his famous comment during World War II that he had not become Prime Minister in order to preside over the liquidation of the British Empire. Finally, and most significantly, his article cast light on his imperial vision at a moment when, in the wake of the territorial expansion triggered by the Great War, the Empire sat on the cusp of irreversible decline. It cannot exactly be counted as philosophical reflection – much of it consisted of a sarcastic diatribe against Wells – but it did see Churchill discussing the Empire in general terms rather than in relation to a specific, current controversy. What, then, was his case in favour of the British Empire?

The striking thing, in fact, is that Churchill had so few concrete things to say for the current state of affairs. He was very good at suggesting that Wells's system of world government would be worse: 'British credit and currency would, for instance, be dissolved in world-federal credits and currency to which German insolvency, French extravagance, Russian rapacity, and Chinese indolence would have loyally made their contributions.' It was only in relation to the role of the King-Emperor (disdained by Wells) that he laid out a positive argument. The Empire, he wrote, was 'a house of many mansions, where there is room for all, and in which the legitimate diversities of national, racial, geographical sentiments and interests may dwell and unfold peacefully and tolerantly side by side'. But formal political arrangements such as a Parliament of the Empire would not command the approval of these different communities. 'There is only one link which is accepted by all. The democratic communities of Australia, the surging progressiveness of Canada, the builders of the Irish Free State, the burghers of the Transvaal, the princes and populations of Hindustan, the inhabitants of fifty tropical dependencies and a thousand ocean-nursed islands, willingly, naturally, gratefully include themselves within the golden circle of an ancient Crown.'[6] In fact, as Wells pointed out, 'One of the chief troubles in the Irish settlement has been the excessive distaste of many Irishmen for the forms of royalty', and one might well ask too how profound the reverence for the monarchy went amongst some of the other groups Churchill mentioned.[7] Churchill was undoubtedly romanticizing the Empire, and here lay the deeper significance of his article. During his subsequent career he would often react with violent hostility to progressive proposals for reform of the Empire, even those more modest than Wells's. His denunciations were brilliant, and his descriptions of the advantages of Empire were colourful if unspecific, but his prescriptions showed little grasp of detail. His belief that 'the future of the British Empire may best be secured by advancing along the old road' was not accompanied by any constructive vision.[8] The bold ideas about economic development sparked by his pre-war African trip had more or less died away. It was this absence of a positive agenda, rather than his continued belief in Empire as such, that increasingly marked him out as a reactionary during the remainder of the inter-war years.

I

Churchill's Indian campaign, in opposition to reforms supported by the Tory leadership, was to be one of the chief hallmarks of the period; but before he could destabilize the Conservative Party from the right, he had first to rejoin it from the left. This was not a straightforward process. He himself claimed that he had been on the point of rejoining in 1922 but had been prevented from doing so by the collapse of the Coalition.[9] In 1923 Bonar Law resigned through ill health and was replaced as Prime Minister by Stanley Baldwin. But, later that same year, Baldwin overplayed his hand by calling a general election, asking for support for a policy of tariffs in order to combat the growing problem of unemployment. The threat to free trade reunited the divided Liberals, and led Churchill to fight a final campaign as a candidate for the party, in Leicester. He pointed out the falsity of Joseph Chamberlain's gloomy predictions about what would happen to the Empire if tariff reform was not adopted. When war had broken out in 1914 'the Empire was found united, heart and hand, after 70 years of Free Trade, in a manner far beyond the brightest and most sanguine dreams of any Imperialist'.[10] He also argued that 'the consolidation and development of the Empire' were not the monopoly of 'Tory Diehards'.[11]

The Tories lost their majority (although they won the largest number of seats), paving the way for a minority Labour government. Churchill was defeated at Leicester, but the overall result removed one obstacle from his path. Baldwin was now forced to drop his tariff policy, making it easier for Churchill to associate himself with the Tories, an alliance made urgent, he could now claim, by the threat the socialist government posed to Britain. In the spring of 1924 Churchill contested a by-election in the Abbey division of Westminster, as an 'Independent and Anti-Socialist' candidate, in conflict with the official Conservative candidate, Otho Nicholson. He tried to solicit Baldwin's help, telling him, 'Mr Nicholson's withdrawal or even the non-interference of the [Conservative] Central office in the fight, wd result in a resounding victory for Conservative & imperial interests & for anti-Socialism.'[12] The appeal was fruitless and Nicholson won the seat, but Churchill did well enough to make it clear that he could be a significant asset to the Tories. During the contest he laid into the Labour government, suggesting that, desirous of appeasing nationalist sentiment within the Empire, it was 'ready to lay down our burden in any one of the great Oriental countries if a stick be shaken at us by any irresponsible chatterbox'.[13] Labour, for its part, claimed that 'Churchill's militarist mind is as dangerous to the workers at home as it is to peace abroad'.[14]

In October there was a further general election, which the Conservatives won by a landslide. Churchill won a seat at Epping, standing nominally as a 'Constitutionalist' but with the support of Tory Central Office. To everyone's surprise, Baldwin, back in Downing Street, made him Chancellor of the Exchequer. Baldwin certainly recognized Churchill's ability, but there may have been deeper calculations. Not only would the appointment cement Churchill's separation from the still-dangerous figure of Lloyd George, it could be seen as a public token of the Conservatives' broad acceptance of the free-trade status quo. Baldwin also appointed Churchill's friend Lord Birkenhead (formerly F. E. Smith), another former Coalitionist, as Secretary of State for India. W. L. Mackenzie King noted that Baldwin had earlier described

Lloyd George, Birkenhead and Churchill privately as 'the three most dangerous men in the Empire', but that now he had taken two of them to his breast.[15]

Churchill had contrasted Labour ministers' desire for good relations with Soviet Russia with the 'frigid repulsion' they supposedly offered to Britain's Dominions.[16] Yet as Chancellor he himself was to meet strong criticism from within his own party for his alleged neglect of the Empire. His chief detractor was Leo Amery, who had strongly opposed his Abbey candidacy and was now Colonial Secretary. ('Though I like him infinitely better than Winston Churchill, for instance, I haven't the same sense of swift power', Gertrude Bell wrote of Amery when he visited Baghdad in 1925. 'On the other hand, I have a sense of great sympathy and consideration and of an earnest desire to do the best thing possible, if only he knew what it was.')[17] A year into the life of the government, Amery recorded in his diary a talk with Baldwin, 'my chief object being to make him understand that we shall get no progress on any Imperial development question unless he can make Winston definitely understand that it is his duty not simply to defend the Treasury point of view in these matters which is congenitally Little England but to override them'.[18]

Baldwin must have come to dread Amery's long letters of protest about Churchill, not to mention the two men's arguments in Cabinet. The issues were often relatively trivial ones, such as the budget of the Empire Marketing Board, spending to encourage emigration, or the question of who would pay for Imperial War Graves.[19] But the basic complaint was always the same. To Amery, Churchill was 'a brilliant talker and military strategist who is frankly incapable of understanding finance or the meaning of Empire development, and is anyhow steeped in free-trade prejudice'.[20] The Chancellor, he believed, was in thrall to his cheese-paring officials, whereas to Churchill Amery was excessively open-handed when it came to disposing of government money. 'I cannot understand why the idea of keeping Palestine in a dole-fed condition at the expense of our taxpayers attracts you', he told him on one occasion.[21] The Prime Minister never lent Amery the support he wanted. 'Whether on the side of Empire development or of domestic protection Baldwin allowed Churchill to paralyse all our actions', Amery told

J. C. Smuts after the fall of the government. 'For me it has been a very trying five years'.[22]

Was there any real foundation for Amery's relentless moaning? It was certainly true that Churchill formed a barrier to any substantive departure from free-trade principles – and Amery was not the only Conservative who thought him doctrinaire – but any such move would at any rate have been very difficult without a further general election to validate it.[23] It was also true that he was no great enthusiast for schemes such as state-subsidized emigration from Britain to her overseas territories, which appealed to some imperialists. 'All experience shows that if people are asked by the Government to emigrate they make a favour of everything and grouse at all the inevitable hardships of life', he observed. 'Having been favoured far above the rest of the population in public money they become almost invariably discontented and beseech the Government for further aid.'[24] Nevertheless, he was not an absolute slave to Treasury orthodoxy. In 1925 Amery proposed a £10-million government-guaranteed loan to support the development of transport in East Africa – exactly the sort of thing that had appealed to Churchill in pre-war days. Churchill did agree to the principle, to the discomfort of his own officials. Yet he also backed his civil servants in their insistence on tight controls on how the money was spent, as against the free hand demanded by Amery, whose big vision was not matched by a firm grasp of financial details.[25] This was the kind of Whitehall battle the Treasury was bound to win, and Amery would almost certainly have been denouncing its supposed short-sightedness no matter who occupied 11 Downing Street.

There was an imperial dimension to one of Churchill's most controversial decisions as Chancellor: the return of the pound to the gold standard in 1925, arguably at the cost of increasing unemployment. (Tying sterling to the dollar at the high fixed rate of of $4.86 to the pound made it harder for Britain to export.) When he made the announcement he pointed out that Canada was already on gold, and that the other Dominions would now join with Britain in the new arrangements. The establishment of a uniform standard of exchange across such a wide area would help revive international and inter-imperial trade, he argued.[26] However, homeland concerns were Churchill's primary focus during this period. Unlike Amery, he did not see Empire development (and the stimulus that it might give to British exports) as a major solution to the problem of the dole queues. Rather, he put most of his faith in balanced budgets and 'sound money', coupled with the reform of taxation and local government finance. He had not abandoned social reform; by extending the system of old-age pensions he made a conscious effort to grasp for the Tories the legacy of the pre-1914 'New Liberalism'.[27] There was little if any talk now, though, of using social policy to strengthen 'the British race'. The provision of social services, it seemed, no longer had to be justified as an imperial benefit. It is equally notable that, during the General Strike of 1926, Churchill saw no need to colour his denunciations of the unions with explicit warnings about the danger posed to the Empire. These absences may have been in line with the concerns of the British people – if we assume, that is, that after the upheavals of the Great War, they were increasingly preoccupied with the domestic over the foreign and imperial.[28] Yet in the 1930s Churchill reverted to the Empire as an issue and stuck with it well beyond the point of political profitability. So we cannot say that his interest in imperial questions simply ebbed and flowed with the spirit of the times.

Instead, we may suggest simply that, during the later 1920s, Churchill found no great imperial question to seize upon and make his own. The power of the Empire may have been strained but, while the Conservative government lasted, it faced no single, dominating threat. Indeed, it seemed to some that it was moving towards a new, happy era. The Imperial Conference of 1926 accepted the so-called 'Balfour Definition', which recognized the Dominions as 'autonomous Communities within the British Empire' while noting that for the time being much responsibility for their defence and foreign policy would continue to rest with Britain.[29] (The definition passed formally into law with the 1931 Statute of Westminster.) This was a mere acknowledgement of reality, and although Churchill may not have liked it much he accepted it with good grace in public at the time. 'The Age of Control is gone, the Age of Comprehension has begun', he declared. 'The Constitution of the British Empire depends now and henceforward solely upon good sense, good will, and loyalty to the Imperial Crown.'[30]

II

The era of control remained in place, of course, in India, the colonies and other dependent territories. But, by the end of the decade, India too seemed to be at a crossroads, as nationalist militancy there increased and British control weakened. In December 1928, against a backdrop of unrest, and in the face of pressure from radicals, Gandhi moved a compromise resolution at the annual meeting of the Indian National Congress. It said that, if Britain did not grant independence within a year, a new campaign of non-violent resistance should be launched. Remarkably, Baldwin seemed to think that Churchill might be the man to deal with the problem. The Prime Minister was planning an election in mid-1929, expected to win it, and thought that afterwards he might move Churchill to the India Office. He told the Viceroy, Lord Irwin (the former Edward Wood), that Churchill 'was very good all through the Irish trouble: he has imagination, courage: he is an imperialist; he is a liberal. BUT – we all know the risk. Should it be taken?'[31] Irwin wrote back saying rather delicately that he thought not. Citing Churchill's attitude to Indians in Kenya as an unhappy precedent, he told the Prime Minister that, 'if I thought that Winston would really be interested, & would really be Liberal minded, about India, I might be different: but I can't bring myself to believe that this is constitutionally likely'.[32] At some stage the Prime Minister personally mentioned the idea to Churchill, who years afterwards recalled: 'Mr Baldwin seemed to feel that as I had carried the Transvaal Constitution through the House in 1906, and the Irish Free State Constitution in 1920, it would be in general harmony with my sentiments and my record to preside over a third great measure of self-government for another part of the Empire.' He added laconically, 'I was not attracted by this plan.'[33]

In the event, the Conservatives lost the election and Baldwin's resolve was never put to the test. (Labour formed another minority administration.) The discussion illustrates, though, that even at this comparatively late date Churchill's reputation on imperial issues was by no means set in stone. Irwin thought him too vigorous an imperialist, Baldwin thought him a liberal, and Amery (who was intriguing to get him moved from the Treasury) thought that he was 'definitely hostile to the Empire'.[34] These three prominent Conservatives could all cite different parts of his record in support of their opinions. Given Churchill's own comments, we can guess that he would have recognized Irwin's portrait of him as closest to the truth, and would have made no apology for it. Nonetheless, it was not until the Conservatives went once more into opposition that he nailed his trousers firmly to the diehard mast.[35]

Shortly after the election the Labour government recalled Lord Lloyd, Britain's High Commissioner in Cairo, and forced him to resign. Lloyd, like Churchill, felt that the granting of self-government to Egypt had been a mistake, and over the previous years his efforts to preserve British influence by browbeating its rulers had annoyed Conservative Foreign Secretary Austen Chamberlain. Churchill thought Lloyd was being punished for his failure to accept Labour's policy of 'sloppy surrender and retreat'.[36] However, Baldwin did not think this was a good issue on which to attack the government, as to do so might drive the Liberals into its arms. Churchill insisted on defending Lloyd but recalled that when he did so 'it was evident I was almost alone in the House. [. . .] So far as I could see, Mr Baldwin felt that the times were too far gone for any robust assertion of British Imperial greatness'.[37] It was the start of a wider breach between the two men.

In August, Churchill departed for a lengthy tour of North America. During the Canadian leg he met Mackenzie King, who noted that he 'made a very good speech [. . .] closing with a very fine & very true peroration re "united we stand, divided we fall" re British Empire'.[38] At the end of October, a few days before Churchill's return to Britain, Baldwin urged the Shadow Cabinet to accept a bipartisan policy on India. The Tories should back Labour's plan to offer eventual Dominion status, he urged, at the same time arguing that this would not involve going beyond previous British pledges. A few days later Irwin formally announced that the government saw Dominion status as 'the natural issue [i.e. result] of India's constitutional progress'.[39] Baldwin then backed this line in the Commons, but many of his own MPs looked on in silent contempt. One former minister, Samuel Hoare, told Irwin, 'Throughout the debate Winston was almost demented with fury and since the debate has scarcely spoken to anyone.'[40]

In mid-November Churchill broke cover with an article in the staunchly imperialist *Daily Mail.* He did not criticize Baldwin or Irwin directly. Rather, he warned that nationalists were interpreting the Irwin declaration as a promise of Dominion status in the near future. This, he wrote, was not practical: it might be desirable as an ultimate object but the journey towards it would have to be 'immense'. Hinduism was a particular object of his criticism:

> Dominion status can certainly not be attained by a community which brands and treats sixty millions of its members, fellow human beings, toiling at their side, as 'Untouchables', whose approach is an affront and whose very presence is pollution. Dominion status cannot be attained while India is a prey to fierce racial and religious dissensions and when the withdrawal of British protection would mean the immediate resumption of mediaeval wars. It cannot be attained while the political classes in India represent only an insignificant fraction of the three hundred and fifty millions for whose welfare we are responsible.[41]

Over the following years he would add to these arguments, but his fundamental message remained consistent: India was not a nation but a 'geographical abstraction',[42] home to multitudes of competing races and religions. Only the rule of disinterested white officials, 'quite impartial between race and race', could hold the ring between them.[43] (He claimed that the deadly Hindu–Muslim riots of 1931 were the result of the belief that the British were about to leave the country.) Britain had brought enormous material and social benefits to the toiling Indian masses; these would be horribly jeopardized were she to depart, as would the economic welfare of Britain as a self-governing India closed its markets. Gandhi's financial backers, the wealthy Indian mill-owners, were hoping to benefit from this at the expense of both the British and the Indian masses. Britain, for its part, had no desire to exploit India, he claimed; the existing relationship was one of mutual benefit, although the British extracted 'only a fraction of the blessings' that the Indians got.[44]

He also came to argue – and this was one of the most compelling parts of his case – that the British government's proposed reforms were excessively complicated and would not in fact satisfy nationalist opinion. Once they were granted, the demand for full independence would inevitably follow. The obvious counter-argument to this was that the very little reform he himself was prepared to grant would satisfy the nationalists even less. Churchill believed, though, that the British should ignore demands for political change and concentrate instead on improving the well-being of the population. The 'plain assertion of the resolve of Parliament to govern and to guide the destinies of the Indian people in faithful loyalty to Indian interests' could bring the existing turmoil to an end.[45] His overarching belief was that British 'abdication' in India would be fatal to the moral authority and the concrete power of the Empire as whole. This was linked to events in Europe and elsewhere and his growing sense that a global crisis of apocalyptic proportions was approaching. 'In my view England is now beginning a new period of struggle and fighting for its life, and the crux of it will be not only the retention of India but a much stronger assertion of commercial rights', he wrote in 1933. 'As long as we are sure that we press no claim on India which is not in their real interest we are justified in using our undoubted power for their welfare and for our own.'[46]

To what extent were such views consistent with those that Churchill had expressed prior to 1929? Critics liked to cite his 1920 Amritsar speech – his most substantive previous post-war comment on India – in order to imply that his views had changed.[47] Churchill responded that he stuck by what he had then said: he abhorred the shooting of unarmed people, 'and nothing is less necessary for the re-establishment of British authority in India'.[48] Opponents also pointed out that he had been a member of the government in 1919 when Edwin Montagu's Government of India Act was passed. (The Act foresaw 'the progressive realisation of responsible government in British India'.) Churchill's response to this was that he had had little direct responsibility for the legislation and that Montagu had at any rate represented it 'as a mere experiment which could be arrested or reversed at any time'.[49] It is worth noting that Churchill did tell Montagu, in October 1921, that 'you are getting into rather deep water with the Dominion of India idea';[50] and he provoked him by saying that Gandhi 'ought to be lain bound hand and foot at the gates of Delhi and then trampled on by an enormous elephant with the new Viceroy seated on its back'.[51] In private he attributed the stiffening of his attitude to the failure of Montagu's reforms to assuage the nationalists. He told a conference of ministers in 1922 that he believed that 'opinion would change soon as to the expediency of granting democratic institutions to backward races which had no capacity for self-government'.[52]

Yet, at the 1921 Imperial Conference, Churchill himself gave a significant hostage to fortune. He said, at a dinner to honour the Dominion premiers and the Indian representatives, that the British 'looked forward confidently to the days when the Indian government and people would have assumed fully and completely their Dominion status'. Irwin later took relish in drawing attention to this speech, and Churchill had great difficulty explaining it away.[53] The true explanation for it is to be found in a letter from Neville Chamberlain describing Churchill's behaviour at the dinner and the reaction to it of one of the Indian delegates, Srinivasi Sastri. According to Chamberlain, Churchill in his speech

> clean forgot about India and talked about 'our race' 'English speaking peoples' and 'the four great Dominions' so that I could not help asking myself What does Mr Sastri think of all this. Towards the end of the speech someone handed up a card on which 'India' was written and Winston then produced an eloquent passage about the day when India would take her place on equal terms with the Dominions. But it was too late and when later on Sastri rose he administered in perfect English and with perfect taste one of the most scathing rebukes I ever heard.[54]

Overall, it is clear that Churchill did not see India as a priority issue at this time. In 1930, by contrast, he told Baldwin that he cared 'more about this [Indian] business than anything else in public life'.[55] The change cannot be put down simply to opportunism but can be explained, at least in part, by ideological and personal influences. One of the former was Katherine Mayo's book *Mother India*, published in 1927. It was a sensational and polemical exposé (written with the cooperation of British officials) of India's supposed incapacity for self-government. Although it dealt with genuine evils such as child marriage, untouchability and poor hygiene it had a profound anti-Hindu bias. Sexual excess, in Mayo's view, lay at the root of Indian society's problems, and had enfeebled Indian men's hands so that they were 'too weak, too fluttering, to seize or to hold the reins of Government'.[56] Churchill told a friend, 'He admires the book Mother India and would have no mercy with the Hindus who marry little girls aged ten.'[57] He subsequently lent the book out to at least one fellow Conservative, and praised Mayo's 'powerful pen and vast knowledge' of India.[58] Clearly, Churchill had been no enthusiast for self-government before reading Mayo, but it seems plausible to suggest that she provided the basis for much of the anti-Hindu tinge of his later arguments. He was to be considerably more positive about the Muslims who, in line with contemporary thinking, he counted amongst India's 'martial races'.[59] During his Indian campaign, Churchill's fear that they and other minorities would be subject to Hindu tyranny led some Muslims to consider him a sympathetic figure.[60]

It seems likely that Lord Birkenhead reinforced the hardening in Churchill's views. Birkenhead was two years older than Churchill. Unlike him, he had failed the Harrow entrance examination. But he did make it to Oxford University, and after early, brilliant success at the Bar he was elected as a Tory MP in 1906. His maiden speech was unconventional in that it was long, controversial, and very, very funny. In spite of their differences over tariff reform, he and Churchill struck up a warm friendship across the floor of the House, which blossomed further as the years went on. As Lord Chancellor in the Coalition government, Birkenhead condemned General Dyer's behaviour at Amritsar, pointing out that if the same methods had been used in Canada or Scotland there would have been outrage.[61] Yet as Secretary of State for India from 1924, he was determined to preserve the status quo. He established a commission, under Sir John Simon, to look into the country's constitutional development precisely because he wanted to forestall possible radical moves by a future Labour government. With great cynicism, Birkenhead wrote privately that his 'highest and most permanent hopes' for the continuation of British rule rested on the permanency of the Hindu–Muslim divide.[62] Churchill later wrote that his friendship with Birkenhead 'kept me in close touch with the movement of Indian affairs, and I shared his deep misgivings about that vast sub-continent'.[63] In 1928 Birkenhead stood down from the Cabinet in order to earn the money needed to fund his lavish lifestyle. Two years later, his health broken by years of heavy drinking, he died, just as India was becoming a major issue. Churchill was devastated. 'Most of all did I deplore his absence during those years when it seemed to me that the future of India was at stake', he recalled.

'With his aid, I believe different and superior solutions might have been reached.'[64]

The increased importance that Churchill attached to India, though, came most of all from the international context. It was the conjunction of events in India with those in the Middle East that persuaded Churchill of the seriousness of the problem. The Labour government's general weakening (as he saw it) on imperial issues risked creating a domino effect. In the summer of 1929 the long-simmering tensions in Palestine broke out into a terrible wave of anti-Jewish violence. In Churchill's view, this was a reaction less to local conditions than to British pusillanimity elsewhere. He claimed that the Arabs had read the dismissal of Lloyd and British proposals to withdraw troops from Cairo and Alexandria as a sign that 'the hour to strike had come'. Furthermore, he argued, 'What has happened in Palestine is only a bloody foretaste of what will undoubtedly happen on a far larger scale throughout the Nile valley, and would happen on a gigantic scale from one end of India to the other once the sober, guiding, and pacifying influence of the British Imperial power were withdrawn.'[65] He warned, 'Any further mistakes made in Egypt will react in India, and from this limited scene the whole stupendous panorama of the East may be thrown into confusion.'[66] In his view, then, the whole future of British power was now at stake.

But although he despaired of Baldwin's reaction to this general imperial crisis, it took a considerable time for him to formalize the break. His timing and choice of issue surely did involve calculation from the point of view of his own career. During 1930 Baldwin ran even deeper into difficulties. Even relatively loyal colleagues such as his likely successor Neville Chamberlain thought him useless as Leader of the Opposition. Churchill's friend (or crony) Lord Beaverbrook, owner of the *Daily Express*, was campaigning for 'Empire Free Trade', a euphemism for a form of imperial preference. He put up candidates against official Conservatives at by-elections and won. In spite of his own opposition to Beaverbrook's views, Churchill helped him draft his public correspondence with Baldwin. ('Amazing performance', noted a Beaverbrook journalist who witnessed this. 'Here is Winston – an ex-colleague of Baldwin in the last Government and still a member of his Shadow cabinet – advising Max [Beaverbrook] how to counter Baldwin's letter.')[67] When, in October, Baldwin produced a stiffer protectionist policy of his own, Churchill found himself in a hole. He seemed ready to resign from the Shadow Cabinet but held back, doubtless calculating that, with the atrophy of popular support for free trade in the face of the slump, he would be on a sticky wicket if he did so.[68]

In the event he took his stand on India instead. In November, the government-sponsored Round Table Conference on the future of India opened. Indian representatives were present but Congress leaders stayed away; Gandhi and Jawaharlal Nehru were at any rate both in jail. Baldwin supported the conference and noted, with a hint of satisfaction, Churchill's gloom about it. 'He wants the Conference to bust up quickly and the Tory party to go back to pre-war and govern with a strong hand', he wrote. 'He has become once more the subaltern of hussars of '96.'[69] In December Churchill did his best to live up to the caricature with a diehard speech to the Indian Empire Society, which had been set up to defend British rule. 'Gandhi-ism and all it stands for will, sooner or later, have to be grappled with and finally crushed', he warned.[70] The speech brought him much criticism – 'But I do not care at all, I am going on with it', he wrote.[71] The government continued to seek compromise. In January 1931 Irwin released Gandhi and his colleagues from prison with a view to starting negotiations. Baldwin's support for this move triggered Churchill's resignation from the Shadow Cabinet. 'Winston has chosen his moment and his excuse for separating from the party very adroitly', wrote Amery some days later, as backbench sentiment welled up against the leadership's stance.[72]

On 17 February Irwin met Gandhi for the first of a series of discussions, prompting one of Churchill's most notorious remarks, in a speech made at the West Essex Conservative Association: 'It is alarming and also nauseating to see Mr Gandhi, a seditious Middle Temple lawyer, now posing as a fakir of a type well-known in the East, striding half-naked up the steps of the Vice-regal palace, while he is still organising and conducting a defiant campaign of civil disobedience, to parley on equal terms with the representative of the King-Emperor.'[73] Later in the same speech Churchill described Gandhi, perhaps even more harshly, as a 'malignant subversive fanatic'; yet it is the 'half-naked fakir' passage that has always resonated. In part this was because Churchill successfully conjured an image that jarred utterly with the popular view of Gandhi as unworldly and, no matter what his faults, sincere. For Churchill, Gandhi's decision to abandon Western dress was repellent, marking a retreat from civilization itself; one would hardly do this, in his view, without some kind of ulterior motive. At the same time it probably confirmed his opinion that the adoption by Hindu Congressmen of Western thought and clothing was merely a veneer. As Churchill put it in another speech, the 'Brahmins who mouth and patter the principles of Western Liberalism' were in fact resolved to keep the Untouchables in 'sub-human bondage'.[74] (He made no acknowledgement of Gandhi's own opposition to untouchability, not even to point out that his claim to speak for the Untouchables was heavily contested by their leader, B. R. Ambedkar. And he struggled to explain Ambedkar's own support for self-government.)[75] In response to the 'fakir' remark Gandhi wrote that 'Mr Churchill has been kind enough to gratuitously advertise my loin-cloth to the world' before going on to explain why he had adopted it. 'European civilization is no doubt suited for the Europeans but it will mean ruin for India, if we endeavour to copy it', he argued.[76]

Churchill was exultant at his speech's reception. He told Clementine: 'There is no doubt that the whole spirit of the Conservative Party is with me, and that much of their dissatisfaction with S.B. turns itself into favour with me.'[77] On 5 March Irwin struck a deal with Gandhi. In exchange for prisoner-release and other concessions, civil disobedience would be halted and Congress would attend the next session of the Round Table Conference. A few hours after the agreement was reached, Gandhi came back to see Irwin looking 'rather depressed'. The more radical Nehru had told him that he, Gandhi, 'had unwittingly sold India'. (There had been no guarantees on future independence.) Irwin recalled: 'I exhorted him not to let this worry him unduly, as I had no doubt that very soon I should be getting cables from England, telling me that in Mr Churchill's opinion I had sold Great Britain.'[78] Baldwin was 'thoroughly bucked' by the pact, which seemed to show that the strategy of negotiation was working.[79]

Press reaction in India to the Conservative Party's internal divisions showed that Churchill's views were not necessarily popular even with white opinion. The London correspondent of the British-run *Statesman* judged that 'Mr Baldwin has done more than any

other man to save the Conservative Party from humiliation and
wreckage and to spare India a feeling of hopelessness and futility'.
The feeling in the Commons, he wrote, was that Gandhi and Irwin
had proved Churchill wrong and that 'by his present campaign of
vituperation against India and her leaders, he is digging his political
grave'.[80] Amongst the vernacular language newspapers, the *Anand*
seemed to accept that an independent India might have a future
within the British Empire. This, though, was subject to qualification:
'If Mr Churchill and his reactionary companions so desire they can
spend more over India by proclaiming martial law and showering
bombs from aeroplanes but so far there is merely the question of
partnership in the Empire but then India will decide to separate
herself completely from it. Does Mr Churchill want to see that day?'
The more radical *Navin Bharat* warned: 'In spite of Mr Baldwin's tall
talk of unity his party consists of enemies of India's freedom like
Churchill who think that India cannot be given anything beyond
provincial autonomy. This shows that the appendix of safeguards
will render independence nominal.'[81] On 19 March the official Tory
candidate triumphed over an anti-Baldwinite at a crucial by-election
in Westminster. '[E]very Englishman in India is glad', claimed the
British-owned *Times of India*.[82] Both Beaverbrook's challenge to
Baldwin and Churchill's (slim) chance of supplanting him as leader
were now dead.

III

In August a major financial crisis involving a collapse of confidence
in sterling forced the resignation of Ramsay MacDonald's Labour
administration. However, MacDonald immediately formed a new
'National Government' which included Tories and Liberals. The
bulk of the Labour Party went into opposition and there was,
predictably, no job for Churchill, who was now merely a government backbencher. He himself was in France when the government
fell. As he set out from London a few days earlier he received the
proofs of *India Insistent*, a book by a fellow Harrovian, Sir Harcourt
Butler. A former Governor of Burma with wide experience of India,
Butler argued 'the need for caution in political advance on western
lines', adding that 'one need not subscribe to the doctrine that the

hands of the clock can never be put back'.[83] Churchill quickly cabled Butler's publishers from Juan-les-Pins: 'I have read with entire agreement – a magnificent work, Churchill.'[84] Within a few days he published a laudatory review of it, warning that 'we should not lose sight of India amid the anxieties of the financial crisis and the excitements of a new Government'.[85] Meanwhile, the more extreme sections of the Indian press affected indifference to the change of government yet nonetheless showed their fear of intensified repression. The *Shakti* wrote: 'India should not expect anything from this national or for that matter any other Government in Britain. The Churchill party has gained in strength and will get stronger.'[86] Gandhi's view, by contrast, was that the British government was facing 'such staggering domestic problems' that it was unlikely to refuse India self-government.[87] Arriving in Britain for the new session of the Round Table Conference, he told journalists that he wanted to meet his enemies, and that he would write to Churchill and *Daily Mail* proprietor Lord Rothermere asking for an interview.[88] But the Churchill–Gandhi meeting of 1906 was not to be repeated.

In October there was a general election in the UK, leading to a startling victory for the National Government. Although MacDonald was still Prime Minister, Baldwin held the whip hand, as 473 of the government's 554 MPs were Conservatives. When Parliament reconvened after the election it debated the Statute of Westminster, formalizing the 1926 Balfour definition of Dominion status. Although Churchill had welcomed the definition at the time, he now backtracked. On the one hand, he feared that Ireland could use the legislation to repudiate the Anglo-Irish Treaty, including the oath of Allegiance to the Crown. (With Eamon De Valera about to take power in Dublin as Prime Minister this was a realistic concern, although 'Dev' was anyway unlikely to be bound by legal niceties.) On the other, he predicted that a 'frightful disaster' would befall India if full Dominion status as set out in the statute were granted to it.[89] He now urged an amendment, restricting the scope of the statute by specifying that it did not affect the Anglo-Irish settlement of 1922, but this attempt to tie Ireland's hands was rejected. On 1 December the Round Table Conference broke up without agreement between Gandhi and the Muslim representatives, who demanded separate electorates for religious minorities. MacDonald announced the government's determination to press ahead regardless and to present, in due course, a reform scheme that would lead onwards to Dominion status. In the Commons debate that followed, Churchill complained that the Conservative Party was now fully committed to the 'Socialist' policy followed by the late Labour government.[90] Again Churchill's diehard line was defeated, this time by 369 votes to 43. Hoare, now Secretary of State for India, wrote of 'the collapse of the Churchill movement in the House of Commons'.[91]

The turn of the year saw a new crackdown in India after Gandhi revived civil disobedience and was again jailed. Churchill continued to warn that 'democracy is totally unsuited to India', but 1932 saw something of a lull in his campaign while he worked on his biography of the first Duke of Marlborough and the government prepared its reform plans.[92] The year was notable, though, for the Ottawa Agreements of the summer. This network of bilateral pacts with Dominion countries greatly extended imperial preference and confirmed Britain's shift towards protectionism. It involved Britain imposing the dreaded 'food taxes' on non-imperial produce. The year before, Churchill had announced his acceptance of tariffs as part of a programme of 'imperial reconstruction', but his conversion was clearly half-hearted.[93] In private he referred contemptuously to 'Rottowa'.[94] His decision to swallow his distaste in public amounted to a realistic acknowledgement that he could not fight the National Government on all fronts at once. Meanwhile, Ottawa helped the Conservative Party buy off its other internal opponents. As Amery put it a little later, 'the Government can only get away with its India policy if on other issues it is definitely imperialist, protectionist, anti-League of Nations, all the things in fact which appeal to the instincts of those who form the strength of the revolt over India'.[95]

A new source of difference arose in January 1933, when Hitler came to power in Berlin. Churchill was rightly concerned about the threat posed by a resurgent Germany, and urged rearmament to deal with it. The government (which did rearm significantly in the years before 1939) presented him as an alarmist. Although it is possible to identify inconsistencies in his thinking, he must be given full credit for having been, at the broadest level, right about the Nazis. At the same time, it must be admitted that his simultaneous predictions of the probable ghastly consequences of the government's India policy devalued his warnings about Germany in the eyes of many. This was an issue he failed to address in his post-war memoirs, which barely touched on his massive effort over India and presented the 1930s as a straightforward story of how his prescience about Hitler had been ignored.[96]

In March 1933 the government's White Paper on India was at last published. The plan was to establish self-government in the provinces as a step towards an all-India federal government. Federation, however, would take place only if enough of the Princely States were willing to join.[97] It is important to emphasize that Churchill's battle against the plan was not the obviously lost cause it might appear in retrospect. In his efforts to combat the scheme, Churchill could count on the support of many rank-and-file Tories and also on the sympathy, if not always on the votes, of a substantial minority of the Conservative membership of the Commons and Lords. In addition, he had the backing of the right-wing *Morning Post* and Rothermere's *Daily Mail*. However, the *Morning Post* was by now virtually moribund, and the Beaverbrook press did not come on board; nor, crucially, did *The Times* or other significant highbrow papers.[98] Furthermore, the BBC only once (in 1935) allowed Churchill to broadcast on the topic of India.[99] This was in line with its policy that political talks should be 'non-controversial'.

Churchill's position was weakened by the distrust with which some of his diehard allies viewed him on account of his Liberal past. Former Party Chairman J. C. C. Davidson recalled that 'although the Tory opponents of the Government's Indian policies welcomed Winston's support, they always rather apologized for the fact that Winston was in their camp'.[100] Viscount Wolmer (later the third Earl of Selborne) complained that Churchill discredited the campaign: '*we* are acting from conviction but everybody knows Winston has no convictions; he has only joined us for what he can get out of it'.[101] By contrast, Henry Page Croft MP, an ardent tariff-reformer whose short-lived right-wing National Party had been reabsorbed by the Conservatives in 1921, was convinced that Churchill was sincere. After all, he argued in his memoirs, Churchill when Chancellor maintained his opposition to protectionism in spite of the damage this did him with the party. Had he been 'the careerist which some tend to assert when discrediting his Indian views, he would surely have swum with the tide and dropped his old Free Trade faith, and so made a great bid to win the confidence of Conservatives'.[102] Arguably, the real difference between Churchill and the right-wingers was not one of sincerity. Rather, he was so passionate about India that he was, unlike them, prepared to use the issue to 'break the Government'.[103] He doubtless hoped that this would be of advantage to him, but in fact he was reckless as to his own best interests. Baldwin once explained privately the reason he had excluded Churchill from the Cabinet: 'he had gone about threatening to smash the Tory party on India, and I did not mean to be smashed'.[104]

Churchill told the Conservative MP Victor Cazalet that 'he felt like cutting people and hating them as he had never hated before in his life. He and his friends were going to fight the White Paper scheme to the bitter end.'[105] (Later, after Cazalet voted for the scheme himself, the formerly friendly Churchill would greet him with no more than a curt nod.)[106] Churchill's strength of emotion, leading him to imagine perhaps that others must feel the same way, may have caused him to overestimate his chances of success. J. C. C. Davidson recollected that on one occasion Churchill stopped him in the House of Commons Smoking Room, told him of his plans for mass agitation against the India Bill and predicted that the government would fall in a fortnight. In Davidson's words:

> He went on to say that the British Empire was a wonderful text to preach from especially if you wanted to preserve it, and I replied bluntly that he wouldn't get a single vote. [. . .] I told him that I thought that the British public was much more interested in the size of their pay-packet on Friday than by great rhetorical appeals to their loyalty to the British Empire. I told him that they might cheer him, but they wouldn't vote for him. He didn't like it a bit.[107]

Churchill had to contend not only with the relative indifference of the British public but also with his own habit of repeatedly shooting himself in the foot. This he did from the very beginning of the debate on the White Paper. On 30 March 1933 he alleged in the Commons that promotion within the Indian Civil Service depended not on merit but on whether officials supported the government's reform programme. When challenged, he failed to substantiate the charge and lost the sympathy of the House. Then, in April, he declined to join the joint select committee (drawn from both the Commons and Lords) that was to draw up detailed reform proposals as part of the White Paper process. He argued that the committee's proposed membership was too heavily stacked on the government's side or, as he put it, in favour of the abdication of British rule in India. He did not, he said, wish to share in responsibility for the 'grievous events' that were bound to follow from this policy.[108] His decision was understandable but surely mistaken, as it made him look like a negative and destructive critic who was unable to present a positive alternative. It was grist to the mill of Hoare, who alleged privately and unfairly that Churchill was convinced 'that England is going Fascist and that he, or someone like him, will eventually be able to rule India as Mussolini governs north Africa'.[109]

Churchill himself gave evidence to the committee over three days in October, remarking afterwards that it was 'the most exhausting thing he had ever done'.[110] He denied that he belonged to 'the Diehard Party', describing this as 'an abusive term which is used by persons who are often found very ignorant of the real foundations of British power and strength'.[111] (In 1922, though, he had blamed the fall of the Coalition on 'the Diehards', and in private he now proudly referred to himself as one.)[112] He presented the committee's members with a memorandum in which he outlined his own plans for reform, sticking fairly closely to the relatively modest proposals of the Simon Commission which had reported in 1930. He was reluctantly prepared to concede 'Home Rule' for the Indian provinces, attended by many safeguards, but there was to be no federation and the central government, over which the Viceroy presided, was to retain strong powers. There should then be no further change for a long period, and there certainly should not be a Dominion constitution for India 'in any period which human beings ought to take into practical account'.[113] This was all quite unrealistic. One India Office official commented: 'It is almost childishly absurd to imagine that after the history of the last few years and declarations far in advance of Mr Churchill's ideas that by any stretch of the imagination India could be got to settle down quietly for a long term of years under a constitution of this kind without further development in the near future.'[114] The plan also drew criticism from the *Times of India* and the nationalist *Bombay Chronicle*, which regretted that Churchill's high intelligence 'should have prostituted its gifts to such base purpose and such an idiotic plan'.[115]

Churchill's interrogation by the committee was notable because it was the one occasion on which he was forced to justify his views directly to Indians, a number of whom (including Ambedkar) were represented on it and asked some 'rather acid questions'.[116] He did not suffer any knock-out blows but, although he put on a good-humoured performance, he failed to show a firm grasp of detail. The Aga Khan (a major figure in Shi'a Islam) told him directly that 'you have what I may call a cursory knowledge' of Indian affairs.[117] The Bombay *Free Press Journal* described Churchill's evidence as a mixture of 'intelligent stupidity and hypocritical sympathy for the India cause'.[118] The London *Times* suggested that after Churchill's deposition the committee would resume its work in the knowledge that the White Paper, 'however susceptible of improvement, stands in its main essentials more invulnerable than ever before'.[119]

Such criticism, of course, was fairly predictable when it came from nationalist sources or even from the India Office or the Baldwin-supporting *Times*. But, notwithstanding the contents of Churchill's own postbag, there was also much to suggest that he was out of kilter with the opinions of even the British in India. For example George Stanley, the Governor of Madras wrote, 'It is amazing to me that people like Winston & Co. cannot realise that India has not stood still during the last few years any more than any other country has done so.' The *Daily Mail*'s description of self-government as a policy of scuttle 'means that the Viceroy and all the Governors of Provinces are "scuttling" because we are all agreed that the White Paper is on the right lines'.[120] When Victor Cazalet visited India he reported to Baldwin: 'I have not met a single individual in a responsible position who did not take the view that the White Paper proposals *must go through*. The hardest-headed conservative-minded political officer has no more use for Churchill than he has for Gandhi.'[121]

It is no surprise, then, that some officials in India saw Churchill's next major assault on the government as 'a dirty attack' and a case of 'Winston as usual'.[122] The press there also reacted scep-tically.[123] Baldwin remarked that 'Winston is fundamentally a blackguard'.[124] However, Churchill's allegations of a conspiracy to suppress evidence to the select committee did raise important issues about the lengths to which the government would go to defeat him and secure the passage of its bill. His claims, which he made public in April 1934, related to events of the previous year. He had documentary proof, he said, that Hoare and Lord Derby (a Conservative peer and an influential figure in Lancashire) had put pressure on the Manchester Chamber of Commerce (MCC) to alter its evidence to the committee. As both Hoare and Derby were members of the committee, he alleged that this was a breach of parliamentary privilege and called for a Commons investigation. In order to understand what all the fuss was about, it is necessary to appreciate the continuing importance of the Lancashire cotton lobby. Although historians debate its strength and significance, it is undoubtedly true that Churchill, who liked to stress his former connection with Oldham, placed much importance upon it.[125] One of his key arguments against increased Indian autonomy was that the higher tariffs that would follow would lead to the impoverishment of Lancashire. In its initial evidence, the MCC argued for restrictions on India's ability to regulate its own trade, which was long established under the so-called fiscal autonomy convention. After Hoare and Derby pointed out that this was straining for the politically impossible, and would do more harm than good, it withdrew this submission and put in a new version, substantially toned down.

It was undoubtedly true that Hoare and Derby did make significant efforts to persuade the MCC. Two questions arise: a) were these efforts the cause of the MCC's change of heart, and b) regardless of their effects, were those efforts improper, or rather, so improper as to constitute a breach of privilege? The Committee of Privileges appointed to investigate found that the answer to a) was 'no'. In fact, the report suggested, advice received from an MCC mission to India had caused the change. The committee's answer to b) was also 'no'. As the joint select committee was not a judicial body there was nothing wrong with its members advising witnesses how to frame their evidence; Hoare and Derby had merely been giving Lancashire advice on how best to pursue its own interests.[126] More recently, this analysis has been challenged, on the basis that important evidence was withheld from the committee. By this argument, Churchill was on the right lines, and might have been able to prove his case beyond doubt had all the facts been known.[127] This is convincing only up to a point, however. Undoubtedly, evidence was suppressed, and the advice of the MCC's India mission was certainly not the decisive factor. Thomas Barlow, a leading figure in the MCC who bore much responsibility for the decision to change its submission, must certainly have had Derby's urgings in mind at the crucial moment. But although it would have been highly embarrassing for the government if Churchill had been able to demonstrate all this, the committee's argument that there had been no breach of privilege may well have been right. Whether or not Hoare and Derby had acted reprehensibly, it is far from clear that, in their original dealings with the MCC, they had broken any formal rules. Moreover, the MCC leaders did not believe – or so they claimed – that they had been subject to improper pressure.[128] And it was always going to be hard for Churchill to present himself as the great defender of Lancashire if he was opposed by Derby, the county's uncrowned king. Churchill insisted on striding onto the pitch and defending someone else's wicket when the team captains preferred to settle the match over tea in the pavilion.[129]

Churchill compounded his difficulties by his ungracious reception of his defeat. When the Privileges Committee's report was debated in the Commons in June he did not accept its conclusions but instead launched into a diatribe. In response, Amery – who was also out of office at this time – made a speech that has become famous. He said that, in making his accusations, Churchill had been faithful to the motto *fiat justitia ruat coelum*. This means 'Let justice be done though the heavens fall', but when Churchill made the mistake of asking for a translation, Amery offered, to loud laughter, 'If I can trip up Sam [Hoare], the government's bust.'[130] Churchill was not in the House when it voted, without dissent, to accept the committee's findings.[131]

In November 1934 the original joint select committee published its own report. This broadly endorsed the approach of the White Paper. In December the Conservative Party's Central Council gave its approval to the policy, by 1,102 votes to 390. In the Commons, 75 Tory MPs rebelled, but this posed no real threat to the government's majority. (The high-water mark of party rebellion had come, in Churchill's absence, at the annual conference in October, with a victory for the leadership of only 543 votes to 520.) The government's legislation still had to pass through Parliament, but it was clear that it would do so in due course. At the start of 1935 Churchill's son Randolph thrust himself into the limelight by standing as an anti-India Bill candidate against an official Conservative at a by-election in Liverpool. Churchill, whose relationship with his son was turbulent, was not best pleased, but gave his reluctant backing. Randolph echoed his father's themes – 'what Lancashire suffers today Britain and the Empire will suffer tomorrow'[132] – and attracted enough support to split the Tory vote and let in Labour. Some of Churchill's Epping constituents started to grumble about his own attitude towards the government.

Churchill described the massive and highly complex Government of India Bill as 'a monstrous monument of sham built by the pygmies'.[133] (He was reported as having used the word 'shame', but he insisted that he had not; his choice of 'sham' suggests he wanted to emphasize that the bill was unworkable, rather than that it was morally reprehensible.)[134] He fought a tough rearguard action against its passage, but it was impossible for him to muster the votes to defeat it. In June, as it reached its final Commons stage, he declared himself unreconciled to it, in a speech that sounded like 'the last despairing cry of a man who has been ignored and who sees nothing but desolation and ruin in consequence'.[135] Just at the point when Indians required 'a far higher measure of disinterested and enlightened autocracy', Churchill argued, they were being offered 'the faded flowers of Victorian Liberalism'. In conclusion he warned that the passing of the bill might sound the death knell of the British Empire in the East.[136] Amery, who spoke next, provided a rejoinder: 'Here endeth the last chapter of the book of the Prophet Jeremiah.' He deplored Churchill's lack of constructive suggestion, and his failure to show any measure of sympathy or understanding towards the aspirations of the Indians.[137] His points were well made and signified important differences with Churchill that were to re-emerge dramatically during World War II. Amery, for his part, was much clearer sighted on India than in his grandiose visions for the Empire as a whole.

In fact, the Act never came fully into force. Although elections for the provincial assemblies took place in due course (resulting in major Congress victories), federation remained a dead letter because of the opposition of the Princes. In the aftermath of his defeat, Churchill made some efforts to appear magnanimous. In August 1935 he was visited at Chartwell, his house in Kent, by the industrialist G. D. Birla, one of Gandhi's big financial backers. (As someone once said, 'it costs a great deal of money to keep Gandhiji living in poverty'.)[138] Birla reported to Gandhi that he had found his host to be 'no fire-eater'. Although 'badly informed about India', Churchill praised Gandhi's work for the Untouchables and said that he hoped the reforms would work: 'you have got the things now; make it a success and if you do I will advocate you getting much more'.[139] Yet if on this occasion he demonstrated the sympathy which Amery accused him of lacking, he would in the next years revert to the bitter tone that had characterized his campaign as a whole.

IV

The later 1930s saw Churchill focus more intensively on foreign policy. When MacDonald retired in 1935, Baldwin became Prime Minister again. 'Winston is rapidly transferring his interest from India to Air!' he wrote – although in fact Churchill had been pressing the government over the problem of air defence for some time.[140] In November Baldwin won another general election, but there was still no place for Churchill in the government; nor did this change when Neville Chamberlain succeeded to the premiership in 1937. In spite of these frustrations, Churchill was not as consistently oppositional as legend would suggest. Nevertheless, his overall stance against the appeasement of Germany and Italy was robust, and this was recognized in some apparently unlikely quarters. Nehru, after a visit to Britain, remarked: 'Irrespective of his politics, Mr Churchill is the ablest politician in England today. [. . .] I am astonished at the foreign policy of His Majesty's Government.'[141] (A few months earlier, when Nehru visited China, Churchill had sent him a goodwill message via a mutual friend.)[142] Churchill alienated some in the Dominions through his misguided support for Edward VIII at the time of the abdication crisis in 1936. The Governor General of Canada, Lord Tweedsmuir, reported to Baldwin that 'Winston has pretty well taken the place of Beaverbrook as Public Enemy No. 1'.[143] By 1939, though, Churchill's popularity at home had soared, as his warnings about the dangers of appeasement increasingly appeared vindicated. There are some signs that he was transcending his image as 'the personification of Empire do-or-die' in the USA as well. In July, *Time* magazine described him as 'An imperialist of the Rudyard Kipling school' and a 'reactionary' on domestic issues.

'But on the one subject of German aggression, now uppermost in British minds, he has followed such a straight, consistent line that in an emergency Winston Churchill might well become Britain's "Man of the Hour." '[144]

How central was the Empire to Churchill's strategic vision at this time? As war approached, he told General Edmund Ironside 'that sometimes he couldn't sleep at night thinking of our dangers, how all this wonderful Empire which had been built up so slowly and so steadily might all be dissipated in a minute'.[145] Irwin, after his Viceroyship ended, had returned to domestic politics and succeeded to the title of Lord Halifax. In 1937 he visited Hitler on behalf of the government and, as one junior minister noted, 'Winston could well discover the same ignominy in seeing a British Cabinet Minister travel wearily to Berchtesgaden, as he saw in the Viceroy of India receiving a man "striding half-naked up the steps of Government House".'[146] Yet, with uncharacteristic restraint, Churchill avoided comparisons of this type; memories of the India campaign were left to fade away.

Churchill had never been a great enthusiast for the League of Nations. Now, however, he spoke often of the requirement to preserve collective security via the League. This should be seen in the context of his efforts to court progressive opinion within Britain and gain Liberal and Labour support for a tough line against the Nazis. In turn, he sounded a moderate note when talking about imperial issues. When asked to broadcast in a series on 'Responsibilities of Empire' he stressed that the Empire power would never be used for any purpose inconsistent with the League's covenant.[147] In a further speech he denied that the Empire was held together by 'outworn Jingoism or grasping Imperialism'. Rather, 'If in these hours of anxiety [. . .] we feel the surge of unity and of duty thrilling the pulses of the British race, it is because we are bound together by principles, themes and conceptions which make their appeal not only to the British Empire, but to the conscience and to the genius of humanity.'[148] Churchill spoke too of the need for the unity of 'the English-Speaking Peoples'. His emphasis on this could be seen as part of an effort to woo US opinion. Churchill's first public reference to 'the unity of the English-speaking races' came in 1911 – when such ideas were already quite common – but it was only in the 1930s that it became one of his most dominant themes, other prominent

politicians having used similar language in the meantime.[149] It was
a seemingly racialized vision in which the Britons of the 'White
Dominions' and America were linked as part of a broader global
community with a common interest in defending freedom.[150]

Churchill did not exactly downplay the Empire in his rhetoric
at this time, but he could, perhaps, have emphasized it more. A
comparison with Amery is instructive here. Amery was a strong
opponent of the National Government's foreign policy. Like
Churchill, he was opposed to disarmament. Like Churchill, he
rejected the idea that Germany's lost colonies should be returned to
her without the consent of the inhabitants. Unlike him, though, he
wanted Britain to keep her distance from European diplomacy and
was scathing about the League of Nations. He wanted to strengthen
the power of the Empire by integrating it as an economic bloc,
while leaving Germany the power to build up her own bloc in
central Europe.[151] Churchill, for his part, ridiculed such views,
observing in a 1934 broadcast on 'The Causes of War':

> There are those who say, 'Let us ignore the continent of
> Europe. Let us leave it with its hatreds and its armaments to
> stew in its own juice, to fight out its own quarrels, and cause its
> own doom. Let us turn our backs upon this melancholy and
> alarming scene. Let us fix our gaze across the oceans and lead
> our own life in the midst of our peace-loving dominions and
> Empire.'
>
> Now there would be much to be said for this plan, if only
> we could unfasten the British islands from their rock founda-
> tions and could tow them three thousand miles across the
> Atlantic Ocean, and anchor them safely upon the smiling coasts
> of Canada.[152]

This was not Little Englandism. Churchill did not believe the
Empire was unimportant; rather he believed that the chief threat to
it came from Europe, not from more distant enemies.

Admittedly, Churchill did underrate other threats. 'But why
should there be a war with Japan?' he wrote in 1924 when battling
to keep naval spending down. 'I do not believe there is the slightest
chance of it in our lifetime.' (In the same memorandum he pointed
out, rather more far-sightedly, that the Japanese would find it very
hard to invade Australia.)[153] 'The Japanese war bogey leaves me

completely cold', he told a Cabinet committee in 1928.[154] In the 1930s he showed himself to be overly sanguine about the strength of Britain's naval base at Singapore, which was seen as an important symbol of Britain's commitment to the defence of Australia and New Zealand.[155] Arguably, though, his broad sense of priorities was correct. In the event of a world war, Britain would need to win first in Europe before turning her attention to the Far East. For him, the British Isles were indeed the starting point of policy, but it was not the case, as Amery liked to allege, that they were the sole end point too.

In July 1939 Mackenzie King – who had returned to office as Prime Minister in Ottawa four years earlier – heard a rumour that Chamberlain had brought Churchill into the government in London. He was terribly worried, because he believed that this would make war inevitable. It seemed possible at this time that the Soviet Union might in that event become an ally of Britain; what should Canada do? 'We would not like to stand behind Churchill – or Russia – it is all a terrible muddle.'[156] The rumour on this occasion proved false; it was only at the outbreak of war in September that Chamberlain appointed Churchill to his old post of First Lord of the Admiralty. But even after Germany invaded Poland, Mackenzie King held Churchill partly responsible for the war.[157] Robert Menzies, the new Prime Minister of Australia, was no unqualified admirer either. A supporter of appeasement, he had met Churchill at Chartwell in 1935 and found him 'an arresting person', but after seeing him in action in the Commons judged that the idol had feet of clay. He wrote in his diary: 'his theme is a constant repetition of "I told you so", and a first class man usually doesn't indulge in this luxury. If a first-rater has once said an important thing, he doesn't need to remind people that he's said it.'[158] Churchill could count on hostility from J. B. M. Hertzog, the South African Prime Minister, but sympathy from Smuts, now Hertzog's deputy. Hertzog's government split when war broke out, and he himself, who supported neutrality, was narrowly defeated in Parliament and replaced by Smuts. With South Africa at war, and Churchill back at the Admiralty, the latter sent a telegram to Smuts: 'I rejoice to feel that we are once again on commando together.'[159]

Churchill was not yet, of course, Prime Minister, and attitudes to him were not necessarily a proxy for attitudes to Britain and to the

Empire. Mackenzie King felt confidence in Chamberlain and Halifax (now Foreign Secretary).[160] His policy was that Canada would support Britain if she went to war, and when hostilities broke out he secured his Parliament's approval for this course; the Canadian declaration of war came a week after those of Britain and France. In Canberra there were no such formalities: for Menzies it was axiomatic that if Britain was at war then Australia was too. New Zealand's anti-appeasing Labour government under Michael Savage also joined the war immediately. But, if Churchill did emerge as Britain's new leader, there was no guarantee that he could count on unqualified support from all parts of the Empire for an uncompromising prosecution of the war. The next years would unleash conflicting forces promoting, on the one hand, imperial military cohesion in the short term and, on the other, the nationalist spirit and economic strain that would seal the Empire's eventual dissolution. It was Churchill's longstanding conviction that 'The British Empire will last so long and only so long as the British race is determined to maintain it.'[161] This revealing assertion, which seemed to assume that British willpower (or the lack of it) was the only factor in world politics, was now to be put to the test.

PART THREE

LIQUIDATION

7

UNDISMAYED AGAINST DISASTER, 1939–1942

A FEW days after the outbreak of war Churchill found the time, in the midst of his new tasks at the Admiralty, to inquire after the health of his old commander, General Sir Bindon Blood, who was now ninety-six. Blood's wife wrote afterwards to thank him for his call. She reported that 'my Bindon' was '*very* feeble & his brain [is] in a shocking muddle, but he knew you had phoned & how pleased he was he looked up and said "Winston is a grand man"'.¹ Blood lived on until the following year and died just six days after Churchill became Prime Minister. His longevity reminds us of the contrast in the scale of the threats the British Empire faced at the start of Churchill's career and at its high-water mark. Churchill himself joked to journalists that 'one may look back with envy to the past, and to the Victorian Age when great controversies were fought about what now seem to us vy minor matters'. At that time great states 'fought little wars' and 'the pugnacious instincts of our people were satisfied with such comparatively harmless objects as Cetewayo, the Mahdi, President Kruger and the Mad Mullah'. The social, economic and military problems of 'this shattering 20th Century' posed an entirely new challenge.² In his public rhetoric, Churchill emphasized the 'vast latent power of the British and French Empires' that equipped them to deal with the German threat. 'We have the freely-given ardent support of the twenty millions of British citizens in the self-governing Dominions of Canada, Australia, New Zealand and South Africa', he said in a broadcast after the first month of war. He added, rather less convincingly, 'We have, I believe, the heart and moral conviction of India on our side.'³

Churchill quickly established a phenomenal work-rate, although he was no slave to formality. One late-night visitor to the Admiralty found him walking about in his socks, smoking a big cigar and with a whisky and soda on his desk; he seemed a little drunk.[4] As ever in need of money, he even found time – with the help of assistants – to labour on his *History of the English-Speaking Peoples*, although it was not completed until after the war. His political fortunes continued to rise, bolstered by strong performances on the radio and in the Commons. Harold Nicolson described how in one speech 'he sounded every note from deep preoccupation to flippancy, from resolution to sheer boyishness. One could feel the spirits of the House rising with every word. [. . .] In those twenty minutes Churchill brought himself nearer the post of Prime Minister than he has ever been before.'[5]

I

Churchill's preoccupation with the submarine menace brought Ireland firmly back into the field of his concern at the oubreak of war. The IRA was engaged in a bombing campaign on the British mainland. 'If they throw bombs in London,' he asked, 'why should they not supply petrol to U-boats?'[6] As Churchill had feared, moreover, De Valera's government committed Éire – as the Free State was officially named in 1937 – to neutrality. It was, however, willing to provide covert cooperation to the British (and Éire also remained a rich source of recruits). But Churchill did not recognize Ireland's right to remain neutral in the first place. Its status was ambiguous, the 1937 constitution failing to make clear whether or not it was a republic. On Churchill's reading of the situation, Éire was technically committed by the King's declaration of war. 'It is not a Dominion', he wrote. 'They themselves repudiate this idea. It is certainly under the Crown. [. . .] Legally I believe they are at "at war but skulking".'[7] At the end of October he told the War Cabinet that Ireland 'should be told clearly that she was at a parting of the ways, and it should be brought home to her what she stood to lose in being declared a foreign power'. If things 'came to such a pass that Eire was expelled from the Commonwealth', Britain should insist on regaining the so-called treaty ports. (These ports, Queenstown, Berehaven and Lough Swilly, had been reserved for Britain's use in 1921 but had been returned to Éire, against Churchill's urging, in 1938.) Churchill's argument had no effect, however. Chamberlain pointed out that De Valera was probably right to claim that no Irish government could survive if it departed from neutrality, and seizure of the ports would be seen in the USA and India as 'highhanded and unwarranted'.[8] During a subsequent meeting with the secret services Churchill urged 'that complete censorship should be imposed on Eire and when opposition was raised on the grounds that this might antagonise the Irish government, he said dramatically, "What is that to the sinking of one of our warships?"'[9]

His table-thumping approach was not to everyone's taste. Anthony Eden, the Secretary of State for the Dominions, complained privately about Churchill's wish to 'drive Eire out of the Empire'. Eden, who had resigned as Chamberlain's Foreign Secretary in 1938, was a political ally of Churchill, but as Oliver Harvey, one of his confidants in the Foreign Office, recorded: 'A.E. is beginning to doubt whether Churchill could ever be P.M. so bad is his judgement in such matters.'[10] Nevertheless, Churchill's outbursts must be kept in proportion, not least in relation to Eden's own epic tantrums. In part, they were a way of venting emotion at a time of great stress, and he was usually persuaded to see reason. Security cooperation from Dublin and the failure to find evidence of U-boat activity on Ireland's west coast in due course assuaged his fears.[11] The IRA, which was the enemy of the Irish government as much as of the British, was ruthlessly suppressed by De Valera. However, Churchill did not buy the idea that Irish unification would end bitterness towards Britain and bring Éire into the war on the side of the Allies. At the start of the war he wrote, 'They [the Irish] will not unite at the present time, and we cannot in any circumstances sell the loyalists of Northern Ireland.'[12]

According to Eden, 'Winston's attitude over India' was 'just as bad' as his attitude to Ireland.[13] One of Churchill's decisions at the Admiralty casts interesting light on his approach to Indian issues. A few weeks into the war he wrote a note on 'Employment of Indians or Colonial Natives in the Royal Navy'. He began with an apparently unambiguous statement: 'There must be no discrimination on grounds of race or colour.' Yet he continued, 'In practice much inconvenience would arise if this theoretical equality had many examples.' Cases should be judged on their merits – that is to say, 'from the point of view of smooth administration'. He concluded: 'I cannot see any objections to Indians serving on HM ships where they are qualified and needed, or if their virtues so deserve rising to be Admirals of the Fleet. But not too many of them please.'[14] This final sentence plainly undermined his initial declaration, for if there was to be *no* discrimination how could the numbers be kept down? The ambivalence was in some ways more revealing than notorious remarks such as his description of the Indians as 'the beastliest people in the world next to the Germans'.[15] It perfectly encapsulated the double standard whereby nominal racial equality within the Empire was vitiated by the supposedly 'practical' considerations that would attend its full enforcement. Individuals' qualifications in the end took second place to 'smooth administration', which too many promotions based on merit might disrupt. This was certainly not apartheid, but it was an official endorsement of the glass ceiling. Not surprisingly, no Indian rose to become an Admiral of the Fleet in the Royal Navy during World War II.

When it came to Indian politics, the focus of Eden's comment, Churchill did not trouble to pay lip service to progressive attitudes. Lord Linlithgow, the conservative, stiff-mannered Viceroy, had with tactless constitutional correctness simply announced that India was at war, without consulting its political leaders or the governments of the provinces. The nationalists were divided. Gandhi, of course, opposed violence but was prepared to give moral support to the British unconditionally. The official Congress leadership, by contrast, was potentially prepared to support the war effort if its conditions on the future of India were met. They were not to be satisfied, though, with Linlithgow's reiteration, coupled with other assurances, that Dominion status remained the British aim. The Congress provincial governments resigned, and it was in due course resolved that Britain was 'carrying on the war fundamentally for Imperialist ends', to which Congress would not become a party.[16] M. A. Jinnah's Muslim League supported the war, however. Jinnah told Linlithgow that 'he was extremely doubtful as to the capacity of India and Indians to look after themselves. [. . .] If the British should by any chance be beaten in the war and driven out of India, India would break into a hundred pieces in three months and lie open, in addition, to external invasion.'[17] The Marquess of Zetland, the Secretary of State for India, pressed Linlithgow to put forward new constitutional proposals to win over Congress. When the issue was discussed by ministers in February 1940, Churchill asked: 'Was it fair that Parliament and the War Cabinet should have to involve themselves in these complications in the midst of a great war?' Linlithgow would doubtless have to see Gandhi, he said, but should not go beyond previous statements. Zetland and Linlithgow had told Gandhi that communal divisions must be settled before Dominion status could proceed. However:

> The First Lord said that he did not share the anxiety to encourage and promote unity between the Hindu and Moslem communities. Such unity was, in fact, almost out of the realm of practical politics, while, if it were to be brought about, the immediate result would be that the united communities would join in showing us the door. He regarded the Hindu–Moslem feud as a bulwark of British rule in India.[18]

The traditional justification for the Raj was that only British rule could keep the different communities from each other's throats. Churchill was now openly arguing that they had to be kept at each other's throats in order to sustain British rule.

On 24 March, at its annual meeting in Lahore, the Muslim League took a momentous step. It passed a resolution declaring that 'the areas in which the Muslims are numerically in a majority, as in the north-western and eastern zones of India, should be grouped to constitute "independent states"'.[19] Perhaps, in making this demand for partition, Jinnah was simply trying to acquire a bargaining chip in order to improve the position of Muslims within a future united India; but it took on a life of its own, and the stage was set for the eventual creation of Pakistan. Zetland was disturbed by the Lahore resolution, but Churchill was sanguine. 'His view was that the awakening of a new spirit of self-reliance and self-assertiveness on the part of the different communities, of which the Moslem League's resolution was a sign, constituted a hopeful development.'[20] According to the Chancellor, Sir John Simon, who was himself something of a hardliner, 'Winston rejoiced in the quarrel which had broken out afresh between Hindus and Moslems, said he hoped it would remain bitter and bloody and was glad that we had made the suggestion of Dominion status which was acting as a cat among the pigeons.'[21] The Cabinet deferred any major step for the time being.

II

The developing war soon pushed imperial issues into the background. On 8 April the Germans invaded Norway and Denmark. The Cabinet, after some dithering, sent troops for operations at Narvik and Trondheim. These proved to be a fiasco but Churchill, who had by now been appointed chairman of the government's Military Co-ordination Committee, successfully escaped the blame. In an unpublished draft of his memoirs he confessed 'it was a marvel – I really do not know how – [that] I survived and maintained my position in public esteem while all the blame was thrown on poor Mr Chamberlain'.[22] In the Commons debate that followed the disaster, Leo Amery – who had not been included in the government at the outbreak of war – delivered one of the most dramatic lines against the Prime Minister. Sensing he had the mood of the House with him, he 'cast prudence to the winds' and quoted Oliver Cromwell's words in dismissal of the Long Parliament: 'You have sat too long here for any good you have been doing. Depart, I say, and let us have done with you. In the name of God, go.'[23] In the vote that followed the government's majority was slashed to 81, and a reconstruction of the government appeared inevitable. Chamberlain hoped to remain Prime Minister, though, and it was only when it became clear that the Labour Party would not serve under him as part of a coalition that he determined to resign. The two plausible successors – as the only candidates likely to be acceptable to Labour – were Churchill and Halifax. The latter was Chamberlain's favoured candidate, but he ruled himself out, not least on the grounds that it would be hard for him to lead the government from the House of Lords. On 10 May, as Germany launched its invasion of Belgium and Holland, the King asked Churchill to form a government. In a justly famous passage he recalled how, on his first night as Prime Minister, he went to bed at 3 a.m. with a deep sense of relief: 'I felt as if I were walking with destiny, and that all my past life had been but a preparation for this hour and for this trial.'[24] Trial it was, for he was quickly forced to take some appallingly tough strategic decisions, having to balance French requests for more fighter squadrons against the danger, as he put it, of denuding 'still further the heart of the Empire'.[25]

Churchill created a broad-based administration stretching, as he boasted, 'from Lord Lloyd of Dolobran on the Right to Miss [Ellen] Wilkinson on the Left'.[26] Chamberlain remained in the Cabinet and continued to lead the Conservative Party until his resignation through terminal ill-health in the autumn. Lloyd became Colonial Secretary, although he too would be dead within a year. Amery became Secretary of State for India and Burma, and Lord Caldecote Dominions Secretary, although he was quickly replaced by Lord Cranborne. Reaction to the new government was generally positive but not universally so. The Labour Party conference, which was meeting at Bournemouth, debated whether or not to endorse its leaders' decision to join the coalition. Emrys Hughes, a future MP who was to publish a sceptical biography of Churchill after the war, spoke in opposition. 'Churchill would tell you honestly that he does stand for imperialism, which this Conference is against. [. . .] He is out for an imperialist policy, and so is Lord Lloyd, who is now in the Government.' Hughes was followed by J. J. Toole of the Bury Labour Party, who boldly declared, to cries of protest, that Churchill was 'the one man who has been right' about Hitlerism. He added: 'If it is an imperialist war, it is Hitler's imperialist war.'[27] The conference voted overwhelmingly to join the coalition.

The reaction throughout the Empire was broadly positive. On taking office, Churchill fired off telegrams to all the Dominion premiers. Churchill reserved the most personal touch for his 'faithful comrade' Smuts: 'It is a comfort for me to feel that we shall be together in this hard and long trek [. . .] and that we shall make a strong laager for all beside the water at the end.' To De Valera he wrote that he looked forward 'with confidence to continued friendship between our two countries'. All this was for public consumption, so it is hardly surprising that the replies were supportive (with even De Valera reciprocating Churchill's message 'cordially'). We can, however, believe Smuts's avowal that he was 'deeply moved'.[28] Mackenzie King was rather less pleased by the change of leadership. Chamberlain, he told his diary, 'would have been a safer guide in the long run than Churchill. I have more confidence in his judgement and guidance'.[29] He, though, was to change his opinion of Churchill quite radically. Furthermore, the new leader of the Canadian Tory Party, which Mackenzie King had just trounced heavily in a general election, proved 'eager to jump on the Empire defense band wagon of Winston Churchill'.[30]

Elsewhere, it was widely felt that – as Jamaica's *Daily Gleaner* put it – 'Under prevailing conditions, Mr Winston Churchill's aggressiveness contrives to make him an admirable individual for the chief position in the government.'[31] The *Canberra Times* said, 'The choice of the new leader was obvious, for Mr Churchill has warned his country for many years of what has now come, and if his services had been availed of earlier, our peril to-day would have been less.'[32] The *Palestine Post* argued, 'It is neither an accident nor a paradox that Labour should have signified its willingness to serve under one who has always stood for a conception of Empire diametrically opposed to its own, for Mr Churchill – Tory, Liberal, Diehard and, since 1933, the foremost foe of Hitlerism – has never been a party man in the narrow sense.'[33] The British-run Calcutta *Statesman* claimed that 'those who have discussed India with him since [he joined the government] last September are aware he is no reactionary', and added optimistically, 'A Government of which he is the head can be relied upon to assist in finding a practical and popular solution of the Indian problem.'[34] Nirad Chaudhuri, a writer whose views on the Raj were later to spark controversy, caused bafflement amongst his friends by hanging a picture of Churchill on his wall.[35]

According to a summary prepared for the India Office, 'The Burmese press welcomed the change of Cabinet and considered the election of Mr Churchill, most hated and feared by Hitler, as the head of affairs a right move at the right time, for it was contended that Mr Churchill was more dashing and decisive than his predecessor and that he could be trusted to make the war effort of the allies more daring and energetic.' But there were also qualifications. The *New Mandalay Sun* argued, 'Although the British are preaching about the evils of Nazism, they do not seem to have realized that for them it is better to be a member of the Empire constituting independent countries than to be under the Nazis. If a definite promise of independence after the war were made, then the subject nations would not grudge to train in the art of fighting with a view to fighting the Nazis.'[36] In a press article in July Nehru welcomed the fact that Chamberlain had been replaced by 'the far abler and more virile Mr Churchill', but still described the war as 'purely imperialist'. Complaining of the British decision to conciliate Japan by (temporarily) shutting the Burma Road supply route to China, he wrote: 'There has been enough appeasement of the aggressor. We want none of it, whether the aggressor is German or Italian or Japanese or British.'[37] The comparison of the British with these other powers was invidious, but Nehru did at least make clear that, were he an Englishman, he would not accept Gandhi's advice to lay down arms, knowing that 'the alternative would be slavery'.[38] Meanwhile, German radio propaganda tried to turn Churchill's imperial past against him, using tendentious quotation from *My Early Life* to depict him as cowardly, cynical and brutal.[39]

On 13 May, in his first speech to the Commons as Prime Minister, Churchill declared 'I have nothing to offer but blood, toil, tears and sweat.' He said boldly that his aim was victory. As he continued, he equated the fate of the Empire with that of human progress, stating that without victory there could be no survival: 'Let that be realised; no survival for the British Empire, no survival for all that the British Empire has stood for, no survival for the urge and impulse of the ages, that mankind will move forward towards its goal.'[40] Six days later, after the Germans had broken through the French defences, he spoke to the British people by radio, 'in a solemn hour for the life of our country, of our Empire, of our Allies, and, above all, of the cause of Freedom'.[41] Then came the near-miraculous escape of the British Expeditionary Force from Dunkirk, completed on 4 June. That day, in his 'fight them on the beaches' speech, he emphasized that 'we shall never surrender. And even if, which I do not for a moment believe, this island or a large part of it were subjugated and starving, then our Empire beyond the seas, armed and guarded by the British Fleet, would carry on the struggle, until, in God's good time, the New World, with all its power and might, steps forth to the rescue and the liberation of the Old.'[42] This final remark was important. Churchill's message was not merely one of defiance, but also held out the hope of ultimate victory, even if the worst-case scenario should come to pass. Enemy propagandists leapt on the phrase, twisting the words in order to suggest that Churchill and his fellow 'plutocratic warmongers' were on the verge of fleeing Britain to conduct the war from territories elsewhere.[43]

On 18 June, after France's army had collapsed and her new government had asked the Germans for an armistice, Churchill made a further speech, to which no superlatives can do justice:

The whole fury and might of the enemy must very soon be turned on us. Hitler knows that he will have to break us in this Island or lose the war. [. . .] Let us therefore brace ourselves to our duties, and so bear ourselves that, if the British Empire and its Commonwealth last for a thousand years, men will still say, 'This was their finest hour.'[44]

In a broadcast in July, warmly welcomed by Australian and New Zealand newspapers, he said that 'all depends now upon the whole life-strength of the British race in every part of the world'.[45] In his famous speech in August during the Battle of Britain ('Never in the field of human conflict . . .') he reminded his listeners of how, during the crisis of May, 'The British nation and the British Empire, finding themselves alone, stood undismayed against disaster.'[46] In October, accepting the leadership of the Conservative Party upon Chamberlain's retirement, he claimed: 'Alone among the nations of the world we have found the means to combine Empire and liberty.'[47] These speeches had a global reach. At this time, Nelson Mandela was at the University College of Fort Hare (the only institution of its kind in South Africa open to black people). In his memoirs he recalled how he and his fellow students would 'huddle round an old radio' late at night to listen to Churchill speaking.[48]

Imperial rhetoric came easily to Churchill. As one scholar has put it, 'If talking about a chip shop in Salford, Churchill would find a way to mention how important its chips were to the Empire.'[49] Sometimes he had to be reminded when it was inappropriate. Halifax, appointed ambassador to Washington at the end of 1940, recalled a wartime occasion when Churchill addressed US legislators. Beforehand, the influential Republican Senator Arthur Vandenberg told Halifax, 'We should all get on much better if you British would stop talking about the British Empire.' When Churchill began his speech in his usual patriotic manner Halifax, by his own account, 'managed to convey telepathically' what Vandenberg had said. 'Whereupon Mr Churchill, turning towards the Senator, went on: "The British Empire – or the Commonwealth of Nations. We keep trade labels to suit all tastes." '[50]

Yet Churchill's apparently almost reflexive use of the word 'Empire' should not distract our attention from the selective way in which he deployed it. His efforts to equate the British Empire with liberty led to some interesting silences. In the 'finest hour' speech, for example, he emphasized the support received from the Dominions, 'who are absolutely free to choose their course, but are absolutely devoted to the ancient motherland'. Menzies, Mackenzie King, Peter Fraser of New Zealand, and 'that wonderful man' Smuts were all 'elected on wide franchises' and thus represented the will of their respective peoples, he said. (Of course, this was hardly true of the franchise in South Africa.) But he made no mention of India, the African colonies, or other territories whose peoples had not been asked for their consent. Clearly, in view of the Indian National Congress's position, it would have been hard for him to reiterate wholeheartedly his earlier claim that Britain had that country's moral support. And his statement that the Dominions were free to choose their own path sat uncomfortably with his attitude to Irish neutrality.

Furthermore, we need not necessarily conclude from his repeated invocations of Empire that his vision for the war as a whole was an imperial one. Of course, imperial resources were highly welcome to him. 'It will be a splendid episode in the history of the Empire if Australia, New Zealand & Canadian troops defend the motherland against invasion', he wrote when Menzies offered soldiers.[51] But in early July 1940 he gave his sanction to a recommendation by the Chiefs of Staff prioritizing the defence of the Middle East, implicitly over that of Singapore and Australasia, a reversal of pre-war strategy. He did assure Fraser and Menzies that if the Japanese invaded their countries 'on a large scale' Britain would cut its losses in the Mediterranean and 'proceed in good time to your aid'. However, the promise was a vague one, intended to offer his fellow Prime Ministers the assurance that it was safe for them to send more troops to help him.[52] Churchill's method – and it was undoubtedly sound strategy – was not to rush all possible help to under-defended outposts, but rather to exploit the imperial periphery in order to defend the metropole. The more he talked up the Empire the easier it was to achieve this, for, if he could offer the Dominions little concrete assistance, at least they could still believe he was thinking about their interests. As George Orwell observed in 1943, it was 'politically necessary to flatter the Dominions, which involves playing down the British'.[53]

Hitler of course was eager to make play with the Empire's

difficulties. Addressing the Reichstag in July, he spoke of his distaste for British leaders and especially Churchill. 'I feel a deep disgust for this type of unscrupulous politician who wrecks whole nations and States. [. . .] Mr Churchill ought perhaps, for once, to believe me when I prophesy that a great Empire will be destroyed – an Empire which it was never my intention to destroy or even to harm.'[54] Supposedly, Germany would be willing to offer Britain peace 'with 95% of the Empire left intact'.[55] His protestations, it hardly need be said, were unconvincing. True, he had expressed some admiration for the British Empire in *Mein Kampf*, arguing that German Great War propagandists had underestimated it woefully. Indeed 'I, as a man of Germanic blood, would, in spite of everything, rather see India under English rule than under any other.'[56] But in 1937, at a conference with his top military leaders, he made it clear that he did not regard the Empire as 'unshakeable' and that he regarded the possibility of its disintegration with equanimity. 'The emphasis on the British Crown as the symbol of the unity of the Empire was already an admission that, in the long run, the Empire could not maintain its position by power politics', he said.[57] He, of course, had imperial designs of his own in Europe.[58] 'No one can say how far Herr Hitler's empire will extend before this war is over,' Churchill told MPs, 'but I have no doubt that it will pass away as swiftly as, and perhaps more swiftly than, did Napoleon's Empire, although, of course, without any of its glitter or its glory.'[59]

III

Throughout the summer of 1940, Churchill did his utmost to secure US involvement in the war. With isolationist sentiment in Congress at his back, and hoping for re-election in November, President Roosevelt offered warm words in private but little tangible aid. Churchill cautioned Mackenzie King, 'We must be careful not to let Americans view too complacently [the] prospect of a British collapse, out of which they would get the British Fleet and the guardianship of the British Empire, minus Great Britain.'[60] Soon, however, a deal was struck whereby Britain would receive fifty old American destroyers in exchange for granting the USA ninety-nine-year leases on military bases in Newfoundland and the Caribbean.

The diplomatic significance was much greater than the value of the hardware, which was negligible. 'Undoubtedly', Churchill observed with satisfaction, 'this process means that these two great organizations of the English-speaking democracies, the British Empire and the United States, will have to be somewhat mixed up together in some of their affairs for their mutual and general benefit.'[61] One radical black writer later complained that, as a consequence of the agreement, land was 'alienated from the Caribbean people without any consultation with them, or with such limited representative governments as had been permitted them by their British rulers'.[62] Actually, Churchill did make some efforts to live up to his public promise of consultation and to protect the local people's interests, although the Caribbean governments were indeed far from representative.[63] Forthright action was perhaps at any rate forgivable in the circumstances.

As ever, Ireland was a complicating factor in Anglo-US relations, given the large Irish-American population. In June the War Cabinet discussed the suggestion made by Smuts that Britain should occupy the Irish Atlantic ports by force. In contrast to his earlier attitude, Churchill said that, although this might be done as a last resort, 'it would be unwise at this moment to take any action that might compromise our position with the United States of America'.[64] Two days later, in contrast to *his* earlier position, the still-influential Chamberlain further raised the possibility of seizing the ports, but urged that a tough approach to De Valera should be coupled with a declaration in favour of Irish unity. In a 'passionate speech' Churchill opposed any coercion of Northern Ireland.[65] 'He would not urge those who had worked [at] self-government loyally within the Empire to join with those who wished to stay outside it.'[66] Nevertheless, the British did now offer De Valera a declaration 'accepting the principle of a United Ireland' in exchange for the use of Irish ports and the stationing of troops and aircraft in Éire. In early July, De Valera turned the deal down, believing that, as the British would not force the Unionists into a united Ireland against their will, a declaration in principle was not worth having. He may also have suspected that the British were going to be beaten.[67] In a draft cable to Roosevelt, never sent, Churchill wrote, 'De Valera and his Party are reconciling themselves to throwing in their lot with the Germans, ~~whom they think are bound to win~~.'[68] *Churchill*

Can Unite Ireland was the title of a pamphlet published that summer by the Irish Republican writer Jim Phelan. It was a vain hope.[69]

In Ireland there were plenty willing to believe 'that Mr Churchill hates Ireland and would not be sorry to set the clock back with a strong hand'.[70] He himself did not help matters when he stated in the Commons in November that Britain's inability to make use of 'the South and West Coasts of Ireland to refuel our flotillas and aircraft and thus protect the trade by which Ireland as well as Great Britain lives' was 'a most heavy and grievous burden and one which should never have been placed on our shoulders, broad though they be'.[71] These remarks found strong support in the House of Commons and the British press, although this was not unanimous: the *National Review* thought Churchill was now paying the price for his earlier support of Irish self-government.[72] Meanwhile, his comments created a storm in Ireland, and undid some of the positive effects that his famous radio broadcasts had achieved there earlier in the year.[73] Sir John Maffey, the UK representative in Dublin, explained them away as 'typically Churchillian', telling the Irish that the Dominions Office had not been asked for its opinion beforehand.[74] In his memoirs, Churchill acknowledged that Britain ultimately survived without the ports – the importance of which declined after America entered the war – but blamed the lack of them for the loss of 'Many a ship and many a life'.[75] A few months later Anglo-Irish relations were further soured by a proposal to extend conscription to Northern Ireland. The plan was dropped, but not before Churchill had told the Irish High Commissioner, as the latter recorded, that 'he had drawn the sword and was definitely opposed to us'.[76]

By the end of 1940 Churchill could breathe a little easier. The Battle of Britain had been won. (As it raged, 'The P.M. expressed delight at the success of our pilots, but said, "It is terrible – terrible – that the British Empire should have been gambled on this." ')[77] Abandoning the attempt to achieve air superiority prior to invasion, the Luftwaffe shifted its attention to the bombing of cities. One supposedly humorous German magazine cover showed Churchill looking out over a blitzed landscape and saying 'Our Empire is so vast, what does it matter if a small island burns down!'[78] In spite of the horrors of the Blitz, the British now enjoyed their first taste of success. In December Roosevelt promised Lend-Lease aid to avert UK bankruptcy. At the start of 1941 British forces scored brilliant victories over the Italians in Libya. When Robert Menzies arrived in Britain in February, he found Churchill in vigorous form, denouncing De Valera as 'a murderer & perjurer' and confident of victory. 'Winston is completely certain of America's full help, of her participation in a Japanese war, and of Roosevelt's passionate determination to stamp out the Nazi menace from the earth.'[79]

The Australian premier's own relationship with Churchill was not an easy one. During the summer of 1940 Menzies wobbled briefly, privately urging a compromise peace before finally pledging to support Britain no matter what the cost.[80] That autumn, a raid on Dakar by British and Free French forces was botched. Menzies was not told about the operation until later, even though an Australian cruiser had taken part. He sent Churchill a 'hectoring' telegram complaining about the lack of consultation and criticizing the 'half-hearted' nature of the attack. Churchill was deeply offended, taking it as a personal assault on his war leadership.[81] Once he had calmed down, he welcomed, or so he said, the prospect of a visit by Menzies to London for consultations. Menzies travelled to Britain via Singapore and the Middle East, where he received a rapturous reception from Australian troops. 'Chips' Channon MP, meeting him in Cairo, recorded that he was 'jolly, rubicund, witty, only 46 with a rapier-like intelligence and gifts as a raconteur'.[82] Menzies was alarmed at the vulnerability of Singapore, and a key purpose of the trip was to seek assurances about the defence of Australia. But that was not his sole motivation. His United Australia Party was reliant for its survival on the support of two independent MPs, and to leave for an extended period might put his position in danger. All the same, the Anglophile Menzies seems to have been sick of domestic manoeuvrings and eager to make a name for himself at the centre of the Empire.

Before his departure, S. M. Bruce, Canberra's High Commissioner in London, had given him a warning. Power in London was increasingly concentrated in Churchill's hands, and although the Prime Minister would treat his Australian counterpart with courtesy, attempts 'to pin him down to definite discussions of fundamental war policy' would lead to him becoming 'discursive and elusive'. Menzies, therefore, would have to choose between forcing 'a considerable show down' and leaving Britain at the end of his mission 'with a sense of frustration'.[83] The point was soon proved. Mussolini had invaded Greece the previous October and German intervention now looked imminent too. Would Britain respond to the Greek requests for help? A few days after his arrival, Menzies recorded a 'Momentous discussion' with Churchill 'about [the] defence of Greece, largely with Australian & New Zealand troops' to be taken from the Middle Eastern theatre.[84] The next day he attended a Cabinet meeting which discussed the possibility of a Balkan expedition. Menzies was 'evidently doubtful, but the general sense' of the meeting 'was to go ahead with it', seemingly as much for moral reasons as strategic ones.[85] The final decision was not taken until early March, by which time the military prospects had deteriorated. Eden (now Foreign Secretary), who was in the Middle East, nevertheless concluded an agreement with the Greeks to give them aid, essentially pledging Australasian troops without consulting their governments. Menzies was angry but accepted the position of Churchill (who had doubts of his own) that there was no backing out. The Cabinet requested from Eden a 'precise military appreciation' of the chances of success; it didn't get one, but approved the expedition anyway.[86] British ministers had been bounced; so had Menzies. The campaign was a disaster. Not only did the British and Dominion troops have to withdraw from Greece after Hitler attacked in April (11,000 men were lost) but the Middle Eastern front was seriously weakened. With the Germans under Erwin Rommel as ·a new force in North Africa, the British were swept back to Tobruk.[87] Menzies had spoken 'plain words' but they had had little effect.[88]

He had equally little luck in his bid to secure air reinforcements for Australia and Singapore and to get specific commitments about the naval defence of the Far East.[89] 'What irresponsible rubbish these Antipodeans talk!' was the private response of Alexander Cadogan, the Permanent Secretary at the Foreign Office.[90] Convinced he could make a contribution to solving the Irish problem, Menzies visited De Valera in Dublin; he liked 'Dev', 'but thought him and all Irishmen crazy',[91] and the impact of his interference was probably only to annoy Churchill. The Australian's morale-boosting speeches to the British people were a success, though, and he was a hit with the press, which did no damage to his barrage-balloon-sized ego. He was not without admiration for Churchill, writing to his own government that the British Prime Minister combined 'remarkable fighting and driving qualities with an astonishing mastery of the details of both plans and equipment'.[92] Yet he also had serious doubts. He told his diary: 'The Cabinet is deplorable – dumb men most of whom disagree with Winston but none of whom dare to say so. [. . .] Winston is a dictator; he cannot be overruled, and his colleagues fear him.'[93] Visiting Lloyd George at his home in Surrey, Menzies discovered that 'we had many ideas in common'. Menzies may not have shared – at least not fully – the former Prime Minister's defeatism and desire for a compromise peace. But the two men could agree that Churchill was a poor strategist, a weak organizer, and that he 'should be at the helm instead of touring the bombed areas'. They also believed that the War Cabinet '*must* contain a Dominions man, for the Dominions type of mind is essential'.[94]

There was little doubt in Menzies's mind that this 'Dominions man' ought to be one R. Menzies. After his return to Australia in May, he continued to press the idea, telling his Cabinet, 'Mr Churchill has no conception of the British Dominions as separate entities. Furthermore, the more distant the problem from the heart of the Empire, the less he thinks of it.'[95] The idea of a permanent Dominion representative found press support in London, but, as Menzies acknowledged, neither Canada nor South Africa was interested, 'Smuts going so far as to say [. . .] that we Dominion Prime Ministers should mind our own business and leave Churchill to mind his.'[96] Peter Fraser thought the proposal 'absurd'.[97] Churchill himself worked hard to frustrate both it and the proposal for a full-scale Imperial War Cabinet that was being floated concurrently. It has been suggested that, having first made his way into the War Cabinet, Menzies aimed to use his position to seize 10 Downing Street for himself.[98] The concrete evidence for this is slight, but even if some such idea did cross his mind, he was only ever an irritant to Churchill, not a serious rival. In August, having failed in his efforts to create a National Government in Australia, and facing growing opposition from within his own party, Menzies resigned. Soon afterwards the Labour Party came to power under John Curtin. A few days before Menzies stood down, Mackenzie King, who was in London, recorded a conversation at Chequers: 'Churchill [. . .] spoke very strongly against Menzies. [. . .] In

speaking strongly, he said he loathes his own people. He says you
cannot hope to be Prime Minister of a people you don't like.'[99]

This was harsh; Menzies came back as Prime Minister in 1949
and stayed in office for sixteen years, hardly possible if he 'loathed'
the Australians. But his criticisms of Churchill's war leadership were
by no means wholly fair either. True, there was much to complain
about, especially Churchill's habit of keeping the top brass up late
at night for long, rambling meetings when they (but not he) had to
be up early the next morning. A fair assessment came from Labour
Party leader and War Cabinet member Clement Attlee, who in his
memoirs challenged Menzies's view. 'Winston was sometimes an
awful nuisance because he started all sorts of hares, but he always
accepted the verdict of the Chiefs of Staff when it came to it, and
it was a great advantage for him to be there driving them all the
time', he recalled. 'Your advisers always tend to say "It can't be
done", and it's as well to have someone who'll tell them it can.'[100]
Churchill made serious mistakes but he was not, as Menzies alleged,
a dictator. The Greek episode actually proved this, as it resulted
from the Cabinet collectively accepting bad advice from the men
on the spot, not from Churchill as an individual overriding other
people's judgement.

IV

Menzies was no lone critic, however. The war was not going well
and Churchill had to work constantly to maintain his position in
Parliament. The German invasion of the Soviet Union in June 1941
brought Britain another ally, but the bigger fish, America, had still
to be landed. In August, Churchill met Roosevelt at a landmark
conference held on board the US cruiser *Augusta* and the British
battle-cruiser *Prince of Wales* at Placentia Bay, Newfoundland.
Churchill would greatly have welcomed a US declaration of war,
but had to be content with the promulgation of the Atlantic Charter,
a joint statement of broad principles about the future of the world.
FDR was eager to use the conference to promote an anti-imperialist
agenda. Although the question of colonial freedom was not discussed
explicitly, two points of the Charter were of crucial significance in
relation to imperial questions.[101]

As finally agreed, Point 4 stated that Britain and America would 'endeavour, with due respect for their existing obligations, to further the enjoyment by all States [. . .] of access, on equal terms, to the trade and to the raw materials of the world which are needed for their economic prosperity'.[102] The original US draft of this was clearly intended as an assault on the imperial preference system, a form of trade discrimination. Churchill's friend Lord Beaverbrook, now Minister of Supply, who was at the conference, was highly concerned.[103] Churchill's own position, as a former free trader, was more than a little ironic. Although he had not been keen on the Ottawa Agreements, he knew that to tear them up without consulting the Dominions would provoke outrage. He was now, furthermore, leader of the Conservative Party. He told Mackenzie King: 'When the tariffs were discussed, while he, himself, was not sympathetic to the Conservative position, he nevertheless had felt it his duty to stand up for it.'[104] The British successfully pressed for the inclusion of the qualifying words about 'existing obligations' and for the removal of a reference to 'discrimination'.[105] This was achieved in spite of the powerful lever the Americans possessed in the form of British dependence on their economic aid. But in spite of Churchill's efforts to protect the interests of the Dominions, he had not actually consulted them on the text of the Charter before its release. Mackenzie King, often touchy about such matters, observed that there had been enough time to run it past the British Cabinet but that Canada had been 'ignored'. He complained to Malcolm MacDonald, Britain's High Commissioner, 'It was the way the British lost their friends, wanting them in foul weather and ignoring them in fair.'[106]

Point 3 of the Atlantic Charter was also to prove controversial, although its text was settled easily enough. Under it, the two governments declared that 'they respect the right of all peoples to choose the form of government under which they will live; and they wish to see sovereign rights and self-government restored to those who have been forcibly deprived of them'.[107] Understandably, some inhabitants of those parts of the Empire that did not have self-government took 'all peoples' to include them. Burmese leaders initially gave the Charter a 'whole-hearted welcome [. . .] on the assumption that it meant full post-war self-government for Burma'.[108] (The country did already have some limited self-government.) The response to the Charter within Churchill's coalition was divided. 'We shall no doubt pay dearly in the end for all this fluffy flapdoodle', wrote Amery.[109] But when Attlee addressed the West African Students' Union in London he emphasized that the Charter's principles would apply 'to all peoples of the world'. He was rewarded with 'loud and prolonged applause', and the student who moved the vote of thanks said, 'West Africans were proud of the Empire and were pleased to march shoulder to shoulder with the British to fight this war.'[110] Churchill acted quickly to squash the raised hopes after he returned to England. He told Amery that he was 'sure' that Attlee 'did not intend to suggest, e.g., that the natives of Nigeria or of East Africa could by a majority vote choose the form of Government under which they live, or the Arabs by such a vote expel the Jews from Palestine. It is evident that prior obligations require to be considered and respected, and that circumstances alter cases.'[111]

In September, Churchill secured the Cabinet's agreement that the Charter 'was not intended to deal with the internal affairs of the British Empire'. (Attlee apparently failed to stand up for his earlier fine words.)[112] Churchill then made his position clear publicly in a statement in the Commons. 'At the Atlantic meeting, we had in mind, primarily, the restoration of the sovereignty, self-government and national life of the States and nations of Europe now under the Nazi yoke, and the principles governing any alterations in the territorial boundaries which may have to be made', he said. 'So that is quite a separate problem from the progressive evolution of self-governing institutions in the regions and peoples which owe allegiance to the British Crown.' He added that in the past the British had made past declarations on constitutional development within the Empire 'which are complete in themselves, free from ambiguity and related to the conditions and circumstances of the territories and peoples affected'.[113] Churchill showed this passage to J. G. Winant, the American ambassador, before he delivered it. Winant thought it 'would simply intensify charges of Imperialism' and begged him to omit it, to no avail.[114] One of the most striking things about the statement, in fact, was the claim that Britain was already committed to progress towards colonial self-government and that the government had previously made unambiguous pledges to this effect. Yet when civil servants tried to answer questions about the commitments to which Churchill had referred, they found the cupboard was bare. 'I do not think the P.M. can have realised the true nakedness of the land when he made the statement', commented junior minister Harold Macmillan. 'The declarations are not complete in themselves, nor are they free from ambiguity. They are scrappy, obscure and jejune.'[115]

Churchill's Commons statement did not allay nationalist pressures. In October, U Saw, Prime Minister of Burma, arrived in London to demand that the Charter be applied to Burma. Churchill met him and told him that if Britain won the war 'liberal ideas would then prevail on the lines of the Atlantic Charter'. However, the Charter was a 'unilateral [sic] declaration which H.M.G. must hold itself free to interpret'.[116] Saw told journalists that Churchill 'was very blunt. I was blunt too.'[117] He left for home disappointed, saying ominously, 'I cannot foresee what the attitude of my people will be when I explain the response of the British Government to my request.'[118] Before he got back to Burma he was arrested by the British after allegedly telling Japanese diplomats in Lisbon en route that he was prepared to lead an anti-British revolt. Churchill wanted him tried for treason but calmer counsel prevailed; Saw was detained in Uganda until 1946.[119]

The Charter controversy also made an impression in Africa. In a 5 November leader article the *West African Pilot* vented its anger at Churchill's words in the Commons: 'That a British prime Minister could utter such a statement during an unparalleled destructive war which has cost Colonial peoples their material resources and manpower is, indeed, a revelation. What, now, must we expect our fate to be after the war?'[120] Nnamdi 'Zik' Azikiwe, the editor of this pioneering Nigerian nationalist newspaper, also cabled Churchill requesting clarification of the discrepancy between Attlee's statement and Churchill's. Did the Charter apply to West Africa or not? Churchill gave instructions for a reply, which, echoing his Commons statement, claimed that the government's Empire policy was 'already entirely in harmony with the high conceptions of freedom and justice which inspired the joint declaration [i.e. the Atlantic Charter]'. Therefore, no fresh statement of policy on Africa was required.[121] But his efforts were to no avail. In 1943 Zik travelled with a delegation to Britain and used the Charter as the basis for a demand for a timescale for complete independence.[122] In the same year the African National Congress demanded that the Charter's principles should be applied to the whole world and pressed for the end of discrimination in South Africa.[123] In 1945 the Pan-African Congress, meeting in Manchester, urged that the tenets of the Charter 'be put into practice at once'.[124] By putting his name to the Atlantic Charter, Churchill had unleashed expectations that he could not control.

V

If the Charter helped undermine the ideological foundations of British colonial rule, the Empire also faced a much more drastic and immediate physical threat. The Japanese attack on Pearl Harbor on 7 December 1941 brought America into the war, a sure guarantee of ultimate victory. Churchill's sense of relief was huge. Intriguingly, one of his first reactions was to send a telegram to De Valera: 'Now is your chance. Now or Never. "A nation once again". Am very ready to meet you at any time.'[125] De Valera recalled his own reaction: 'On being handed the written text I concluded that it was Mr Churchill's way of intimating "now is the chance for taking action which would ultimately lead to the unification of the country". [. . .] I did not see the thing in that light. I saw no opportunity at the moment of securing unity, that our own people were determined on their attitude of neutrality, etc.'[126] The barriers to unification had certainly not gone away, and the cable could easily be read as a classic piece of Churchillian emotionalism; certainly it was vague, and De Valera concluded from his further contacts with the British that there was no chance of a bargain over Northern Ireland.[127] After discussing things with members of his government, De Valera decided not to go to London.[128] His failure to respond warmly to Churchill's initiative cannot be seen as the high-handed rejection of a great opportunity to achieve Irish unity. Arguably, the real significance of Churchill's telegram can be derived from the fact that the text was copied to Roosevelt, who was 'Delighted'.[129] If it achieved nothing else, the message at least appeared to show the Americans that the British were making an effort.

Ireland, of course, was a fairly minor concern for Churchill by this stage, as Japan's assault on British territories in the Far East proved devastating. The sinking on 10 December of HMS *Prince of Wales* and HMS *Repulse* – recently despatched to Singapore in a failed attempt at deterrence – was a foretaste of disasters to come.[130] By the New Year, Japan had seized Hong Kong and a substantial part of Malaya and had also made gains in Burma. Churchill's priority, though, was Europe, and in Washington – where he travelled before Christmas to consult with the President – he secured a commitment from the Americans to a 'Germany first' strategy. As a result the Australians felt profoundly exposed and criticized the reinforcements planned for the Far East as wholly inadequate.[131] Ian Jacob, a military aide to the British War Cabinet noted in his diary: 'Throughout the time of our visit to Washington the Prime Minister received a series of most exasperating telegrams from Mr Curtin, the Prime Minister of Australia.' Jacob wrote that during the war the Australian government had 'taken a narrow, selfish and at times a craven view of events', in contrast to the New Zealanders, who had been 'a tower of strength'. However, he conceded:

> I fear that the Prime Minister's treatment of Mr Menzies is somewhat to blame. He has never really understood the Far East problem and has deliberately starved Singapore in favour of home and the Middle East, without paying enough attention to the feelings of Australia. His policy was undoubtedly right, but he should have taken great pains to make Australia understand what was being done, and give them the impression that he was really taking them into his confidence.[132]

In a New Year message to his people, Curtin declared that Australia refused to 'accept the dictum that the Pacific struggle must be treated as a subordinate segment of the general conflict' and that the country now looked 'to America, free of any pangs as to our traditional links or kinship with the United Kingdom'.[133]

Churchill was 'deeply shocked' by Curtin's 'insulting' comments.[134] At the point he heard about them, he was paying a triumphant visit to Ottawa. In Washington he had suffered some kind of heart attack, a diagnosis which his doctor kept secret even from him. This did not stop him enjoying 'meeting the crowds and adopting characteristic poses with cigar in his mouth, hat on end of cane, making the sign "V" with his two fingers, and generally stirring up enthusiasm like a 10-year old'.[135] His discussions with

Mackenzie King went smoothly, although 'the P.M. is not really interested in Mackenzie King. He takes him for granted.'[136] (Malcolm MacDonald had observed some months earlier that for his part the devout, abstemious King admired Churchill 'enormously' but did not 'like him much'.)[137] Churchill addressed the Canadian Parliament, telling of the prediction of defeatist French generals in the summer of 1940: 'In three weeks England will have her neck wrung like a chicken.' 'Some chicken!' he observed. 'Some neck!'[138] Asked by journalists the next day if he thought Singapore could hold on, he answered, 'I sure do.'[139]

In fact, the island fortress was doomed. Although supposedly impregnable, its defences were in chaos. The British population, still trying to live the imperial high-life, did not seem to take the war seriously, and the local commander was incompetent. As the end neared, Churchill instructed that the battle was to be fought to the bitter end: 'Commanders and Senior Officers should die with their troops. The honour of the British Empire and of the British Army is at stake.'[140] But the position was hopeless, and on 15 February 1942 the British surrendered. Around 130,000 men were taken prisoner, including the Australian Eighth Division.[141] In his memoirs, Churchill wrote of it as 'the worst disaster and largest capitulation in British history'.[142] German propagandists had a field day, talking of 'Winston Churchill, the undertaker of the British Empire.'[143] The situation in the Far East continued to deteriorate. Japan's takeover of Burma was complete by the end of May, and a puppet regime was established in Rangoon, initially with the backing of the nationalist Thakin party. A few months earlier a visiting US journalist had detected that 'the population was so venomously anti-British that it would welcome a Japanese occupation. Winston Churchill's photograph in the newsreel theatres was hissed; Hitler's was applauded.'[144]

A British public opinion survey by Mass-Observation, the sociological research organization, shortly after the fall of Singapore, threw up some interesting findings about attitudes to Empire. It found that many respondents felt a degree of guilt about the Empire and the way it had been administered. The collapse in the Far East, some of them felt, was a case of chickens coming home to roost. According to the report, however, there was a paradoxical consequence: 'This feeling, in some cases, seems to mitigate any apprehension or regret people may feel at the present precarious position of parts of the Empire.'[145] In other words, the catastrophe did not do as much damage to British morale as it might have done, because it helped assuage uneasy consciences. By contrast, Singapore's fall left the Australians feeling exposed and even betrayed. ('Australia in greatest possible flap', wrote Oliver Harvey.)[146] Their fears were heightened when, a few days later, the Japanese launched a major air attack on Darwin. Relations between Curtin and Churchill became increasingly fractious; some of their 'acid and embarrassing' exchanges of cables were made public at Curtin's behest.[147] H. V. Evatt, the Australian Minister for External Affairs, eager to bring about conciliation, complained, 'The continuous rowing over unfortunate things and attempt to hector over more important things gravely impair Empire solidarity.'[148] Churchill reacted badly to Australian pleas for a stronger commitment to her defence. He subjected High Commissioner Bruce to a 'tirade' in which he denounced the Curtin government as 'impossible and quite unhelpful'. (As an example of unhelpfulness he cited the insistence on withdrawing Australian troops from besieged Tobruk in 1941, which in fact had been initiated by Menzies's government.) He claimed that 'they had pinned their hopes on the U.S.A., but now having found in Washington that those hopes were not likely to be realised they were falling back on the old country'.[149]

Curtin later told journalists 'that Australia was Churchill's "forgotten land"', but Churchill's failure to do more for its defence can be justified.[150] Japanese attacks on the country continued until November 1943 – yet, as even the Australian historian most critical of Churchill appears to concede, the country was too big and too far away from Japan to make a full-scale invasion practical.[151] The concentration on the Middle East and Europe was sound warwinning strategy. If Australia's worst fears proved exaggerated, however, the British did not handle them well. They were good at providing generalized assurances that, if a full-scale invasion occurred, they would drop everything they were doing and head off to help right away. This was an effective method of fobbing off requests for more immediate and concrete defence assistance, but it was bound to create bad feeling in the longer run. Churchill, who was under astonishing stress and physically unwell, can of course be forgiven for his dismissive approach to what must have seemed like remote problems. He shared, however, British officialdom's patronizing attitude to the Australians, fulminating privately that – as the descendants of convicts – they 'came of bad stock'.[152] In spite of everything, Churchill remained an icon to be admired for many in Australia, although he was to be a more politically divisive figure there than he was in Canada and New Zealand.[153]

VI

The collapse in the Far East also pushed India up Churchill's agenda. There had been little political progress there since he had entered Downing Street and Amery the India Office. Amery, indeed, had not really wanted the job, believing that Churchill made the offer in order to 'side track' him from 'the real conduct of the war'.[154] The appointment had had a somewhat mixed reception in India. Sir Maharaj Singh, who had been at Harrow with Amery, wrote to the Calcutta *Statesman* saying that Amery's attitude to Indians when Colonial Secretary had been unsympathetic. 'Latterly, however, his views broadened and he opposed Mr Winston Churchill in parliament on the Government of India Act of 1935. When I last saw him he frankly admitted that he saw no future for India except responsible Government.'[155] Writing from India in May 1940, Linlithgow agreed with Amery that it was important to demonstrate that Britain was still committed to its earlier promises. He wrote that 'there have, not unnaturally, been many suggestions that with Winston in the chair, a movement to the right was to be anticipated: and while your utterances, which have been very well received here, have done a good deal to offset that, the suspicion is still lurking, and the sooner the position is made clear, the better'.[156] As his past record and his 'flapdoodle' comments on the Atlantic Charter indicated, Amery was no reforming radical, but even his modest efforts in support of change quickly brought him into conflict with the Prime Minister.

Amery believed that France's capitulation in July 1940 had reawakened Congress sympathies for Britain, and that its leaders would be responsive to a promise of self-government after the war, if this were matched by an increased role for them immediately in the running of Indian affairs. None of this went far beyond what

Zetland had proposed earlier in the year. But when Churchill discovered that Amery had been discussing these ideas with Linlithgow – who had acceded to them with a degree of reluctance – he accused him of misleading the Cabinet.[157] Amery described in his diary how Churchill 'said he would sooner give up political life at once, or rather go out into the wilderness and fight, than to admit a revolution which meant the end of the Imperial Crown in India'.[158] In the end, Churchill agreed to redraft the statement himself, and although some of the substance was kept the wording became 'rather woolly and lacking in precision'.[159] The 1940 'August offer', as it became known, did promise the expansion of the Viceroy's Council, the creation of an Advisory War Council, and moves after the war to devise a new constitution.[160] But the pledges as to the future seemed vague and – as Congress would only accept full independence – the offer proved a dead letter.

Gandhi then relaunched civil disobedience, although it did not receive much popular success. (Congress did not actively disrupt recruiting and by January 1941 the Indian army reached a strength of 418,000 – 37 per cent Muslim, 55 per cent Hindu.)[161] In October 1940 Nehru was imprisoned. 'I admire Winston Churchill for his ability and courage and determination and I admire the British people for the spirit they have shown in defence of their own freedom', he wrote to the anti-colonialist MP Josiah Wedgwood. 'But that admiration does not lead me to accept the British Prime Minister's dictation in regard to India.'[162] Although, by the end of the year, he and other political prisoners had been released and civil disobedience abandoned, British military setbacks further undermined confidence in the established order. By early 1942 even the moderate non-Congress nationalist Sir Tej Sapru was holding forth 'with unusual bitterness, re. (1) lack of foresight for protection of Burma and Malaya, (2) stupidity of Government in India'.[163] These remarks were recorded by Professor Reginald Coupland, the leading imperial historian of the age, who was visiting India to examine the constitutional situation. Coupland also found evidence of the 'intensification of bitterness v. England, especially since [the] Atlantic Charter fiasco'.[164] Nevertheless, there were some signs that Congress was looking for an opportunity to throw its weight behind the war effort.[165]

Sapru was to play a part in kick-starting the political process once more. In January 1942 he and other liberals sent an open telegram to Churchill, urging him to make 'some bold stroke [of] far-sighted statesmanship' in order to enlist India's wholehearted cooperation in the war.[166] Churchill was predictably reluctant to discuss constitutional issues in India 'at a moment when [the] enemy is at the frontier'. He told Attlee that the Indian liberals would not be able to deliver the goods and that changes which put Congress in charge would not enhance the war effort. 'The Indian troops are fighting splendidly, but it must be remembered that their allegiance is to the King Emperor, and that the rule of the Congress and Hindoo Priesthood machine would never be tolerated by a fighting race.'[167] Linlithgow and Amery were agreed in not wanting any major new step, although the latter at least thought it important that Churchill say something conciliatory to correct the impression that he 'means to concede nothing and therefore has deliberately avoided speaking about India'.[168] Yet there were also other forces at work. Attlee, in line with the views held by others in the Labour Party, demanded something more concrete.[169] Roosevelt too made his views clear. When Churchill visited Washington at Christmas 1941, the President raised the topic of India with him. Churchill recalled: 'I reacted so strongly and at such length that he never raised it verbally again.'[170] But this did not stop the President applying pressure in other ways. In a broadcast in February he asserted that the Atlantic Charter applied to 'the whole world'. When journalists asked if he had been talking about India, he pointedly declined to comment.[171] Furthermore, the fall of Singapore forced Churchill to reconstruct his government. Sir Stafford Cripps MP, who had just returned from his posting as Ambassador to the USSR, was appointed to the War Cabinet. Cripps was on the crest of a wave of public popularity and seemed a potential rival to the embattled Prime Minister. He also had distinct sympathies with Congress. Commenting on the origins of the so-called 'Cripps offer', Amery noted how 'the pressure outside, upon Winston from Roosevelt, and upon Attlee & Co. from their own party, *plus* the admission of Cripps to the War Cabinet, suddenly opened the sluice gates, and the thing moved with a rush'.[172] Alexander Cadogan wrote, 'Poor old Winston, feeling deeply the present situation and the attacks on him, is losing his grip, I fear.'[173]

In March, then, the Cabinet authorized Cripps to proceed to India to negotiate with political leaders there on the basis of a substantial new plan (the details of which were not immediately made public). Under this, a constituent assembly would be established after the war so that India could move forward to self-government. No province would be forced to join the new arrangement that emerged – this amounted to a concession of the principle of Pakistan – and questions of war strategy would be kept in British hands until the close of hostilities.[174] 'We have resigned ourselves to fighting our utmost to defend India in order, if successful, to be turned out', commented Churchill mordantly.[175] Roosevelt chose his moment to send Churchill a long telegram comparing the problems of the United States between 1783 and 1789 to contemporary India, which Churchill reprinted in his memoirs with a sarcastic comment: 'This document is of high interest because it illustrates the difficulties of comparing situations in different centuries and scenes where almost every material fact is totally different'.[176] Smuts expressed concern that the plan left open the possibility of partition, but Curtin and Mackenzie King both expressed their pleasure at the proposals.[177] In India – in the absence of exact details of the British position – reaction to the Cripps mission ranged from warm welcome to angry scepticism. Sir Ramaswami Mudaliar, a prominent member of the Viceroy's Council, took a pessimistic view. 'Winston must have been so preoccupied with war that he succumbed to C.'s pressure,' he told Reginald Coupland. 'C. a dubious choice because, when in India in 1939, he was thought to be in Nehru's pocket, and it is said that Jinnah wrote to Winston that, whoever came, it mustn't be C. Yet not such a bad choice *if* he brings concessions to the Moslems.'[178] The tensions inherent in the mission were evident to journalists, who asked Cripps, after he had arrived in Delhi, about his 'sharp differences' with Churchill over India. 'I and Mr Churchill absolutely agree', he affirmed. To laughter, one reporter shot back, 'Which of you has changed?'[179]

Yet, if anyone could complete the task, it was Cripps. From a wealthy background, he had succeeded brilliantly as a barrister, which provided his route into politics. Having abandoned his youthful Conservative leanings, he was appointed Solicitor-General under the second Labour government and stayed loyal to the party in the split of 1931. He then swung violently to the left and was expelled from Labour soon before the outbreak of war, serving as an independent MP before his return to the fold in 1945. There was little love lost between him and Churchill, but the latter nonetheless appointed him to the Moscow embassy, once observing that 'he was a lunatic in a country of lunatics and it would be a pity to move him'.[180] As a teetotaller and vegetarian, Cripps had a reputation for 'quirkiness, extreme austerity and cold aloofness', although he could also demonstrate a lively sense of humour.[181] Hitler told his inner circle that he preferred 'the undisciplined swine' Churchill as an adversary to the ascetic, 'drawing-room Bolshevist' Cripps. 'From Churchill one may finally expect that in a moment of lucidity – it's not impossible – he'll realise that the Empire's going inescapably to ruin, if the war lasts another two or three years. Cripps, a man without roots, a demagogue and a liar, would pursue his sick fancies although the Empire were to crack at every corner.'[182] Goebbels, for his part, thought that the Cripps mission was a cunning plan to pacify India via divide and rule: 'It is quite clear that this mess has been cooked up in Churchill's kitchen.'[183]

Cripps spent three weeks in India cajoling the party leaders to accept the scheme that he had brought with him. At one point the agreement seemed tantalizingly close even though, early on, Gandhi referred to the offer of self-government after the war as 'a post-dated cheque'. (Some wag of a journalist added 'on a failing bank'.)[184] After the mission broke down, Cripps commented that 'Gandhi was anything but a saint and had determined to wreck the negotiations from the beginning. He had succeeded.'[185] Others placed the blame elsewhere. Even before the final collapse in April, 'high-placed Americans were angrily saying that Churchill had butted in to prevent a reasonable settlement!'[186] The truth was more complex. Certainly, both Amery and (especially) Churchill lost confidence in Cripps, feared that he might be exceeding his brief, and began to communicate with Linlithgow behind his back. The involvement of Colonel Louis Johnson, Roosevelt's personal representative in India, complicated things further. But there was no single decisive and wrecking Churchillian intervention. Perhaps the most crucial barrier to agreement was the suspicion that the Congress leaders felt towards Linlithgow (who for his part did not trust Cripps). They did not believe that, once they had been admitted to a new, more thoroughly Indianized Viceroy's Council, the Viceroy himself would allow them meaningful power. Nehru recalled that: 'During the Cripps-Congress negotiations, I accepted some impossible things but I and those who were with me, found out very soon that those in power in Britain still possessed the mind and mentality of the Victorian period and I came to a definite conclusion that it was impossible to arrive at any settlement with the British rulers.'[187]

Political weakness had forced Churchill to accept the initiative of the Cripps mission and he had clearly been discomfited by being driven away from his diehard position. He thus bore the news of the breakdown, he recalled in his memoirs, 'with philosophy'.[188] The outcome for him was not without advantage. As Cripps's official biographer remarks perceptively, 'It is clear that, spared the necessity of going through with the Cripps offer, what was now uppermost in the Prime Minister's mind was the effect upon American opinion of having made it.'[189] In other words, there was a propaganda benefit in having made an apparently generous proposal and having had it turned down. Furthermore, a little of the shine had now been taken off Cripps's halo. As Amery commented when the mission was first planned, 'I am by no means sure [. . .] that Winston doesn't think it a good thing to send off this dangerous young rival on the errand of squaring the circle in India.'[190]

The problem of India remained. After the fall of Tobruk in North Africa in June, Churchill faced a vote of no confidence in Parliament (which was defeated overwhelmingly). In Nehru's contention, the 'real explanation' for British military setbacks was 'Empire' and the remedy for them was 'the complete liquidation of that Empire'.[191] On 8 August 1942 the All-India Congress Committee passed a resolution calling on the British to 'Quit India' and launched a new wave of civil disobedience. Forewarned, the British acted swiftly, arresting Gandhi, Nehru and other Congress leaders the next day. Riots erupted all over the country, Europeans were attacked, and railways were sabotaged.[192] At the end of the month, Linlithgow told Churchill, 'I am engaged here in meeting by far the most serious rebellion since that of 1857'.[193] Subhas Chandra Bose, the extremist leader who had broken with Congress and established a Free India Centre in Berlin, congratulated the rebels in a propaganda broadcast, and mocked Churchill for visiting Stalin in Moscow. Britain, he said, would 'debase herself to any extent and stoop to any humiliation, so long as she can retain her hold over India. That is why Mr Winston Churchill, the high priest of

imperialism, the arch-enemy of Indian nationalism and the sworn
opponent of all forms of Socialism, swallowed his imperialist pride
and presented himself at the gates of the Kremlin.'[194]

The swift and brutal British reaction ensured that peace was
restored in India by the autumn. Thousands were killed or wounded
and multitudes were imprisoned. On several occasions mobs were
machine-gunned from the air.[195] According to the Cabinet Secretary's notebook Churchill observed:

> Indian show-down v. satisfactory. Recruiting v. favourable.
> Congress shown unable to move the masses – a great flop. They
> have come out as a revolutionary movement: influenced or
> working with Japanese: and have failed. Shows that Congress
> don't represent India – only Congress caucus and Hindu priest-
> hood.[196]

According to Amery, 'From this he rambled on to the suggestion
that it would really pay us to take up the cause of the poor peasant
and confiscate the rich Congressman's lands and divide them up.'[197]
Labour ministers made remarks on similar lines. Churchill was
surprised to learn that there was no inheritance tax in India and the
Cabinet agreed that the Viceroy should be asked to put forward
some proposals.[198] Amery, aware that many of these questions were
in fact now the responsibility of the Provinces, and eager 'to get on
with the real business', sat silent.[199] It was a telling moment. In the
face of large-scale violence, the British government had taken note
of India's enormous social divisions and made a vague, not especially
well-informed, resolution to do something about them. But after
further discussion over the next weeks it was decided it would be
too expensive. There could be no question of spending money on
Indian social reform 'any more than on Canadian social reform',
Amery wrote.[200]

Equally telling was the minute Churchill wrote about Sir Ramaswami Mudaliar and the Maharaja Jam Saheb of Nawanagar, both
of whom had earlier been invited to represent India at the War
Cabinet as 'a generous gesture to loyal Indians' and who arrived
in Britain in September. 'Though I shall naturally invite them
to attend our Monday meetings on general war affairs, it must not
be assumed that I shall feel able to invite them to Meetings when
Indian affairs are to be discussed', Churchill warned his colleagues.

'We have already had several such meetings, and may have more, at which the presence of Indian representatives would be highly embarrassing.'[201] They, certainly, felt the difficulties of their own position. Churchill was due to make a statement in the Commons on the disturbances on 10 September. The day before, Mudaliar and the Jam Saheb were taken to be photographed with him in the Downing Street garden. While they were there, Amery asked Churchill if he had read the note he had sent him in preparation for the statement. The Prime Minister reacted angrily, saying he had read it but that he would speak on his own lines. 'If we ever have to quit India we shall quit it in a blaze of glory, and the chapter that shall be ended then will be the most glorious chapter of that country, not merely in relation to the past but equally in relation to the future, however distant that may be. That will be my statement on India tomorrow.' No one else could get a word in edgeways, and when the Indians went back to their hotel they considered quitting and going home if the statement was as bad as they feared it would be.[202] In the end, Amery's influence prevailed to some extent; Churchill toned down his public statement. In private, though, the Prime Minister remained as intransigent as ever, 'I hate Indians', he suddenly burst out, 'They are a beastly people with a beastly religion.'[203]

Churchill began his modified Commons statement by saying that the declaration of principles that formed the basis of the Cripps mission 'must be taken as representing the settled policy of the British Crown and Parliament'. In other words, the government stood by its offer. But, Churchill pointed out, Cripps's 'good offices' had been 'rejected by the Indian Congress Party', which was at any rate unrepresentative even of the Hindu masses. Furthermore:

> The Congress Party has now abandoned in many respects the policy of nonviolence which Mr Gandhi has so long inculcated in theory, and has come into the open as a revolutionary movement designed to paralyse the communications by rail and telegraph and generally to promote disorder, the looting of shops and sporadic attacks upon the Indian police, accompanied from time to time by revolting atrocities – the whole having the intention or at any rate the effect of hampering the defence of India against the Japanese invader who stands on

the frontiers of Assam and also upon the eastern side of the
Bay of Bengal. It may well be that these activities by the
Congress Party have been aided by Japanese fifth-column work
on a widely extended scale and with special direction to
strategic points.

Towards the end of his statement, he referred to the continued
high levels of recruitment to the Indian army: 'It is fortunate,
indeed, that the Congress Party has no influence whatever with
the martial races, on whom the defence of India apart from British
Forces largely depends.' And in his concluding remarks, he noted
that large numbers of reinforcements had reached India and that
'the numbers of white soldiers now in that country, though very
small compared with its size and population, are larger than at
any time in the British connection'. Therefore, 'the situation in
India at this moment gives no occasion for undue despondency or
alarm'.[204]
     According to Amery, Churchill's statement 'evoked ringing
cheers' from Conservatives but 'greatly upset many of the Labour
people, including a good many moderates'.[205] The reaction of the
Indian nationalist press was predictably angry. It pointed out that,
having negotiated with Congress for so long, not least during the
Cripps mission, it was a bit rich for the British government to start
denouncing it as unrepresentative. The *Hindu* claimed that Churchill
had packed more half-truths and venom into a few hundred words
than he had given to the Commons during the passage of the India
Bill.[206] The Calcutta *Sunday Statesman*'s 'Indian Observer' – a columnist billed as holding 'a representative Indian central point of
view' – remarked more thoughtfully that 'such anger, such fury,
such desperation have many times preluded the sullen but inevitable
reversal of an unworkable policy'.[207] For its part, the Congress-
supporting India League, based in London, produced a pamphlet
designed as a point-by-point answer to what Churchill had said.[208]
Jinnah criticized the speech too. He, of course, agreed with
Churchill that Congress was unrepresentative but argued that the
British government attached insufficient value to Muslim cooperation. Churchill had referred to the 90 million Muslims opposed to
Congress and had said that they had a right of self-expression.
But, Jinnah asked rhetorically, 'Is this the only value you attach to

the Mussalmans and the Muslim League, that they are opposed to the Congress, which is a fact, and they have the right to self-expression, which is a self-evident truth? Is that all he has to say?'[209]

The impact in America was also negative. 'Winston's statement on India will not have done us much good here', Halifax complained to Eden. 'Why must he talk about *white* troops, when "the British army in India" would have served his purpose just as well?'[210] Cripps, who felt that he was being sidelined from the running of the war, was at this time pondering resignation. He realized, though, that he could not resign over India. 'Churchill's speech harmful and foolish; but it contains the specific pledge in words that the Cripps offer holds.'[211] This, perhaps, is the correct way to read Churchill's statement. Although he used it as opportunity to encourage his Tory supporters and to vent some of his longstanding prejudices, he also ensured that he protected his political flank. Indeed, his reiteration of the Cripps offer was highly significant, not because there was any chance that it would now be accepted, but because he now associated himself personally with the promise of independence after the war. It was evidence that his political weakness during 1942 had dragged him from his entrenched position, although he drew attention away from this with his verbal pot-shots at Congress.

VII

In October 1942 Smuts arrived in London for consultations, at Churchill's pressing invitation. Invited to address both Houses of Parliament, he was introduced by the doddering Lloyd George who, if not actually on his last legs, was certainly on his penultimate ones. Afterwards, Chips Channon saw all three men sitting together in the Smoking Room. 'Winston and Smuts, who had once fought each other in the Boer War, were having a drink together, and there were glasses before them. Of the three only the bronzed South African looked fit.'[212] According to taste, Smuts's speech was either a) full of 'every commonplace that we have all been trying to avoid for years' (Harold Nicolson), or b) 'finely phrased and inspired by a lofty conception of what the British Commonwealth means today' (Leo Amery).[213] It did contain at least some substance, in the form of a clear hint that an offensive against Hitler was coming.[214] Two days later, on 23 October, the British Eighth Army under General Montgomery attacked Axis forces at El Alamein. (Over half of Monty's 195,000 men were British, and most of the rest came from India, Australia, New Zealand and South Africa.) Eleven days of fierce fighting followed, at the end of which Rommel began to retreat – and carried on for 1,500 miles. On 7 November British and US troops landed in Morocco and Algeria.[215] 'Now this is not the end', Churchill said in a speech at the Mansion House in London on 10 November. 'It is not even the beginning of the end. But it is, perhaps, the end of the beginning.'[216]

A later passage in the same speech is equally famous:

> We mean to hold our own. I have not become the King's First Minister in order to preside over the liquidation of the British Empire. For that task, if ever it were prescribed, someone else would have to be found and, under democracy, I suppose the nation would have to be consulted.[217]

According to *The Times*, his comments were greeted with loud cheers.[218] The context for the remarks deserves some consideration. In general, they can be seen as a rejection of the contemporary (and particularly American) demand that in future colonies should be subjected to some form of international control or 'trusteeship'.[219] More specifically, they may well have been intended as a rebuttal of Wendell Willkie, the Republican candidate defeated by Roosevelt in 1940, who had called for the 'orderly but scheduled abolition of the colonial system'.[220] It is also worth noting that they came immediately after a passage in which Churchill emphasized that Britain would not exploit its military triumphs to gain territory at the expense of France – she had no 'acquisitive appetites or ambitions' in North Africa or anywhere else, he said.[221] Thus his insistence that Britain retain existing possessions was modulated by the assurance that she was not engaged upon a war of conquest. On the other hand, his observations about democracy were not merely benign musings about the workings of the system.[222] Churchill was well aware of the prestige he could now command and was implicitly threatening colleagues that, if they opposed him on imperial issues, he would be prepared to force a general election, even during wartime. In any such election, he may well have thought, they, not he, would be swept away.

With his position strengthened immeasurably by the first clear signs of victory, Churchill was able to demote Cripps, who had argued with him over military strategy, from the War Cabinet to the Ministry of Aircraft Production. His challenges as Prime Minister were still enormous. At home, the publication of William Beveridge's famous report, calling for a major post-war expansion of social services, helped trigger a groundswell of radical opinion that would in due course sweep the Conservatives from office; Churchill himself saw such planning for peacetime as a distraction from the current war effort. At the same time, his 'liquidation' remarks drew inevitable criticism. 'The Indians will come to dislike Allied successes if they merely increase British arrogance, as evidenced by Mr Churchill's speech', said Chakravarti Rajagopalachari, a prominent Indian politician known for his support for the war.[223] Nehru wrote in his prison diary that he was pleased with Churchill's plain speaking as it at least made the situation obvious: 'How can any decent Indian submit to this or agree to cooperate with Churchill and his underlings passes my comprehension.'[224] Wendell Willkie slammed Churchill's defence of 'the old imperialistic order', and there were other signs of a revival in the USA of the picture of Britain 'as a stronghold of reactionary imperialism'.[225] Nevertheless, the criticism was not all one way. There was, of course, support from some fairly predictable quarters, such as the *National Review* and the British Empire Union in Australia.[226] The Liberal MP Jimmy de Rothschild emphasized his friend Churchill's belief that the Empire must march hand in hand with freedom: 'Such is the Empire which he does not wish to liquidate.'[227] Perhaps more surprisingly, the *Washington Post* said Willkie was talking nonsense, as Churchill had not been defending the old order but only 'the right of the British Empire to exist as an entity'. In many countries the Empire had demonstrated its liberality over the years, and as regards India, 'about which so much emotional confusion exists in this country', Churchill and his government were pledged to give it freedom after the war. The *Post* believed Britain would live up to this promise.[228]

Of course, it was the reaction in the White House that was especially crucial. Mackenzie King, visiting Roosevelt there in December, discussed Churchill's speech with the President. According to Mackenzie King:

He said really the thing that did do harm was the reference to the liquidation of the Empire. I said that was an answer to Willkie. I said it gave him a great internal kick to say certain of these things. We had a laugh over it. He said he [Churchill] is sort of a puck, and spoke of his being a sort of cherub in appearance here after being up late at night.[229]

In other words, Churchill had more or less got away with it, aided by his reputation for mischief and by the fact (or perception) that his wicked words had been intended as a poke in the eye for one of FDR's adversaries. Roosevelt could easily afford him a little indulgence. But as the balance of power shifted from Britain to America in the final years of the war, it seemed increasingly likely that Churchill would be forced to preside over imperial liquidation after all.

8

HANDS OFF THE BRITISH EMPIRE,
1942–1945

AT THE end of 1943, a year which had seen a string of Axis defeats, Josef Goebbels wrote an article in the newspaper *Das Reich* under the headline 'Tottering Colossus'. 'Britain will lose this war in the political sphere, even if she should succeed in winning it in the military sphere.' He argued: 'The British Empire is selling out, and one day its friends and foes will join to swallow it up.' Although Churchill could have obtained a 'cheap peace' in 1940 he had recklessly continued the war: 'Now Britain, having reached the point when she cannot back out, finds herself forced to give in to the ambitions of her more powerful Allies.'[1] The idea that the British Empire was 'dissolving like a lump of sugar in the Roosevelt teacup' had been a theme of Axis propaganda for some time.[2] More recently, such claims have found an echo at the right-wing end of the historiographical spectrum, in the suggestion that Churchill pursued a false path, 'mortgaged' Britain to the United States and failed to preserve the Empire.[3] (The fact of economic dependence on the USA has also been a cause of regret on the left, even if the Empire itself is not missed.) Yet, if Britain emerged from the war hugely weakened and overshadowed by America and the Soviet Union, it is misleading to suggest that Churchill's grand strategy was to blame for this. German talk of a 'cheap peace' was naturally quite empty – and so, although at times he seemed to place excessive faith in the Atlantic Alliance and in his personal relationship with Roosevelt (and also in that with Stalin), there was no alternative course Churchill could have taken that would have preserved the power of the British Empire in the longer run. The final years of the war were to see his dawning but incomplete realization of the unpalatable fact of its decline.

I

Some imperial problems appeared to Churchill as a distraction from the war effort. In January 1943 Gandhi announced his intention to fast for twenty-one days. Although he was not planning to fast to death, it seemed a likely outcome for a frail man of seventy-three. If this were to happen while he was still in custody, calamity threatened. As Cripps told the Cabinet, Gandhi was 'such a semi-religious figure' that his death in British hands would be 'a great blow and embarrassment to us'.[4] When the fast began on 10 February, Churchill suspected it was a sham. 'I have heard that Gandhi usually has glucose in his water when doing his various fasting antics', he cabled Linlithgow, asking if this could be verified.[5] 'This may be the case but those who have been in attendance on him doubt it', the Viceroy replied; the point was never proved, but Churchill remained sceptical.[6] With Gandhi apparently close to death, Hindu India followed the disquieting bulletins with high-pitched anxiety. Towards the end of February, Gandhi agreed to drink a small amount of fruit juice mixed with water and his health thus recovered somewhat; he broke the fast formally on 3 March. Churchill – himself suffering from pneumonia – succeeded in warding off the threat of American intervention in the crisis. 'Am feeling definitely better now', he told Harry Hopkins, FDR's right-hand man, at the end of February. 'So is Gandhi. [. . .] I am so glad that you did not get drawn in.'[7] 'What fools we should have been to flinch before all this bluff and sob-stuff', he told Smuts exultantly.[8] He even prepared some remarks on these lines for a broadcast. He had always been sure, he said, that Gandhi 'had not the slightest intention of starving himself to death or running any risk of squandering the world's record nuisance value. [. . .] So the Battle of Gandhi is over, and all parties can rejoice in the victory.'[9] He had the good sense, however, not to use this passage when the time came to deliver the speech.

By refusing to back down in the face of Gandhi's tactics, the Raj may have regained a limited amount of prestige after the setbacks of earlier years. The Bengal famine of 1943–4, however, offered a further severe blow to its moral authority. In addition to the loss of rice imports from Burma, an existing shortfall in agricultural production had been worsened by a major cyclone in Bengal in

October 1942. Nonetheless, a classic, Nobel Prize-winning analysis of the causes of famine argues that in this instance there was no actual shortage of food; wartime inflation combined with mismanagement by the authorities triggered unnecessary hoarding.[10] At a broader level, according to this reasoning, India's lack of democracy at the time can be blamed on the fact that, without the need to win elections, its British rulers lacked the incentive to avert catastrophe. More recent work has argued that war conditions did lead to a genuine shortage and that tales of hoarding (retailed by the authorities at the time in order to justify their refusal to divert food to India) were illusory.[11] Nevertheless, it seems impossible to avoid the conclusion that maladministration made the consequences worse than they need have been, and that Churchill's own reaction was grossly inept and, it is tempting to add, callous.

Administrative and political problems within the Bengal government exacerbated a situation already made worse by severe transport difficulties and the loss of supplies from Japanese-occupied Burma.[12] In the face of the famine, the British authorities were appallingly slow to act. Even after Amery woke up to the seriousness of the problem he struggled to convince the War Cabinet to allocate extra shipping and supplies. Churchill 'spoke scathingly of India's economic inefficiency which made it necessary to supply it with food which otherwise might not be needed' and offered unhelpful comments about 'Indians breeding like rabbits'.[13] Lord Wavell, the new Viceroy, faced the problem with the requisite seriousness, but struggled terribly to get the backing he needed. He told Amery in February 1944, when arguing for more imports: 'I warn His Majesty's Government with all seriousness that if they refuse our demands they are risking a catastrophe of far greater dimensions than [the] Bengal famine [. . .] They must either trust the opinion of the man they have appointed to advise them on Indian affairs or replace him.'[14] Even this veiled threat of resignation did not get him the help he wanted. His figures were questioned by Churchill's scientific adviser Lord Cherwell, 'that old menace and fraud', as the Viceroy called him. 'The fact is that the P.M. has calculated his war plans without any consideration at all of India's needs', Wavell protested. 'I am afraid that he may be courting a first-class disaster to the Empire, unless we are very lucky.'[15] It was not until that April that, in Amery's words, 'Winston was at last seriously perturbed and convinced that something would have to be done.'[16] Fortunately, although the government's eventual response was extremely belated, a further season of famine was avoided.

Wavell's willingness to confront London on this crucial issue was proof of his fitness for the job. He had not been Churchill's first choice. A career soldier, he had been Commander in the Middle East (1939–41) and then India, and was promoted to field marshal at the start of 1943. The Prime Minister blamed him, probably unfairly, for the failure of the Arakan offensive into Burma at the end of 1942. Many other names had been canvassed for the succession to Linlithgow including Attlee, Eden, and Amery (who, not uncharacteristically, had suggested himself).[17] Churchill, indeed, quickly came to regret his choice. During the months he spent in England before taking up his post, Wavell made it clear that he was not content to be a do-nothing viceroy, but wanted authority to pursue constitutional advance with India's political leaders. He secured this in vague general terms. Churchill reluctantly provided him with a set of instructions which was 'mostly meaningless, e.g. it exhorted me to get on with the war, to improve the lot of the Indian, to make peace between Moslem and Hindu, and indicated right at the end that political progress during the war was not barred'. Having read it, Amery told Wavell that 'you are wafted to India on a wave of hot air'.[18]

Many observers felt that the mere mention of India brought out a streak of unpleasantness or even irrationality in Churchill. In March 1943 R. A. Butler, the Education minister, visited him at Chequers. The Prime Minister 'launched into a most terrible attack on the "baboos", saying that they were gross dirty and corrupt'. He even declared that he wanted the British to leave India, and – this was a more serious remark – that he supported the principle of Pakistan. When Butler argued that the Raj had always stood for Indian unity, Churchill replied, 'Well, if our poor troops have to be kept in a sweltering, syphilitic climate for the sake of your precious unity, I'd rather see them have a good civil war.' At this, Clementine protested that he didn't mean what he was saying, and Churchill admitted this was true: 'but when I see my opponents glaring at me, I always have to draw them out by exaggerated statements'.[19] Such a technique was all very well when he was dealing with subordinates, but it was risky and counterproductive when he employed it on

representatives of foreign powers. Not long after his encounter with
Butler, he had a meeting with Roosevelt's personal representative
William Phillips, who had visited the subcontinent on the President's
behalf. Phillips suggested to Churchill that the time was ripe to
promote discussions between Gandhi and Jinnah. Phillips recalled:

> Churchill was annoyed, and annoyed with me; that was clear.
> He got up and walked rapidly back and forth. 'My answer to
> you is: Take India if that is what you want! Take it by all
> means! But I warn you that if I open the door a crack there
> will be the greatest blood-bath in all history. Mark my words,'
> he concluded, shaking a finger at me, 'I prophesied the present
> war, and I prophesy the blood-bath.'

Phillips was 'puzzled', not to say astonished. 'Never had I
mentioned the sudden withdrawal of British power and yet he
insisted upon assuming that that was my proposal. It was only too
clear that he had a complex about India from which he would not
and could not be shaken.'[20] Meanwhile, Churchill could take little
comfort from the tides of opinion in India. In December 1943
Jinnah urged the British to 'divide and quit'. 'Mr Churchill said
he did not preside over the British Government to liquidate the
Empire', he observed. 'But voluntary liquidation is more honourable
than a compulsory one, and the British Empire will be liquidated
one day.'[21]

One factor that increased Churchill's resentment towards India
was the issue of the sterling balances. These were British debts
chalked up in London in exchange for goods and services required
for the war effort. These grew, in total, from £1,299 million in
December 1941 to £3,355 million in June 1945, of which around
one-third was owed to India.[22] From one perspective, this was very
good news for the UK. She was, in effect, extracting an enormous
forced loan which she was unlikely to have to repay in the near
future. (One German propaganda leaflet aimed at Indian troops
portrayed Churchill escaping the bombing of London with a wagon
containing India's riches.)[23] From Churchill's perspective, however,
Britain was accumulating vast obligations towards India in exchange
for the privilege of protecting her against Japan. 'Are we to incur
hundreds of millions of debt for defending India in order to be
kicked out by the Indians afterwards?' he would demand of Amery.

'This may be an ill-contrived world but not so ill-contrived as all that.'[24] At one stage he came up with the idea of announcing publicly that Britain would make some kind of counter-claim against India. 'It may be honourable or necessary to bilk your cabby when you get to the station, but I cannot see how it helps telling him through the window that you mean to bilk him when you get there', noted the long-suffering Secretary of State, who knew both that India was massively impoverished and also that the current system was essential in order to maintain the flow of her goods and men.[25] When Wavell was present during one of these diatribes, Amery passed him a note saying that Churchill 'knows as much of the Indian problem as George III did of the American Colonies'. Wavell's contribution to the discussion was to point out that, during the first two years of the war, Indian soldiers had defended Britain in the Middle East rather than Britain defending India.[26]

Churchill was, of course, right to be anxious about Britain's financial position, which was a matter of diplomacy and of home politics as well as of economics. The American government was determined to extract, as the price of their help, commitments to a new global order in finance and trade. Open, multilateral trade and payments regimes, they believed, would safeguard against the restrictionism and slump that had bedevilled the interwar years. In particular, they wished to do away with Britain's imperial preference system, opposition to which was personified by Roosevelt's Secretary of State, Cordell Hull. In early 1942 the details of the Mutual Aid Agreement were finalized. Article VII committed Britain, as quid pro quo for Lend-Lease, to 'the elimination of all forms of discriminatory treatment in international commerce, and to the reduction of tariffs and other trade barriers'.[27] However, the British only agreed to this after the President wrote to Churchill stating explicitly that his government was not asking for 'a commitment in advance that Empire preference will be abolished'.[28] Churchill had made it clear that, although he himself 'did not believe that preferences served any useful purpose' and was prepared to negotiate for their abolition, he objected to any appearance 'that Empire ties would be bartered away or sold in exchange for goods which Britain needed to wage war'.[29] The effect was that, although the British were now pledged to future trade talks, they would not have to get rid of preferences unless the Americans cut their own tariffs to a satisfactory extent. All this, moreover, was highly important from the point of view of Churchill's domestic political position.

For, in dealing with these topics, he faced a balancing act. Most Labour ministers favoured cooperation with the USA's liberalizing agenda, as did some key Tory figures such as Eden and John Anderson. However, Amery, Lord Beaverbrook and others maintained the dream of economic self-reliance within the Empire and viewed Hull's free-trade obsession with hostility. They were also sceptical of the other aspect of the reform plans, negotiated jointly by Harry Dexter White of the US Treasury and, on the British side, John Maynard Keynes. This was the proposed International Monetary Fund (IMF) and International Bank that were eventually agreed at the Bretton Woods conference of 1944. Opponents attacked the Fund (which involved fixing exchange rates) as a return to the gold standard. This was a canard, but it was a point about which Churchill, given his record as Chancellor, may well have been sensitive. When ministers discussed the plans a few months before Bretton Woods, there was chaos. Labour minister Hugh Dalton recorded that many present, including Churchill, had not read the relevant report: 'the Beaver begins to shout headlines, "It is a gold fund", "The Bank says it is the gold standard", "We are giving up our economic empire"' and so forth. The meeting descended into pandemonium with several ministers shouting at once. The question was urgent because civil servants needed instructions for their talks with Dominion officials. Churchill, though, said the Cabinet should not be hustled 'just because a few officials from the Dominions are here; they can be entertained for a few days, and given drinks, and taken round to see the bomb craters'.[30]

The episode raises the question of whether Churchill really understood the issues at stake, which (in comparison to the tariff debates of the Edwardian era) were often highly technical. Amery, unsurprisingly, liked to suggest that he did not, and Churchill certainly did not follow all the twists and turns of the argument.[31] Keynes, on the other hand, felt that when Churchill did make an effort he could be 'quite magnificent' and capable of 'thoroughly understanding the points at issue'.[32] Perhaps what is most important is that, even if Churchill's attitude to the Atlanticist economic agenda at times seemed defensive and almost negative, he never intervened decisively against it. For, as the war drew on, he was increasingly appreciative of the fact that Britain was 'broke', and knew perfectly well that future US help would be conditional on pledges of economic good behaviour in the international sphere.[33] Unlike Amery and Beaverbrook, though, he did not think that responding to American pressure on these issues compromised the future of the Empire. For him – as in the pre-1914 era – an open global economy was compatible with a healthy British imperialism. Efforts by Americans in this direction therefore did not offend him in the same way that their interventions on India did.

II

From Churchill's point of view, the concept of 'the English-speaking peoples' was one way to preserve British influence in a world in which growing American power was a reality. In May 1943 he visited Washington for talks with Roosevelt and also addressed Congress. His speech, 'acclaimed universally as a masterpiece', allayed political pressure for a 'Pacific first' strategy by emphasizing British support for the defeat of Japan after the war in Europe had been won.[34] (This also helped reassure the Australians – foreign minister H. V. Evatt was in the audience – and Churchill further took the trouble to meet Commonwealth representatives at the White House, speaking of 'our beloved Australia and New Zealand'.)[35] During his stay, he recalled in his memoirs, he proposed to US officials 'some common form of citizenship, under which citizens of the United States and of the British Commonwealth might enjoy voting privileges after residential qualification'.[36] This did not go down well with all concerned. Vice-President Henry Wallace was treated to Churchill's musings on the theme after an official luncheon. The Prime Minister spoke of 'freedom to travel in any part of the United States or the British Empire for citizens of both countries' and also made it clear 'that he expected England and the United States to run the world' after the war. Wallace recorded:

> I said bluntly that I thought the notion of Anglo-Saxon superiority, inherent in Churchill's approach, would be offensive to many of the nations of the world as well as to a number of people in the United States. Churchill had had quite a bit

of whiskey, which, however, did not affect the clarity of his thinking process but did perhaps increase his frankness. He said why be apologetic about Anglo-Saxon superiority, that we were superior, that we had the common heritage which had been worked out over the centuries in England and had been perfected by our [United States] constitution. He himself was half American, he felt that he was called on as a result to serve the function of uniting the two great Anglo-Saxon civilizations in order to confer the benefit of freedom on the rest of the world.

Churchill in turn disapproved of Wallace's suggestion that Latin American countries could be included in the scheme for a passport-free zone. 'He said if we took all the colors on the painter's palette and mix them up together, we get just a smudgy grayish brown.' Wallace accused him of believing in 'the pure Anglo-Saxon race or Anglo-Saxondom ueber Alles'. Churchill, perhaps now on the defensive, replied that 'his concept was not a race concept but a concept of common ideals and common history'.[37] But, given his talk of mixing up the colours, it is hardly surprising that Wallace had taken him to be speaking racially.

Churchill's efforts to strengthen cooperation between America and the British Empire were replete with difficulty. It was not just a question of differences in ideology, as in the Wallace episode. (The views of the idealistic, left-wing Vice-President were not exactly typical anyway.) Rather, the British faced a dilemma, not least with regard to the growing problem of post-war planning. A strong bilateral relationship between Britain and America, with Churchill and Roosevelt at the apex, could seem, from Ottawa or Canberra, to have the effect of excluding the Dominions. On the other hand, if the British insisted on Commonwealth consultation, the Americans might suspect a collective 'ganging up' against US interests. Churchill felt it necessary to emphasize to the President that 'different parts of the Empire could meet together and discuss matters of common concern to them without, in any way, being assumed to be taking a stand against the United States or any other countries'.[38] Churchill, though, did not tend to err on the side of excess solicitude towards those he claimed to regard as his 'kith and kin'.[39] When the Australians asked to take part in discussions about the fate of post-war Europe, his immediate reaction was that this would 'have the effect of paralyzing foreign policy' and that the British 'must be accorded reasonable latitude'. Attlee, by contrast, spoke up for the Dominions' right to be heard.[40]

Particularly revealing was Churchill's comment, made around this time, about 'the troublesome attitude of the Colonies'. He was actually talking about the Dominions.[41] It is also telling that he clearly preferred 'Empire' to 'Commonwealth', although here he was prepared to compromise. When he received the freedom of the City of London in June he said that 'the expression British Commonwealth and Empire may well be found the most convenient means of describing this unique association of races and religions, which was built up partly by conquest, largely by consent'. And, in another implied hit at anti-imperialists of the Wendell Willkie type, he added that the 'universal ardour of our Colonial Empire to join in this awful conflict' was 'the first answer that I would make to those ignorant and envious voices who call into question the greatness of the work we are doing throughout the world'. He emphasized, too, though, that 'Upon the fraternal association and intimate alignment of policy of the United States and the British Commonwealth and Empire depends, more than on any other factor, the immediate future of the world.'[42]

But the path of fraternal association did not always run smooth, even within the Commonwealth. Tensions with Canada were in evidence in the run-up to the Anglo-American strategy conference – codenamed 'Quadrant' – held in Quebec in August 1943. For some time the Canadians had been growing restive. They were giving Britain substantial economic help, which was to amount to a quarter of what the US (with a much, much larger population) provided under Lend-Lease.[43] Canada also provided many volunteers for the fighting services: by the time of Pearl Harbor it already had 120,000 troops stationed in the UK. The demands of morale created pressure to give them something to do, and one result was the Dieppe Raid of August 1942. Commanded by the youthful, glamorous Admiral Lord Louis Mountbatten – too highly promoted by Churchill – fewer than half of the 5,000 raiders returned.[44] The Canadians were put to far better use in the invasion of Sicily in July 1943. Unfortunately, the draft public announcement of the action did not mention them, referring only to 'British-American' troops. Worse still, owing to a communication muddle, Mackenzie King became convinced, wrongly, that the British had rejected his request for a correction. The dispute became public, and the enraged premier complained to the High Commissioner that Churchill and his colleagues trampled roughshod over Canada's interests. In the end, Churchill agreed to make a Commons statement smoothing things over, but the Canadians also suffered other slights, real and imagined, and made their feelings known.[45] General Sir Alan Brooke, Chief of the Imperial General Staff, felt that Canada's government and its military had 'made more fuss than the whole of the rest of the Commonwealth concerning the employment of Dominion forces!'[46]

For Churchill to hold a conference with Roosevelt on Canada's soil was one way to help restore Mackenzie King's sense of dignity. The latter was sidelined from the key parts of the Quadrant talks, though; the not unreasonable argument against including Canada in Anglo-American military planning was that to do so would be unfair to the other Dominions. Mackenzie King recalled that he had been 'not so much a participant in any of the discussions as a sort of general host', whose job 'was similar to that of the General Manager of the Château Frontenac' (a renowned Quebec City hotel).[47] All the same, Churchill did make serious efforts to soothe Mackenzie King's *amour propre* and to help him meet his domestic critics' allegations that Canada's voice was being ignored. King found him 'very understanding on matters of this kind'.[48] Churchill also helped secure Ottawa a seat on the Allied committee that dealt with the development of the atomic bomb.[49] Such demonstrations of consideration may have contributed to Mackenzie King's effusiveness towards him: 'I said when we were talking that I believed he was the one man who had saved the British Empire. He said no, if I had not been here someone else would have done it. I said I did not believe that was so.'[50] It all showed that Churchill could be diplomatic (and even modest!) when he saw the necessity.

Quadrant resulted in important decisions on Operation Overlord (the planned invasion of France) and on Anglo-American nuclear cooperation. It was also agreed to create the South-East Asia Command (SEAC) under Mountbatten; eventually to reconquer Burma, the Americans nicknamed it 'Save England's Asiatic Colonies'.[51] (Orde Wingate, the arrogant but brilliant commander of the 'Chindits' – a force which undertook long-range penetration behind Japanese lines – was part of the British team in Quebec; he was to be killed in an air crash in March 1944.) Meanwhile, Churchill developed a misguided obsession with capturing the northern tip of Sumatra, from which, he believed, it would be possible to bomb Singapore. Brooke, driven to distraction, reflected in his diary on his boss's make-up: 'It is a wonderful character – the most marvellous qualities and superhuman genius mixed with an astonishing lack of vision at times, and an impetuosity which if not guided must inevitably bring him into trouble again and again. [. . .] he is quite the most difficult man to work with that I have ever struck, but I should not have missed the chance of working with him for anything on earth!'[52]

Roosevelt and Churchill met again in Egypt in November, together with the Chinese leader Chiang Kai-shek. The three men issued a joint communiqué, known as the Cairo Declaration, stating their intention that Japan be stripped of Pacific islands she had occupied since 1914 and that lost Chinese territories should be restored. The British had done their best to temper American generosity towards China, but failed to secure any mention of the return of their own possessions. (Australia and New Zealand were annoyed that they had not been involved in these decisions, which prompted a new assertiveness by them in foreign policy.)[53] From Cairo, the President and the Prime Minister moved on to Tehran for a meeting with Stalin. There, Churchill would see further evidence of FDR's determination to withhold his favours from the British.

This was the first meeting of the 'Big Three', or, as was increasingly the case – given the realities of Soviet and American power – the 'Big $2^{1}/_{2}$'.[54] Roosevelt was determined to establish a warm relationship with (or indeed suck up to) Stalin, if need be at Churchill's expense. He refused Churchill's request for an initial bilateral meeting and insisted on meeting with Stalin instead. A 'Grumbling but whimsical' Churchill told Averell Harriman (US ambassador to Moscow) 'that he was glad to obey orders; that he had a right to be chairman of the meeting, because of his age, because his name began with C and because of the historic importance of the British Empire which he represented'. Nevertheless, he said, he was prepared to waive his claims but would insist on giving a dinner party on 30 November, his sixty-ninth birthday.[55] The

Roosevelt–Stalin meeting on the 28th saw the two leaders reach accord on the future of territories liberated from the Japanese. The president criticized French rule in Indochina and raised the possibility of 'a system of trusteeship' there 'which would have the task of preparing the people for independence within a definite period of time, perhaps 20 to 30 years'. According to the US record of the talks, 'Marshal Stalin completely agreed with this view.' Roosevelt warned his new friend not to raise the topic of India with Churchill, and Stalin 'agreed that this was a sore spot with the British'.[56] They were both happy to needle him on other issues, though. That night at dinner Stalin said that the 'entire French ruling class' was 'rotten to the core'. Indeed, 'It would be unjust and positively dangerous to leave them in possession of their former Empire'. Churchill's protest that 'he could not conceive of the civilized world without a flourishing France' was rejected with contempt.[57]

The formal sessions of the conference dealt with military questions, Stalin pressing for a firm date for Overlord, and the future of Europe. But at dinner on the 29th imperial issues came up again. Roosevelt asserted that, after the war, 'bases and strong points in the vicinity of Germany and Japan' should be held under trusteeship. Churchill clearly suspected that some of these proposed bases might be on British territory, and he resented the idea that they might be subjected to international control:

> THE PRIME MINISTER stated that as far as Britain was concerned they do not desire to acquire any new territory or bases, but intended to hold on to what they had. He said that nothing would be taken away from England without a war. He mentioned specifically, Singapore and Hong Kong. He said a portion of the British Empire might eventually be released but that this would be done entirely by Great Britain herself, in accordance with her own moral precepts.

He thus did not depart from the line laid down in his 'liquidation' speech, that Britain would hold her own but not seek new territory. Stalin claimed to favour 'an increase in the British Empire, particularly the area around Gibraltar', but Churchill failed to rise to the bait.[58] Churchill's dinner on the 30th passed off well, and the next day British and Indian troops, together with employees of the Anglo-Persian Oil Company, gave him a birthday parade.[59]

On the final day of the conference, though, Roosevelt teased him mercilessly, to Stalin's great enjoyment, 'about his Britishness, about John Bull, about his habits'. By Roosevelt's account, it was this that defrosted his relations with Stalin: 'From that time on our relations were personal'.[60] The whole experience was scarring for Churchill. 'I realised at Teheran for the first time what a small nation we are', he told a friend afterwards. 'There I sat with the great Russian bear on one side of me, with paws outstretched [. . .] and on the other side the great American buffalo, and between the two sat the poor little British donkey, who was the only one of the three who knew the right way home.'[61]

The question of international trusteeship for colonial areas, raised in passing at Tehran, had been under official discussion in both Britain and the USA for some time. The pressure, of course, came from the latter, and the British discussions were much concerned with moderating any such proposals to the point of acceptability. The Cabinet Secretary's notes record Churchill's resentment of this: 'Time taken off the war in order to find a formula to gratify the Americans. Why shd. we apologise? We showed the world a model of Colonial development.' In his view, the only legitimate criticism was 'that we haven't spent enough in Colonies'.[62] The Colonial Office strategy was to move the Americans away from the idea of a single world organization towards one of regional bodies, which might be less threatening to Britain's interests; Churchill himself thought in terms of councils for Europe, the Americas and the Pacific, subordinate to a Supreme World Council.[63] Scepticism about the American attitude was not confined to him. The US was keen to acquire bases in the Pacific and, whatever Roosevelt might say casually, had little intention of subjecting control of these to international oversight. It seemed to some that the Americans were all too ready to point the finger at the evils of European colonialism, while pursuing a covert neo-imperialist agenda of their own. American double standards were neatly exposed by Oliver Stanley (Colonial Secretary from 1942) in a conversation at the White House towards the end of the war. Roosevelt, criticizing Churchill's 'what we have we hold message', told Stanley: 'I do not want to be unkind or rude to the British but in 1841, when you acquired Hong Kong, you did not acquire it by purchase.' Stanley immediately answered,

'Let me see, Mr President, that was about the time of the Mexican War.'[64]

III

The Americans were not the only supporters of trusteeship, though. New Zealand's Peter Fraser spoke up for it firmly at the conference of Dominion Prime Ministers in London in May 1944. He argued that reports on colonial administration should be submitted to and discussed by an international organization. Oliver Stanley and John Curtin both dissented (although Curtin was here at odds with the views of his colleague Evatt). Churchill blandly summarized the discussion by saying that much agreement had been reached.[65] Blandness, in fact, was the keynote of the conference, although increasingly desperate German propagandists tried to portray the meeting as a 'gathering round the death-bed of the imperial mother'.[66] India was hardly mentioned.[67] Curtin's scheme for an imperial secretariat was quietly sidelined. With British ministers still at odds over international post-war economic issues, it was hard for Churchill to make much progress on these.[68] A slight note of discord entered proceedings when the premiers discussed the proposed new international organization (the Dumbarton Oaks conference that was to lay the foundations for the UN took place later in the year). Churchill made it clear that he wished the British Empire as a whole to be represented on the new body, rather than for its component nations to have individual seats. Mackenzie King, backed by Smuts, faced down this centralizing plan. 'It was the hardest battle of the conference thus far because it required very straight and direct talking to and differing from Churchill on the things he feels most deeply about', noted King. 'The truth is, he speaks of Communism, etc. being a religion to some people, the British Empire and Commonwealth is a religion to him.'[69]

There were also other tensions. The Australian government, facing a manpower crisis, wanted to release men from the forces in order to produce food (much of the country's exports were needed by Britain). Churchill was angered by this. He felt that the Australian war effort was 'a very poor show', although his advisers were to provide him with evidence to the contrary. Meeting with Curtin at Chequers, Churchill refused to allow servicemen to return from Europe and the Middle East, although he did subsequently offer some concessions.[70] Curtin also had other anxieties, but Churchill seems to have won him over completely.[71] The *Canberra Times* reported, 'The assurances of Mr Churchill have dispelled Australian fears that Britain might be disinclined to enter wholeheartedly in the Far Eastern struggles after the fall of Germany.'[72] Actual British plans for this next stage remained unsettled, not least because of arguments in Whitehall about strategy. In spite of this, Curtin was eager, doubtless for domestic reasons, to obtain a public statement that they had been agreed. But when Mackenzie King, who knew this, pressed him to spell out what had actually been decided, the Australian used the words 'The British Government is to consider what it is going to do.' Mackenzie King was incredulous, and told Curtin sardonically, 'I assumed they would wish Canada to take some part in the war against Japan and certainly our plans were not settled at all.'[73]

In Churchill's mind Far Eastern problems naturally took a lower priority at this moment than the coming launch of Overlord. American troops had been massing in Britain for a long time, a new social fact that was the cause of much official introspection. The government failed in its efforts to persuade the Americans to restrict the numbers of black troops sent. (When the executive secretary of America's National Association for the Advancement of Colored People cabled Churchill to ask if it was true that such a request had been made, he received no reply because it was impossible to give an honest denial.)[74] Britain's non-white population at this time was tiny. Nevertheless, there were those who felt that the British – with their experience of Empire – could teach the Americans – who maintained widespread segregation – a thing or two about race relations. Most ministers hoped that Britons could be persuaded to maintain a social distance from black soldiers, making formal segregation unnecessary. In October 1942 the question came up at Cabinet, when the War Secretary, P. J. Grigg, proposed that British soldiers should be 'educated' to adopt the racial attitudes of their white US counterparts. In response, Lord Cranborne pointed out the difficulties of what he called the '"not too matey" principle'. Not only were significant numbers of black Canadians already present in Britain, but 'If it can be said we have advocated "colour bar" all the coloured people here fr. our Empire will go back discontented and preach disaffection there.'[75] He drew attention to the case of a black Colonial Office official who 'had always lunched at a certain restaurant which now, because it was patronised by U.S. Officers, kept him out'. Churchill said, 'That's all right: if he takes a banjo with him they'll think he's one of the band!'[76] The War Office largely got its way, and the government in effect colluded with the segregation maintained by the US army.

On 6 June 1944 the invasion of France began. By the end of that day 73,000 American and 83,000 British and Canadian troops had landed in Normandy.[77] Within a few days the beachhead was secure enough for Churchill to make an inspection, together with Brooke and Smuts. (The latter's tendency to support Churchill's strategic ideas over those of the Americans doubtless added to his congeniality as a companion.) Victory in Europe, although requiring terrible sacrifices of human life, was now largely a matter of time. But when Churchill contemplated the future of the continent he was assailed by doubt. Should he beg Roosevelt to take a tougher line against resurgent Russia, or throw out the hand of friendship to Stalin instead?[78] On his way to Canada for a further conference with Roosevelt in Quebec – codenamed 'Octagon' – he looked 'old, unwell and depressed'.[79] John Colville recorded, 'The P.M. produced many sombre verdicts about the future, saying that old England was in for dark days ahead, that he no longer felt he had a "message" to deliver'.[80] He was bucked up by his reception when his ship arrived at Halifax. After making a short speech he 'led community singing, beating time with his cigar'. The crowd then broke into 'God Save the King'.[81] He was further buoyed by the news on 12 September that Canadian troops had taken Le Havre. At lunch with the President and others that day he spoke of India, blaming the famine on 'the hoarding of food by the people themselves for speculative purposes' and telling stories against Gandhi.[82]

Harmony at the conference was not absolute. Mackenzie King, again not included in the Anglo-US talks, was as concerned as ever about Churchill's attempts at imperial centralization. Mackenzie King was adamant that although Canadian troops could fight the Japanese in the Central or Northern Pacific theatres, they should not do so in South-East Asia. He wrote: 'Our people, I know, would

never agree to paying out of taxes for Canadians fighting [. . .] for
the protection of India, [and] the recovery of Burma and Singapore.' He added: 'I understand the Americans feel Singapore,
Burma and all is a side-show to save the British prestige, and that
there is a possibility of American troops actually conquering Japan
before the conquest of Singapore might be effected.'[83] Meanwhile,
Churchill, who had held on to his obsession with Sumatra, plagued
his own advisers with accusations that they were conspiring with the
Americans against him.[84] At the same time, though, he recognized
the danger for post-war Anglo-American relations if Britain's efforts
against Japan appeared to be 'limited to the pursuit of her own
selfish interests in Burma, Malaya and Hong Kong'. Therefore he
offered to send a fleet to the Central Pacific to operate under US
command. This was opposed by the notoriously irascible Admiral
King, US Chief of Naval Operations, who allegedly 'did not want
anyone else to intervene in his own pet war'. But Roosevelt accepted
Churchill's gesture without hesitation. 'The British delegation
heaved a sigh of relief, and the story went the rounds that Admiral
King went into a swoon and had to be carried out.'[85]

Churchill described Octagon as a 'blaze of friendship and unity';
certainly, it was an overall success from the British point of view.[86]
Beforehand, Roosevelt had been told of the full extent of Britain's
financial difficulties; he joked that the news was 'very interesting
[. . .] I will go over there and make a couple of talks and take over
the British Empire'.[87] In Quebec, though, he agreed that Lend-
Lease should be continued during 'Stage II' – the period between
the end of the war with Germany and the final defeat of Japan.[88] It
was a necessary but generous offer, contradicting the notion that the
Americans never missed an opportunity to use their power to put
their British allies in financial bondage. When Colville suggested to
Churchill that the advantages obtained for Britain were beyond the
dreams of avarice, he replied 'Beyond the dreams of justice.'[89]

IV

But this last autumn of the war also brought its share of troubles.
Churchill returned home to the news that the First Airborne Division had met its destruction at Arnhem. (Churchill nonetheless told

Smuts that the battle had been 'a decided victory').[90] Moreover, Churchill's October conference in Moscow with Stalin was at best a partial success. On the way back, he dined in Cairo with his friend Lord Moyne, the British Minister-Resident in Cairo, who had served under him as a Treasury minister in 1924–5. It was the last time he would see him. On 6 November Moyne was returning home for lunch when two gunmen shot his driver dead and then fired through the car door at Moyne, hitting him three times. That same day, Churchill told the Cabinet 'the bad news that an attempt had been made on Walter Moyne's life, apparently by Jewish extremists, and that his condition was serious'. News of his death came that same evening.[91] When arrested, the assassins confessed that they were from the group Fighters for the Freedom of Israel, formerly known as the Stern Gang.[92] Moyne had not been devoid of sympathy for Zionism, but he had attracted the wrath of the militants in part through a speech in which he said that to force Arabs to live under a Jewish regime would be contrary to the Atlantic Charter.[93] The Jewish Press in Palestine reacted to the crime with horror. 'No enemy of the Jewish people could have done more to undermine the foundations upon which our work is reared than the murderers of Lord Moyne have contrived to do', declared *Haaretz*. In its view, the killing was the work of a 'tiny group' which had 'gone insane'.[94] It was a view shared by the pro-Zionist Leo Amery, who wrote in his diary: 'It is tragic that a man of such devotion to duty and kindliness to all men should be murdered by insane fanatics who have inflicted a possibly fatal injury on their own cause. If they had only known how helpful Walter has been in all the Palestine discussions in finding fair and workable lines of solutions.'[95]

Churchill's Commons tribute to Moyne seemed to confirm that the atrocity had been counterproductive. His eulogy was clearly marked by personal grief, and the House listened in grim silence.[96] On 17 November he followed it up with a further statement to MPs:

> This shameful crime has shocked the world. It has affected none more strongly than those, like myself, who, in the past, have been consistent friends of the Jews and constant architects of their future. If our dreams for Zionism are to end in the smoke of assassins' pistols and our labours for its future to

produce only a new set of gangsters worthy of Nazi Germany, many like myself will have to reconsider the position we have maintained so consistently and so long in the past.[97]

Moyne's murder led to a sea-change in Churchill's attitude to Zionism. It is, however, important to remember that, in spite of the extravagance of some of his language, his support for it had always had limits. Earlier in the war, primed by Chaim Weizmann, he had lent his support to the idea that a Jewish Palestine could be included in a wider Arab Federation to be headed by King Ibn Saud of Saudi Arabia. That plan foundered – inevitably – on the rock of Ibn Saud's opposition.[98] Subsequently, Churchill told the Cabinet that he was 'committed to [the] creation of a Jewish National Home in Palestine'. This should be proceeded with, he said, adding that at the end of the war, 'we shall have plenty of force with which to compel the Arabs to acquiesce in our designs'.[99] In 1944 the Cabinet reached agreement on the principle that Palestine should be partitioned into Arab and Jewish areas, which arguably fulfilled the 'National Home' pledge. Yet this did not satisfy the Zionists – who wanted the Jews to achieve a majority in the whole of Palestine through immigration – as Weizmann made clear in a meeting with Churchill two days before Moyne was shot. Churchill though, refused to listen to his arguments and made it plain that no more favourable plan was on offer. After Moyne's murder – which Weizmann condemned – Churchill instructed that discussion of even this scheme be put to one side. Although Roosevelt found him 'as strongly pro-Zionist as ever', in the spring of 1945, Churchill (perhaps influenced by Smuts's opposition to it) refused to revive the partition plan.[100] That July, he reacted to US criticisms of his government's policy in Palestine by suggesting that Britain should give up responsibility 'for managing this very difficult place'. He wrote: 'I am not aware of the slightest advantage which has ever accrued to Great Britain from this painful and thankless task. Somebody else should have their turn now'.[101] Significantly, he never met Weizmann again, in spite of describing him in the Commons as 'a very old friend of mine'.[102]

The suggestion of international involvement in Palestine made, of course, a strong contrast with Churchill's normal antipathy to outside interference in the Empire's affairs. On the last day of 1944, after an American request for British proposals on the colonial question, he wrote a minute about the trusteeship issue:

> There must be no question of our being hustled or seduced into declarations affecting British sovereignty in any of the Dominions or Colonies. Pray remember my declaration against liquidating the British Empire. If the Americans want to take Japanese islands which they have conquered, let them do so with our blessing and any form of words that may be agreeable to them. But 'Hands off the British Empire' is our maxim and it must not be weakened or smirched to please sob-stuff merchants at home or foreigners of any hue.[103]

The showdown on trusteeship came in February 1945 at the Big Three conference at Yalta in the Crimea.[104] (Beforehand, Churchill and Roosevelt had met at Malta – which earlier in the war had earned the admiration of both by withstanding a devastating siege – although the ailing President, who had only weeks to live, avoided substantive talks on political questions.)[105] The foreign ministers of all three countries were able to agree that, prior to the forthcoming conference that was to establish the UN organization, the great powers should consult each other on the establishment of trusteeships. But when Edward Stettinius (who had replaced Cordell Hull as Secretary of State) reported this to Stalin, FDR and Churchill, the latter declared that he would never 'consent to forty or fifty nations thrusting interfering fingers into the life's existence of the British Empire'.[106] Furthermore, 'After we have done our best to fight in this war and have done no crime to anyone I will have no suggestion that the British Empire is to be put into the dock and examined by everybody to see whether it is up to their standard.'[107] In his memoirs Eden described how Stalin 'got up from his chair, walked up and down, beamed, and at intervals broke into applause'.[108]

Yet in spite of the pyrotechnics, Churchill slipped up when it came to the detail. Eager to calm him down, Stettinius reassured him that the trusteeship proposal related to the stripping of Japan of islands it held under League of Nations mandates and told him, 'We have had nothing in mind with reference to the British Empire.'[109] These comments were not intended to deceive, but they appear to have lulled Churchill into a false sense of security. He went on to approve a formula whereby trusteeship would apply to a) existing League mandates, b) territory taken away from enemy states as a consequence of the war, and c) any territories that might be placed under trusteeship voluntarily. As Britain did hold existing mandates, for example Tanganyika, the proposal clearly did apply to parts of her Empire, regardless of what Stettinius had said.[110] It is unclear whether Churchill ever realized his error; either way, he convinced himself that there was 'Not much to fear' as the new world organization would 'make a mess' of its responsibilities.[111] He was too sanguine. Over the coming years the UN's Trusteeship Council was to create many opportunities for vocal international criticism of Britain's colonial policies, contributing significantly to the growing movement for rapid decolonization.[112] The episode shows that, although Churchill was more vocally committed to the maintenance of the Empire than many of his fellow politicians, he was by no means immune to the pressures to which later governments were forced to succumb.

Churchill returned from Yalta via Cairo. While in Egypt he met King Ibn Saud of Saudi Arabia, joining him for an enormous lunch. The British were given whisky and soda, albeit in coloured glasses and described as 'medicine' in order not to offend Islamic sensibilities.[113] Churchill raised the question of Palestine (which shows he had not lost interest in it altogether). According to the King, 'Mr Churchill opened the subject confidently wielding the big stick', drawing attention to the subsidies given him in the past and urging compromise with Zionism. The King said that such a compromise would be 'an act of treachery to the Prophet' and that at any rate it would do Britain no good, 'since the promotion of Zionism from any quarter must indubitably bring bloodshed, wide-spread disorder in the arab lands, with certainly no benefit to Britain or any one else'. Ibn Saud observed: 'By this time Mr Churchill had laid the big stick down.'[114]

Egypt's King Farouk, whom Churchill met next, was more pliable. The conversation was recorded by Lord Killearn, the British High Commissioner. Farouk was young, sybaritic and ineffectual. Although the head of a nominally independent state, it was clear where the power lay. In 1942, Killearn (then Sir Miles Lampson) had forced Farouk to choose between abdication or the formation of a new government acceptable to the British, making the position clear by surrounding his palace with tanks. Churchill spent a fair part of the discussion telling Farouk

> that he should take a definite line in regard to the improvement of the social conditions in Egypt. He ventured to affirm that nowhere in the world were the conditions of extreme wealth and extreme poverty so glaring. What an opportunity for a young Sovereign to come forward and champion the interests and living conditions of his people? Why not take from the rich Pashas some of their superabundant wealth and devote it to the improvement of the living conditions of the fellaheen?

This was highly revealing of Churchill's attitudes, and not only because it showed that his concern with economic development, which had been especially strong during the Edwardian period, was still present. Equally striking was his romantic conception that the problems could easily be taken in hand by a progressive 'young Sovereign', ignoring both the corrupt nature of the regime and the likely difficulties that Farouk would have faced even if he had been serious about tackling poverty. Churchill also urged the execution of Lord Moyne's assassins, who had been sentenced to death but who had not yet been hanged.[115] He had previously complained to Killearn about the delay, saying that failure to carry out the executions (which in due course went ahead) would be a 'gross interference with the course of justice' and would likely cause a breach in Anglo-Egyptian relations.[116] Churchill does not seem to have reflected that his own pressure was itself an attempted interference with the judicial process.

In March 1945 another of Killearn's visitors was Wavell, returning to London for consultations. The Viceroy wanted to discuss with ministers his ideas for constitutional progress. Churchill had agreed to this only reluctantly. Wavell's credibility with the Prime Minister had been dented by his decision in May 1944 to release Gandhi on medical grounds. His prediction that 'Gandhi is unlikely ever to be an active factor in politics again' had soon been falsified, which led to 'a peevish telegram' from Churchill asking 'why Gandhi hadn't died yet!'[117] A letter from Gandhi to Churchill received no reply.[118] Wavell had continued to press for some political initiative and Churchill had in turn denounced him in Cabinet 'for betraying this country's interests in order to curry favour with the Indians.' (On that occasion Amery told the Prime Minister 'to stop talking damned nonsense'; previously he had said that he 'didn't see much difference between his outlook and Hitler's'.)[119] Eventually, Amery joined forces with Cripps to make the Prime Minister accept that Wavell's desire for forward movement could no longer be ignored. Having given in, Churchill wrote a letter to his wife from Malta, while on his way to the Crimea. In this he confided his 'feeling of despair about the British connection with India' and about what would happen if it were broken. 'Meanwhile we are holding onto this vast Empire, from which we get nothing, amid the increasing criticism and abuse of the world, and our own people, and increasing hatred of the Indian population, who receive constant and deadly propaganda to which we can make no reply. However out of my shadows has come a renewed resolve to go on fighting on as long as possible and to make sure the Flag is not let down while I am at the wheel.' These thoughts had been prompted by reading a book by the author Beverley Nichols, *Verdict on India* (1944). The book denounced the Hindus, so it is not too surprising that Churchill agreed with it. More striking is the fact that – as he also told Clementine – he agreed with its support for the principle of Pakistan.[120] His remarks on similar lines to Butler in 1943 had not been merely casual ones.

Wavell's sojourn in London was not a happy one. One caller found that he cut a rather sad figure in the 'cheerless' room granted him at the India Office and noted, 'The girl messenger who was looking after his visitors did not know how to spell his name.'[121] The Viceroy was not a natural politician – he was disconcertingly lacking in small-talk – and he had to contend with the fact that Churchill and many of his ministers were uninterested in discussing India. At his (somewhat belated) first meeting with the Prime Minister, Churchill said, 'you must have mercy on us', and suggested that, in view of the government's many difficulties, constitutional progress in India 'could be kept on ice'. Wavell stated firmly that the issue was urgent, which prompted 'a long jeremiad' from Churchill in which he indicated his support for partition. 'He talked as if I was proposing to "Quit India", change the Constitution, and hand over India right away,' Wavell noted, 'and I had to interrupt him a number of times.'[122] Excluded from key meetings and denied the chance to see key documents, the Viceroy soon felt like 'an Untouchable in the presence of Brahmins'.[123] He did, however, have significant support from the unholy alliance of left-wing Cripps and right-wing Amery. Amery took care to ensure Churchill knew that if Wavell was forced to resign then he and Cripps would too.

For the time being, Churchill remained intransigent, haranguing the Cabinet, denouncing Wavell and attempting to disclaim the Cripps offer. ('Winston frankly takes the view that we made the offer when in a hole and can disavow it because it was not accepted at the time', observed Amery.)[124] On 7 May the news came that Germany had surrendered unconditionally. This was followed by the withdrawal of Labour and Liberal ministers from the coalition, as they were determined to secure the political independence of their respective parties. Churchill then formed a new caretaker administration, pending a general election. In spite of some last-minute attempted backtracking by Churchill, the new government agreed action. As Wavell pointed out to Amery, the 'P.M. could not expect me to return to India empty-handed, and [. . .] surely it would be unfortunate if from an electioneering point of view India came into party politics'. That would have been hard to avoid if Wavell's plans had been turned down, as the Labour leaders knew the details of all the discussions that had taken place.[125] The deal struck involved Wavell calling a conference of Indian political leaders with a view to creating an Indianized Viceroy's Council comprising members drawn from their ranks. This would be an interim solution before full agreement on a new constitution was reached. However, the conference, held at Simla, broke down in mid-July. Congress was keen to prove that the Muslim League did not have a monopoly of Muslim support and therefore wanted a representative who was not a member of it to be appointed to the Council; Jinnah refused to allow this, triggering the talks' failure. Amery wrote later that the 'immediate wrecker was Jinnah' but that perhaps the real wrecking factor was the long delay before Wavell had been allowed to make his effort; on this analysis, Amery made clear, the genuine culprit was Churchill.[126]

Just before Churchill embarked on his general election campaign he had to tackle another crisis, an episode which serves as a reminder that the British Empire was not the only one facing difficulties at this time. In 1941 British and Free French troops had entered the Levant, ousting the Vichy regime from control. (France held the area under the League of Nations mandate system.) But although Syrian and Lebanese independence was then declared in the name of General de Gaulle, this proved to be more nominal than real, in spite of British pressure. Much friction between the two Allied powers ensued. When the French arrested the Lebanese President and Prime Minister in 1943, Churchill was predictably outraged, complaining to Roosevelt, apparently without irony, that France's actions were 'entirely contrary to the Atlantic Charter'.[127] Churchill's friend Edward Spears, appointed British minister in Syria and Lebanon, was suspected by the French of agitating against them; the Prime Minister reluctantly sacked him at the end of 1944, believing that he was suffering from Francophobia.[128] In spite of French fears, the British had no territorial ambitions in the region, as Churchill's 'liquidation' speech made clear. London's policy was to sit on the fence – to support a privileged position for the French in the Levant *if* the countries' governments were prepared to concede this by treaty (which was very unlikely, given the depth of local anti-French feeling). In late May 1945 violence broke out in Syria and, when the French authorities failed to bring it under control, British troops moved in to restore order. Although Churchill had been far from keen to do this, de Gaulle interpreted it as a plot to present Britain as the protector of the Arabs and to impose public humiliation on France.[129] It had been no such thing, although it is only fair to observe that Churchill regarded Arab aspirations in the Levant far more sympathetically than he did nationalist movements in British territories. He was not scheming for the liquidation of the French Empire but he could regard the prospect of its decline with a certain detached equanimity. During the crisis, ironically, de Gaulle echoed Churchill's own language at Yalta: 'he would not allow France to be put into the dock before the Anglo-Americans'.[130]

V

To many observers, Churchill's victory in the forthcoming election looked like a foregone conclusion. In the view of the *Washington Post*, he hardly needed an issue to campaign on beyond his record of military victory and having 'saved Britain and the British Empire from what seemed certain extinction'.[131] On 4 June he opened his campaign with a broadcast that quickly became notorious. A socialist government, he said, 'would have to fall back on some form of Gestapo, no doubt very humanely directed in the first instance'.[132] In a brilliant riposte, Attlee suggested that this remark showed the difference 'between Winston Churchill, the great leader in war of a united nation, and Mr Churchill, the party leader of the Conservatives'; Labour, he argued, was the true national party.[133] Even Churchill's own supporters were dismayed by his gaffe. 'Winston jumped straight off his pedestal as a world statesman to deliver a fantastical exaggerated onslaught', noted Amery. His younger son Julian, himself a Conservative candidate, started to wonder if he was on the right side![134] Critics were able to point out that Australia and New Zealand both had Labour governments and that no dire consequences had resulted.[135] The speech may have contributed to the subsequent refusal of Ben Chifley (Australian Prime Minister after Curtin's death in office) to permit an Opposition motion thanking Churchill for his services to the Empire during the war.[136]

Imperial issues did not generate a great deal of excitement during the election. Although the Simla conference started towards the end of the campaign, India did not seem to be of much interest to the voters. Instead, domestic questions tended to dominate.[137] Churchill was keen to show that he was still a social reformer, and his rhetoric retained a slight trace of the National Efficiency theme that had preoccupied him before 1914. In his second broadcast he highlighted contemporary concerns about the falling birth-rate: 'Our future as a nation, and future as the centre of a great Empire, alike depend upon our ability to change the present trend in our population statistics.' It was essential to 'encourage by every means the number of births' and, through health policy, to 'fight for a healthy and well-nourished race of citizens'.[138] On the Empire itself, the Conservative manifesto offered some progressive-sounding generalities. It spoke of framing plans 'for granting India a fuller opportunity to achieve Dominion Status' and said that Britain's responsibility to the colonies was 'to lead them forward to self-governing institutions'. Not that Labour policy was any more specific; its manifesto talked of 'the advancement of India to responsible self-government, and the planned progress of our Colonial Dependencies'. Only the Liberals mentioned 'complete self-government for India'.[139]

The Tory manifesto was also vague on questions of international economic policy. During the campaign itself, Churchill's public reticence on these was flagged up by the economist Roy Harrod, fighting as a Liberal in Huddersfield. Harrod alleged that there was a serious danger in returning the Conservatives to power, as it was probable that those Tories (such as Amery and Beaverbrook) who opposed greater freedom of trade would get their way. The prospects for the British economy would thus be frustrated: 'Churchill, whose own ideas on these topics might be perfectly sound, would be a prisoner in the Conservativep.' At the behest of the incumbent Liberal National MP, who wanted support for his own declaration that the government stood by its previous commitments to international economic liberalization, Churchill was moved to describe Harrod's accusations as 'mischievous'.[140] Talk of Churchill as a 'prisoner' of his party on international economic issues was an exaggeration, but, as peacetime was to show, Tory divisions over Empire trade and finance were not yet dead.

Votes were cast on 5 July but the results were not announced until the 26th, in order to allow time for the votes of servicemen abroad to be counted. The outcome was a landslide for Attlee's Labour Party. Leo Amery was amongst those who lost their seats. (He had been faced in his constituency 'with very serious Left wing opposition which has been worked up against me as the oppressor of India', though it seems unlikely that this was decisive in his defeat.)[141] Churchill's defeat provoked widely differing reactions. Robert Menzies declared his departure from the international scene to be a tragedy.[142] Mackenzie King – who had recently won yet another election himself – confessed to his diary his relief 'that at Imperial Conferences and Peace Conferences I know I will not have to be bucking centralized Imperialism again'.[143] Gandhi later gave the Labour victory as an instance of the kind of mass intellectual conversion that he believed non-violence could bring about: 'To me it is a sufficient miracle that in spite of his oratory and brilliance, Churchill should cease to be the idol of the British people who till yesterday hung on his every word.'[144] But, although many Indians welcomed Labour's victory, some were sceptical. V. D. Savarkar, a Hindu nationalist later acquitted of involvement in Gandhi's murder, feared that Attlee would 'out-Churchill Churchill'.[145] Churchill did have his Indian admirers. Nirad Chaudhuri recalled:

'I was shocked, because I could never imagine that the British people would so unceremoniously reject the man who had led them to victory from an almost hopeless situation.'[146]

In America, 'The news of Mr Churchill's sweeping defeat was received with a shock of astonishment that was almost reminiscent of the reactions to the Pearl Harbor Bombing.' Sensational changes in foreign policy were not anticipated, but there was the expectation of changes in the British attitude on some issues, including India, the colonies, and Palestine. According to the British Embassy, 'The Zionists were quick to announce their pleasure at the turn of events and expressed confidence in the new Government.'[147] Republicans were alarmed by the spread of socialism. Presumably, though, the Tory defeat held a silver lining for former isolationists such as Senator Bob La Follette, Jr, who had recently censured 'Mr Churchill's dogmatic and at times arrogant refusal to discuss any definite plans for freedom for the subject people of the British Empire'.[148] However, it was not immediately clear how radical a shift could be expected from Labour. A few months after taking office, the senior minister Herbert Morrison was asked by American journalists if the new government intended to 'preside over the liquidation of the Empire'. Morrison replied: 'No fear. We are great friends of the jolly old Empire and are going to stick to it.'[149]

In contrast to the glory and heroics of 1940, the final years of World War II can appear as a forlorn tale, even though they culminated in comprehensive military victory. 'Churchill stood for the British Empire, for British independence and for an "anti-Socialist" vision of Britain', one historian has observed. 'By July 1945 the first of these was on the skids, the second was dependent solely upon America and the third had just vanished in a Labour election victory.'[150] Yet it is also important to remember that the war did evince genuine popular enthusiasm from within the Empire – and this was not restricted to the self-governing Dominions. Consider, for example, this poem on the war, written by Boishwerelo Yane, a teacher in the Bechuanaland protectorate:

When things were just about to begin,
At a time when the bells call worshippers to go and pray,
There was heard a whistle-call, that travelled
All the way from Mr Churchill, the head of the Government.

In response came out Mongwaketse, Mokwena, Mokgatla and
    Mongwato,
And the chiefs of smaller tribes in the Protectorate.
Their answer was, 'Do not wait to be asked!'
Hitler of Germany stood up in anger, the dog raised his tail.

He has put his paws on the little ones, like Poland,
Raise your voices and say, 'You dog! You have comrades,
But so too does Mr Churchill,
He has comrades who will come to oppose you.'

This was one of thirty-nine entries in a verse competition to
mark the launch of the first Setswana-language newspaper in 1944;
twenty-eight of them took the war as their subject matter. Those
who wrote them were clearly highly literate and surely had a much
firmer grasp of the causes and personalities of the war than most of
their less well-educated fellow countryfolk.[151] Equally obviously,
the half-million Africans who joined the British army had strong
economic motives to do so, yet we cannot discount the idea that
principle or indeed Empire loyalty may also have played a part in
the thinking of at least some of them.[152] Furthermore, it must not
be forgotten that support for the war and burgeoning support for
colonial liberation were not necessarily incompatible. As the Gold
Coast nationalist Kwame Nkrumah wrote in later years, 'All the fair
brave words spoken about freedom that had been broadcast to the
four corners of the earth took seed and grew where they had not
been intended.'[153] The final decade of Churchill's career was to see
him battling demands and changes in part unleashed by his own
inspiring rhetoric.

9

ONCE MAGNIFICENT AND STILL CONSIDERABLE, 1945–1955

ON 8 October 1948 Winston and Clementine Churchill arrived at the Grand Hotel, Llandudno, North Wales, accompanied by their poodle, Rufus. They were there for the Conservative Party's annual conference. Loss of power had not dimmed Churchill's celebrity status. The entire staff lined up to welcome him, and they spared no effort to ensure his comfort even at this time of harsh post-war austerity. Reportedly, one Tory worthy 'stood by the elevator gate and watched the car go up eight times, carrying only a waitress with heavy trays. Finally, the elevator boy shouted through the gate: "Sorry, sir, but it's Mr Churchill's dinner." '[1] Churchill's keynote speech the next day provided the assembled delegates with a satisfying meal of their own. He gave a bravura performance, combining strong words on the Soviet threat coupled with an attack on the 'guilty men' of the Labour government, who, he claimed, had neglected Britain's defences. He also looked forward with hope. In a well-known passage, he described 'the existence of three great circles among the free nations and democracies':

> The first circle for us is naturally the British Commonwealth and Empire, with all that comprises. Then there is also the English-speaking world in which we, Canada, and the other British Dominions and the United States play so important a part. And finally there is United Europe. These three majestic circles are co-existent and if they are linked together there is no force or combination which could overthrow them or even challenge them.

The fact that Great Britain stood at the point where the three circles overlapped created an opportunity for it to exercise global leadership. 'If we rise to the occasion in the years that are to come it may be found that once again we hold the key to opening a safe and happy future to humanity, and will gain for ourselves gratitude and fame.'[2]

Anthony Eden had already spoken to the conference of the 'three unities': 'unity within the British Commonwealth and Empire, unity with western Europe, and unity across the Atlantic'.[3] Churchill's achievement was to rearticulate this in a more colourful fashion. His rhetoric served two important functions. First, for his national audience, it offered reassurance amid the post-war gloom. The speech seemed to show how (under Conservative leadership, it went without saying) Britain could play a pivotal world role in spite of the decline of her imperial power. Second, it helped smooth over divisions within the Conservative Party itself. There was significant anti-Americanism amongst Tories at this time, which manifested itself partly in hostility to US efforts to prod Britain into engaging in European integration.[4] Churchill had himself declared in favour of a 'United States of Europe' two years earlier. He now made clear, though, that 'I cannot think [. . .] that the policy of a United Europe as we Conservatives conceive it can be the slightest injury to our British Empire and Commonwealth or to the principle of Imperial Preference which I so carefully safe-guarded in all my discussions with President Roosevelt during the war.'[5] His insistence that there was no incompatibility between a strong Empire, a united Europe and Anglo-American unity was a way of reconciling the competing ideological instincts of different groups of Tories.

His decision to give a *tour d'horizon* of foreign affairs at this point, rather than a speech on domestic matters, was characteristic. As *The Times* noted, this allowed him to avoid committing himself to the economically interventionist 'new Conservatism' associated with figures such as R. A. Butler.[6] He was not, in fact, a very dynamic Leader of the Opposition, and left much of the legwork to Eden. In part, this was an understandable reaction to the shock of electoral defeat. But it also reflected his greater comfort in his role as an international visionary than in dealing with the parochial issues that are the stuff of much party politics. Although many Conservatives became frustrated with his hands-off approach, it was not a bad strategy. His slow climb back to power, in fact, owed much to his assiduous cultivation of his image as a world statesman.

I

It was an arduous and uncertain path. The first months of peace were especially difficult for Churchill, as he struggled with the adjustment to life after Downing Street and with fractures within his party. The war with Japan had ended suddenly in August 1945, the surrender pre-empting the British operation to recapture Malaya. One consequence of the cessation of hostilities was that President Truman's administration cut off Lend-Lease aid to Britain. As no alternative source of help had been put in place, this action seemed to threaten 'stark ruin' to the national economy.[7] It also revealed divisions within the Conservative ranks. Churchill's reaction to the American announcement seemed to be one of shock.[8] However, Leo Amery (still a figure of some weight although out of Parliament) felt satisfaction. He told his diary: 'It looks as if all my objections to Bretton Woods, multilateral low tariff schemes etc. and my advocacy of reliance on sterling will now be justified and that sheer necessity will force Attlee and Co onto a policy of Empire trade: "And not through Eastern windows only"!'[9] In fact, the government took steps in the opposite direction, despatching Keynes to Washington to negotiate a dollar loan, which the Americans made conditional on trade and currency liberalization and on the ratification of Bretton Woods. The US embassy in London noted that the proposal to link the progressive elimination of imperial preferences with the reduction of American tariffs would be fought by 'the Amery group of Tory imperialists and the Beaverbrook clique who are fighting for an exclusive sterling area, Empire preference and bilateral bargaining'.[10] Although this posed no threat to the British government's acceptance of the deal, it was a serious headache for Churchill. Amery did his best to exploit 'the wonderful opportunity offered by the present situation', and was eager to develop 'a really effective campaign for educating both the Conservative Party and the public at large'.[11] To him, Churchill's economic views were those of a mid-Victorian Liberal, while Eden, who shared them, was 'tiresomely internationalist'.[12]

It was amazing, in fact, that Amery could summon the concentration to engage in politics at this time. His deeply troubled elder son John had spent the war in Europe and – believing that Britain should join with Germany to save civilization from communism – had broadcast on German radio. He argued that Churchill's government was throwing away 'the priceless heritage of our fathers, of our Empire-builders' in the course of a war that served no British interests.[13] He also made pathetically ineffective efforts to recruit a British *Freikorps* to fight the Soviets. He was now awaiting trial for treason. In due course, knowing his case was hopeless, he pleaded guilty, and on 19 December he was hanged at Wandsworth prison. Leo Amery had naturally been mortified at John's actions and, at the time of his initial broadcast in 1942, had offered to resign. Churchill had assured him that he could not be held responsible for his adult son's behaviour.[14]

During this appalling personal crisis, Amery Senior may have found some mental release in compulsive political activity. His misgivings about the US loan were not eccentric, being widely shared amongst Tory MPs and peers. Churchill 'was instinctively for taking the American money', as were Eden and other key figures, but backbench discontent was rife.[15] Hugh Dalton, now Chancellor, believed that Tory frontbenchers had had 'great rows behind the scenes with Winston'.[16] The unexpected outcome was that the Shadow Cabinet decided to recommend abstention when Parliament voted on the loan. Yet Churchill could not enforce even this rather unheroic line. His appeal to abstain was 'urged and repeated with almost desperate earnestness', to little avail.[17] When the vote was called, dozens of Tories joined a smaller number of Labour rebels in the 'No' lobby; a handful supported the government motion, which passed comfortably. Dalton relished the sight of Churchill and his senior colleagues sitting 'miserably on their backsides' while their MPs defied them.[18] The Conservative Harry Crookshank noted, 'Winston is very upset, talks of giving up etc.'[19] Amery recorded, 'In spite of his very urgent appeal 71 Conservatives voted against Winston's advice – a great shock to his leadership which now, in peace, is unnatural. The 71 may yet save the Conservative Party.'[20] The *News Chronicle* offered the realistic assessment that Churchill was unlikely to resign: 'Nor is the party likely to press for such a drastic step. All one can say is that when Mr Churchill does decide to step down there is not now likely to be much attempt to dissuade him.'[21]

Churchill's authority with his MPs had already been undermined by a recent weak performance against Attlee in the Commons and by his poor attendance record at the House. Urged by the backbench 1922 Committee to promise to show up more often, he had defiantly announced that he intended to go to the USA for several months' visit.[22] He set sail for New York on 9 January 1946. The highlight of his trip was the lecture in March at Westminster College, Fulton, Missouri. Here he gave his famous warning about the Soviet menace: 'From Stettin in the Baltic to Trieste in the Adriatic, an iron curtain has descended'. In order to counteract the threat, he called for the 'the fraternal association of the English-speaking peoples'. This, he said, meant 'a special relationship between the British Commonwealth and Empire and the United States of America'. More specifically, he pointed out that the USA already had a permanent defence agreement with Canada. (He had consulted Mackenzie King – who was highly supportive – before making the speech.) This, he said, should be extended to all Commonwealth countries 'with full reciprocity'.[23]

Churchill's speech provoked, at first, considerable hostility in the US. He was widely understood to be calling for a formal military alliance, something he denied. The celebrated columnist Walter Lippmann argued that there would be no difficulty for the USA in making a defence agreement covering the British Isles and the Dominions. The problem lay in the idea of extending US protection to the dependent Empire. This was because 'a united front in that part of the world' would not be the kind of equal partnership that was possible with Canada or other self-governing countries.[24] The Republican Senator Arthur Capper said that Churchill was apparently 'intent on using the United States as a threat against Russia to stop Russia's march across Europe and into Asia – and at the same time to arouse the people of the United States to commit this country to the task of preserving the far-flung British Empire'.[25] But, as the Canadian ambassador to Washington noted, the most violently anti-British sections of US opinion tended also to be anti-Russian. 'Therefore, the vehement disapproval such elements would normally show towards Mr Churchill's proposal for an Anglo-Saxon alliance has been modified in this case by their approval of the strong line he adopted against Russia. In their reaction to Mr Churchill's speech, these elements find it difficult to combine their favourite pastimes of "Redbaiting" and "Lion tail twisting".'[26]

The 'iron curtain' speech thus achieved much of the effect that

Churchill desired, once the initial fuss had died down. Although he had not mentioned the Anglo-American loan – which had yet to be approved by Congress – opposition to it in Washington now weakened. *The Economist* noted that if the loan passed, the balance in its favour would have been tilted by the belief that it represented an investment in security against Russian expansion: 'This may well be the first fruit of Fulton.'[27] Furthermore, Churchill made concerted efforts to ensure that the loan passed. On 10 March, Lord Halifax (then still British ambassador) hosted a dinner attended by Churchill and nine key Democratic and Republican Senators and Congressmen. According to the official who kept a record of the conversation, Churchill set the record straight about his own attitude to the loan: 'There were indeed certain aspects of the Agreement which he did not like but that was a far cry from saying that he did not wish to see the Loan approved as was believed, he thought, in this country.' He urged Americans to be 'more understanding' in their approach to imperial preference – even though, as he said, he was not a believer in it himself. His main emphasis, however, was on the trade war which, he said, would be bound to follow on rejection of the Loan by the United States:

> The United States with its economic power would clearly win such a fight but it would indeed be a pyrrhic victory. [. . .] if the Loan were not granted, England would nevertheless come through somehow – belts would have to be tightened still further and austerity endured for much longer but England would come through and with her Empire remain as always one of the great forces in the world for stability, justice and freedom.

The Senators and Congressmen seemed 'definitely impressed by all that Mr Churchill had to say'.[28] It is notable that, with the exception of Arthur Capper, all those present subsequently supported the loan, some of them vociferously. No doubt some would have done so without Churchill's intervention, but not, perhaps, the influential Republican Arthur Vandenberg, whose surprise announcement of his intention to vote in favour was crucial in shifting the debate.[29] The loan eventually passed the Senate in May and the House of Representatives in July. The impact of Churchill's efforts on this outcome is hard to quantify, but it was undoubtedly meaningful. One Congressman later told him, 'It was realization that the best of all that is Britain is represented in you which prompted my tearing up and discarding a speech prepared in opposition to the loan, and my vote in favour of it.'[30] Some US lawmakers, though, were never to shake off their conviction that Churchill was a 'cunning foreign propagandist' who wanted to 'persuade Americans to underwrite the British Empire'.[31] Their suspicions of him might have been confirmed had they heard his off-the-record speech to the University Club in New York during his 1946 visit. According to a British official who was present:

> He defended the Empire and its principles with brilliance and vigour, and was warmly applauded for his presentation of its objectives. He deplored Britain's being 'talked out' of her rich estate in India [. . .] but acknowledged the early need to advance India to nationhood. He expressed fears as to India's future, however, which he considered obscure: her people might have cause to regret any hasty assumption of the responsibilities of nationhood.[32]

Churchill returned home towards the end of March. Throughout the rest of the year, internal Tory opposition to his economic views faded away. Amery published a book attacking the loan agreement, in which he declared, 'No more than Mr Churchill am I prepared to acquiesce in the liquidation and break up of the British Empire'.[33] The Empire Industries Association, of which he was president, launched an 'Empire Unity Campaign' but it made little impact on the Conservative policy. Amery noted in November: '[Robert] Boothby [MP] brought rather a depressing account of the Party's Finance Committee which he said is drifting back hard to multilateralism and all the rest of it.'[34] The critics were later able to claim a measure of vindication. One of the conditions of the loan was that sterling should be made convertible into other currencies, including the dollar, in order to help free up trade. But after convertibility was introduced in 1947 it was quickly abandoned after a run on the pound. Churchill (who had expressed his own doubts about this part of the deal during the Commons debate) had more justification for his position, though, because there was no realistic alternative to the loan and the economic agenda that went with it. Although the empire preference gang did not disband completely –

Amery remained a fixture at Tory conferences to the end of his
life – Churchill from now on kept moderate opinion on his side.
He achieved this in part through his continued (albeit limited and
conditional) public defence of the very imperial preference system
in which he claimed not to believe. In this way, ironically, he put
himself fairly close to the Labour government's position. During
post-war trade talks, ministers stubbornly held on to a scaled-down
version of imperial preference, not through ideological commitment
but because they felt that US tariff concessions were not enough to
justify scrapping it.[35]

II

Churchill's behind-the-scenes assistance to the Labour government
over the loan showed his capacity to act in a non-partisan way on
issues of national importance. However, his behaviour in the Commons at times appeared erratic, causing some observers to worry
about his mental state. In May 1946 the Liberal Party leader,
Clement Davies, wrote a letter to a colleague describing Churchill's
reaction to a government statement on the food situation. 'Winston
began a sort of tirade. His manner of uttering it was worse than the
actual words he used. Knowing the terrible state in Europe and in
India, the impression I got from Winston was that he was not prepared to make any further sacrifices for either of those two places'.
Davies had then spoken, dissenting from Churchill's point of view;
afterwards Churchill 'walked across to me swearing and abusing all
and sundry'. Davies was, he said, 'deeply concerned about Winston.
He is a great man, a great figure and an outstanding personality, but
something is going amiss. Sometimes he behaves like an ill-mannered
gamin, making faces and putting out his tongue and so on.'[36] The
day after the episode Davies related, Churchill lost his temper during
a debate on the government's proposal to withdraw troops from
Egypt, and stuck his tongue out at Ernest Bevin, the Foreign Secretary.[37] (The negotiations with Cairo later broke down, because
of Egypt's insistence that its sovereignty over the Sudan be recognized.)[38] This was all probably less the result of mental deterioration
than of the frustrations of Opposition. 'I fear, once the immense
responsibility of the Prime Ministership and the war are off Winston's

20. *Above.* Gandhi outside
10 Downing Street. Arriving in
Britain for discussions on the future
of India in 1931, he told journalists
that he wanted to meet his political
enemies. But the Churchill–Gandhi
meeting of 1906 was not to be
repeated.

21. *Above, right.* Leo Amery as
secretary of state for India in 1940.
His long relationship with Churchill
got off to a poor start when the future
Prime Minister pushed him into the
Harrow School swimming pool.

22. *Right.* Failed mission:
Cabinet minister Sir Stafford Cripps
with Jawaharlal Nehru (later first
Prime Minister of independent India)
in 1942. Cripps took with him to
India a British offer of self-government
after the war; Gandhi dismissed this
as 'a post-dated cheque'.

23. Australian Prime Minister Robert Menzies with Churchill in 1941. Did Menzies dream of taking the keys to Downing Street for himself?

24. This World War II poster carries the slogan *"We will win"* – *Mr. Winston Churchill, the Prime Minister of Britain*. It is better known in its English version, *Let Us Go Forward Together*.

«انا لمنتصرون»
المستر ونستون تشرشل
رئيس الوزارة البريطانية

25. During a visit to the Western Desert in 1942, Churchill presented one of his cigars to Private S. Collins of Australia.

26. An RAF Consolidated B24 Liberator bomber flown by an Australian crew based in India, with nose-art depicting Churchill as a bulldog.

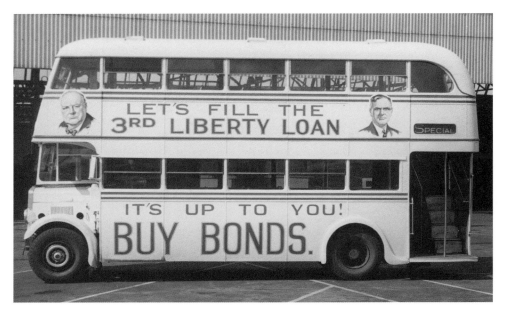

27. A bus in Sydney carrying pictures of Churchill and Australian PM John Curtin, 1943. The British found Curtin's telegrams to Churchill about Australia's defence needs exasperating.

28. Churchill in the amphitheatre at Carthage during his visit to the First Army, North Africa, 1943.

29. Roosevelt and Churchill with Canadian Prime Minister W. L. Mackenzie King (rear left) and Canadian Governor-General the Earl of Athlone, during the 'QUADRANT' Conference in Quebec 1943.

30. Tehran, November 1943. The Shah of Persia (centre) greets Churchill on the occasion of his 69th birthday. Churchill was in Tehran to meet with Roosevelt and Stalin.

31. The Dominion conference, London, 1944. Surrounding Churchill, left to right, are Mackenzie King, Smuts, Peter Fraser of New Zealand, and Curtin.

32. Factory worker laying out flags, 1945. Five years earlier, Churchill had observed that the British Empire and the United States would 'have to be somewhat mixed up together in some of their affairs'.

Gad, sir, Lord Velveteen is right. The Socialists have given the Empire away to a lot of self-governing Dominions! When Winston comes back he will send a battleship and shove 'em all back into the Empire

33. This cartoon appeared a few months before Churchill returned to office at the election of 1951. Back in power, Churchill could do little to stem the tide of Britain's imperial decline.

34. Prisoners of the British during the Mau Mau uprising in Kenya (1952–60).
This photo dates from 1954. Churchill could not understand the change that had overcome
the 'happy, naked and charming' Kikuyu people he had met during his 1907 visit.

35. Queen Elizabeth II with her Prime Ministers at the 1955 Commonwealth conference,
shortly before Churchill's retirement. Nehru is second from right; Robert Menzies
is on Churchill's right.

36. *Left.* Kwame Nkrumah
first Prime Minister of independent
Ghana, 1957. The forces of
nationalism could no longer be
ignored, but Churchill disapproved of
Harold Macmillan's renowned
'wind of change' speech.

37. *Below.* Macmillan, newly appointed
prime minister, shakes hands
with Churchill in 1957.

shoulders he will relapse into the bad judgement and recklessness of pre-war days', wrote Amery.[39] Those frustrations partly resulted from the fact that the Labour government had launched a policy of retreat from Empire of which he strongly disapproved yet could do nothing to arrest. For him, India remained the truly emotive issue. Wavell, in London once more in August 1945 for consultations, met with Churchill, who 'gave forth the usual jeremiad' and bade him farewell with the words 'Keep a bit of India'.[40]

In private, Churchill could be fatalistic. 'India must go', he told one guest at the villa he took in Italy for his holiday that autumn. 'It is lost. We have been consistently defeatist. We have lost sight of our purpose in India.'[41] 'India breaks my heart', he told Amery the following year.[42] The government's real problem now was to convince Indian politicians that they were serious about granting independence and to get them to agree amongst themselves about the shape that the future might take. From March to June 1946, Stafford Cripps headed a Cabinet Mission to India aimed at striking a deal. It seemed that the Muslim League could, on conditions, be persuaded to accept a United India, but the bargain was scuppered by Gandhi's provocative insistence that a Congress Muslim be included in the interim government. After it was announced that such a government was to be formed anyway, protests by the League led to violence in which thousands were killed. Nehru became Prime Minister in September, and the following month Jinnah joined his government, but the coalition did not succeed. In January 1947, with progress on a new constitution deadlocked, Attlee summarily dismissed Wavell and appointed Mountbatten as Viceroy in his stead. In February, hoping to induce the Indians to agree a constitutional plan amongst themselves, the British government announced its intention to withdraw from India by 30 June 1948. Churchill denounced these developments in the Commons. Claiming that communism as well as corruption had grown apace under the interim administration, he declared that it had been 'a cardinal mistake to entrust the government of India to the caste Hindu, Mr Nehru'. The new time limit did not give Mountbatten a fair chance, moreover. 'What is the policy and purpose for which he is to be sent out, and how is he to employ these 14 months?' Churchill demanded. 'Is he to make a new effort to restore the situation, or is it merely Operation Scuttle on which he and other distinguished officers have been despatched?' As an alternative to unilateral withdrawal, he suggested entrusting the problem to the United Nations. That, however, was to him a second-best expedient, as his striking peroration made clear:

> It is with deep grief I watch the clattering down of the British Empire, with all its glories and all the services it has rendered to mankind. [. . .] We must face the evils that are coming upon us, and that we are powerless to avert. We must do our best in all these circumstances, and not exclude any expedient that may help to mitigate the ruin and disaster that will follow the disappearance of Britain from the East. But, at least, let us not add – by shameful flight, by a premature, hurried scuttle – at least, let us not add, to the pangs of sorrow so many of us feel, the taint and smear of shame.[43]

'Winston was his unique self –' wrote one Tory observer, '& that self was magnificent, restrained but imaginative' and, 'toward the end, deeply moving'.[44] Another (himself an ardent supporter of British rule) thought it 'a good speech' and 'less violent than one might have expected'.[45] Churchill's colleagues, indeed, lived in some trepidation, constantly anticipating that his next speech would bring his 'antediluvian' opinions to the surface.[46] Words like 'scuttle' and 'squalid' were his stock in trade, together with predictions of civil war.[47] He tried, unconvincingly, to back-pedal his original acceptance of the 1942 Cripps Offer. He encouraged his backbenchers to attack the 'cowardly abandonment of our duties' in India.[48] Yet in truth his engagement with the Indian issue in 1946–7 was somewhat intermittent.[49] Furthermore, although he let off steam with violent outbursts in private, senior Tories generally heaved a sigh of relief after he spoke in the Commons. 'On the whole Winston might have been worse' is a typical comment from Amery's diary at this time.[50] It should also be noted that some Indians showed appreciation for Churchill's approach. B. R. Ambedkar, who visited him at Chartwell, thanked him for 'the kindness and courtesy you have shown me' and for 'the sympathy you have evinced for the cause of the Untouchables'.[51]

Ultimately, it was restraint that won out. In May 1947 Mountbatten returned to Britain with the news that Congress, and most likely Jinnah, would accept partition and Dominion status in return for a much accelerated transfer of power. He and Attlee met Churchill, Eden and Lord Salisbury (formerly Cranborne) and requested a pledge that the Tories would not try to delay the legislation to implement this. Having consulted other colleagues, Churchill sent a letter to the Prime Minister stating that the Conservative Party would not oppose the bill. What accounted for this remarkable decision? There were plenty of senior Conservatives who, fundamentally, agreed with Churchill over India, whatever their doubts about his methods of controversy. He was not, therefore, pressured into capitulation by more moderate colleagues. Primarily, it was a question of political tactics. The leadership as a whole, including Churchill, did not see much electoral advantage in the issue, preferring to focus its energies on domestic questions. Indian leaders' acceptance of Dominion status provided the Tories with a fig leaf to cover their retreat.[52] Churchill was therefore angered when he learnt that the legislation was to be called the 'Indian Independence Bill', although in fact he swallowed even this.[53]

Independence on 15 August was followed by forced population transfers accompanied by a wave of mass killings. Partition was a deeply contentious process: although it was clear on the whole which provinces should go to India and which to Pakistan, two with mixed populations, Bengal and the Punjab, needed to be divided. Over the next months, 5.8 million Muslims found refuge in Pakistan and nearly as many Hindus and Sikh refugees headed for India. Up to a million people were killed.[54] Churchill did not hesitate to blame Attlee's government for the 'hideous massacres, the like of which have never stained the British Empire in all its history'.[55] (One Labour MP in turn reproached him with the Bengal famine.)[56] Furthermore, when India's constituent assembly described the country as a 'sovereign independent republic', Churchill was in two minds about whether it should be allowed to stay in the Commonwealth.[57] The British government was ready to permit it to do so, and appeared willing to drop the word 'British' from the term 'British Commonwealth' in order to ease its path.[58] Churchill decried this in the Commons: 'At present there are not many Conservative Prime Ministers in the British Empire but it may be that this proportion will be reversed in the near future and that a more robust spirit will prevail.'[59] Even George VI thought this speech 'unwise and troublesome', as did Mackenzie King, a Liberal of course, now at the very end of his premiership and in London for his final Commonwealth conference.[60] Attlee told Churchill privately 'that it would be a disastrous step to meet India's desire for continued association with a blank negative'. In Attlee's words, 'Mr Churchill in response at once went off the deep end with his usual attitude on Indian matters, and suggested that India should now be a foreign power'.[61] However, he calmed down and in due course agreed to the unwieldy but tactful formulation whereby India became an independent republic associated with the Commonwealth, recognizing the British monarch as its head. Churchill wrote to Smuts, who was now in Opposition himself, about the issue. 'When I asked myself the question: "Would I rather have them in even on these terms or let them go altogether", my heart gave the answer, "I want them in." Nehru has certainly shown magnanimity after sixteen years imprisonment.'[62]

Churchill did come to recognize that a phase of history was over. Julian Amery recorded a lunch in 1952 at which Churchill engaged in his favourite game of historical 'what if?':

> He went back to the war-time years and said what he had hoped to do in India. He argued that with very small forces the Congress rising of 1942 had been successfully suppressed without in any way interfering with the recruitment of volunteers for the Indian Army. He believed, therefore, that with a comparatively small force we could have maintained law and order in India after the war. We could then have held a Constituent Assembly with British troops holding the ring, in which the Princes, the Untouchables, the Moslems and others would have made their influence felt much more effectively than they did in the chaos that followed our withdrawal.

However, when Amery suggested the British would yet get the Indian Empire back, Churchill replied, 'No, it is gone, gone for ever'.[63] Post-independence, Churchill established a good relationship with Nehru who, even when in prison, had considered him 'an honourable enemy' with 'fine qualities apart from the question of India or the East'.[64] In 1961 he told the US ambassador to Delhi that his relations with Churchill had been influenced 'by the old school tie. He thought Churchill had been generous in saying that he, Nehru, had forgotten both how to fear and how to hate.'[65]

This is not to say that Churchill was immediately overcome by a warm, autumnal magnanimity towards his former adversaries. In 1948 Gandhi was assassinated by a Hindu fanatic. (Jinnah died of cancer later the same year.) In his memoirs of World War II – the writing of which preoccupied him for much of his time in Opposition – Churchill showed little inclination to let bygones be bygones. His advisers managed to get him to moderate his early drafts, but he still published the assertion that Gandhi had taken glucose during his 1943 fast. When the volume in question came out in 1951, Gandhi's doctors disputed this, and the claim was removed from future editions.[66] The comment of the *Indian News Chronicle* was typical of the rage the allegation provoked: 'Mr Churchill has proved to be both a false prophet and a poor historian. He has tried to sub-edit history, over-dramatise events to glorify himself, and presented a perverted version of facts.'[67] Amery's view of the book's Indian coverage was that 'it might be worse and happily slurs over a great deal'.[68] Later academic critiques of the whole memoirs, more cautiously expressed than this, have tended to substantiate the charge of 'sub-editing history'.[69]

III

To Churchill, India was not the only case of 'scuttle' from responsibility by Attlee and Co. The issue of Burma was, of course, closely related. During the war, Churchill had reacted negatively to official planning for the post-reconquest future. In 1943 Amery wrote that 'he has an instinctive hatred of self-government in any shape or form and dislikes any country or people who want such a thing or for whom such a thing is contemplated. So far from being pleased with the thought of continued direct rule for a period of years, all he sees in it is that we are to spend money in order to be, as he puts it, kicked out by the Burmese afterwards.'[70] Churchill feared during this period that 'we are being urged to take steps in miniature in Burma which will afterwards bring the destruction of our Indian Empire'.[71] Nevertheless, in the spring of 1945, with India much more to the forefront of his mind, he let Amery's Burma proposals pass through the Cabinet 'with singularly little argument'.[72] The White Paper promised 'complete self-government within the British Commonwealth' but was vague as to timing.[73] The new Labour government was forced to speed things up dramatically, faced with the threat of rebellion under the leadership of the charismatic young nationalist (and former Japanese collaborator) Aung San. Churchill, recalling his father's role in the annexation of Upper Burma, lamented the ongoing 'decline and fall of the British Empire'.[74]

In May 1947 Aung San demanded a date for withdrawal early in 1948 and revealed that the new Burma would be a republic.[75] (Unlike India it never did join the Commonwealth.) The British could do little to arrest the rush to independence, but Aung San never got the chance to become a respected Nehru-type figure. On 19 July he and five of his ministers were gunned down together. Former premier U Saw was alleged to be behind the plot and was later hanged. Independence proceeded regardless, and this time the Conservatives opposed the bill when it was brought before the Commons in November. In his speech Churchill regretted that there was no provision for even a temporary stage of Dominion status. Referring to the ongoing dollar shortage, he observed, 'The British Empire seems to be running off almost as fast as the American Loan.' Given his former role as the head of a Japanese 'Quisling army', Aung San's hands, he said, had been 'dyed with British blood and loyal Burmese blood'.[76] This was, perhaps, not exactly the ideal way to extend the hand of friendship to the Burmese people, who revered their murdered leader. Clement Davies reproached Churchill accordingly: 'We all remember the tragedy of Ireland, but the right hon. Gentleman and his colleagues shook hands with the man who was regarded up to that moment as a traitor and who died as a result of extending the hand of friendship, Michael Collins. So it does no good to indulge in these recriminations.'[77] One civil servant involved in the Burmese negotiations described Churchill's speech as 'outrageous', adding, 'One's only hope is that it will have been discounted on the spot as coming from Winston'.[78] Churchill did not even have the full support of his own MPs. Three voted with the government and some, including Harold Macmillan and R. A. Butler, abstained. The bill passed its second reading by 288 to 114, and the Burmese selected 4 January 1948 as their independence day, believing it to be astrologically auspicious.[79] Having granted independence to violent Burma, the government could hardly deny it to peaceable Ceylon, which got its freedom, within the Commonwealth, that same February. The Conservative Party actually supported this, although Churchill did not turn up for the debate.

The developments in India and Burma unfolded against the backdrop of crisis in Palestine and negotiations with Egypt over the future of British forces there. Churchill linked these questions repeatedly. His line on Palestine was not that withdrawal should be avoided at all costs. The Zionists' high hopes of the Labour government had been disappointed: Bevin had incurred their wrath by resisting US-backed demands for high levels of new Jewish immigration. In July 1946 Jewish terrorists blew up the King David Hotel, the British HQ in Jerusalem, killing and wounding dozens. In the Commons, Churchill declared that he had not abandoned the Zionist cause, but that terrorism was putting British support for it at risk: 'It is perfectly clear that Jewish warfare directed against the British in Palestine will, if protracted, automatically release us from all obligations to persevere, as well as destroy the inclination to make further efforts in British hearts.' He noted that Britain was apparently ready to 'scuttle' from Egypt as well as India, 'but now, apparently, the one place where we are at all costs and at all inconveniences to hold on and fight it out to the death is Palestine'. He concluded: 'I think the Government should say that if the United States will not come and share the burden of the Zionist cause [. . .] we should now give notice that we will return our Mandate to U.N.O. and that we will evacuate Palestine within a specified period.'[80] Amery lamented that he was no longer in the Commons and had no chance of 'preventing Winston talking the nonsense he did about throwing up the mandate'.[81] In February 1947 Britain did ask the UN to find a solution, British troops remaining in the country for the time being.

Churchill returned to the argument that March in reaction to the initial timetable laid down for withdrawal from India. He declared it incomprehensible that there was a time limit for India but not one for Palestine, which he viewed as much less strategically significant. 'Two bottles of powerful medicine have been prepared,' he said, 'but they are sent to the wrong patients.'[82] During the debate on the Burma Independence Bill he claimed that 'Half, perhaps one-third, or one-quarter, of the British troops squandered in Palestine' would have been enough 'to enable the transfer of power to a Burmese Government, on the basis of Dominion status, to be carried out by regular and measured steps'.[83] The logic of this argument – which he also deployed in relation to India – was doubtful. If it was impossible for these troops to maintain order in minute Palestine, how could they hope to do so in massive India or jungle-clad Burma?[84]

After the UN's plan for partition was rejected by both Arabs and Jews, the British left in May 1948, triggering the war that resulted in the creation of the state of Israel. In January 1949 Churchill urged the formal British recognition of Israel, while at the same time suggesting that it would have been possible to agree a partition plan immediately after the war that would have resulted in a better deal for the Arabs.[85] Amery told Chaim Weizmann – now elected President of the country he had done so much to create – that Churchill's speech had been made in a helpful spirit. He wrote: 'You must remember that, in an unfortunate moment, no doubt upset by the actions of the terrorists, he himself had suggested scuttling, and has therefore had to turn the particular corner with some circumspection.'[86] The suggestion that Churchill's doubts had merely been a temporary aberration was, of course, more than a little misleading.

It was natural for the Attlee government to present the steps it took towards dismantling the Empire as part of a planned process aimed at securing a smooth transfer of power. 'If Churchill were in power he would lose the Empire,' opined the junior minister Patrick Gordon Walker in 1947, 'just as George III lost the thirteen colonies. The aim of the Labour government is to save the empire; this will be achieved by giving the colonies self-government.'[87] The reality was considerably messier than this implied. Labour's immediate ambitions for reform had been relatively modest. In the face of military overstretch, economic crisis and nationalist pressures from within the Empire, the government was driven to concede much more, much more quickly, than it had ever intended. To this extent, Churchill's charge of 'scuttle' had some truth in it, but Attlee's ministers do deserve an enormous amount of credit for recognizing the inevitable and bowing to it when it came. It is hard to avoid wondering what Churchill himself would have done had he won the 1945 election. He liked to suggest that, had he been in charge, progress towards self-government would have been more orderly and slower – exactly how much slower was left rather vague. But he no longer disputed the principle of self-government as a long-term goal; it would have been hard to do so, given the various pledges in this direction that his own government had made. It seems probable, then, that – just as he had been forced, kicking and screaming, to accept constitutional initiatives for India during the war – he would have been unable to overcome the momentum of post-war events. He would have been made to preside over the liquidation of a substantial part of the Empire, albeit without the Attlee government's good grace. Another possibility is that he might have drawn the line at conceding Indian independence and staged a dramatic resignation when his colleagues attempted to compel him to see sense. This seems unlikely, though, given what we know of his tenacious hold on the post of Leader of the Opposition, despite the hopes of many of his colleagues that he would bow out into a graceful retirement.

Churchill, of course, still had many admirers amongst the public, although in the early post-war period his popularity seemed to fade. A 1947 survey by Mass-Observation – whose methods were admittedly not terribly scientific – found a steep decline in approval from the peak reached in 1943. 'I have always regretted that Winston Churchill whom it is impossible not to like, did not retire on the crest of the wave', commented one young woman. 'I find it impossible to agree with his politics, and his grief at the break up of the British Empire leaves me cold.'[88] (Approval of the Empire itself, however, was generally high; wartime doubts about it, such as they were, had seemingly evaporated.)[89] In August 1949, at the age of seventy-four, Churchill suffered a stroke, although he staged a decent recovery and the news was hidden from the public. The following February the government called a general election, in the face of continued domestic austerity and the ongoing Cold War, and in the aftermath of the shock devaluation of the pound. Churchill insisted that all his youthful daydreams had been accomplished and that he had 'no personal advantage to gain by undertaking once more the hard and grim duty of leading Britain and her Empire through and out of her new and formidable crisis.' But it was, he said, his duty to try.[90]

The campaign mainly focused on the economy and on Churchill's suggestion of a summit conference with the Soviet Union. The

Conservatives made little effort to attack Labour's decolonization record. The party manifesto spoke of developing Empire trade and pledged to maintain 'whatever preferences or other special arrangements may be necessary'.[91] Nothing was said about the political future of Britain's colonies. Churchill did, however, make some play with the failure of the government's scheme to grow groundnuts in Tanganyika, a piece of attempted Empire development gone expensively wrong.[92] He also criticized the practice of sending so-called 'unrequited exports' – goods for which no payment was received – to Egypt and India by way of paying off wartime debts. He appeared to hint that some of these sterling balances should be written off in consideration for the expense to which Britain had been put in shielding the countries concerned from invasion.[93] The election resulted in a narrow Labour majority, sufficient to allow the government to limp on for some time.

Over the next months, Labour's problems got worse. The outbreak of the Korean War in June set back economic recovery, forcing tough choices about how rearmament would be paid for. Early in 1951, Chancellor Hugh Gaitskell's insistence on introducing prescription charges in the National Health Service led to the resignation of the fiery socialist health minister Aneurin Bevan. In May, a new crisis emerged in Iran, a country which could fairly be described as part of Britain's informal empire. (Informal empire is the domination of one nominally independent nation by another country, especially by virtue of economic control.) For years there had been much political meddling. In 1941, the British had deposed the Shah and replaced him with his son. The Anglo-Iranian Oil Company (AIOC) was also of vital importance. Before World War I, Churchill, as First Lord of the Admiralty, had played a part in securing a majority government stake in the company, a move intended to help secure the Royal Navy's oil supplies.[94] Now, AIOC was Iran's most sizeable foreign investor. Its refinery at Abadan was the world's biggest and represented Britain's largest overseas investment.[95] Many Iranians felt, with some justification, that they did not get a fair deal from the existing concession agreement. After the British refused to allow moves that would have increased Iran's annual payment, Mohammed Mossadegh's nationalist government announced it would nationalize AIOC's operations in the country. The Attlee government did consider military action, but concluded that it would be unwise without US backing. This was not forthcoming; at this stage the Americans saw Mossadegh as a buffer against communism. Churchill had a difficult line to steer too. On the one hand, he had to satisfy backbenchers eager to lay into the government for pusillanimity. On the other, he too saw the need not to act without US support, and he wanted to avoid the 'warmonger' label that Labour was keen to pin on him.[96]

On 19 September Attlee called another general election. Things then developed fast. On the 26th the Iranians issued an ultimatum, demanding the withdrawal of AIOC's remaining personnel from Abadan. The British complied within a week. Churchill now had a clear reason to revive the charge of 'scuttle'. A few days later Egypt denounced its 1936 treaty with Britain, and proclaimed King Farouk to be King of the Sudan.[97] (In practice, the British ignored this and its troops remained in the Suez Canal Zone.) Churchill spoke of 'the great decline of British prestige and authority in the Middle East which followed inevitably from the loss of India'. Now it was known that Britain would 'not in any circumstances offer physical resistance to violence and aggression' it was to be expected that 'Egypt will treat us more roughly still'.[98] This in turn helped Labour make use of the 'warmonger' card. The *Daily Mirror* had already cast the issue in terms of 'Whose finger on the trigger?' Was it to be calm, methodical Mr Attlee or the unpredictable Churchill? Herbert Morrison, the Foreign Secretary, stopped short of saying that the Tories actually wanted war: 'I do not accuse the average Conservative of being a warmonger [. . .] it would not be fair and it would not be true. But it is their temperament; it is the background of their mental outlook – the old imperialist outlook.'[99] Churchill, for his part, tried to rebut the charge that, had he been returned in 1945, Britain would have become involved in a war with the Indian people. At that time, he said, all parties had been pledged to granting India Dominion status, 'carrying with it the right to secede from the British Empire and Commonwealth. The only question was how the transference of power was to be made.'[100] This was an interesting reading of history, given that there had been no unequivocal Tory pledge in 1945 (although at that time Churchill had publicly lauded Amery's efforts 'to bring India to the status of a Dominion').[101] Churchill had, of course, spent many years opposing Dominion status precisely because it carried with it an implicit right of secession.

It is not clear whether either side drew a clear advantage from such rows. Amery observed at the end of the campaign that 'Winston has wound up with an impassioned defence of himself as a lover of peace. I am sure he does in principle, but he has always thoroughly enjoyed a war.' He added the charge, 'Naturally, as usual, the Empire might be non-existent so far as his speeches are concerned' – an apparently absurd accusation best understood in terms of Churchill's failure to talk constructively about imperial development in the future.[102] After the election dust had settled, the *Manchester Guardian* suggested that, although the warmonger charge had not brought much response from voters, the crises in Iran and Egypt helped the Tories less than once they would have done. Moreover, 'The Empire, still fragrant with the aroma of groundnuts, was hardly in the picture.'[103] Austerity and the cost of living were the major issues, and Churchill worked hard to portray Bevan as a left-wing extremist who would call the shots in a new Labour government. 'Abadan, Sudan and Bevan are a trio of misfortune', he said.[104] Polling day was 25 October. Labour won a majority of the votes cast but, owing to the vagaries of the first-past-the-post electoral system, the Conservatives won a seventeen-seat majority in the Commons. At the age of seventy-six, Churchill was back in Downing Street.

IV

In Canada the news was greeted warmly by the press, although the Liberal government of Louis St Laurent, Mackenzie King's successor, was more doubtful. Churchill's talk of Commonwealth solidarity was thought to raise the old threat of centralization.[105] In Australia, Robert Menzies had been back in power since 1949 while Labour had been defeated in New Zealand by the opposition National Party. The *Canberra Times*, welcoming Churchill's comeback, suggested, 'Within the British Empire the disappearance of socialist governments may pave the way to a more closely knit and effective organisation'.[106] In India there was some scepticism about his return, but it was generally viewed with a slight sense of detachment. The *Hindustan Times* said that it was no secret that Asian countries would have preferred Labour to stay in power: 'As far as India is concerned, she cannot forget Mr Churchill's references to the scaling down of her sterling balances [. . .] Now that Mr Churchill is at the head of the British government, he will have to undo his own past mischief if the faith in Britain is to be preserved.'[107] Some reassurance was offered by Churchill's appointment of Lord Ismay, his wartime military secretary, as Secretary of State for Commonwealth Relations. In 1947 Ismay had risked Churchill's disapproval by acting as Mountbatten's Chief of Staff, but it appears that he won the confidence of Indians. The *Times of India* felt that the Tories could help the cause of international peace, but warned Churchill not to 'reimpose some of the outmoded concepts of Empire and colonialism'.[108] Nehru himself was relaxed.[109] African nationalists, who had yet to win their independence, felt a greater sense of alarm. According to the *West African Pilot*: 'As the return of the "old war horse" means to Britain "more raw materials from the colonies" and [a] greater rearmament drive, so too to the West Africans, it symbolises the era of greater youth solidarity; it is the climax of our struggle; it is the period when, perhaps like the Americans of 1776, we might have to sing one tune, and one tune only: "independence in our life time".'[110] The Soviets, unsurprisingly, portrayed the Tory victory as a sign of imperialism's menacing progress.[111]

At home, the installation of the new government coincided with a moment of national optimism. In February 1952 George VI died of lung cancer and was succeeded by his daughter Elizabeth. In his broadcast tribute to the late King, Churchill gave a subtle reworking of an old theme. 'The Crown has become the mysterious link – indeed, I may say, the magic link – which unites our loosely bound but strongly interwoven Commonwealth of nations, States and races', he said. 'People who would never tolerate the assertions of a written constitution which implied any diminution of their independence, are the foremost to be proud of their loyalty to the Crown.'[112] With Britain fading as a great power, Churchill stressed the moral authority of the Crown as a substitute for military might. He spoke effectively to the public sense that the new reign might usher in an era of British resurgence. It seemed highly symbolic, for example, that, on the eve of the coronation in 1953, news came through that Edmund Hillary and Tenzing Norgay had conquered Mount Everest. The former was from New Zealand and the latter from Nepal, but Churchill was far from unique in hailing their climb as a 'memorable British achievement'.[113]

Such episodes could boost optimism about a 'new Elizabethan age', but the Empire could not survive on prestige alone. The economic situation was serious. At a time of global shortage, Britain could no longer rely on cheap supplies of raw materials from the colonies. Oliver Lyttelton, the new Colonial Secretary, told the Cabinet, 'Amery economics are no longer applicable.' He also warned that financial constraints made colonial economic development 'impossible'.[114] Far from launching a new rearmament drive, the new government was forced to retrench the existing programme inherited from Labour. In July 1952 – by which time the government had already ditched a bold plan, Operation ROBOT, to free up the economy by floating the pound – Churchill told a rowdy House of Commons of his concerns.

> Tragic indeed is the spectacle of the might, majesty, dominion and power of the once magnificent and still considerable British Empire having to worry and wonder how we can pay our monthly bills. I fully admit I am tortured by this thought and by the processes which I see around me, and I shall do everything in my power – [Hon. Members: 'Resign!'] – to bring home to the mass of our race and nation the sense of peril and the need for grave and far-reaching exertions.[115]

Meanwhile, nationalist pressures were making themselves felt in many parts of what was left of the Empire. Perhaps the most pronounced crisis was the communist insurgency in Malaya, where a state of emergency had been in place since 1948. Just prior to Churchill's re-election the High Commissioner, Sir Henry Gurney, had been shot dead when his car was ambushed. The man appointed to replace him was General Sir Gerald Templer, who is generally credited with devising the strategy that eventually defeated the insurgency. 'You must have power – absolute power – civil and military power,' Churchill said to him at the outset. 'And when you've got it grasp it, grasp it firmly. And then never use it. Be cunning – very cunning. That's what you've got to be.'[116]

Sitting above all these problems was that of America. Churchill returned to power at the tail-end of the Truman era. The 1952 election race was between the Democrat Adlai Stevenson and, for the Republicans, Dwight Eisenhower, with whom Churchill had worked closely during World War II. The sculptor Oscar Nemon was visiting the Prime Minister at Chequers when the news of the result was due and, according to Nemon's unpublished memoirs, Churchill was hoping for a Stevenson victory. He was looking at his tropical fish tanks when an assistant told him of Eisenhower's win. 'And now I shall also have a fish that can talk', he said. Nemon replied that he did not know that any such fish existed. 'Believe me it does,' answered Churchill, 'and this one speaks with an American accent.'[117] Whatever his reservations about the new President, Churchill understood the importance of cultivating him, although his efforts to this end were rather transparent. Eisenhower noted in his diary that Churchill had 'fixed in his mind a certain international relationship he is trying to establish – possibly it would be better to say an atmosphere he is trying to create'. He felt that Churchill's hope that Britain and the Commonwealth would receive privileged treatment from the US was inappropriate and was reluctant to be seen to be propping up colonialism. 'In some instances immediate independence would result in suffering for people and even anarchy', he acknowledged, but, 'In this situation the two strongest Western powers must not appear before the world as a combination of forces to complete adherence to the status quo.' He concluded: 'Much as I hold Winston in my personal affection and much as I admire him for his past accomplishments and leadership, I wish that he would turn over leadership of the Conservative Party to younger men'.[118]

However, whenever British and American interests coincided, Eisenhower was happy to collude with Churchill's efforts to shore up Britain's power. This was the case in Iran, where attempts to reach a negotiated settlement had failed. The threat of a coup by the Iranian Communist Party, which was lending its support to Mossadegh, helped convince Washington that it was necessary to strike first. Eden, as Foreign Secretary, was cautious. In June 1953 he flew to Boston for medical treatment. Churchill used his absence to approve Anglo-American plans to remove Mossadegh with the cooperation of the Shah. On the 23rd Churchill suffered a massive stroke, which took him out of action for several weeks. His illness was kept secret from the public. The Iranian coup which brought down Mossadegh went ahead in August. Initially, things went wrong and the Shah briefly fled. However, the CIA orchestrated street protests that ended with the Shah's return and with Mossadegh in jail.[119] Kermit Roosevelt (grandson of Theodore and distant relation of Franklin) was the plot's CIA mastermind. After it was over, he visited Churchill at Downing Street where he found him in bed, propped up by pillows. As he related the tale of the coup, the Prime Minister sometimes listened attentively and at others nodded off, 'consumed alternately by curiosity and by sleepiness'. 'Young man,' he said when the story was over, 'if I had been but a few years younger, I would have loved nothing better than to have served under your command in this great venture!'[120]

The problem of Egypt proved more difficult. In 1952 King Farouk was forced to abdicate following a nationalist coup. General Mohammed Neguib and Colonel Gamal Abdul Nasser were key figures in the regime that replaced him; in due course Nasser dispensed with his rival. Through all this the British, who still had many troops in the Canal Zone, remained eager to negotiate a new Anglo-Egyptian treaty to secure their future military presence in the region. The Egyptians had little incentive to negotiate, as the existing treaty was due to expire in 1956, at which point they could hope to see the back of the troops. The Americans were not prepared to do much to help the British, as they did not want to risk driving Egypt into the Soviet camp. Eden's efforts to strike a deal could therefore only be an exercise in saving face: it was not realistic to think that the soldiers could remain. In spite of this, Churchill talked tough, although he cleverly modulated his message. In 1953 Leo Amery, still watching affairs from the sidelines, described how 'Winston [. . .] made a splendid speech on Monday which entirely captured the opposition by his suggestion of discussions with Russia and a new [Treaty of] Locarno, and the Right by being firm with Neguib.'[121] To his fellow Commonwealth Prime Ministers Churchill insisted that Britain's interest in the Near East was 'No case of so-called imperialism.' Britain was in Egypt 'for international reasons', in order to protect an international waterway and to maintain a base important to NATO.[122]

Churchill's 'no surrender' attitude may have been a good parmentary tactic but, in general, it did not make Eden's job any easier. It was already hard enough. Churchill's troubled relationship with his Foreign Secretary was rotting the government from within. Having anointed Eden as his successor during World War II, he stubbornly refused to relinquish the throne. At times he could be positively malicious about this. An eminent doctor who was lunching with him told him, after watching him eat and drink, that he had the glands of a man of forty: 'Whereupon Winston at once said, "Pass the glad tidings on to Anthony!"'[123] His diehardism on Egypt was certainly the product of conviction. (As a parliamentary candidate in 1899 he had declared that England would 'leave Egypt when the pyramids fell down, and not before'.)[124] But it was also a very effective way of needling Eden. On one occasion – when Eden was not present – he went into 'a rage against A.E., speaking of "appeasement" and saying he never knew before that Munich was situated on the Nile'. Churchill seemed to regard the quest for agreement as a sign of weakness and even to positively want the talks to break down.[125] He was particularly resistant to including in any agreement the termination of joint Anglo-Egyptian rule of the Sudan – the legacy of Kitchener's River War campaign in which he had fought. The majority of the Cabinet was against him, and he knuckled under, although, as the negotiations progressed, he continued to tell colleagues: 'I care far more about Sudan (a great & living trust) than about [the] Canal Zone.'[126] By conceding the principle of Sudanese independence – which came in 1956 – the Egyptians were able to eliminate the vestiges of British control there.

Churchill's attitudes had much in common with the so-called Suez Group of Tory backbenchers. Much influenced by the experience of the Abadan crisis, they demanded a halt to imperial retreat.[127] Prominent amongst them was Julian Amery, who had been elected in 1950. 'I thought the base in Suez was the key to our position in the Middle East and in Africa', he recalled. 'And I made a rather bitter attack on a speech Eden had made foreshadowing withdrawal.' The next morning Amery received a phone call from No. 10, but he did not get the 'rocket' he anticipated. Instead the Prime Minister's secretary told him, 'Mr Churchill asked me to let you know that he's read your speech and he is very impressed by it!' Moreover, Amery remembered, in 'subsequent conversations in the House, on three or four occasions, when I was leading this campaign against the withdrawal from the base, he would say, "Keep it up! I agree!"'[128]

There were, of course, limits to how far Churchill could go in undermining his own government's policy. He muttered about acting as Foreign Secretary himself should Eden resign, but he could hardly have withstood such a calamity. So he unenthusiastically accepted Eden's line. Finally, an agreement between Britain and Egypt was reached whereby the troops would be evacuated by June 1956, but they would be allowed to return in the event of war. Civilian technicians would stay for seven years after the withdrawal to keep the base facilities in good order.[129] It must have been a bitter moment for Churchill.[130] When a meeting of backbenchers discussed the deal, and started to become truculent, the government Chief Whip found the Prime Minister and told him, 'I think you ought to go up. Our side is in trouble!' With a grunt, Churchill replied, 'I'm not sure I am on our side!' But he did go and, reluctantly backing Eden, carried the meeting.[131] 'You cannot maintain prestige with folly', he told the would-be rebels.[132]

When the agreement was announced in the Commons in July 1954, Churchill 'sat glum and with bowed head'. Labour MPs taunted him with cries of 'No scuttling!' When Attlee pointedly asked him if the agreement had his consent, he rose slowly, looking hurt, and the House fell quiet. He opened his arms wide and said, 'I am convinced that it is absolutely necessary.'[133] In debate the next day he declared that the claim that he had encouraged the Suez Group 'under the table' was 'an absolute untruth'. He rationalized his change of heart by claiming that the advent of the H-bomb had rendered the Suez Canal Base obsolescent.[134] That was not a terribly convincing argument. However, his ultimate willingness to bite the bullet of withdrawal forms a reminder of the pragmatism that his wilder outbursts often obscured.

V

His relations with Commonwealth leaders similarly demonstrated his ability to adjust to new realities. He continued to develop the good relationship with Nehru that he had begun to establish in Opposition after 1947. 'I get on very well with him', he told Lord Moran. 'I tell him he has a great role to play as the leader of Free Asia against Communism.' Moran asked how Nehru reacted to this. After all, he was to be a key figure in the Non-Aligned Movement of countries that were determined not to take a side in the Cold War. 'He has a feeling that the Communists are against him, and that', Churchill explained with a smile, 'is apt to change people's opinions.'[135] In fact Nehru's appreciation of Churchill was based in part on his sense that, as a Cold Warrior, he was by no means completely hard-line.

Perhaps less surprisingly, now that the tensions of the war period were past, Churchill achieved an amicable bond with Robert Menzies. The thaw had set in with a 1948 visit to Chartwell at which the Australian had been granted a preview of the 'three circles' concept. Although Menzies thought that Churchill really ought to retire, he made sure to cultivate the link of friendship.[136] He contributed an essay on 'Churchill and the Commonwealth' to a volume published to celebrate the great man's eightieth birthday in 1954. Noting that the Prime Minister had not been identified with 'great Empire economic policies' – Churchill was 'much too European for that' – Menzies offered a slightly backhanded tribute to his wartime imperial rhetoric. 'The great Imperialists in half a dozen countries had made millions think [of] the Empire', he wrote; 'it was left to Winston, the Englishman and European, to make scores of millions feel it with passion and will.'[137] Churchill also retained his fondness for Canada, which he visited in 1952 and again in 1954. He was, however, deeply upset by the decision that the Canadian navy should abandon the playing of 'Rule Britannia'. He told Lester Pearson, the country's minister for external affairs, of his bitter disappointment and, to drive the point home, 'recited all the verses of "Rule Britannia", and, inspired by this, went on to recite several Harrow patriotic songs he had learned sixty years ago'.[138] On his visits, the Canadian authorities tactfully ensured that the anthem was played for him on every possible occasion.

Churchill even got on well with Eamon De Valera on the one occasion that he met him. At the close of World War II, the two men had clashed over the airwaves. In his May 1945 victory broadcast Churchill had lambasted Ireland's decision to stay out of the war, and spoke of how Britain, instead of seizing the ports, had restrainedly 'left the De Valera government to frolic' with German and Japanese representatives in Dublin.[139] In response De Valera had offered a dignified vindication of Irish neutrality. Their September 1953 encounter, when the Taoiseach visited London, was surprisingly cordial, although they did not make any great diplomatic breakthrough. When De Valera raised the question of Irish unification, which in theory Churchill still favoured, the latter pointed out the obstacle posed by Ulster and Conservative Party opinion. To the request for the return of the bones of the Irish patriot Sir Roger Casement, hanged for treason by the British in 1916, Churchill implied that he favoured the idea, but afterwards did not act on it. (Casement was finally reburied in 1965.)[140] One other point of interest came up. In 1949, when De Valera had been out of power, Ireland had left the Commonwealth for good. He now told Churchill that he would not have taken this step himself.[141] Perhaps this contributed to Churchill's beneficent reaction to his former adversary. 'A very agreeable occasion', he said afterwards, 'I like the man.'[142]

On racial issues, though, he made no effort to adjust to modernity.[143] When asked if he had seen the film *Carmen Jones*, a musical with a black cast, he replied that he had walked out early on as he didn't like 'blackamoors'.[144] This was not just a private prejudice: it had implications for policy. Labour's 1948 British Nationality Act had confirmed wide rights – which had previously been available to Empire subjects – for Commonwealth citizens to settle in Britain. It received little debate at the time, but immigration soon increased rapidly. Many of the new arrivals were from the West Indies. By the early 1950s the issue of 'coloured' immigration was rising up the political agenda and the Conservative Cabinet discussed it on several occasions. The Cabinet Secretary's notebook records Churchill's view in 1954. He spoke of the problems which 'will arise if many coloured people settle here. Are we to saddle ourselves with colour problems in UK?' Immigrants, he said, were 'attracted by the Welfare State', and 'Public opinion in U.K. won't tolerate it [immigration] once it gets beyond certain limits.' At this stage, however, he thought it would be 'politically wise to allow public feeling to develop a little more' before taking action.[145] The following year Harold Macmillan noted a further discussion on Caribbean immigrants: 'A bill is being drafted – but it is not an easy problem. P.M. thinks "Keep England White" a good slogan!'[146] In fact, restrictive legislation was not passed until some years after Churchill left office. He complained to the editor of the *Spectator* that he thought immigration was 'the most important subject facing this country, but I cannot get any of my ministers to take any notice'.[147] In reality, many of them shared his (undoubtedly exaggerated) concerns. His inability to get anything done probably owed much to the fact that, by this stage, his diminishing energies were focused mainly on foreign policy. Arguably, it also owed something to the difficulties of drawing up a law that would have the effect of excluding black people while appearing to be non-discriminatory.[148] (Race was clearly the issue: ministers showed no concern about continuing large-scale Irish migration, even though the Republic of Ireland was now outside the Commonwealth.) Churchill disliked the idea of a 'magpie society', as he called it, which he thought 'would never do'.[149] Ironically, lack of decisive action to halt black and Asian migration meant that he presided, however unwillingly, over the beginnings of Britain's multicultural society.

At the international level, the advent of the apartheid regime in South Africa in 1948 added an unpleasant new dimension to discussion of race. Smuts's electoral defeat that year followed by his death two years later had deprived Churchill of a reliable friend. Once back in office himself, the Prime Minister he had to deal with (until 1954) was the National Party's D. F. Malan. In addition to its well-known segregation laws, Malan's government sought to weaken South Africa's connection with Britain, for example by making it harder for British immigrants to be granted citizenship. Churchill's government did not approve of apartheid but, at the same time, it did not want South Africa to leave the Commonwealth and was wary of alienating Malan's regime. Officially, apartheid was a South African internal question.[150] David Hunt, one of Churchill's private secretaries, recalled the Prime Minister 'sending a telegram to Dr Malan and asking me whether he should say sardonically, "My dear Mr President [*sic*], *Alles sal reg kom* (everything will be all right). Keep on skelping the kaffirs!"' The joke was clearly in poor taste, but it does hint at a slight sense of awkwardness on Churchill's part. He may have been, in Hunt's words, 'on the whole rather anti-black', but overt, institutionalized racism was a source of embarrassment and uneasiness.[151] Yet it was not an issue that Churchill wanted to confront directly, or even one that he was happy to see others confront. When the Archbishop of Canterbury, Dr Geoffrey Fisher, denounced apartheid as 'a sort of slavery', Malan protested vigorously. Lord Swinton (Ismay's replacement at the Commonwealth Relations Office) brought the matter to Cabinet, warning that Malan

might object to sitting with the Archbishop at the forthcoming coronation. Churchill said that Fisher should be reproved, and that he
would be 'well advised to stick to spiritual matters'.[152]

However, the government did hold firm against the South
African desire to take control of Basutoland, Bechuanaland and
Swaziland (known collectively as the High Commission Territories).
The threat that they would be swallowed up was longstanding. In
1941, Churchill had written that if this occurred they would be run
'in accordance with very old-fashioned ideas'.[153] When the South
Africans brought the issue of the territories up again in 1954, he
told the Cabinet, 'We will not hand these over to Malan.' He
believed that if South Africa renounced its allegiance to the Crown,
Natal, a strongpoint of British loyalism, might secede from the
Union, but he correctly predicted that Malan would not react
violently to a refusal.[154] He then made it clear in the Commons that
the demands would not be met: 'I therefore sincerely hope that Dr
Malan and his Government, with whom we have hitherto happily
co-operated on so many problems we share in common, will not
needlessly press an issue on which we could not fall in with their
views without failing in our trust.'[155] Churchill also took a firm line
in negotiations over the Simon's Town naval base near Cape Town.
'No weakening of our rights over Simonstown should be tolerated',
he urged, and argued there should be no NATO involvement there.
'The Americans are getting a footing in many parts of what was
once our Empire but I do not think our weakness has yet become
so pronounced as to require American protection to preserve our
rights in Simonstown in any period which we need to consider at
this moment.'[156] Agreement was finally reached in 1955, shortly
after Churchill's retirement, on terms more advantageous to the
British than might have been expected. Although the South Africans
gained control of the base, the Royal Navy kept the right to use its
facilities in peacetime and was guaranteed their availability in time
of war, even a war in which South Africa was not involved.[157]

There has been much debate over the 1951 government's
African policy as a whole. Did it represent a continuation of the
Attlee administration's decolonization agenda, or did it seek to
turn back the clock? There is a strong argument for continuity,
albeit in the sense that Labour had in reality been reactive rather
than radical and that this dynamic did not change much under

the Tories. Certain decisions, such as the creation of the doomed Central African Federation (of Northern and Southern Rhodesia and Nyasaland) were a continuation from the previous regime.[158] The case of the Gold Coast is also instructive. There, Kwame Nkrumah had founded the Convention People's Party (CPP) in 1949. Pointing out that the Labour government was relatively sympathetic to African demands, and desiring immediate self-government, he urged striking while the iron was hot. Citing Churchill's 'liquidation' speech, he warned that if the Conservatives were returned to power 'our struggle for independence might be suppressed'.[159] He was imprisoned for supporting an illegal strike, but was released when his party won the country's first general election in 1951. The following year, Nkrumah became Prime Minister, and in 1957 he led his country to independence. Now known as Ghana, it was the first African country to win its freedom from Britain. Much of the progress was owed to the colony's far-sighted Governor, Sir Charles Arden-Clarke. He knew that Conservative ministers were doubtful about the pace of change but he got his way anyway, in the absence of a workable alternative policy.[160] Naturally, his efforts helped stoke up demands elsewhere in British Africa. If the Gold Coast had its own Prime Minister, why shouldn't, say, Nigeria have one too? Churchill thought that it was 'Crazy' to give universal suffrage to 'these naked savages'. Lyttelton hoped to 'retard' constitutional development in Nigeria and cited the principle of 'divide et impera'.[161] There was no big new wave of decolonization for the time being. However, the real question by this stage was when the various colonies would get independence, not if. The government's strategy was to apply the brakes whenever practicable, not to engineer a major change of course.

VI

Of the many African issues the government had to confront, the worst was the Mau Mau revolt in Kenya. It was probably also the one that involved Churchill most emotionally, as the memory of his 1907 visit gave him a sense of connection to the country. The image he had gained then of its inhabitants as happy, childlike people conformed with the prevailing stereotype. In the face of horrific

Mau Mau violence, this was suddenly replaced with a stereotype of Africans as primordial savages, in the grip of some form of collective psychosis. The blood-curdling nature of Mau Mau oaths (often taken unwillingly) helped justify the use of 'primitive barbarity' as a simplistic, catch-all explanation. In fact, Mau Mau's origins owed much to land hunger, exacerbated partly by the reservation of the highlands to the settlers, as approved by Churchill years earlier. However, the rebellion should not be understood exclusively as an anti-imperial revolt but rather as a civil war within the Kikuyu, the ethnic group chiefly affected. Many Africans stayed loyal to the British regime, including, for example, Harry Thuku, the nationalist whose deportation Churchill had sanctioned in the 1920s. Only thirty-two European civilians were killed in Mau Mau attacks, in comparison with at least 1,819 African deaths. The British response to the crisis was brutal. Communities were subjected to collective punishments. Members of the security forces – black as well as white – committed terrible brutalities. The death penalty was extended to a wide range of offences, including administering Mau Mau oaths, carrying weapons, or 'consorting' with the group's members. A total of 1,090 Kikuyu were executed for such crimes during the course of the emergency, many of them after trials that were patently unfair. At least 150,000 people passed through the detention camps, almost always being held without trial.[162] Unsurprisingly, such measures were counterproductive, forcing thousands of Kikuyu to take to the forests and transforming sporadic Mau Mau violence into a full-scale guerrilla campaign.[163]

How much responsibility did Churchill and his ministers bear for the major abuses that took place? One Nairobi journalist has written recently, 'Churchill's role in the atrocities against the Kenyans is too obvious.' This is because 'He was the man who appointed and gave moral and institutional support to a number of war criminals', including Sir Evelyn Baring, the Governor of Kenya from 1952. Furthermore, 'Churchill was the head of an unrelenting Conservative Government that believed in its arrogant "civilising mission" to Africans, even as it reduced them to sub-humans.'[164] To those who are inclined to see the decolonization process as essentially benign, such anger comes as a salutary reminder of the deep resentment that some people still feel about the British role. It is, moreover, undoubtedly true that Churchill bore some general moral responsibility for the things done in his government's name. Beyond this broad responsibility, there is the question of his detailed involvement, how extensive it was, and whether or not his attitude was truly 'unrelenting'. There was certainly an element of diehardism in his views, but close examination of his role in the crisis shows that at times he showed a surprising level of sympathy towards the rebels.

Churchill had no direct part in instigating the state of emergency. This was asked for by the newly arrived Baring in October 1952, after the murder of Paramount Chief Waruhiu wa Kungu, the latest in a rash of Mau Mau killings. Baring was under pressure from the settlers, who, he feared, might take the law into their own hands in the absence of strong official action. Lyttelton agreed to his request.[165] Churchill's own early interventions prove, on the one hand, that he was concerned about Kenyan affairs and that, on the other, his efforts had little effect. In a typical move, he suggested that an exercise for parachutists should be held in Kenya, feeling that a display of air power would make an impression on the population and improve confidence in the British regime. The Chiefs of Staff rejected this as unnecessary.[166] He continued to worry away at the idea, although it was never implemented: 'What I propose is that small parties of 20 or so should be dropped in selected places and that two or three cross-country vehicles should come and pick them up after they had interviewed the local natives.'[167] Far better judged, but equally ineffectual, was the minute he sent to Lyttelton about cattle taken from the Kikuyu as a form of collective punishment. He asked if it was true that they were dying from lack of attention: 'they must be fed, watered and milked; who is doing this? Remember they belong to the innocent as well as the guilty.'[168] Such sentiments were worthy, but he did not succeed in getting the people on the ground to take much notice of them.

In March 1953 a large group of loyal Kikuyu was massacred at Lari.[169] 'Today's Mau Mau atrocities in Kenya show the urgency for getting troops there', Churchill wrote. 'At the same time there are advantages in staging a battalion en route for a few days at Khartoum and thus imprinting upon the minds of the Egyptian dictators the fact that we can quite easily cut them off entirely from the Sudan out of which they hope to talk, bribe and swindle us.'[170] As always, he resented criticisms of the British and there was a chill in his relations with Nehru when, on the anniversary of the Amritsar massacre, the latter spoke up in support of Mau Mau.[171] 'I never expected anything better from a Congress governed India', Churchill wrote.[172] But he was not willing to allow the settlers carte blanche. In mid-1953 General Sir George Erskine was appointed as Kenya's Commander-in-Chief. Erskine took a very dim view of the settlers: 'I hate the guts of them all, they all are middle-class sluts.'[173] Churchill equipped him with a letter giving him the power to impose martial law. Erskine never used it, but he made sure its existence was known. He kept it in his glasses case, and when he wanted to bring settlers or members of Baring's government into line, he would do so by pointedly snapping the case open and shut.[174]

Churchill's own instinct was to find some way to negotiate with the Mau Mau. His quest for a Michael Collins-type leader with whom to strike a deal helps to explain his support for clemency for one of the movement's most notorious leaders, Wahuriu Itote, known as 'General China'. To understand this episode fully, we also need to be aware of Churchill's attitude to capital punishment. He was a firm supporter of hanging. However, as Home Secretary – with the power to reprieve condemned criminals – he had been modestly lenient.[175] Much later, in Opposition in 1947, he was one of several MPs who intervened on behalf of five men in the Gold Coast who had been condemned to death for ritual murder. He objected to the fact that several times they had been on the brink of execution, only to be granted a stay at the last minute. He criticized this as ' "cat and mousing" men up to the scaffold'.[176] (Three of the five were later hanged.)[177] In respect of Mau Mau, then, he had no objection to executions as such, but he did sound a note of caution. In May 1953 Baring pressed for measures to speed up trials, and Lyttelton warned the Cabinet that up to two hundred hangings might take place as a consequence of the Lari massacres.[178] Churchill told the Cabinet that 'care should be taken to avoid the simultaneous execution' of large numbers of people as 'Public opinion in this country would be critical of anything resembling mass executions.' It is important to emphasize that he was objecting here, not to large numbers of executions per se, but to large numbers of people being hanged *at the same time*. Lyttelton promised that he 'would seek the advice of his Cabinet colleagues if any question arose of carrying out simultaneously death sentences imposed on more than, say, twelve persons'.[179] He also tried to use Churchill's views as a means to restrain Baring's zeal.

'All of this is likely to be a troublesome question,' he told the Governor, 'and I wanted to give you the earliest warning of the PM's attitude.'[180] But the warning had little effect. Very soon after, rules for new fast-track courts were approved in Nairobi, without being scrutinized in London.[181]

Churchill may have felt some reservations about developments in Kenya, but he never said so openly. He did, however, seize the chance to advocate mercy when it could be justified in terms of policy. This opportunity presented itself with the capture of General China. China had served with the King's African Rifles during World War II, but afterwards became disillusioned with the lack of prospects for ex-servicemen in Kenya. In 1950 he took a Mau Mau oath and not only oathed others in turn but killed those regarded as traitors to the cause. When the emergency was declared he and a small band of followers had already sought refuge from the police in the Mount Kenya forest. As the numbers of forest fighters grew – he eventually commanded four thousand of them – he played a key role in attacks on European farms and on the loyalist Kikuyu Home Guard. In January 1954 his luck ran out when he was wounded in a battle with the security forces. Expecting to die of his injuries, he gave himself up. His capture was a major intelligence coup for the British, as he provided crucial information on the numbers and disposition of the Mau Mau forces to his interrogator, Assistant Superintendent Ian Henderson, who managed to win his trust. Within little more than a fortnight he was tried and sentenced to death. He would have been hanged, as so many others were, but Henderson was convinced that he would be more useful alive, and that he might even be able to help broker a surrender pact with the Mount Kenya armies.[182] The hope of a large-scale capitulation was the background to the British Cabinet's discussions of China's fate.

In the background too was Churchill's concern about press attacks regarding the use of the death penalty in the fight against Mau Mau. On 10 February Churchill told his colleagues that there was much in the criticisms. Executions, he said, should 'serve a public service', the implication being that sometimes a greater good could be served by giving a reprieve.[183] According to the formal minutes of the meeting he said that Baring, in considering whether or not to reprieve China, 'should give due weight' to the fact that it was now being claimed on his behalf that he had given himself up in response to the amnesty that already had been offered to fighters who surrendered. That claim was untrue. However, Churchill asked, 'In view of the importance of convincing Mau Mau supporters generally of the reliability of this offer, might it not be advantageous to exercise clemency in General China's case, even though the Government did not in fact accept his claim to have surrendered under the terms of the amnesty?' The minutes also record Lyttelton's reply: 'he was in full agreement with the Governor's view that commutation of the sentence would have a deplorable effect in Kenya, particularly among the Government's Kikuyu supporters'.[184] The Cabinet Secretary's notebook upon which the minutes are based record a franker exchange. Churchill spoke critically of 'Execution of men who fight to defend their native land' to which Lyttelton replied 'But this is armed rebellion.'[185] At this stage the balance of opinion was to let the execution go ahead.

However, by the following week Baring had changed his tune, and cabled London to say that it seemed possible that China could negotiate the surrender of gangs not only in his own area but in Kenya as a whole. Under these conditions, commutation of his sentence was desirable. Taking a firmer line against the settlers than was his wont, he said that the violent criticism that this was likely to produce should be ignored.[186] Churchill raised the issue again in Cabinet, and said that once negotiations had been opened with China on the basis proposed he should not be hanged even if the talks broke down: 'you can't bargain with a man under sentence of death and hang him if he doesn't come across'. Lyttelton said that he still disapproved of the whole thing, but that he would leave the decision to Baring. It was possible that only a few fighters would lay down their arms: 'He will get a bad bargain if only a few come across & you have to let him [China] off.'[187] However, even Lyttelton came round once he had arrived in Kenya himself on a tour of inspection.[188] China's reprieve was announced on 4 March.[189] Settler leader Michael Blundell declared, 'The record of "General China" was one of murder, butchery, and arson, and from what has happened one could only conclude that the hallmark of the Government was expediency, and that they had no principles at all.'[190]

Blundell's own visit to Churchill in Downing Street took place that December. The parley conducted via General China with other rebel leaders had not led to large-scale surrenders, in part because a detachment of the King's African Rifles had attacked a group who were waiting to give themselves up. It looked as if British promises could not be trusted.[191] Nevertheless, the Mau Mau were now on the back foot militarily. This did not put an end to Churchill's desire for negotiations; again and again he urged Blundell to find someone to do a deal with. 'I'm sure that you need negotiation', he insisted, asking repeatedly if there was any possible partner: 'You must find someone to negotiate with. I'd like to come and do it myself.' He also spoke of 'the bad odour that the shootings, the brutalities and the detention camps gave to Britain in the world'.[192] Churchill's last significant contribution on Mau Mau occurred early in 1955. The government promulgated a new amnesty for all crimes committed by both sides prior to January that year. This has been viewed as a very one-sided offer. Although spared the death penalty, surrendering fighters would be subject to indefinite detention, whereas loyalists who had committed atrocities would get off scot free.[193] In Cabinet, Churchill raised a similar objection, saying it was a pity to confuse the surrender offer with the withdrawal of proceedings against loyalists. Alan Lennox-Boyd, who had replaced Lyttelton as Colonial Secretary, replied that it would be impossible to defend the first without the second. Kikuyu Home Guard members would desert and the settlers would be affronted. Churchill returned to the point, asking if it would not be enough merely to suspend proceedings against loyalists until it was clear whether or not there had been a general Mau Mau surrender. Lennox-Boyd again rebuffed him, saying that it could not be allowed to appear that the fate of loyalists depended on the success of the surrender appeal.[194]

There was to be no end to the rebellion before Churchill left office in 1955. The bulk of the fighting was over by 1957, although the formal State of Emergency continued until 1960. In sum, it is true that, as Prime Minister at the head of the whole system, Churchill presided over some appalling abuses committed by the imperial regime, but he did not actively will them. In fact, he showed signs of being troubled by them and made some efforts to prevent them. It is worth remembering that as a young and vigorous Colonial Office minister in the Edwardian era he had railed against similar abuses, on a smaller scale, often without being able to do much to stop them. His failure to do so now can in part be explained by the fact that he was growing increasingly decrepit and had many other questions to deal with. His sense of the urgency of colonial issues at this time is hinted at by his response to Lennox-Boyd's request for a new Colonial Office building. All that was needed, Churchill thought, was a suite of rooms with 'a large sitting room, a fine kitchen and dining room'.[195] His remaining energies were spent mainly on problems of Cold War politics, and although his occasional fits of interest in Kenya were largely benign, only a more concentrated effort could have made a real difference.

VII

Churchill's final months in power formed an inglorious end to a great career. Colonial policy was not much to the fore. After Stalin's death in 1953 he had sought a summit meeting with the new Soviet leaders. He clearly hoped that, if he brought a thaw to the Cold War, he could then retire in a blaze of glory. Nehru endorsed the summit idea warmly, telling the Indian parliament that 'fear-laden humanity will bless those who will rid it of these terrible burdens and lead it to peace and happiness'.[196] Churchill's pursuit of a rapprochement with the Russians was a way of trying to prove that Britain – positioned at the point of overlap of the 'three circles' – could still be a key player. However, the idea was not viewed warmly by the Americans or even by Churchill's own colleagues, and it died a prolonged death. In July 1954, in an attempt to sidetrack him from it, Eisenhower suggested to Churchill that his hope for 'a fitting climax' to his career could be satisfied by other means. Colonialism, the President wrote to him, was 'on the way out as a relationship between peoples'. Churchill should make a speech on this: 'If you could say that twenty-five years from now, every last one of the colonies (excepting military bases) should have been offered a right to self-government and determination, you would electrify the world.'[197] In a caustic reply, Churchill denied, implausibly, that he was 'looking about for the means of making a dramatic exit or of finding a suitable Curtain'. Furthermore:

> I read with great interest all that you have written me about what is called Colonialism, namely: bringing forward backward races and opening up the jungles. I was brought up to feel

proud of much that we had done. Certainly, in India, with all its history, religion and ancient forms of despotic rule, Britain has a story to tell which will look quite well against the background of the coming hundred years.

As a matter of fact the sentiments and ideas which your letter expresses are in full accord with the policy now being pursued in all the Colonies of the British Empire. In this I must admit I am a laggard. I am a bit sceptical about universal suffrage for the Hottentots even if refined by proportional representation. The British and American Democracies were slowly and painfully forged and even they are not perfect yet. I shall certainly have to choose another topic for my swan song: I think I will stick to the old one 'The Unity of the English-speaking peoples.' With that all will work out well.[198]

Churchill continued to hang on in office, driving his ministers to distraction by his refusal to set a firm date for his departure. Harold Macmillan, exaggerating somewhat, said that Churchill's 'almost child-like determination to get his way at all costs and regardless of other results must be, partly at any rate, a result of his mental illness'.[199] Eden, of course, was the chief sufferer. According to Oscar Nemon, the Prime Minister would sit gazing into space and mumbling half-aloud, 'Those hungry eyes. Those hungry eyes! I really should resign. One cannot expect Anthony to live forever.'[200] Churchill-admirer Nirad C. Chaudhuri saw him in the Commons in what was one of his final appearances as Prime Minister. 'He looked very much like his figure on a Toby jug, but was much more rosy, white-haired, and child-like than I could have imagined him to be', Chaudhuri wrote. 'It was surprising how successfully he had divested himself of all atmosphere, of all suggestion of being not only a writer, historian, and political thinker, but also a statesman and war leader.' He later added that he had intended these words in a complimentary sense, saying that he saw Churchill as 'an English incarnation of one of the early heroes of Rome, Cincinnatus', a model of virtuous simplicity.[201]

Churchill finally stood down in April 1955. Leo Amery, even now keeping an eye on events, wrote, 'It cannot be said that he has been a great Prime Minister this last time,' but thought that he would 'always live by his war leadership' and by his great post-war speeches.[202] (By the end of the year Amery himself had succumbed to old age, earning a tribute from Churchill as 'above all, a great patriot.')[203] The evening before his formal resignation, the soon-to-be-ex-Prime Minister played host to Queen Elizabeth at a dinner party at No. 10. In proposing a toast to Her Majesty, Churchill said, 'Madam, I should like to express the deep and lively sense of gratitude which we and all your peoples feel to you and to His Royal Highness the Duke of Edinburgh for all the help and inspiration we receive in our daily lives and which spreads with ever-growing strength throughout the British Realm and the Commonwealth and Empire.'[204] The news of his retirement made headlines throughout the world, but not in London; Fleet Street was in the throes of a newspaper strike. There were some critical voices on the left. F. A. Ridley, writing in the *Socialist Leader* (which was unaffected by the strike), poured scorn upon Churchill: 'He tried to hold Ireland by force, and it is now an independent republic; he helped to conquer South Africa, and it is now treading the republican road; he assisted to garrison Egypt, and he himself had to sign the agreement abandoning the Suez Canal. An unbroken record of disaster!'[205] In France, *l'Humanité* made a similar point: 'all his life, Churchill has fought against the emancipation of the colonial peoples, and these today have risen up against their oppressors; all his life, Churchill has sought to defend the privileges of British capitalism, and this has led him ultimately to mortgage his country's national independence to American imperialism.'[206] However, a perhaps more authentic note of popular feeling was struck by the Gold Coast's *Daily Graphic*. It observed that Churchill still liked to be controversial, but it added that 'the years have mellowed old antagonisms and he is regarded now with affection and respect by everyone, even those who opposed his policies most bitterly'.[207] In this, the paper surely spoke for many throughout the now all-but-liquidated Empire.

EPILOGUE

IN RETIREMENT, Churchill told his cousin, the sculptor Clare Sheridan, that his life's work had 'all been for nothing. [. . .] The Empire *I* believed in has gone.'[1] This pessimism was surely in part the product of the depression induced by his departure from office and worsening health, but his gloom about British decline was not wholly misplaced. Even though his compatriots were benefiting from low inflation, full employment and increasing living standards, affluence at home seemed to some to be poor compensation for the concurrent collapse in influence abroad. That collapse, if inevitable in the long run, was dramatically accelerated by the actions of Anthony Eden. Churchill had expressed his own private doubts about his successor on his last night in Downing Street. Sitting on his bed after his dinner with the Queen, still wearing his knee-breeches and decorations, he was silent for several minutes before suddenly exclaiming, 'I don't believe Anthony can do it.'[2]

At first it seemed that this prediction would be falsified. Eden seemed glamorous, even dynamic, and won a decisive general election victory in May 1955, just weeks after taking over. Soon, however, he appeared to be drifting. One *Daily Telegraph* journalist lamented the absence of the 'smack of firm government'.[3] Living in the shadow of Churchill's myth, Eden was greatly irritated by such comments, which does much to explain his spectacular over-reaction to the events of July 1956. He also, of course, had to contend with the right-wing Suez Group of backbenchers that Churchill had previously encouraged behind the scenes. His desperation to avoid any accusation of weakness conditioned his response to Egypt's nationalization of the Suez Canal, which was owned by an Anglo-French company. This act – highly provocative but not illegal – came just weeks after the withdrawal of British troops under the

1954 treaty that Eden himself had negotiated. His determination to undo the humiliation by facing down Nasser was to lead him to disaster.

The government began planning military action while maintaining a façade of negotiation. Eden kept Churchill informed of developments. 'I am pleased with the policy being pursued about Suez', the latter told Clementine in early August, 'We are going to do our utmost.'⁴ On the 5th of that month the hawkish Harold Macmillan, now Chancellor of the Exchequer, visited Churchill at Chartwell. When Churchill asked his opinion of the government's existing military plan, Macmillan said that it was not bold enough. As he recorded in his diary, he suggested involving Israel: 'Surely, if we landed we must seek out the Egyptian forces; destroy them; and bring down Nasser's Govt. Churchill seemed to agree with all this'.⁵ Indeed, Churchill was so excited that the next day he rushed off to see Eden at Chequers. Eden's wife Clarissa – who was also Churchill's niece – recalled, 'It turned out he had dictated "a plan" on the road and the secretary had miraculously managed to type it as they were going along.' She was not impressed: 'Naturally Anthony had covered everything Winston mentioned in his plan – which turned out to be Harold's anyway.'⁶ The following day the Prime Minister was in a bad mood, and Macmillan concluded 'that the source of the trouble was the Churchill visit. Eden no doubt thought that I was conspiring with C against him.'⁷ Even though Eden himself wanted to overthrow Nasser, he resented anyone else appearing to outdo his fervour. His longstanding resentment of Churchill was undoubtedly mixed up in this.

The Americans were not keen on Nasser, but neither were they eager to see him deposed by force. Eisenhower, running for re-election, wanted to present himself as the man who had restored peace to the world. Eden therefore made a show of exhausting the diplomatic options, but in October he decided to act behind the backs of the Americans. A secret pact with France and Israel committed the latter to invade Egypt. Anglo-French forces would then move in, under the guise of 'separating the combatants'. Coming just days before November's presidential election, the invasion was met with hostility in Washington. One of Eisenhower's first reactions was to wonder 'if the hand of Churchill' was behind the operation, 'inasmuch as this action is in the mid-Victorian style'.[8] In fact, Churchill would never have come up with a plan that involved deceiving the US government on such a scale. He was supportive of Eden in public, releasing a statement which spoke of his confidence that 'our American friends will come to realize that, not for the first time, we have acted independently for the common good'.[9] However, American opposition quickly combined with a weakening British financial position to bring the invasion to an abrupt halt. Eden's resignation, on grounds of ill-health, followed in January 1957. In private, Churchill said he thought the whole Suez operation had been appallingly badly conceived and carried out. Asked whether, had he still been Prime Minister, he would have done what Eden had, he replied, 'I never would have dared; and if I had dared, I would certainly never have dared stop.'[10] His friend Violet Bonham Carter recorded: 'I think he is very sad about everything poor darling – & though he began by being critical & fully realizing the Govt's blunder, he now cannot endure or admit defeat *for this country*'.[11]

'After Suez', according to Clementine Churchill, her husband 'specifically set out to mend fences with the United States', through visits, public statements, and discussions with key American figures.[12] His faith in Anglo-American unity was undimmed, and his four-volume *History of the English-Speaking Peoples*, published between April 1956 and March 1958, formed a testament to it. He had originally conceived it in the 1930s and, as he explained then, 'What is common to the history of the whole race will form the staple of a narrative comprising their origin, their rise, their quarrels and their comradeship, which I trust may long continue.'[13] After it had been put on ice during the war, work began again in 1953. Much of it was written by ghost-writers.[14] In 1963 President Kennedy awarded Churchill honorary citizenship of the United States. In his statement of thanks – probably drafted for him – the former prime minister rejected 'the view that Britain and the Commonwealth should now be relegated to a tame and minor role in the world'. He added: 'Mr President, your action illuminates the theme of unity of the English-speaking peoples, to which I have devoted a large part of my life.'[15] It is worth comparing these comments with a remark he made in a letter to his brother over sixty years earlier, in which he spoke of 'this great Empire of ours – to the maintenance of which I shall devote my life'.[16] Naturally, he viewed maintenance of the

Empire and the unity of the English-speaking peoples as wholly
compatible, indeed mutually reinforcing. But it is interesting to note
how, as the Empire declined, the theme of 'the English-speaking
peoples' eclipsed it in his public rhetoric at the last.

Eden was replaced as Prime Minister by Harold Macmillan,
whose government's approach to the Empire was unromantic: if
the costs of holding a particular territory outweighed the benefits
it should be dispensed with. After Macmillan secured a third term
for the Tories in 1959, he appointed Iain Macleod as Colonial
Secretary. The differences between the Macleod era and what had
gone before can be overstated but, even if he was simply bringing
earlier policies to their logical conclusion, he did so at a greatly
accelerated rate. By the time Macmillan moved him in 1961,
appointing him as Conservative Party Chairman and Leader of the
House of Commons, the key decisions had already been taken.
Nigeria gained independence in 1960; Tanganyika, Kenya, Nyasaland (as Malawi) and Northern Rhodesia (as Zambia) soon followed
in its wake. Even the Prime Minister himself may have been alarmed
at what he had unleashed. Nevertheless, Macmillan made his own
contribution to the spirit of reform with his famous speech to the
South African parliament in 1960, making clear the British government's disapproval of apartheid. 'The wind of change is blowing
through the continent', he said. 'Whether we like it or not, this
growth of national consciousness is a political fact.'[17] Churchill saw
this as needless antagonism of the South African government. 'Why
go and pick a quarrel with these chaps', he asked.[18] Violet Bonham
Carter noted that 'he is alas very anti-black & didn't like Harold's
Cape Town speech'.[19] He was also sceptical about the government's
1961 decision to apply for membership of the European Economic
Community (EEC), a course of action seen by many as a betrayal
of Britain's Commonwealth links. Robert Menzies wrote to him
expressing his fears regarding this, and also criticizing what he saw
as the dictatorial tendencies of Kwame Nkrumah as President of
Ghana. Churchill sent what was, at this stage in his life, an unusually
long reply, agreeing completely with Menzies. He thought Ghana
would leave the Commonwealth, although he was 'not convinced
that would be a great loss'.[20] When Montgomery visited Churchill
in hospital after a fall in 1962, he asked him if he favoured Britain
joining the EEC. He received a straight 'No'. However, when

Monty told the press of this, Churchill's secretary put out a statement reiterating Churchill's formal position, which was supportive of the government, while emphasizing that Britain's Commonwealth role should not be put in jeopardy. Britain should apply, because the negotiation process was the only way of finding out whether the conditions of membership were acceptable.[21]

Another episode of Churchill's retirement is worth noting, if only for its oddity.[22] This was his contribution to the 1957 motion picture *Something of Value*. The movie was adapted from the Robert Ruark's book of the same name, and told the story of a white settler (Rock Hudson) and his one-time boyhood friend (Sidney Poitier), a Kikuyu who becomes involved in Mau Mau. When the director, Richard Brooks, visited Kenya to scout for locations an African lawyer he met introduced him to the anthropologist Louis Leakey. Leakey in turn took him to meet the imprisoned Jomo Kenyatta, later independent Kenya's first President. Between them they persuaded Brooks that Ruark's novel, which was sympathetic to the white settler viewpoint, did not portray the situation in the country accurately, and that he should change his script. 'Leakey and Kenyatta said that unless the Europeans could get along with the Africans, the Europeans would have to get out of Africa', recollected Brooks. 'Leakey told me that might be difficult to believe, so he gave me a book written by Winston Churchill which said the same thing.' Although Brooks's interpretation of it might seem hard to recognize, the book was *My African Journey*. Deeply impressed by what he read, the director spent months trying to get hold of Churchill on the telephone. When at last he did so, he overcame the former Prime Minister's initial scepticism and persuaded him to provide a short, filmed prologue.[23] 'Forty-nine years ago I visited Africa', Churchill said in this. 'In my book *My African Journey* I wrote "the problems of East Africa are the problems of the world". This was true in nineteen-hundred and seven. It is true today.' However, this introductory monologue went down badly with test audiences. As Brooks recalled, a difficult meeting with MGM studio executives followed:

> One of them said, 'Before we start talking about what we think is rotten about this movie, I want to tell you something right now. You have got to get rid of this fucking Englishman ...'

I said, 'What are you talking about? Who?' He said, 'The guy at the beginning of the movie! That's who! Out! Out of the picture!' I said, 'Are you talking about Sir Winston Churchill?' He said, 'Whoever the fuck he is, I don't care!' I said, 'He's the greatest statesman in the world.' He said, 'I don't care. Out of the movie!'[24]

And so the Greatest Living Englishman ended up on the cutting-room floor.[25]

In 1964, not long before his ninetieth birthday, Churchill finally left the House of Commons. Harold Wilson's Labour Party won the general election that took place that October and thereafter continued the decolonization agenda. On 10 January 1965 Churchill suffered a massive stroke, and lingered on for two weeks before passing away on the anniversary of Lord Randolph's death. Around the world there was an outpouring of emotion. As on his retirement, there were dissenting voices. A few days before he died, the Iraqi newspaper *Al-Thawra al-Arabiyya* printed an unpleasant cartoon captioned 'Churchill Struggles with Death'. It showed Churchill sitting with his 'daughter' Israel on his knee, demanding to take her with him. 'Imperialism', in the guise of Uncle Sam and John Bull, insists that he leave her behind 'so that we may torment the Arabs with her'.[26] Eamon De Valera, now holding the largely ceremonial post of President of Ireland, acknowledged that 'Sir Winston Churchill was a great Englishman, one of the greatest of his time'. But he added that 'we in Ireland had to regard Sir Winston over a long period as a dangerous adversary. The fact that he did not violate our neutrality during the war must always stand to his credit, though he indicated that, in certain circumstances, he was prepared to do so.'[27] Neither he nor the Taoiseach, Seán Lemass, attended Churchill's funeral, and the Minister of External Affairs was sent instead.[28] The ambivalent Irish attitude was nicely captured by University College Dublin's Literary and Historical Society, which resolved to send a telegram of sympathy to Clementine Churchill 'by 59 votes to 23, with nine abstentions'.[29] There was also a hint of such ambivalence to be found in India. President Sarvepalli Radhakrishnan talked of the Indian people's 'profound sorrow', but former minister Krishna Menon saw fit to recall Churchill's 'belligerent days against Indian nationalism'. (Nehru had died the previous year but had stated that he would attend Churchill's funeral were he to outlive his old adversary and fellow Harrovian.) African reaction was somewhat less equivocal. Nkrumah of Ghana spoke of his 'deep regret'.[30] Michael Okpara was one of several leading Nigerian politicians who paid tribute: 'He said Sir Winston's qualities were admired by all African nationalists who could not agree with him on the question of their complete freedom.'[31]

Although the tributes to him naturally focused on World War II, the Empire dimension of his life also received an airing. Harold Macmillan, for example, in a BBC broadcast, spoke of Churchill's 'love of Britain, of the Empire, his pride in its glorious past, his confidence in its future'.[32] (However, in a radio talk prepared for the USA and Canada, he did not mention the word 'Empire', instead speaking of 'his love of Britain and the Commonwealth, and his sincere belief in the common purpose of all English-Speaking Peoples'.)[33] Likewise, Robert Menzies, in his widely praised broadcast, spoke of Churchill as 'a great Commonwealth statesman' and not as an Empire statesman.[34] But if Macmillan and Menzies were a touch reticent about using the term Empire, two other commentators were less shy. Interestingly, they were both Americans. Eisenhower – who could easily have chosen to be more anodyne – said that Churchill was 'the embodiment of all that was best in the British Empire'.[35] And Joseph C. Harsh, the US journalist who provided commentary on ITV's coverage of Churchill's state funeral, was even more forthright: 'Before the days of Winston Churchill, many an American saw Britain as a selfish imperial taskmaster ... During the Churchill era that image has been transformed.' Thanks to Churchill more than any other man, he said, 'we Americans who once thought of Britain as rapacious, insolent and domineering now think of Britain as sturdy, brave and above all honourable'.[36]

The funeral itself, which took place on 30 January, could be seen as Britain's last great imperial pageant. In Salisbury, the capital of (Southern) Rhodesia, there was a splendid memorial service, attended by the country's political elite. This has been described as 'perhaps the last great "establishment" occasion in Rhodesia when the great and the good could feel part of the British tradition of which they had been so proud'.[37] A few months later the white minority regime in Rhodesia, desperate to avoid the imposition by London of majority rule, illegally and unilaterally declared independence. It was a moment that symbolized the British government's inability to control the destinies of its former imperial subjects. The following year the country's leader, Ian Smith, declared, 'If Sir Winston Churchill were alive today, I believe he would probably emigrate to Rhodesia – because I believe that all those admirable qualities and characteristics of the British that we believed in, loved and preached to our children, no longer exist in Britain's future as the centre of a great empire'.[38]

There were plenty of other interpretations of Churchill and his legacy. The day after Churchill's death the journalist and historian John Grigg, a somewhat unconventional Conservative, argued that he had been the architect of a 'delusive victory'. Grigg did not doubt that Churchill had saved Britain from defeat and dishonour, but believed he had failed to save it from its friends. 'Though he claimed – and doubtless believed – that he had not become the King's first Minister to preside over the liquidation of the British Empire, he had no choice but to acquiesce in a state of affairs that made that liquidation inevitable. He presided, in fact, over the inauguration of the American empire.'[39] (No one seems to have taken exception to these comments at the time, but when the right-wing historian John Charmley made a similar argument nearly thirty years later he provoked a storm of controversy.)[40] By contrast, the journal *Round Table*, which had been founded by Lord Milner and his followers in 1910, offered a subtle defence of Churchill. Commonwealth subjects, it suggested, had a simplified image of him, which was not closely related to the many controversies in which he had engaged. To them, it argued, he was simply a patriot: 'He was the great fighter, and the cause for which he fought was their own. In the end, they saw him as the universal deliverer, the protector of the liberty of the Commonwealth to choose its own path; and none of them cared, few of them realized, that the path they actually chose to follow was transforming the Commonwealth in a sense directly opposed to the conception of it that prevailed in Churchill's mind.'[41] Richard B. Moore, an American black rights activist born in Barbados, offered a very different but similarly thoughtful take in the journal *Liberator*. 'The most able and voluble spokesman of the imperial mode of thought, Winston Churchill was nevertheless its prisoner', he wrote. Moore condemned severely many aspects of Churchill's record, including his willingness 'to degrade and persecute the militant leaders of nationalist colonial movements'. Yet he also found much to praise, including Churchill's 'sage warnings', his 'eloquent and inspiring' speeches in 1940, and his building of alliances with the USA and the USSR. How could these great contributions to human welfare be produced by such a narrow, hidebound imperialist? Moore explained that this was due to 'a most rare and fortunate coincidence', that is, 'the agreement at that specific moment and in that particular conjuncture of events, of the vital interests of the British Empire with those of the great overwhelming majority of mankind'.[42] Here we see Moore struggling to reconcile his admiration for Churchill on the one hand and his opposition to Empire on the other. The acknowledgement that the interests of the British Empire and those of humanity in general *could* have coincided, even if only under very particular conditions, was surely a very significant concession for a radical anti-colonialist to make.

In the years since his death, Churchill has remained an iconic figure. US presidents have repeatedly invoked his name in support of their own goals. For George W. Bush, he was a man who 'knew what he believed' and 'really kind of went after it in a way that seemed like a Texan to me'.[43] However, when British and American politicians call upon Churchill's memory, the imperial aspect of his career tends to be airbrushed out of a picture in which his battles against Nazism are heavily foregrounded. His early military heroics may be celebrated – as in the film *Young Winston* – but the attitudes that attended them are not. Nevertheless, Bush was vulnerable to reproaches such as 'Even Churchill Couldn't Figure Out Iraq'.[44] By contrast, politicians outside the Western world are not reticent in addressing Churchill's imperialism. In 2005, in a speech made in Sudan, President Thabo Mbeki of South Africa launched into a stinging denunciation, quoting Churchill's early remarks on the 'fanatical frenzy' of Muslims as evidence of the 'terrible legacy' of British colonialism. By depicting Africans as savages, he argued, Churchill and other imperialists had inflicted devastating divisions upon the Empire's subject peoples. These 'eminent representatives of British colonialism' had done 'terrible things wherever they went, justifying what they did by defining the native peoples of Africa as savages that had to be civilised, even against their will'.[45] Yet, even if his criticisms had a measure of validity, just as Bush's praise of

Churchill did, Mbeki too was using historical memory for his own
ends. While deploring the past evils of colonialism, he noticeably
failed to draw attention to the contemporary horrors being perpet-
uated with Sudanese government connivance in Darfur. It should
also be noted that there have been others willing to criticize
Churchill's imperial record from a very different perspective. In
1990 a BBC documentary team received an anonymous letter from
a South African woman of English descent in response to a call for
information. She wrote: 'It was Churchill who, in his most "glorious" years, threw away the entire British Empire with the stroke of
a pen and he should be held responsible for the rape of not only the
entire African continent but also of India and Asia. Orderly British
rule [was] handed over carte blanche to primitive savages.'[46] This
opinion may have been bizarre, but it was not necessarily unique in
South Africa during the final collapse of apartheid.

How, then, should Churchill's lifetime involvement with the
Empire be assessed? His defenders amongst historians are certainly
right to argue that the picture is more complicated than his diehard
image would suggest. That reputation, acquired from the 1920s
onwards, overlay an earlier picture of him as an imperial conciliator,
based on his South African and Irish accomplishments. When at the
Colonial Office before World War I he was even seen for a brief
time as a 'danger to the Empire'. Nevertheless, his detractors'
arguments also have merit. If Churchill became seen as a diehard,
this was in part because of choices that he deliberately made,
positioning himself unashamedly with reactionary elements in the
Conservative Party. He used his own background selectively to
reinforce the stance he now adopted. At the risk of sounding
flippant, we might say that it was in the years between the wars that
he decided to become a Victorian. This is not to play down the
importance of his actual Victorian background but rather to emphasize that it cannot be used as a catch-all explanation, or excuse, for
all the imperial attitudes he struck in later life.

It is true that his background provided him with some founda-
tional beliefs from which he never departed. His 1953 statement,
'Wherever it had grown, British imperialism had meant steady
progress for the masses of the people and the establishment and
enforcement of just laws' could easily have come from the mouth of
his headmaster, Mr Welldon, in the 1880s.[47] Yet, far from instilling

in him a uniform set of principles which he applied remorselessly throughout life, his upbringing and early career provided him with two different sets of assumptions which were hard to square with one another. The first was the confident, Whiggish assumption of inevitable human progress. The second was a dark, pessimistic view of life as a harsh, evolutionary process that pitted human beings against each other in atavistic conflict.

An interesting clue to the way in which Churchill tried to reconcile these assumptions in his own mind can be found in speech notes he prepared for a debate on India in March 1943. These remarks – aimed at 'a particular class of simpleton by no means all resident in the British Isles' – included the expected sideswipes at Gandhi and at the Indian capitalists who supported him. Yet there was also a more subtle passage in which he examined the idea of Indian independence. One might as well say 'Give Europe her independence', he said. Europe had in fact been given such independence with the final collapse of the Roman Empire, he argued, and she had used it to embark on a nearly 'unending succession of bloody and devastating wars, of which we are at present passing through the latest'. He hoped, however, that after the war there would emerge a new regional organization, 'some sort of central residing power' which would put a check on such miseries. This had to be a force 'external to Europe itself'; that was why 'we seek so earnestly to bring the detached vast steadying power of the United States into the new Council of Europe'. He then turned more explicitly to the question of Empire. He acknowledged that in the past there had occurred the 'exploitation of the weaker races by the white man' and 'the wicked and brazen exploitation of colonies and conquests'. However, 'the broad, shining, liberating and liberalizing tides of the Victorian era' had put an end to this. 'For the last 80 years – four generations – the British have had no idea whatever of exploitation in India, but only service. In fact British rule has rendered to India exactly that function of central control, including an external element, which is what we seek to create in Europe.'[48]

The speech was never completed or delivered, in part due to pressure of work and in part due to Churchill's realization that it 'might be contentious'.[49] It raised as many questions as it answered. After all, he himself proved deeply hostile to the idea of making British colonial rule accountable to an external force, in the form of the United Nations. But the speech notes did provide at least a partial account of how a despairing view of human nature could be harmonized with a belief in the feasibility of progress. Progress was possible, but it needed to be imposed by a benign, disinterested outside force. Even in the face of clear abuses, some of which he denounced as such himself, he never lost faith that rule of others by the British fitted the bill in this respect. In that sense, he was a true imperialist, however much critics such as Leo Amery might cast doubt on his credentials. For him, moreover, running the Empire was not just about the careful weighing of policy options. It was an emotive issue. Charles de Gaulle put his finger on it during a discussion towards the end of World War II in which Churchill sought to damp down French ambitions in the Levant:

> CHURCHILL: Colonies today are no longer a pledge of
>   happiness, or a sign of power. India is a very heavy burden
>   to us. Modern squadrons are worth more than overseas
>   territories.
> DE GAULLE: You are right. And yet you wouldn't exchange
>   Singapore for squadrons.[50]

But what of Churchill's concrete successes and failures? As a young officer and journalist he was not as much of a maverick as is usually suggested, but nor were his writings those of a mindless imperialist lackey. Unlike many other correspondents of the same stripe, he provided more than a chronicle of inspiring events. In the words of one contemporary, he went on his own lines: 'Churchill reviews the past, and attempts to look into the future. He is original and instructive, as well as interesting.'[51] As a young Tory MP he proved unable to conform successfully. His decision to plump for free trade and the Liberals may have involved an element of opportunism but – even though he did not stick to them with complete tenacity later – his beliefs on the issue were sincere. His efforts as a junior minister to conciliate South Africa after the Boer War were in some ways far-sighted, yet the failure to do more for the rights of the non-white population appears to modern eyes as a blot on the record. His grand visions for East Africa in the same period were well meaning but rather superficial and paternalistic. By the time that he returned to the Colonial Office after the Great War his attitudes had hardened and, although he was not a straightforward pushover for the Kenyan settlers, his decision over the land issue contributed to the country's later problems. He has, however, been criticized too harshly over the creation of Iraq; he did not draw up the new Middle East map out of his own head but rather put his imprimatur on a problematic solution that had been placed before him by apparent experts. Likewise, his Palestine White Paper may have been an unsatisfactory response to an intractable problem but something quite similar would most probably have emerged under a different minister. His actions over Ireland at this time are more obviously praiseworthy. If the Anglo-Irish war was unnecessarily cruel and bloody, he and Lloyd George did at last grasp the need for negotiation and implemented a settlement in the face of much Tory hostility. It was, of course, an imperfect answer, but it was about the best that could have been achieved in the circumstances.

In the 1930s, it almost seems that we are confronted with two Churchills: the far-sighted one who boldly warned against the rise of Germany, and the reactionary one who inveighed against constitutional progress. In his own mind there was no contradiction. In that undelivered 1943 speech he observed: 'For ten years before the war, I warned our British people against Hitler and Gandhi.'[52] Yet few modern commentators will be prepared to grant the equivalence. It is certainly possible to pluck out meritorious aspects of Churchill's critique of the government's Indian policy, such as his statements of concern for the Untouchables. One can even point to the massacres that attended independence and partition as a kind of vindication of his predictions of chaos. However, his belief that India was unsuited to democracy was to be conclusively disproved. (Admittedly, Pakistan's relationship with democracy has been troubled, but it seems highly doubtful that its problems could have been avoided if British rule had been prolonged.) If his continued rearguard action against reform during World War II is not much to his credit, this pales almost into insignificance next to his failure to respond adequately to the Bengal famine. Here he displayed genuine callousness, and short-sightedness to boot. This terrible episode must, however, be viewed alongside the many positive aspects of his war leadership, not least his capacity to inspire peoples throughout the Empire and beyond in the struggle with fascist tyranny.

Even during the war itself, Churchill was forced to face the eclipse of Britain's role as the superpowers rose. During his oppo-sition years his attacks on 'scuttle' in its various forms may have been good politics but they do not look convincing in retrospect. Back in office after 1951 he found that the Empire's atrophy could not be easily reversed. And some of the positions he adopted showed a retreat from diehardism, notably his (comparatively) conciliatory stance over Mau Mau. It is to his credit too that, in spite of his private encouragement of the Tory rebels, he finally bit the bullet and approved the treaty with Egypt. His efforts to foster the 'special relationship' with the United States are harder to judge. He deluded himself if he thought that this could ever approach an equal partnership. But if so it was a less damaging delusion than that which was to be suffered by Eden during the Suez crisis – the idea that bold unilateral action could be the means to reverse the tides of history and restore the British Empire to its place in the sun. Arguably, the achievement of Churchill's final years was to cover a necessary and pragmatic retreat from Empire with a mixture of 'no surrender' bluster and sentimental appeal to Anglo-American unity.

However, his most significant achievement of all was something broader. 'Change was in the air in the 1940s', recalled Nelson Mandela in his memoirs. 'The Atlantic Charter of 1941, signed by Roosevelt and Churchill, reaffirmed faith in the dignity of each human being and propagated a host of democratic principles.' Although some in the West viewed the Charter as hollow rhetoric, he wrote, this was not true of 'those of us in Africa'. Rather, he and his ANC colleagues were inspired by it: 'We hoped that the government and ordinary South Africans would see that the principles they were fighting for were the same ones we were advocating at home.'[53] This, of course, was an unintended conse-quence: Churchill did not mean the Charter to be interpreted as a promise of imperial liberation. But by putting his name to the crucial pledge of national self-determination, he helped unlock the forces of anti-colonialism. The spirit of freedom, which he articu-lated so eloquently on so many occasions, escaped the bounds he would have set upon it. The decline of Churchill's Empire, much as the man himself regretted it, can be seen in part as a tribute to the power of beliefs that he himself prized dearly.

Notes

Abbreviations used in the notes (see bibliography for further details):

CV Companion volume to Churchill's official biography by
    Randolph Churchill/Martin Gilbert
CWP *Churchill War Papers*
DAFP *Documents on Australian Policy, 1937–49*
FDR Franklin Delano Roosevelt
FRUS *Foreign Relations of the United States*
IOR India Office Records
MKG Mohandas K. Gandhi
NA The National Archives, Kew, London: CAB Cabinet records;
    CO Colonial Office records; DO Dominions Office records;
    FO Foreign Office records; PREM Prime Ministers' files
TOPI *India: The Transfer of Power, 1942–7* (ed. Nicholas Mansergh)
WSC Winston Spencer Churchill
WSC CW *The Collected Works of Sir Winston Churchill*

Unless otherwise stated, all Churchill's speeches, statements and radio broadcasts cited are from *Winston S. Churchill: His Complete Speeches, 1897–1963*, ed. Robert Rhodes James.

PROLOGUE

1 The account here is taken from Michael Blundell's *A Love Affair with the Sun: A Memoir of Seventy Years in Kenya*, Kenway Publications, Nairobi, 1994, pp. 108–10, with additional details from his earlier book, *So Rough a Wind*, Weidenfeld & Nicolson, London, 1964, pp. 183–5. For a critique of Blundell's liberal pretensions, see David Anderson, *Histories of the Hanged: Britain's Dirty War in Kenya and the End of Empire*, Weidenfeld & Nicolson, London, 2005, p. 54.
2 'Arrest & Impeachment of Mr Churchill', *Manchester Guardian*, 27 Sept. 1920.
3 Lord Winterton to Leo Amery, 11 June 1953, Leo Amery Papers, 2/1/49.

4 Ronald Hyam judges that Churchill 'was not all that interested in the empire, apart from its rhetorical potentialities, and as distinct from what he regarded as the larger and more portentous issues of international relations': *Britain's Declining Empire: The Road to Decolonisation, 1918–1968*, Cambridge University Press, Cambridge, 2006, p. 172.

5 John Barnes and David Nicholson (eds.), *The Empire at Bay: The Leo Amery Diaries, 1929–1945*, Hutchinson, London, 1988, p. 993 (entry for 4 Aug. 1944).

6 Mark Pottle (ed.), *Daring to Hope: The Diaries and Letters of Violet Bonham Carter, 1946–1969*, Weidenfeld & Nicolson, London, 2000, p. 137 (entry for 29–30 May 1954).

7 WSC, minute of 23 Jan. 1906, NA, CO 446/52/2224, quoted in Ronald Hyam, *Elgin and Churchill at the Colonial Office, 1905–1908: The Watershed of the Empire-Commonwealth*, Macmillan, London, 1968, p. 208.

8 'Conference of Prime Ministers and representatives of the United Kingdom, the Dominions and India, held in June, July and August, 1921', Cmd. 1474, August 1921, p. 39. It should be noted that 'Secretary of State for the Colonies' was the formal title of the office. In this book, however, the simpler term 'Colonial Secretary' is used frequently. Similarly, the Secretary of State for the Dominions (a post which existed between 1925 and 1947) is often referred to here as the 'Dominions Secretary'. These usages, although informal, were regularly deployed by contemporaries.

9 Speech of N. M. Samarth, Indian Legislative Assembly Debates, vol. II, no. 31, 9 Feb. 1922, p. 2319, copy in NA, CO 533/287.

10 Ashley Jackson makes this point persuasively. It is, however, more common to assert that the Empire reached its maximum extent during the interwar years: *The British Empire and the Second World War*, Hambledon Continuum, London, 2006, p. 5.

11 Technically, South Africa after 1910 was a 'union' and Southern Ireland from 1922–49 was a 'free state', but in effect both had Dominion status.

12 For more detailed explanations see Alan Palmer, *Dictionary of the British Empire and Commonwealth*, John Murray, London, 1996, pp. 87, 109, 172.

13 See, for example, Peter Clarke, *The Last Thousand Days of the British Empire*, Allen Lane, London, 2007, p. 506.

14 WSC, *Lord Randolph Churchill* [originally published by Macmillan, London, 1906], CW, vol. VI, p. 487.

15 J. E. C. Welldon, 'The Imperial Aspects of Education' (paper delivered on 14 May 1895), *Proceedings of the Royal Colonial Institute*, 26 (1894–5), pp. 322–39, at 324–5.

16 Speech of 21 Feb. 1942, *Selected Works of Jawaharlal Nehru*, vol. XII, B. R. Publishing Corporation, Delhi, 1979, p. 134.

17 This can be seen especially on the left, for example Clive Ponting, *Churchill*, Sinclair-Stevenson, London, 1994, p. 23. For a right-wing critic's take on Churchill's Victorian mindset, see John Charmley, *Churchill, The End of Glory: A Political Biography*, Hodder & Stoughton, London, 1993, p. 16.

18 John Colville, preface to WSC, *The River War*, Sceptre, London, 1987 (first published 1899), pp. 9–10.

19 Roland Quinault, 'Churchill and Black Africa', *History Today*, June 2005, pp. 31–6, at 36.

20 W. L. Mackenzie King diary, 5 March 1932.

21 Mark Pottle (ed.), *Champion Redoubtable: The Diaries and Letters of Violet Bonham Carter, 1914–1945*, Weidenfeld & Nicolson, 1998, p. 252 (entry for 6 Jan. 1943).

22 Kirk Emmert's *Winston S. Churchill on Empire* (Carolina Academic Press, Durham, NC, 1989) does not offer such a survey but rather attempts to outline Churchill's views on Empire 'as he would have had he set out his views systematically' (p. xvii). Raymond A. Callahan's *Churchill: Retreat from Empire* (Scholarly Resources Inc., Wilmington, DE, 1984) deals only with the years 1940–55.

23 In the former category, Ronald Hyam, 'Churchill and the British Empire', in Robert Blake and Wm. Roger Louis (eds.), *Churchill*, Oxford University Press, Oxford, 1993, pp. 167–85, an extended version of which will be published in Hyam's forthcoming book *Understanding the British Empire*, and Piers Brendon, 'Churchill and Empire', unpublished lecture. (I am grateful to Dr Brendon for providing me with a copy of his text.) Of the numerous books in the latter category, special mention must be made here of Hyam's magisterial *Elgin and Churchill at the Colonial Office, 1905–1908*. He did consider writing a book on Churchill and the Empire more broadly but was discouraged by the comparative paucity of archival records for Churchill's second Colonial Office period in 1921–2: letter to the author, 25 Oct. 2008.

24 Norman Rose, *Churchill: An Unruly Life*, Simon & Schuster, London, 1994, p. 40.

25 'Mr Churchill – Imperialist!' (review of *My African Journey*), *Observer*, 6 Dec. 1908.

26 See 'Men and Things', *Palestine Post*, 10 Oct. 1948.

27 Ryszard Kapuscinski, *The Shadow of the Sun: My African Life*, Penguin, London, 2002 (first published 2001), p. 321.

28 Wm. Roger Louis, *In the Name of God, Go! Leo Amery and the British Empire in the Age of Churchill*, W. W. Norton & Co., New York, 1992, p. 30.

29 Leo Amery diary, 28 Sept. 1951, Leo Amery Papers, 7/45.

30 For example John Ramsden excludes India from his analysis in *Man of the Century: Winston Churchill and His Legend since 1945*, HarperCollins, London, 2002, giving his reasons on p. xvi.

31 As Hyam points out in 'Churchill and the British Empire', p. 167.

1. LEARNING TO THINK IMPERIALLY

1 Nigel Nicolson (ed.), *Harold Nicolson: Diaries and Letters, 1930–1939*, Collins, London, 1966, pp. 396–7 (entry for 14 June 1939).
2 Chamberlain advised his fellow citizens to 'Learn to think Imperially': 'Mr Chamberlain in the City', *The Times*, 20 Jan. 1904.
3 Paul Addison, *Churchill: The Unexpected Hero*, Oxford University Press, Oxford, 2005, p. 17.
4 Geoffrey Best, *Churchill: A Study in Greatness*, Penguin, London, 2002 (first published by Hambledon, London, 2001), p. 24.
5 Elizabeth Everest to WSC, 8 April 1894, CV I, part 1, p. 463.
6 'Music, Dancing, and Theatre Licences', *The Times*, 11 Oct. 1894.
7 WSC, *My Early Life: A Roving Commission* [originally published by Thornton Butterworth, London, 1930], CW, vol. I, p. 71.
8 WSC to Jack Churchill, 7 Nov. 1894, CV I, part 1, p. 532.
9 WSC, *My Early Life*, p. 71.
10 Gordon Halswell to WSC, 6 Oct. 1933, CV V, part 2, p. 661.
11 WSC to Lady Randolph Churchill, 24 May 1887, and J. W. Spedding to WSC, 10 July 1890, CV I, part 1, pp. 133, 205.
12 Speech of 26 July 1897. These last words were a fairly direct borrowing from William Whewell, *A Sermon preached on Trinity Monday, June 15 1835, before the Corporation of the Trinity House*, London 1835, p. 15: 'Can we suppose otherwise, than that it is our office to carry civilization and humanity, peace and good government, and, above all, the knowledge of the true God, to the uttermost ends of the earth?' I am grateful to Boyd Hilton and the archivist of Trinity College, Cambridge for assistance on this point.
13 WSC, *Thoughts and Adventures* [first published by Thornton Butterworth, London, 1932], CW, vol. XIII, p. 32.
14 Roland Quinault, 'Churchill, Lord Randolph Henry Spencer (1849–1895)', *Oxford Dictionary of National Biography*, Oxford University Press, Oxford, 2004 [http://www.oxforddnb.com/view/article/5404, accessed 13 Aug. 2007]; WSC, *My Early Life*, p. 125.
15 *The Times*, 3 Dec. 1874, CV I, part 1, p. 1.
16 WSC, *My Early Life*, p. 16.
17 WSC, *Lord Randolph Churchill*, pp. 448–50.
18 'Satan Absolved' (1899), in *The Poetical Works of Wilfrid Scawen Blunt: A Complete Edition*, vol. II, Macmillan, London, 1914, p. 285.
19 Wilfrid Scawen Blunt, 'Randolph Churchill: A Personal Recollection', *Nineteenth Century and After*, 59 (1906), pp. 401–15, at 403.
20 Parliamentary Debates, House of Commons, 4th Series, vol. 280, 8 June 1883, col. 49.
21 WSC, *Lord Randolph Churchill*, p. 207.
22 Ibid., p. 208.
23 'Lord R. Churchill At Chatham', *The Times*, 7 June 1883.

24 Lord Randolph Churchill, speech of 15 April 1884, quoted in WSC, *Lord Randolph Churchill*, p. 227.

25 Lala Baijnath, *England and India*, Jehangir B. Karani & Co., Bombay, 1893, pp. 88–9.

26 Letter of 3 March 1885, quoted in WSC, *Lord Randolph Churchill*, p. 796.

27 Roy Foster, *Lord Randolph Churchill: A Political Life*, Clarendon Press, Oxford, 1981, pp. 169, 171.

28 Lord Randolph Churchill, speech of 6 Aug. 1885, quoted in WSC, *Lord Randolph Churchill*, p. 376.

29 'The Primrose League', *The Times*, 20 April 1885; WSC, 'The Scaffolding of Rhetoric' (unpublished article), 1897, CV I, part 2, p. 820.

30 Blunt, 'Randolph Churchill', p. 412.

31 N. G. Chandavarkar, *English Impressions* (1887), pp. 44–5, quoted in Foster, *Lord Randolph Churchill*, p. 409.

32 Lord Randolph Churchill, speech of 21 Nov. 1885, quoted in Foster, *Lord Randolph Churchill*, p. 204. A baboo – or babu – was a native Indian clerk, defined by Winston Churchill as 'the Oriental embodiment of Red Tape': *The Story of the Malakand Field Force: An Episode of Frontier War* [first published by Longmans, Green & Co., 1898], CW, vol. II, p. 163n.

33 Lord Randolph Churchill to Oscar Browning, 14 March 1890, Oscar Browning Papers, OB/1/345/C.

34 Brian Roberts, *Churchills in Africa*, Hamish Hamilton, London, 1970, pp. 4, 14.

35 Ibid., p. 30. Rather hypocritically he then spent £2000 on a diamond necklace himself: 'I don't mean to give it to Jennie, but she can wear it at times, and if we get hard up I shall sell it.' Lord Randolph Churchill to his mother, 30 Nov. 1891, Lord Randolph Churchill Papers, Add. 9248/27/3787.

36 Lord Randolph Churchill, *Men, Mines and Animals in South Africa*, Sampson, Low, Marston & Co., London, 1893, p. 25.

37 Ibid., p. 94.

38 Lord Randolph Churchill to WSC, 27 June 1891, CV I, part 1, p. 248.

39 WSC to Lord Randolph Churchill, 22 July 1891, ibid., p. 260.

40 WSC to Lord Randolph Churchill, 27 Sept. [1891], ibid., p. 270.

41 Churchill, *Men, Mines and Animals*, p. 92.

42 Lord Randolph Churchill to his mother, 15 July 1891, Lord Randolph Churchill Papers, Add. 9248/27/3761.

43 Churchill, *Men, Mines and Animals*, p. 120.

44 Lord Randolph Churchill to his mother, 30 Sept. 1891, Lord Randolph Churchill Papers, Add. 9248/27/3786.

45 Earl of Rosebery, *Lord Randolph Churchill*, Arthur L. Humphreys, London, 1906, pp. 72, 181.

46 WSC, *Thoughts and Adventures*, p. 32.

47 Aylmer Haldane, *A Soldier's Saga*, William Blackwood & Sons, Edinburgh and London, 1948, pp. 119–20.

48 See Foster, *Lord Randolph Churchill*, pp. 382–403.

49 Blunt, 'Randolph Churchill', p. 406.

50 WSC, *Lord Randolph Churchill*, pp. 102, 214.

51 Ibid., p. 487. This remark was endorsed by Rosebery: *Lord Randolph Churchill*, p. 117.

52 Lord Randolph Churchill to WSC, 9 Aug. 1893, CV I, part 1, p. 391.

53 WSC, *My Early Life*, p. 20.

54 See especially John MacKenzie (ed.), *Imperialism and Popular Culture*, Manchester University Press, Manchester, 1986, and J. A. Mangan, *'Benefits bestowed': Education and British Imperialism*, Manchester University Press, Manchester, 1988.

55 See Bernard Porter, *The Absent-Minded Imperialists: Empire, Society, and Culture in Britain*, Oxford University Press, Oxford, 2004.

56 John Colville, *The Fringes of Power: Downing Street Diaries, 1939–1955*, Hodder & Stoughton, London, 1985, pp. 320, 444 (entries for 18 Dec. 1940 and 28 Sept. 1941).

57 E. D. W. Chaplin (ed.), *Winston Churchill and Harrow*, Harrow School Book Shop, Harrow-on-the-Hill, 1941, pp. 71, 77.

58 WSC, 'Back to the Spartan Life in Our Public Schools', *Daily Mail*, 1 Dec. 1931, in WSC, *The Collected Essays of Sir Winston Churchill*, ed. Michael Wolff, 4 vols., Library of Imperial History, London, 1976, vol. IV, pp. 86–7.

59 J. E. C. Welldon to Oscar Browning, 4 May 1885, Browning Papers, OB/1/1728A.

60 Haldane, *A Soldier's Saga*, p. 131.

61 L. S. Amery, *My Political Life*, vol. I: *England before the Storm, 1896–1914*, Hutchinson, London, 1953, p. 40.

62 J. E. C. Welldon, *Recollections and Reflections*, Cassell, London, 1915, pp. 144–5.

63 J. E. C. Welldon to Harcourt Butler, c. 1890, Harcourt Butler Papers, MS Eur. F11/27.

64 Welldon to Harcourt Butler, 5 Sept. 1923, ibid.

65 J. E. C. Welldon, 'The Imperial Aspects of Education' (paper delivered on 14 May 1895), *Proceedings of the Royal Colonial Institute*, 26 (1894–5), pp. 322–39, at 333.

66 Ibid., pp. 325, 333.

67 Notably Reginald Bosworth Smith, who campaigned against British withdrawal from Uganda, for which he was praised by Welldon in front of the school. Churchill drew Bosworth Smith's activities to Lord Randolph's attention. R. Bosworth Smith, 'The Continuity Of Moral Policy' (letter to the editor), *The Times*, 25 Oct. 1892; WSC to Lord Randolph, 5 Nov. 1892, CV I, part 1, p. 346; 'Lecture by Mr H. M. Stanley', *Harrovian*, 17 Nov. 1892.

68 'The Oldham Election', *Manchester Guardian*, 28 June 1899.

69 Jim Golland, *Not Winston, Just William? Winston Churchill at Harrow School*, The Herga Press, Harrow, 1988, p. 13; Robert Somervell, *Chapters of Autobiography*, Faber & Faber, London, 1935, p. 103.

70 WSC, 'Influenza', 1890, quoted in Golland, *Not Winston, Just William?*, pp. 11–12.

71 Churchill's history notebook, c. 1892, Churchill Papers, CHAR 1/11. This may have been singled out for preservation because it describes, amongst other things, the military exploits of his ancestor, the first Duke of Marlborough.

72 J. E. C. Welldon, *Forty Years On: Light and Shadows (A Bishop's Reflections on Life)*, Ivor Nicolson & Watson, London, 1935, p. 120.

73 WSC to Lord Randolph Churchill, [30 March 1892], CV I, part 1, p. 329; 'Lecture by Mr H. M. Stanley', *Harrovian*, 17 Nov. 1892.

74 'The Toryism of Tomorrow: An interview with Lord Randolph Churchill', *Pall Mall Gazette*, 27 Nov. 1884, in Foster, *Lord Randolph Churchill*, p. 407.

75 WSC to Lady Randolph Churchill, 6 April 1897, CV I, part 1, p. 751. See also WSC to Bourke Cockran, 12 April [1896], in Michael McMenamin and Curt J. Zoller, *Becoming Winston Churchill: The Untold Story of Young Winston and His American Mentor*, Greenwood World Publishing, Oxford/ Westport, CT, 2007, p. 87, and, for the 1920s, Parliamentary Debates, House of Commons, 5th Series, vol. 149, 15 Dec. 1921, cols. 181–2.

76 WSC's speech of 16 Aug. 1929, in David Dilks, *'The Great Dominion': Winston Churchill in Canada, 1900–1954*, Thomas Allen, Toronto, 2005, p. 75. See also WSC, *My Early Life*, p. 56.

77 J. E. C. Welldon to Harcourt Butler, 27 June 1923, Harcourt Butler Papers, MS Eur. F11/27.

78 William D. Rubinstein, 'The Secret of Leopold Amery', *Historical Research*, 73 (2000), pp. 175–96.

79 Amery, *My Political Life*, vol. I, p. 35.

80 WSC, *My Early Life*, p. 32.

81 WSC to Lord Curzon, 3 June 1901, Lord Curzon Papers, MS Eur. F111/272.

82 His obituarist, in drawing attention to this devotion, stated that it was 'of the Pickwick-Sam Weller type': 'Bishop Welldon: A Great Personality', *The Times*, 19 June 1937.

83 J. A. Mangan, '"The grit of our forefathers": Invented Traditions, Propaganda and Imperialism', in MacKenzie, *Imperialism*, pp. 115–39, at 121; David Gilmour, *Curzon*, John Murray, London, 1994, pp. 170–1, 207.

84 WSC to J. E. C. Welldon, 16 Dec. 1896, CV I, part 2, p. 714.

85 Welldon to Harcourt Butler, 27 June 1923 and 2 Jan. 1924, Harcourt Butler Papers, MS Eur. F11/27.

86 Welldon to Maud Hoare, 10 May 1935, Templewood Papers, Anderson Collection, File 9.

87 M. Philips Price, *My Three Revolutions*, George Allen & Unwin, London, 1969, p. 289.

88 Douglas S. Russell, *Winston Churchill: Soldier*, Conway, London, 2006 (first published 2005), p. 44.

89 WSC, *My Early Life*, p. 58.

90 For example 'Kaffir', WSC to Jack Churchill, [11 July 1891], CV I, part 1, p. 257.

91 WSC to Lady Randolph, 19 Oct. [1893], ibid., p. 592.

92 Penny Summerfield, 'Patriotism and Empire: Music-Hall Entertainment, 1870–1914', in MacKenzie, *Imperialism*, pp. 17–48, at 29.

93 WSC to Lady Randolph, 2 March 1899, CV I, part 2, p. 1012.

94 WSC, *My Early Life*, p. 96.

95 WSC, 'The Insurrection in Cuba', *Daily Graphic*, 13 Jan. 1896, CV I, part 1, pp. 616–17.

96 McMenamin and Zoller, *Becoming Winston Churchill*, pp. 83–7.

97 WSC, *My Early Life*, p. 94.

98 George R. Aberigh-Mackay, *Twenty-One Days in India or The Tour of Sir Ali Baba K.C.B.*, W. Thacker & Co., London, 1910 (first published 1880), pp. 3–4, 41.

99 WSC to William Phillips, 15 Dec. 1942, in William Phillips, *Ventures in Diplomacy*, John Murray, London, 1955, p. 221.

100 George Chesney, *Indian Polity: A View of the System of Administration in India*, Longmans, Green & Co., London, 1868, p. 212. Churchill cited the book in *The Story of the Malakand Field Force*, p. 160.

101 Golland, *Not Winston*, p. 8; Russell, *Winston Churchill*, p. 19.

102 Lord Ismay, *The Memoirs of Lord Ismay*, Heinemann, London, 1960, pp. 15–16.

103 The serialization was published in book form as *The Happy Warrior*, Hulton Press, London, 1958. See also John Marsh, *The Young Winston Churchill*, Evans Brothers Ltd, 1955, to which Leo Amery provided the foreword.

104 Constance Leslie to H. Rider Haggard, 11 Feb. 1888, and WSC to Haggard, n.d., Churchill Papers CHAR 1/178/59–60.

105 WSC, *Story of the Malakand Field Force*, p. 144.

106 WSC to Lady Randolph, 2 March 1899, CV I, part 2, p. 1013.

107 Rudyard Kipling to Max Aitken, 15 Jan. 1914, in Thomas Pinney (ed.), *The Letters of Rudyard Kipling*, vol. IV: *1911–19*, Macmillan, Basingstoke, 1999, p. 218.

108 Rudyard Kipling to George Saintsbury, 23 Dec. 1922, in Thomas Pinney (ed.), *The Letters of Rudyard Kipling*, vol. V: *1920–30*, Macmillan, Basingstoke, 2004, p. 134.

109 Speech of 17 Nov. 1937.

110 Kipling to George Bambridge, 14 Feb. 1935, in Thomas Pinney (ed.), *The Letters of Rudyard Kipling*, vol. VI: *1931–36*, Macmillan, Basingstoke, 2004, p. 333.

111 Kipling to Bambridge, 26–27 Feb. 1935, ibid., p. 340.

112 Speech of 17 Nov. 1937.

113 WSC to Lady Randolph, 14 Oct. [1896], CV I, part 2, p. 688.

114 WSC, *My Early Life*, p. 119.

115 J. Moray Brown and T. F. Dale, *The Badminton Library of Sports and Pastimes: Polo* (1901), pp. 254–5, quoted in Patrick F. McDevitt, *May the Best Man*

Win: Sport, Masculinity, and Nationalism in Great Britain and the Empire, 1880–1935, Macmillan, New York, 2004, p. 39.

116 McDevitt, *May the Best Man Win*, ch. 3.

117 WSC, *Story of the Malakand Field Force*, p. 160.

118 WSC to Lady Randolph, 31 Aug. [1895], CV I, part 1, p. 585.

119 Roland Quinault, 'Winston Churchill and Gibbon', in R. McKitterick and R. Quinault (eds.), *Edward Gibbon and Empire*, Cambridge University Press, Cambridge, 1997, pp. 317–32. Quotation at 332.

120 Lord Macaulay, *Critical and Historical Essays*, vol. II, Longmans, Green & Co., London, 1866, p. 185.

121 WSC, *Story of the Malakand Field Force*, p. 3.

122 Parliamentary Debates, House of Commons, 5th Series, vol. 131, 8 July 1920, col. 173.

123 Paul Addison, *Churchill on the Home Front, 1900–1955*, Pimlico, London, 1993, p. 10.

124 Winwood Reade, *The Martyrdom of Man*, Watts & Co., London, 1934 (first published 1872), p. 431.

125 David. C. Smith, *H. G. Wells: Desperately Mortal: A Biography*, Yale University Press, New Haven and London, 1986, pp. 14–15.

126 WSC, *My Early Life*, p. 129; Joseph Spence, 'Lecky, (William) Edward Hartpole (1838–1903)', *Oxford Dictionary of National Biography*, Oxford University Press, 2004; online edition, 2009.

127 Paul Addison, 'Destiny, History and Providence: The Religion of Winston Churchill', in Michael Bentley (ed.), *Private and Public Doctrine: Essays in British History Presented to Maurice Cowling*, Cambridge University Press, Cambridge, 1993, pp. 236–50; Philip Williamson, 'Christian Conservatives and the Totalitarian Challenge, 1933–40', *English Historical Review*, 115 (2000), pp. 607–42.

128 See Addison, *Churchill on the Home Front*, p. 10.

129 Andrew S. Thompson, *Imperial Britain: The Empire in British Politics, c. 1880–1932*, Longman, Harlow, 2000, p. 24.

130 Reade, *Martyrdom*, p. 129.

131 Ibid., p. 309.

132 Ibid., pp. 309–10.

133 Ibid., p. 407.

134 WSC, *My African Journey* [first published by Hodder & Stoughton, London, 1908], CW, vol. I, pp. 23, 27, 42.

135 Reade, *Martyrdom*, p. 289. Reade may have taken this paraphrase of William Wilberforce's celebrated speech of 25 April 1789 from Thomas Clarkson's *History of the Rise, Progress and Accomplishment of the Abolition of the African Slave Trade by the British Parliament* (1808).

136 Reade, *Martyrdom*, p. 405.

137 Addison, *Unexpected Hero*, pp. 89–90.

138 'Midland Conservative Club: Mr Churchill's Presidential Address', *Birmingham Daily Post*, 2 June 1899.

139 WSC to Lady Randolph, 31 March [1897], CV I, part 2, p. 746.

140 WSC, 'Comments on *Annual Register,* early 1897', ibid., pp. 760, 763.

141 WSC, *Great Contemporaries* [first published by Thornton Butterworth, London, 1937], CW, vol. XVI, p. 27.

142 WSC to Lady Randolph, 6 April [1897], CV I, part 2, p. 751.

143 WSC to Lady Randolph, 14 Oct. 1896, ibid., p. 688.

144 ibid., p. 688n.

145 WSC to Jack Churchill, 20 March [1898], ibid., p. 893.

146 WSC to Lady Randolph, 29 Dec. 1898, ibid., p. 996.

147 WSC to Lady Randolph, 4 Nov. [1896], ibid., p. 697.

148 WSC, *My Early Life*, p. 118.

149 Lord Moran, *Winston Churchill: The Struggle for Survival, 1940–1965,* Constable, London, 1966, p. 370.

150 WSC to Lady Randolph, 18 Nov. [1896], CV I, part 2, p. 704.

151 WSC to Lady Randolph, 14 Jan. 1897, ibid., p. 724.

152 'Author's Preface', in WSC, *My Early Life.*

153 Lord Irwin to Stanley Baldwin, 28 March 1929, Stanley Baldwin Papers, vol. 103, ff. 20–3, partially reproduced in CV V, part 1, p. 1452.

154 Penderel Moon (ed.), *Wavell: The Viceroy's Journal,* Oxford University Press, Karachi, 1997, p. 4 (entry for 24 June 1943).

155 John Barnes and David Nicholson (eds.), *The Empire at Bay: The Leo Amery Diaries, 1929–1945,* Hutchinson, London, 1988, p. 49 (entry for 4 Aug. 1929).

156 Moran, *Struggle for Survival*, p. 131.

2. JOLLY LITTLE WARS AGAINST BARBAROUS PEOPLES

1 Speech of 14 Dec. 1929.

2 Editorial, *The Times*, 28 July 1897.

3 H. B. Hanna, 'The Lesson of the Swat Rising', *The Times*, 10 Aug. 1897.

4 See, for example, 'Mr [John] Morley at Arbroath', *The Times*, 29 Sept. 1897, and 'Sir William Harcourt at Kirkcaldy', *The Times*, 27 Nov. 1897.

5 'Outlook: The Frontier Fallacy', *Daily Mail*, 30 March 1898.

6 See, for example, Viscount Fincastle and P. C. Eliott-Lockhart, *A Frontier Campaign: A Narrative of the Malakand and Buner Field Forces, 1897–8*, R. J. Leach & Co., London, 1990 (first published 1898), p. 223.

7 See WSC, *The Story of the Malakand Field Force: An Episode of Frontier War* [first published by Longmans, Green & Co., 1898], CW, vol. II, ch. 3.

8 Frederick Woods (ed.), *Young Winston's Wars: The Original Despatches of Winston S. Churchill, War Correspondent, 1897–1900*, Leo Cooper, London, 1972, p. 10 (despatch of 6 Sept. 1897).

9 WSC, *My Early Life: A Roving Commission* [originally published by Thornton Butterworth, London, 1930], CW, vol. I, p. 143.

10 WSC to Lady Randolph 21 Oct. [1897], CV I, part 2, p. 807.

11 Bindon Blood to WSC, 22 Aug. 1897, ibid., p. 780.
12 F. Maurice and George Arthur, *The Life of Lord Wolseley*, Doubleday, Page & Co., New York, 1924, p. 66. See also Joseph J. Matthews, 'Heralds of the Imperialistic Wars', *Military Affairs*, 19 (1955), pp. 145–55, at 153.
13 WSC to Frances, Duchess of Marlborough, 25 Oct. 1897, CV I, part 2, p. 810.
14 WSC, *Story of the Malakand Field Force*, p. 199.
15 He then described this type of bullet as 'particularly cruel' and 'improper': Woods, *Young Winston's Wars*, p. 269 (despatch of 9 March 1900).
16 Michael MacDonagh, 'Can We Rely on Our War News?', *Fortnightly Review*, 63 (1898), pp. 612–25.
17 Woods, *Young Winston's Wars*, p. 3 (despatch of 3 Sept. 1897).
18 WSC, *My Early Life*, p. 139.
19 Woods, *Young Winston's Wars*, pp. 31–4 (despatch of 23 Sept. 1897); WSC to Lady Randolph, 19 Sept. [1897], CV I, part 2, p. 792; WSC, *My Early Life*, pp. 156–7.
20 WSC to Lord William Beresford, 2 Oct. [1897], CV I, part 2, p. 798.
21 WSC, *My Early Life*, p. 162.
22 WSC to Frances, Duchess of Marlborough, 25 Oct. 1897, CV I, part 2, p. 810.
23 WSC to Reginald Barnes, 14 Sept. 1897, ibid., p. 788.
24 WSC, *Story of the Malakand Field Force*, pp. 167–8.
25 WSC to Lady Randolph, 19 Oct. [1897], CV I, part 2, p. 797.
26 Woods, *Young Winston's Wars*, pp. 39, 52 (despatches of 28 Sept. and 8 Oct. 1897).
27 WSC, *Story of the Malakand Field Force*, pp. 3–4, 168, 192–3.
28 Woods, *Young Winston's Wars*, p. 30 (despatch of 21 Sept. 1897). For Churchill's comments on women see *Story of the Malakand Field Force*, p. 6.
29 WSC to Lady Randolph, 19 Sept. [1897], CV I, part 2, p. 793.
30 WSC, *Story of the Malakand Field Force*, p. 230.
31 'Churchill's Mysore Home', *Sunday Statesman*, 25 July 1943.
32 Manuscript of *The Story of the Malakand Field Force*, Churchill Papers, CHAR 8/2, f. 23. Piers Brendon drew attention to this point in *The Decline and Fall of the British Empire, 1781–1997*, Jonathan Cape, London, 2007, p. 205.
33 CV I, part 2, p. 913.
34 See, most recently, Warren Dockter, 'Winston Churchill and the Islamic World: Early Encounters', *Historian*, 101 (Spring 2009), pp. 19–21.
35 Ted Morgan, *Churchill: Young Man in a Hurry, 1874–1915*, Simon & Schuster, New York, 1982, p. 94.
36 Peter De Mendelssohn, *The Age of Churchill: Heritage and Adventure, 1874–1911*, Thames & Hudson, London, 1961, p. 103.
37 Roland Quinault, 'Winston Churchill and Gibbon', in R. McKitterick and R. Quinault (eds.), *Edward Gibbon and Empire*, Cambridge University Press, Cambridge, 1997, pp. 317–32. Quotation at 322.

38 In support of his claim about the Malakand expedition he quotes a letter from Churchill to his mother which in fact refers to the separate Tirah expedition, for which see below. Martin Gilbert, *Churchill: A Life*, Heinemann, London, 1991, pp. 80, 82; WSC to Lady Randolph, 19 Jan. 1898, CV I, part 2, p. 860.

39 Kirk Emmert, *Winston S. Churchill on Empire*, Carolina Academic Press, Durham NC, 1989, p. 9.

40 WSC, *Story of the Malakand Field Force*, p. xii.

41 Review of *The Story of the Malakand Field Force*, *United Service Gazette*, Broadwater Collection.

42 Woods, *Young Winston's Wars*, p. 28 (despatch of 21 Sept. 1897).

43 Both Churchill and Lady Randolph referred to the '5th letter' as the controversial one, yet that comprised a description of military action with no contentious content; it is the seventh letter that tallies with their discussion.

44 WSC to Lady Randolph, [2 Nov.] 1897, CV I, part 2, pp. 813–14.

45 'Sir George White on Indian Frontier Policy', *The Times*, 4 Oct. 1897.

46 Woods, *Young Winston's Wars*, p. 65 (despatch of 16 Oct. 1897).

47 Review of *The Story of the Malakand Field Force*, *United Service Gazette*, Broadwater Collection.

48 WSC to Lady Randolph, 21 Oct. [1897], CV I, part 2, p. 807. Martin Gilbert creates a misleading impression by quoting only the part from 'Financially' to 'blunder': *Churchill's Political Philosophy*, Oxford University Press, Oxford, 1981, p. 9.

49 WSC to Lady Randolph, [2 Nov.] 1897, CV I, part 2, p. 814.

50 WSC to Lord William Beresford, 2 Nov. [1897], ibid., p. 821.

51 WSC, *Story of the Malakand Field Force*, p. 150.

52 Ibid., pp. 213–15.

53 'Impressions of Books', *Daily Mail*, 15 March 1898; Review of *The Story of the Malakand Field Force*, *Outlook*, 26 March 1898. The latter is in the Broadwater Collection.

54 Review of *The Story of the Malakand Field Force*, *United Service Gazette*, Broadwater Collection.

55 'With Sir Bindon Blood', *Pall Mall Gazette*, 18 March 1898, Broadwater Collection.

56 Review of *The Story of the Malakand Field Force*, *Review of Reviews*, April 1898, Broadwater Collection.

57 'Indian Frontier Warfare', *Daily News*, 14 March 1898, Broadwater Collection.

58 Review of *The Story of the Malakand Field Force*, *Scotsman*, 17 March 1898, Broadwater Collection.

59 'The Riddle of the Frontier', *Times of India*, 5 May 1898, Broadwater Collection.

60 Lovat Fraser, 'Winston as War Lord', *Sunday Pictorial*, 15 April 1923. Emphasis in original.

61 WSC, 'The Ethics of Frontier Policy', *United Service Magazine*, Aug. 1898, in *The Collected Essays of Sir Winston Churchill*, ed. Michael Wolff, Library of Imperial History, London, 1976, vol. I, p. 34.
62 WSC to Ian Hamilton, [?18 April 1898], CV I, part 2, p. 912.
63 WSC, *My Early Life*, p. 179.
64 Parliamentary Debates, House of Lords, 4th Series, vol. 53, 8 Feb. 1898, col. 42. Similarly, see 'Mr [Arthur] Balfour in Manchester', *The Times*, 11 Jan. 1898.
65 'Banquet at the Guildhall', *The Times*, 10 Nov. 1888.
66 Churchill offered a very slight variant on Salisbury's words as reported in *The Times*, and misdated the speech to 1892.
67 'Lord G. Hamilton on India', *The Times*, 11 Nov. 1897.
68 'Sir H. H. Fowler on India', *The Times*, 22 Nov. 1897.
69 Ian Hamilton, *Listening for the Drums*, Faber & Faber, London, 1944, pp. 238–9.
70 WSC to Lady Randolph, 19 Jan. 1898, CV I, part 2, p. 860.
71 George H. Cassar, 'Hamilton, Sir Ian Standish Monteith (1853–1947)', *Oxford Dictionary of National Biography*, Oxford University Press, Sept. 2004; online edition, May 2006 [http://www.oxforddnb.com/view/article/33668, accessed 17 Oct. 2007]; Ian B. M. Hamilton, *The Happy Warrior: A Life of General Sir Ian Hamilton*, Cassell, London, 1966, p. 458.
72 WSC, *My Early Life*, pp. 172–3; Hamilton, *Listening for the Drums*, p. 239.
73 Aylmer Haldane, *A Soldier's Saga*, William Blackwood & Sons, Edinburgh and London, 1948, p. 119.
74 WSC to Lady Randolph, 7 March [1898], CV I, part 2, p. 886.
75 WSC to Lady Randolph, 18 and 31 March [1898], ibid., pp. 891, 908.
76 Haldane, *A Soldier's Saga*, pp. 119–20.
77 Hamilton, *Listening for the Drums*, p. 237.
78 Ibid., p. 239.
79 Haldane, *A Soldier's Saga*, p. 120.
80 WSC, *My Early Life*, p. 174.
81 'Eyewitness', 'The Tirah Campaign', *Fortnightly Review*, 375 (1 March 1898), pp. 390–400.
82 WSC, *My Early Life*, pp. 174–5; WSC to Lady Randolph, 31 March [1898], CV I, part 2, p. 908.
83 WSC, 'The Tirah Campaign', 30 March 1898, published in *The Times*, 3 May 1898, reproduced in CV I, part 2, pp. 903–6.
84 *Westminster Gazette*, 3 May 1898, Broadwater Collection. See also the *Critic*, 14 May 1898, and 'Comments', *Broad Arrow*, 7 May 1898.
85 Peter Clark, 'The Battle of Omdurman in the Context of Sudanese History', in Edward M. Spiers (ed.), *Sudan: The Reconquest Reappraised*, Frank Cass, London, 1998, pp. 203–21, at 210–11; 'Ismat Hasan Zulfo, *Karari: The Sudanese Account of the Battle of Omdurman*, Frederick Warne, London, 1980, p. 27.
86 Woods, *Young Winston's Wars*, p. 136 (despatch of 12 Sept. 1898).

87 Clark, 'The Battle of Omdurman', p. 208.

88 Woods, *Young Winston's Wars*, p. 136 (despatch of 12 Sept. 1898).

89 See Spiers (ed.), *Sudan*, and also Terje Tvedt, *The River Nile in the Age of the British: Political Ecology and the Quest for Economic Power*, I. B. Tauris, London, 2004, ch. 1.

90 'Lord Kimberley on Foreign Affairs', *The Times*, 28 Feb. 1898; 'Lord Herschell at Brighton', *The Times*, 1 March 1898.

91 WSC, *The River War: An Historical Account of the Reconquest of the Sudan*, 2 vols, Longmans, Green & Co., London, 1899, vol. I, p. 277.

92 G. W. Steevens, *With Kitchener to Khartum*, Thomas Nelson & Sons, London, n.d. (first published 1898), p. 72.

93 Ian F. W. Beckett, 'Kitchener and the Politics of Command', in Spiers, *Sudan*, pp. 35–53, at 42.

94 Matthews, 'Heralds', p. 149.

95 H. L. Mencken, *Newspaper Days, 1899–1906* (1942), p. 12n, quoted ibid., p. 155.

96 WSC, *My Early Life*, p. 227.

97 Roger T. Stearn, 'G. W. Steevens and the Message of Empire', *Journal of Imperial and Commonwealth History*, 17 (1989), pp. 210–31, at 225 and 231, n. 139.

98 WSC, *My Early Life*, pp. 227–8. G. W. Steevens, 'From the New Gibbon', *Blackwood's Edinburgh Magazine*, 165 (1899), pp. 241–9.

99 G. W. Steevens, 'The Youngest Man in Europe' (first published in the *Daily Mail*, 2 Dec. 1898), in Charles Eade (ed.), *Churchill, By His Contemporaries*, Reprint Society, London, 1955 (first published 1953), pp. 34–7.

100 For some perceptive observations, making the case in Churchill's favour, see 'The Historian of This War', *Toronto Daily Star*, 31 March 1900.

101 Woods, *Young Winston's Wars*, p. 278 (despatch of 10 March 1900).

102 WSC to Lady Randolph, 4 & 17 Sept. 1898, CV I, part 2, pp. 974, 982.

103 Zulfo, *Karari*, p. 94.

104 Michael Asher, *Khartoum: The Ultimate Imperial Adventure*, Penguin, London, 2006 (first published 2005), p. 401.

105 Clive Ponting, *Churchill*, Sinclair-Stevenson, London, 1994, p. 29.

106 Woods, *Young Winston's Wars*, p. 112 (despatch of 6 Sept. 1898); WSC, *My Early Life*, pp. 203–10; WSC, *River War*, vol. II, pp. 138, 142–3.

107 WSC to Lady Randolph, 10 Aug. 1898, CV I, part 2, p. 963.

108 WSC to Lady Randolph, 4 Sept. 1898 and WSC to Ian Hamilton, 16 Sept. 1898, ibid., pp. 973, 978.

109 WSC to Lady Randolph, 17 Sept. 1898, ibid., p. 981.

110 John Pollock, *Kitchener*, Constable, London, 1998, p. 132.

111 Steevens, *With Kitchener*, pp. 344–5.

112 Woods, *Young Winston's Wars*, p. 133 (despatch of 11 Sept. 1898).

113 Keith Wilson, 'Young Winston's Addisonian Conceit: A Note on the "War on the Nile" Letters', in Spiers, *Sudan*, pp. 223–8, at 227.

114 Woods, *Young Winston's Wars*, p. 149 (despatch of 20 Sept. 1898).

115 Ibid., p. 126 (despatch of 10 Sept. 1898).

116 Steevens, *With Kitchener*, p. 332. The sentiment had earlier been summarized by Kipling in a poem of 1890: 'So 'ere's *to* you, Fuzzy-Wuzzy, at your 'ome in the Soudan/ You're a pore benighted 'eathen but a first-class fightin' man'.

117 Woods, *Young Winston's Wars*, p. 126 (despatch of 10 Sept. 1898).

118 WSC to Hamilton, 16 Sept. 1898, CV I, part 2, p. 979.

119 'The Editor of *Concord*' to the *Westminster Gazette*, 19 Oct. 1898; WSC to the *Westminster Gazette*, 24 Oct. 1898.

120 Ernest N. Bennett, *The Downfall of the Dervishes, or, The Avenging of Gordon: Being a Personal Narrative of the Final Soudan Campaign of 1898*, Negro Universities Press, New York, 1969 (first published 1898), p. 183.

121 Woods, *Young Winston's Wars*, p. 114 (despatch of 8 Sept. 1898).

122 Ernest Bennett, 'After Omdurman', *Contemporary Review*, 75 (1899), pp. 18–33. Quotation at 23.

123 WSC to the Duke of Marlborough, 24 Jan. 1899, Marlborough Papers, 1/52.

124 WSC to Lady Randolph, 26 Jan. 1898, CV I, part 2, p. 1004.

125 WSC, *River War*, vol. II, pp. 195–7.

126 Churchill's recollections were recorded by Wilfrid Scawen Blunt, *My Diaries: Being a Personal Narrative of Events, 1888–1914: Part Two* [1900–1914], London, Martin Secker, n.d., p. 400 (entry for 21 Oct. 1912).

127 WSC, *My Early Life*, p. 242.

128 'Midland Conservative Club: Mr Churchill's Presidential Address', *Birmingham Daily Post*, 2 June 1899.

129 'The Mahdi's Head', *Daily News*, 5 June 1899.

130 WSC, *River War*, vol. II, pp. 212, 214.

131 See David Jablonsky, 'Churchill's Initial Experience with the British Conduct of Small Wars: India and the Sudan, 1897–98', *Small Wars and Insurgencies*, 11 (2000), pp. 1–25.

132 WSC to Lord Salisbury 14 Aug. 1899, and Salisbury to WSC, 17 Aug. 1899, CV I, part 2, p. 1042.

133 Pollock, *Kitchener*, p. 150.

134 'The River War', *Daily Telegraph*, 8 Nov. 1899 and 'Pages in Waiting', *World*, 8 Nov. 1899, both in Broadwater Collection.

135 F. I. Maxse, 'Inaccurate History', *National Review*, 35 (1900), pp. 262–75.

136 'The River War: Mr Winston Churchill's Severe Criticism of Lord Kitchener', *Star*, 7 Nov. 1899, Broadwater Collection.

137 Geoffrey Best, *Churchill and War*, Hambledon, London, 2005, p. 23. In 1950 a scholar wrote to Churchill asking him why the criticisms of Kitchener had been cut out; a reply from a secretary failed to give an answer. Churchill was not necessarily being evasive; he may have been too busy to give an explanation or, by this stage, he could have simply

forgotten the reason. Marjorie Perham to WSC, n.d., and Jo Sturdee to Perham, 29 Jan. 1950, Marjorie Perham Papers, 295/9.

138 WSC, *River War*, vol. I, p. 19.

139 'The Real History of the Soudan War', *Pall Mall Gazette*, 6 Nov. 1899 and 'The River War', *Star*, 7 Nov. 1899, both in Broadwater Collection.

140 WSC, *The River War*, vol. II, p. 396.

141 'Reviews: Out of Egypt', *Outlook*, 18 Nov. 1899, Broadwater Collection.

142 WSC, *The River War*, vol. II, pp. 398–9.

143 Ibid., pp. 400–1.

144 WSC, 'The Fashoda Incident', *North American Review*, Dec. 1898, in *Collected Essays*, vol. I, p. 40.

145 Speech of 31 Oct. 1898.

146 WSC, *Story of the Malakand Field Force*, p. 157.

3. A CONVENIENT WAY OF SEEING THE EMPIRE

1 Lord Moran, *Winston Churchill: The Struggle for Survival, 1940–1965*, Constable, London, 1966, p. 236.

2 'Mr Churchill – Imperialist!', *Observer*, 6 Dec. 1908.

3 WSC to Curzon, n.d. but September/October 1899, Lord Curzon Papers, MS Eur. F111/272.

4 WSC, *My Early Life: A Roving Commission* [originally published by Thornton Butterworth, London, 1930], CW, vol. I, pp. 108, 113.

5 WSC, 'Our Account with the Boers', n.d. but 1896–7, Churchill Papers, CHAR 1/19/2–20. Short extracts are quoted in Randolph S. Churchill, *Winston S. Churchill*, vol. I: *Youth, 1874–1900*, Heinemann, London, 1966, pp. 449–50, and subsequent writers have generally relied on these.

6 'Cardiff Politics', *Western Mail*, 18 May 1899.

7 Quoted in Lewis Broad, *Winston Churchill, 1874–1951*, Hutchinson, London, 1951, p. 25.

8 Quoted in 'Echoes of the Fight: From Today's Papers', *Oldham Daily Standard*, 26 June 1899.

9 'In the Arena: Splendid Meeting at the Theatre Royal', *Oldham Daily Standard*, 28 June 1899.

10 'Mr Churchill and the Government', *Oldham Evening Chronicle*, 27 June 1899.

11 'The Conservative Candidates', *Manchester Guardian*, 1 July 1899.

12 Paul Addison, *Churchill: The Unexpected Hero*, Oxford, Oxford University Press, 2005, p. 22; Roy Jenkins, *Churchill*, Macmillan, London, 2001, pp. 48–9; Clive Ponting, *Churchill*, Sinclair-Stevenson, London, 1994, p. 32; WSC, *My Early Life*, p. 239.

13 There is some discussion of this aspect of the campaign in Henry Pelling, *Winston Churchill*, Macmillan, London, 1974, pp. 71–3. See also Peter

Clarke, *Lancashire and the New Liberalism*, Cambridge University Press, London, 1971, p. 43.

14   'The Conservative Candidates', *Manchester Guardian*, 28 June 1899.

15   'The Oldham Election', *Oldham Evening Chronicle*, 29 June 1899.

16   P. Harnetty, 'The Indian Cotton Duties Controversy, 1894–1896', *English Historical Review*, 77 (1962), pp. 684–702.

17   'Theatre Royal Meeting', *Oldham Daily Standard*, 28 June 1899.

18   'At Greenacres Co-op', *Oldham Daily Standard*, 30 June 1899.

19   Penderel Moon (ed.), *Wavell: The Viceroy's Journal*, Oxford University Press, Karachi, 1997, p. 12 (entry for 27 July 1943).

20   'The Men for Oldham', *Oldham Daily Standard*, 26 June 1899.

21   'Mr Chamberlain on the Transvaal', *The Times*, 27 June 1899.

22   Peter T. Marsh, *Joseph Chamberlain: Entrepreneur in Politics*, Yale University Press, New Haven and London, 1994, p. 464.

23   'The Oldham Election', *Manchester Guardian*, 30 June 1899.

24   'Grand Meeting at Chadderton', *Oldham Daily Standard*, 4 July 1899.

25   'At the Conservative Club', *Oldham Daily Standard*, 7 July 1899.

26   Speech of 17 Aug. 1899.

27   See, for example, Bindon Blood to Lady Randolph Churchill, 28 Aug. 1899, Churchill Papers, CHAR 28/67/5–6: 'No doubt there is plenty of gold in the Transvaal to pay all [war] expenses, and the business ought to be a very simple one if it is undertaken with sufficient means.'

28   WSC, *My Early Life*, p. 246.

29   Keith Surridge, *Managing the South African War, 1899–1902: Politicians v. Generals*, Royal Historical Society, London, 1998, p. 4.

30   WSC to Evelyn Wood, 10 Nov. 1899, CV I, part 2, p. 1059.

31   WSC, *The Boer War: London to Ladysmith Via Pretoria/Ian Hamilton's March* [both titles originally published by Longman's Green & Co, London, 1900], CW, vol. IV, p. 10 (despatch of 1 Nov. 1899).

32   Ibid., p. 19 (despatch of 6 Nov. 1899).

33   The best account of the episode is Celia Sandys, *Churchill Wanted Dead or Alive*, HarperCollins, London, 1999, ch. 5, to which I am indebted.

34   L. S. Amery, *Days of Fresh Air*, Jarrolds, London, 1939, pp. 141–2.

35   Aylmer Haldane, *A Soldier's Saga*, William Blackwood & Sons, Edinburgh and London, 1948, p. 142.

36   John Black Atkins, *The Relief of Ladysmith*, Methuen & Co., London, 1900, pp. 74–5.

37   Haldane, *A Soldier's Saga*, p. 147.

38   See especially Peter Warwick, *Black People and the South African War, 1899–1902*, Cambridge University Press, Cambridge, 1983, and John Gooch (ed.), *The Boer War: Direction, Experience and Image*, Frank Cass, London, 2000, chs 6 and 7.

39   Thomas Pakenham, *The Boer War*, Weidenfeld & Nicolson, London, 1979, pp. 406–7.

40 M. K. Gandhi, *An Autobiography, or, The Story of My Experiments with Truth*, Penguin, London, 1982 (first published 1927–9), p. 204.

41 William Nasson, 'Africans at War', in Gooch, *Boer War*, pp. 126–40, at 127.

42 WSC to Joseph Chamberlain, 16 Nov. 1900, CV I, part 2, p. 1216.

43 Parliamentary Debates, House of Commons, 4th Series, vol. 101, 21 Jan. 1902, col. 477.

44 Speech of 5 April 1906.

45 WSC, *Boer War*, pp. 60–1 (despatch of 30 Nov. 1899).

46 For example, Roland Quinault, 'Churchill and Black Africa', *History Today*, June 2005, pp. 31–6, at 33–4.

47 'Mr Winston Churchill's Letters on the War', *Spectator*, 26 May 1900, Broadwater Collection.

48 'Mr Winston Churchill's Ladysmith Book', *Pall Mall Gazette*, 15 May 1900.

49 Violet Bonham Carter, *Winston Churchill as I Knew Him*, Reprint Society, London, 1966 (first published 1965), p. 58.

50 'The Book of the War', *Freeman's Journal*, 15 May 1900, Broadwater Collection.

51 WSC, *Boer War*, p. 219 (despatch of 10 March 1900).

52 See H. R. Fox Bourne, *Blacks and Whites in South Africa: An Account of the Past Treatment and Present Condition of South African Natives under British and Boer Control*, 2nd edition, P. S. King & Son, London, 1900. For an alternative perspective, acknowledging multiple abuses in British areas but emphasizing that (unlike in the Transvaal) they did not receive legal sanction, see Josephine Butler, *Native Races and the War*, Gay & Bird, London, 1900.

53 Parliamentary Debates, House of Commons', 4th Series, vol. 77, 19 Oct. 1899, col. 271.

54 Speech of 22 Feb. 1906.

55 WSC, *My Early Life*, p. 272.

56 Aylmer Haldane, *How We Escaped from Pretoria*, William Blackwood & Sons, Edinburgh and London, 1901, p. 16.

57 WSC, 'Our Account with the Boers'.

58 WSC to Bourke Cockran, 30 Nov. 1899, CV I, part 2, p. 1083.

59 J. W. B. Gunning to Louis de Souza, 22 Nov. 1899, Churchill Additional Papers, WCHL 2/1/12. An English translation of the letter and Churchill's (undated) draft telegram can also be found in this file.

60 Sandys, *Churchill Wanted*, p. 84.

61 Aylmer Haldane, 'Note', 29 Oct. 1935, CV I, part 2, p. 1115.

62 'Our London Correspondence', *Manchester Guardian*, 30 July 1900.

63 WSC, telegram of 21 Dec. 1899, in the *Morning Post*, 27 Dec. 1899.

64 *Natal Mercury*, 25 Dec. 1899, quoted in Sandys, *Churchill Wanted*, p. 137.

65 WSC, *My Early Life*, pp. 311, 313.

66 'Notes on the War', *Daily News*, 30 Dec. 1899.

67 WSC, telegram of 23 Dec. 1899, in the *Morning Post*, 30 Dec. 1899.

68 'London Letter', *Western Mail*, 16 June 1900.

69 WSC to Pamela Plowden, 10 Jan. 1900, CV I, part 2, p. 1144.

70 WSC, telegram to the *Morning Post*, 27 Jan. 1900, quoted in 'Boer and Briton', *Freeman's Journal*, 2 Feb. 1900.

71 'Winston Churchill as Lecturer', *Western Mail*, 1 Nov. 1900. Churchill also challenged the self-exculpatory account of Sir Charles Warren, who was in charge of the battle: 'The Spion Kop Disaster', *Jackson's Oxford Journal*, 1 Sept. 1900.

72 William Birdwood to Janetta Birdwood, 12 March 1900, William Birdwood Papers, Ref 670/19–227. Emphasis in original.

73 'From Our Special Correspondent [in Cape Town]', *The Times*, 9 April 1900.

74 'Straight Talk from a *Times* Correspondent', *Reynolds's Newspaper*, 15 April 1900; WSC, 'The British Officer', *Pall Mall Magazine*, 23 (1901), pp. 66–75, at 67.

75 Frederick Woods (ed.), *Young Winston's Wars: The Original Despatches of Winston S. Churchill, War Correspondent, 1897–1900*, Leo Cooper, London, 1972, p. 272 (despatch of 9 March 1900).

76 Ibid., p. 284 (despatch of 10 March 1900).

77 'Current Notes', *Freeman's Journal*, 4 April 1900.

78 'The War', *Jackson's Oxford Journal*, 21 April 1900; 'London Letter', *Western Mail*, 18 April 1900.

79 See WSC, *Boer War*, p. 221 (despatch of 10 March 1900).

80 'Future of South Africa', *Western Mail*, 7 March 1900, reproducing WSC to J. M. Maclean MP, 5 Feb. 1900; WSC, *My Early Life*, p. 316.

81 WSC to the *Natal Witness*, 29 March 1900, CV I, part 2, pp. 1163–4. Churchill's telegram to the *Morning Post* of 24 March 1900 is reproduced in WSC, *My Early Life*, pp. 344–5.

82 Editorial, *Manchester Guardian*, 2 April 1900.

83 'The Halt at Ladysmith: From the *Chronicle* War Correspondent to the *Leeds Mercury*' (despatch of 4 April), *Leeds Mercury*, 30 April 1900.

84 'London Correspondence', *Freeman's Journal*, 6 April 1900.

85 Jack Churchill to Lady Randolph, 3 April 1900, CV I, part 2, pp. 1165–6.

86 Ian Hamilton, *Listening for the Drums*, Faber & Faber, London, 1944, p. 248.

87 'Mr Winston Churchill Home from the Front', *Jackson's Oxford Journal*, 28 July 1900.

88 'Mr Winston Churchill at Oldham', *Manchester Guardian*, 26 July 1900.

89 WSC to Milner, 8 September 1900 (typed copy), Alfred Milner Papers, Dep. 184, ff. 112–14.

90 Alfred Milner to WSC, 8 Oct. 1900, CV I, part 2, p. 1209.

91 'A Timely Intervention', *Manchester Guardian*, 21 Aug. 1900, repeating a story from the *Westminster Gazette*. For evidence on the leaflet, see 'Politics and Society', *Leeds Mercury*, 21 Sept. 1900.

92 'Soldiers of the Empire', *Oldham Daily Standard*, 20 Sept. 1900.

93 'Mr Winston Churchill at Cardiff', *Western Mail*, 30 Nov. 1900.

94 WSC, 'To the Electors of the Parliamentary Borough of Oldham', *Oldham Daily Standard*, 24 Sept. 1900.

95 The most useful comments are to be found in Paul Addison, *Churchill on the Home Front, 1900–1955*, Pimlico, London, 1993 (first published by Jonathan Cape, 1992), p. 13.

96 WSC, 'To the Electors of the Parliamentary Borough of Oldham', *Oldham Daily Standard*, 24 Sept. 1900; 'Under the Unionist Flag', *Oldham Daily Standard*, 25 Sept. 1900.

97 See Paul Readman, 'The Conservative Party, Patriotism, and British Politics: The Case of the General Election of 1900', *Journal of British Studies*, 40 (2001), pp. 107–45.

98 'Soldiers of the Empire', *Oldham Daily Standard*, 20 Sept. 1900.

99 'Turtle for Tories', *Oldham Evening Chronicle*, 21 Sept. 1900.

100 'Politics and Society', *Leeds Mercury*, 21 Sept. 1900.

101 WSC, *My Early Life*, p. 374.

102 'New Book by Mr Winston Churchill MP' (review of *Ian Hamilton's March*), *Glasgow Herald*, 12 Oct. 1900.

103 WSC to Lord Rosebery, 4 Oct. 1900, CV I, part 2, p. 1206.

104 Churchill, *Winston S. Churchill*, vol. I, p. 541.

105 'Mr Winston Churchill, MP at Middlesbro', *Northern Echo*, 12 Nov. 1900.

106 'Mr Winston Churchill in Leeds', *Leeds Mercury*, 16 Nov. 1900. Joubert, who had been Commandant General of the Transvaal, had in fact died in March.

107 'Statement by Mr Cockran', *New York Times*, 15 Dec. 1900.

108 'How Lieut. Churchill Escaped from the Boers', *New York Times*, 13 Dec. 1900.

109 WSC, *My Early Life*, p. 375.

110 *Montreal Gazette*, 24 Dec. 1900, quoted in David Dilks, *'The Great Dominion': Winston Churchill in Canada, 1900–1954*, Thomas Allen, Toronto, 2005, p. 13.

111 Moran, *Struggle for Survival*, p. 19.

112 Gustav Ohlinger, 'Winston Spencer Churchill: A Midnight Interview', *Michigan Quarterly Review*, 5 (1966), pp. 75–9. Quotation at 77.

113 WSC to Milner, 31 Dec. 1900, Milner Papers, Dep. 184, ff. 155–7.

114 WSC, *My Early Life*, p. 369.

115 Parliamentary Debates, House of Commons, 4th Series, vol. 89, 18 Feb. 1901, col. 406.

116 Ibid., col. 408.

117 WSC to the editor of *The Times*, 25 June 1901 (published 28 June), CV II, part 1, p. 75. Emphasis in original.

118 Parliamentary Debates, House of Commons, 4th Series, vol. 89, 18 Feb. 1901, col. 407.

119 WSC, *My Early Life*, p. 379.

120 WSC to Milner 17 March 1901, quoted in Addison, *Churchill on the Home Front*, pp. 17–18.

121 Speech of 4 Oct. 1901.
122 'Sir E. Grey on Political Questions', *The Times*, 12 Oct. 1901.
123 *Montreal Gazette*, 24 Dec. 1900, quoted in Dilks, *'The Great Dominion'*, p. 16.
124 WSC, *My Early Life*, p. 249.
125 'Mr Winston Churchill MP at Oldham', *Manchester Guardian*, 20 May 1901.

4. THAT WILD WINSTON

1 Ramsay MacDonald to the *Leicester Pioneer*, quoted in 'Mr Churchill and the Colonies', *The Times*, 21 March 1906.
2 Quoted in 'Mr Winston Churchill's Indiscretions', *Public Opinion*, 23 March 1906.
3 'Lord Elgin and South African Affairs', *Wanganui Herald*, 27 April 1906.
4 Editorial, *The Times*, 26 April 1906.
5 Quoted in 'Mr Churchill's Speech: Strong Colonial Comments', *The Times*, 17 March 1906.
6 Lord Selborne to Lord Northcote, 15 July 1906, D. George Boyce (ed.), *The Crisis of British Power: The Imperial and Naval Papers of the Second Earl of Selborne, 1895–1910*, The Historians' Press, London, 1990, p. 273.
7 'Mr Winston Churchill', *Tuapeka Times*, 17 February 1906.
8 WSC to Lady Randolph, 6 April [1897], CV I, part 2, p. 751.
9 'Mr Winston Churchill, MP', *Manchester Guardian*, 20 May 1901.
10 The following account draws on Lowell J. Satre, 'St John Brodrick and Army Reform, 1901–1903', *Journal of British Studies*, 15 (1976), pp. 117–39.
11 Parliamentary Debates, House of Commons, 4th Series, vol. 93, 13 May 1901, cols. 1571, 1573.
12 Ibid., col. 310.
13 See especially 'The Problem of the Army, I: The Military Position of the Empire', *The Times*, 21 Jan. 1903 and 'The Problem of the Army, XI: Summary', *The Times*, 24 Feb. 1903. The articles were originally anonymous, but Amery subsequently published them under his own name as *The Problem of the Army* (1903). See also WSC to Leo Amery, 10 Jan. 1903, Leo Amery Papers, 2/1/31.
14 Lord George Hamilton to Lord Curzon, 25 April 1901, quoted in Satre, 'St John Brodrick', p. 123.
15 'The Earl of Rosebery', *Manchester Guardian*, 24 Feb. 1902.
16 WSC to Lord Rosebery, 10 Oct. 1902, CV II, part 1, p. 168.
17 'Mr Chamberlain in Birmingham', *The Times*, 16 May 1903.
18 Speech of 21 May 1903.
19 WSC to John St Loe Strachey, 23 May 1902, John St Loe Strachey Papers, STR/4/10.
20 Leone George Chiozza (later Leo Chiozza Money), *British Trade and the Zollverein Issue*, The Commercial Intelligence Publishing Co., London, 1902,

esp. p. 65. For Money's influence on Churchill, and for the subsequent development of the latter's thinking, see Richard Toye, *Lloyd George and Churchill: Rivals for Greatness*, Macmillan, London, 2007, pp. 27–9.

21 Speech of 11 Nov. 1903.

22 Speech of 7 May 1907 in WSC, *Mr Brodrick's Army and Other Early Speeches*, CW, vol. VII, pp. 168, 171, 173.

23 This echoed a comment made by Rosebery in 1897, although on one occasion Churchill incorrectly attributed it to Chamberlain in his pre-tariff reform days. Ibid., pp. 181, 378; 'Lord Rosebery on Free Trade', *The Times*, 2 Nov. 1897.

24 WSC to Strachey, 4 June 1903, Strachey Papers, STR/4/10.

25 'The Tory Split in Oldham', *Oldham Evening Chronicle*, 26 Nov. 1903, Broadwater Collection.

26 WSC, *The Story of the Malakand Field Force: An Episode of Frontier War* [first published by Longmans, Green & Co., 1898], CW, vol. II, p. 183.

27 Review by WSC of Seebohm Rowntree, *Poverty: A Study of Town Life* (1901), CV II, part 1, p. 111.

28 WSC to J. Moore Bayley, 23 Dec. 1901, ibid., p. 104.

29 Although in 1900 Churchill had spoken in favour of a state pension system, and Chamberlain had given clear hints that something might be done, nothing happened. See John Hulme, 'Winston Churchill, MP: A Study and . . . a Story', *Temple Magazine*, 5 (Jan. 1901), pp. 291–6.

30 'In Angel Meadow', *Manchester Guardian*, 8 Jan. 1906; reproduced in Randolph Churchill, *Winston S. Churchill*, vol. II: *Young Statesman, 1901–1914*, Heinemann, London, 1967, pp. 123–4.

31 Toye, *Lloyd George and Churchill*, p. 36.

32 J. E. C. Welldon to WSC, 13 Dec. 1905, CV II, part 1, p. 414.

33 W. L. Mackenzie King diary, 17 Dec. 1905.

34 See 'Churchill's Appointment Unpopular', *Wanganui Herald*, 18 Dec. 1905.

35 Edward Marsh, *A Number of People: A Book of Reminiscences*, London, William Heinemann, 1939, p. 50.

36 Ronald Hyam, *Elgin and Churchill at the Colonial Office, 1905–1908: The Watershed of the Empire-Commonwealth*, Macmillan, London, 1968, pp. 7–35.

37 WSC, *Story of the Malakand Field Force*, p. 51.

38 Marsh, *A Number of People*, p. 150.

39 Flora Lugard to Frederick Lugard, 20 March 1906, quoted in Margery Perham, *Lugard: The Years of Authority, 1898–1945*, Collins, London, 1960, p. 269.

40 Sir Harry Verney, 'Liberal Minister', undated extract from the *Harrovian* (c. 1965), in Violet Bonham Carter Papers, MS 297.

41 Lord Elgin to Lady Elgin, 16 June 1907, quoted in R. Hyam, 'Bruce, Victor Alexander, Ninth Earl of Elgin and Thirteenth Earl of Kincardine (1849–1917)', *Oxford Dictionary of National Biography*, Oxford University Press, Sept. 2004; online edition, Jan. 2008.

42 Hyam, *Elgin and Churchill*, pp. 66–9.

43 WSC to Lord Selborne, 17 March 1906, in Boyce, *Crisis of British Power*, p. 254.
44 WSC to Joseph Chamberlain, 26 Feb. 1906 and Chamberlain to WSC, 1 March 1906, CV II, part 1, pp. 432–3.
45 'Mr Churchill', *Manchester Guardian*, 12 Jan. 1906. For the slogans, see 'Manchester', *Manchester Guardian*, 2 Jan. 1906.
46 WSC to the Electors of North-West Manchester, 1 Jan. 1906, CV II, part 1, p. 423; Hyam, *Elgin and Churchill*, p. 77, n. 5.
47 Speech of 22 Feb. 1906.
48 *Liverpool Daily Courier*, 7 March 1906, Broadwater Collection.
49 Speech of 9 Jan. 1906.
50 Hyam, *Elgin and Churchill*, pp. 76–7.
51 'Parliament', *The Times*, 15 March 1906.
52 WSC to an unnamed correspondent, 15 March 1906, quoted in 'The Fall in South African Shares', *The Times*, 17 March 1906.
53 A summary of South African press reaction, including the quotations above, can be found in 'Mr Churchill's Speech: Strong Colonial Comments', *The Times*, 17 March 1906.
54 'The Colonial Office and the Colonies', *Evening Post* (New Zealand), 5 June 1906.
55 'The Blenheim Pup', *Pall Mall Gazette*, 17 March 1906.
56 Joseph Chamberlain to the editor of *The Times*, 19 March 1906.
57 WSC to an unnamed correspondent, 15 March 1906, CV II, part 1, p. 527.
58 'The onslaught on Churchill', *Toronto Daily Star*, 4 May 1906.
59 WSC to Selborne, 17 March 1906, in Boyce, *Crisis of British Power*, p. 255.
60 Marsh, *A Number of People*, p. 151.
61 'Political Situation in South Africa: The Native Question', *Daily Telegraph*, 2 March 1906.
62 Cited in 'Churchill's Famous Speech', *Hawera & Normanby Star*, 24 March 1906.
63 WSC to Selborne 24 March 1906, Selborne Papers (2nd Earl), MS 54, ff. 117–20.
64 Hyam, *Elgin and Churchill*, pp. 240–1.
65 *New York Times*, 30 March 1906 (untitled article).
66 Hyam, *Elgin and Churchill*, pp. 241–3.
67 Flora Lugard to Frederick Lugard, 6 May 1906, Lugard Papers, 4/1.
68 'Parliament: House of Commons', *The Times*, 19 July 1906.
69 WSC, minute of 25 May 1907, NA, CO 179/241/18285, quoted in Hyam, *Elgin and Churchill*, p. 251.
70 'Mr Churchill', *Manchester Guardian*, 16 April 1908.
71 'House of Commons', *The Times*, 6 April 1906.
72 'Ministers and the New Colonies', *The Times*, 9 April 1906.
73 'Mr Churchill on Australia', *The Times*, 30 May 1906; 'The Colonial Office and the Colonies', *Evening Post* (NZ), 5 June 1906.

74 'The Colonial Vote', *Transvaal Leader*, 11 June 1906.

75 'The 1900 Club', *The Times*, 26 June 1906.

76 WSC, memorandum, Jan. 1906, CV II, part 1, p. 498.

77 Shula Marks, 'White Masculinity: Jan Smuts, Race and the South African War', *Proceedings of the British Academy*, 111 (2001), pp. 199–223, at 204, 206.

78 WSC, memorandum, Jan. 1906, CV II, part 1, p. 499.

79 Lord Moran, *Winston Churchill: The Struggle for Survival, 1940–1965*, Constable, London, 1966, p. 146.

80 J. C. Smuts, speech of 1895, in *Selections from the Smuts Papers*, vol. I: *June 1886–May 1902*, ed. W. K. Hancock and Jean van der Poel. Cambridge University Press, Cambridge, 1966, p. 83.

81 See Saul Dubow, 'Smuts, the United Nations and the Rhetoric of Race and Rights', *Journal of Contemporary History*, 43 (2008), pp. 45–73.

82 Francis Williams, *Nothing So Strange: An Autobiography*, Cassell, London, 1970, p. 229.

83 Mackenzie King diary, 12 Sept. 1944.

84 J. C. Smuts to M. C. Gillett, 1 Feb. 1906, in *Selections from the Smuts Papers*, vol. II: *June 1902–May 1910*, ed. W. K. Hancock and Jean van der Poel, Cambridge University Press, Cambridge, 1966, p. 228.

85 Hyam, *Elgin and Churchill*, pp. 124–36; Ronald Hyam and Peter Henshaw, *The Lion and the Springbok: Britain and South Africa since the Boer War*, Cambridge University Press, Cambridge, 2003, ch. 3.

86 J. C. Smuts to Margaret Clark, 25 March 1906, CV II, part 1, p. 536.

87 WSC to Lord Elgin, 15 March 1906, ibid., p. 530.

88 Parliamentary Debates, House of Commons, 4th Series, vol. 162, 31 July 1906, col. 753.

89 Ibid., vol. 152, 28 Feb. 1906, col. 1243.

90 Stanley Trapido, 'African Divisional Politics in the Cape Colony, 1884 to 1910', *Journal of African History*, 9 (1968), pp. 79–98, at 81.

91 Parliamentary Debates, House of Commons, 4th Series, vol. 152, 28 Feb. 1906, col. 1236.

92 Ibid., cols. 1233, 1243–4.

93 Abdullah Abdurahman to WSC, 13 June 1906 and enclosed petition, NA, CO 291/112.

94 'South African Native Question', *The Times*, 24 July 1906.

95 Parliamentary Debates, House of Commons, 4th Series, vol. 162, 31 July 1906, cols. 746–7; Hyam, *Elgin and Churchill*, p. 158.

96 Abdullah Abdurahman, speech of 7 Jan. 1907, in R. E. van der Ross, *Say It Out Loud: The APO Presidential Addresses and other Major Political Speeches, 1906–1940, of Dr Abdullah Abdurahman*, Western Cape Institute for Historical Research, University of the Western Cape, Bellville, 1990. Text available at www.sahistory.org.za.

97 'Mahatma' was an honorific title, which he acquired later.

98 Kathryn Tidrick, *Gandhi: A Political and Spiritual Life*, I. B. Tauris, London and New York, 2006, ch. 1.

99 M. K. Gandhi, *An Autobiography, or, The Story of My Experiments with Truth*, Penguin, London, 1982 (first published 1927–9), p. 203.

100 Louis Fischer, *The Life of Mahatma Gandhi*, HarperCollins, London, 1997 (first published 1952), p. 78.

101 WSC, minute of 4 Nov. 1906, NA, CO 291/103, quoted in Hyam, *Elgin and Churchill*, p. 266.

102 Telegram from Elgin to Selborne, 27 Nov. 1906, NA, CO 291/105; Hyam, *Elgin and Churchill*, p. 266.

103 William Godfrey and C. M. Pillay to Selborne, 15 Oct. 1906, NA, CO 291/104; MKG, 'Deputation Notes – I', *Indian Opinion*, 8 Dec. 1906, in *Collected Works*, 100 vols., Government of India Publications Division, New Delhi, 1960–1994, vol. VI, p. 62.

104 'House of Commons', *The Times*, 15 Nov. 1906.

105 M. K. Gandhi and H. Ally to Elgin's private secretary, 12 Nov. 1906, and 'H.W.J[ust]', minute of 19 Nov. 1906, NA, CO 291/104.

106 WSC, minute of 21 Nov. 1906, NA, CO 291/105.

107 MKG, 'Deputation Notes – IV', *Indian Opinion*, 29 Dec. 1906, in *Collected Works*, vol. VI, pp. 257–8.

108 G. D. Birla to WSC, 23 Sept. 1935, CV V, part 2, p. 1265.

109 MKG, 'Deputation Notes – IV', *Indian Opinion*, 29 Dec. 1906, in *Collected Works*, vol. VI, p. 259.

110 Parliamentary Debates, House of Commons, 4th Series, vol. 173, 2 May 1907, col. 1059.

111 'From Private Correspondence', *Scotsman*, 16 May 1907.

112 MKG, 'Churchill's Speech', *Indian Opinion*, 25 May 1907, in *Collected Works*, vol. VI, p. 495.

113 WSC to Selborne, 2 Jan. [1908], Selborne Papers, MS 70, ff. 136–7.

114 'From Private Correspondence', *Scotsman*, 16 May 1907.

115 Minutes of 1 and 3 April 1906, NA, CO 225/71, quoted in Ronald Hyam, 'The British Empire in the Edwardian Era', in Judith M. Brown and Wm. Roger Louis (eds.), *The Oxford History of the British Empire: The Twentieth Century*, Oxford University Press, Oxford, 1999, pp. 47–63, at 50.

116 Selborne to the Earl of Middleton (St John Brodrick), 22 Aug. 1907, in Boyce, *Crisis of British Power*, p. 327.

117 WSC, minute of 3 Feb. 1908, quoted in Hyam, *Elgin and Churchill*, p. 215.

118 Hyam, *Elgin and Churchill*, pp. 208, 225–34, 289–303.

119 Flora Lugard to Frederick Lugard, 6 May 1906, Lugard Papers, 4/1.

120 Hyam, *Elgin and Churchill*, pp. 198–9, 208–9.

121 WSC to Lord Northcliffe, 24 Jan. 1907, Churchill Papers, CHAR 28/117/18.

122 WSC to Elgin, 8 Jan. 1907, CV II, part 1, p. 610.

123 David Lloyd George to William George, 6 May 1907, William George Papers, 1896.

124 'Winston Day by Day', *Punch*, 20 Nov. 1907.

125 'Unofficial Despatches', *Crown*, 23 Nov. 1907, Broadwater Collection.

126 Elgin to Crewe, [?] May 1908, CV II, part 2, p. 797.

127 WSC to Sir Francis Hopwood, 17 Oct. 1907, Francis Hopwood (Lord
     Southborough) Papers, Box 5.

128 Edward Marsh to Cynthia Charteris, 11 Dec. 1907, in Christopher
     Hassall, *Edward Marsh: Patron of the Arts: A Biography*, Longman's, London,
     1959, p. 139.

129 'Woman Went over Roosevelt's Route', *New York Times*, 13 March 1909.

130 Hesketh Bell, *Glimpses of a Governor's Life*, Sampson, Low, Marston & Co.,
     London, n.d., p. 170 (diary entry for 25 Nov. 1907).

131 WSC to Lady Randolph Churchill, 6 Nov. 1907, CV II, part 2, p. 693.

132 James Sadler to Elgin, 9 Dec. 1907, NA, CO 533/33.

133 'In Wild Uganda', *Daily Graphic*, 17 Jan. 1908, Broadwater Collection.

134 Bell, *Glimpses*, p. 170 (diary entry for 22 Nov. 1907).

135 'The Arrival at the Capital', *Star of East Africa*, 9 Nov. 1907.

136 WSC to Edward VII, 27 Nov. 1907, CV II, part 2, p. 712.

137 'Answers to Correspondents', *Star of East Africa*, 30 Nov. 1907.

138 'The Party – Not the Man', ibid.

139 WSC, *My African Journey* [first published by Hodder & Stoughton, London,
     1908], CW, vol. I, p. 32.

140 See the review of *My African Journey* in the *Spectator*, 19 Dec. 1908, which
     noted that even 'The worst politician in Nairobi' did not actually advocate
     mass murder.

141 See, for example, Elspeth Huxley, *White Man's Country: Lord Delamere and the
     Making of Kenya*, vol. I: *1870–1914*, Chatto & Windus, London, 1953 (first
     published 1935), pp. 206–8.

142 Submission by Lord Delamere et al., n.d., NA, CO 533/33.

143 Elgin to James Sadler, 17 July 1906, NA, CO 533/14/21797, quoted in
     Hyam, *Elgin and Churchill*, p. 418.

144 'Mr Churchill's Tour', *Manchester Dispatch*, 14 Jan. 1908, Broadwater
     Collection.

145 Parliamentary Debates, House of Commons, 4th Series, vol. 165, 22 Nov.
     1906, col. 994.

146 WSC, *My African Journey*, pp. 34, 37, 39; C. E. Lawrence, 'Mr Churchill's
     Travels' (review of My African Journey), *Daily Chronicle*, 30 Nov. 1908.

147 'Old and New Africa' (review of *My African Journey*), *Morning Leader*, 30 Nov.
     1908, Broadwater Collection.

148 WSC to Lewis Harcourt, 13 Sept. 1911, Harcourt Papers, Dep. 462,
     ff. 231–3.

149 WSC to Edward VII, 27 Nov. 1907, CV II, part 2, p. 712.

150 WSC, *My African Journey*, p. 77.

151 Ibid., p. 40.

152 Ibid., p. 41.

153 Ibid., p. 27.

154 Speech of 18 Jan. 1908.

155 WSC, *My African Journey*, p. 75. For further early examples of this well-

known rhetorical trope see Ronald Hyam, 'Winston Churchill before 1914', *Historical Journal*, 12 (1969), pp. 164–73, at 173.

156 'Mr Churchill – Imperialist!' (review of *My African Journey*), *Observer*, 6 Dec. 1908.

157 'If Philosophers Were Kings: Mr Churchill in Africa' (review of *My African Journey*), *Daily News*, 30 Nov. 1908.

158 WSC to J. A. Spender, 22 Dec. 1907, J. A. Spender Papers, MS 46388, ff. 220–1; Paul Addison, *Churchill on the Home Front, 1900–1955*, Pimlico, London, 1993 (first published by Jonathan Cape, 1992), p. 59.

159 Speech of 18 Jan. 1908.

160 Both cited in 'Unpopularity of Mr Winston Churchill', *Taranaki Herald*, 15 April 1908.

161 Elgin, draft letter of 29 April 1908, quoted in Hyam, *Elgin and Churchill*, p. 511.

162 Lord Elgin to Lord Crewe, [?] May 1908, CV II, part 2, p. 797.

163 WSC to Hopwood, 22 Oct. 1907, Hopwood Papers, Box 5.

164 Wilfrid Scawen Blunt, *My Diaries: Being a Personal Narrative of Events, 1888–1914: Part Two* [1900–14], Martin Secker, London, n.d., p. 283 (entry for 25 Nov. 1909).

165 WSC to Hopwood 3 Oct. 1907, Hopwood Papers, Box 5; WSC to Elgin, 4 Oct. 1907, CV I, part 2, p. 685.

166 Blunt, *My Diaries: Part Two*, p. 284 (entry for 25 Nov. 1909).

5. THE FATE OF AN EMPIRE

1 Speech of 27 Jan. 1922.

2 Edwin Montagu to WSC, 31 Jan. 1922 and Lord Reading to Montagu, 6 Feb. 1922, CV IV, part 3, pp. 1743–7, 1756–7.

3 'Indians in Kenya: Mr Churchill's Recent Statement', *Madras Weekly Mail*, 9 Feb. 1922.

4 Speech of N. M. Samarth, Indian Legislative Assembly Debates, vol. II, no. 31, 9 Feb. 1922, p. 2319, copy in NA, CO 533/287; 'Indians in Kenya: A Madras Protest', and 'Indians in Kenya: The Churchill Controversy', *Madras Weekly Mail*, 16 Feb. 1922. See also 'India's Political Salvation', *The Times*, 16 Feb. 1922. For the resolution on Indian equality – from which, unsurprisingly, the South African delegation dissented – see 'Conference of Prime Ministers and representatives of the United Kingdom, the Dominions and India, held in June, July and August, 1921', Cmd. 1474, 1921, p. 8.

5 Speech of 8 July 1920.

6 WSC, memorandum, 25 Oct. 1919, CV IV, part 2, p. 939.

7 Speech of 4 Sept. 1909.

8 WSC to J. C. Robertson, 27 Oct. 1922, CV IV, part 3, p. 2094.

9 Edward David (ed.), *Inside Asquith's Cabinet: From the Diaries of Charles Hobhouse*, John Murray, London, 1977, p. 76 (entry for 7 March 1909).

10 WSC, *My African Journey* [first published by Hodder & Stoughton, London, 1908], CW, vol. I, p. 41.

11 Speech of 4 Sept. 1909.

12 'Mr Winston Churchill: Barnardo Homes and the Problem of Boy Labour', *Daily Chronicle*, 27 Nov. 1908.

13 Speech of 11 Oct. 1906.

14 WSC to H. H. Asquith, Dec. 1910, quoted in Paul Addison, *Churchill on the Home Front, 1900–1955*, Pimlico, London, 1993 (first published by Jonathan Cape, 1992), p. 125.

15 Wilfrid Scawen Blunt, *My Diaries: Being a Personal Narrative of Events, 1888–1914: Part Two* [1900–1914], p. 401 (entry for 21 Oct. 1912).

16 Lord Charles Beresford, 'The Naval Outlook: Mr Churchill's Promises and Performances', *Empire Review*, 26, 154 (Nov. 1913), pp. 217–24.

17 Nicholas Lambert, 'Economy or Empire? The Fleet Unit Concept and the Quest for Collective Security in the Pacific, 1909–14', in Greg Kennedy and Keith Neilson (eds.), *Far-Flung Lines: Essays on Imperial Defence*, Frank Cass, London, 1997, pp. 55–83.

18 Ibid., pp. 70–1.

19 WSC to Lewis Harcourt, 29 Jan, 1912, Harcourt Papers, Dep. 468, ff. 113–20.

20 Speech of 15 May 1912. Although the *Complete Speeches* gives 'guard and control', it seems more likely that Churchill said 'patrol', as reported in 'An Empire Navy', *The Times*, 16 May 1912.

21 'Rulers of the Sea', *Evening Post* (New Zealand), 20 May 1912; 'Canada and the Navy', 'Imperial Considerations First', and 'Mr Churchill and the Dominion Navies', *The Times*, 20 May, 1912.

22 *Sydney Morning Herald*, quoted in 'Australia and Naval Defence', *The Times*, 19 July 1912.

23 'Mr Borden's Position', *The Times*, 4 July 1912.

24 'Canada and Imperial Defence', *The Times*, 6 July 1912.

25 WSC to R. L. Borden, 29 Aug. 1912, Asquith Papers, 24, ff. 164–5.

26 'A Half-Century of Tribute', *Globe* (Toronto), 6 Dec. 1912.

27 'Winston Churchill Again Changes Mind', *Ottawa Free Press*, 6 Dec. 1912.

28 'Concerning that "Emergency" Discovered by Mr R. L. Borden', *Toronto Daily Star*, 11 Jan. 1913.

29 'Correspondence between the First Lord of the Admiralty and the Prime Minister of the Dominion of Canada', Cd. 6689, HMSO, London, 1913.

30 F. B. Carvell, quoted in *Toronto Daily Star*, 11 March 1913.

31 Henry Emmerson, quoted in 'Canada and Defence', *Evening Post* (NZ), 13 March 1913, citing the Press Association.

32 'Imperial Patrol', *Evening Post* (NZ), 7 May 1913.

33 Borden to WSC, 23 March 1913, CV II, part 3, p. 1805.

34 'The Pacific Danger', *The Times*, 14 May 1914.

35 'Dominion Navies', *Evening Post* (NZ), 30 April 1913.

36 'Canada Rejects Naval Aid', *New York Times*, 31 May 1913.

37 'The Meeting-Place of Continents', *The Times*, 14 May 1914.

38 Donald C. Gordon, 'The Admiralty and Dominion Navies, 1902–1914', *Journal of Modern History*, 33 (1961), pp. 407–22, at 422.

39 Graham Freudenberg, *Churchill and Australia*, Macmillan, Sydney, 2008, pp. 46–50.

40 Leo Amery, *My Political Life*, vol. I: *England before the Storm, 1896–1914*, Hutchinson, London, 1953, p. 196.

41 'Perils of the Pacific', *Evening Post* (NZ), 13 May 1913.

42 Borden to WSC, 31 Dec. 1913, CV II, part 3, p. 1814.

43 C. P. Scott diary, 15 Jan. 1914, C. P. Scott Papers, MS. Add. 50901, f. 91.

44 'A Brilliant and Memorable Achievement', *Evening Post* (NZ), 3 May 1915.

45 Edward J. Erickson, 'Strength against Weakness: Ottoman Military Effectiveness at Gallipoli, 1915', *Journal of Military History*, 65 (2001), pp. 981–1011, at 1009.

46 WSC, *The World Crisis, Part Two: 1915* [first published by Thornton Butterworth, London, 1923], CW, vol. IX, p. 366.

47 WSC to H. H. Asquith, 21 May 1915, CV III, part 2, p. 926.

48 Lord Reading diary, 27 May 1915, Lord Reading Papers, MS Eur. F118/152.

49 Speech of 5 June 1915.

50 Henry W. Nevinson, *Last Changes, Last Chances*, Nisbet & Co. Ltd, London, 1928, p. 56.

51 Wilfrid Scawen Blunt diary, 14 Aug. 1915, Wilfrid Scawen Blunt Papers, MS 15–1975.

52 Scawen Blunt diary, 29 April 1917, Blunt Papers, MS 17–1975.

53 Despatch of 10 Sept. 1915, quoted in 'Gallipoli Struggle: Prime Reasons of Failure', *Evening Post* (NZ), Oct. 1915.

54 'German Gibes at Churchill', *New York Times*, 14 Nov. 1915.

55 Martin Gilbert, *Winston S. Churchill*, vol. III: *1914–1916*, Heinemann, London, 1971, pp. 563, 565–6.

56 T. H. Buck to Ralph David Blumenfeld, 21 Nov. [1915], Ralph David Blumenfeld Papers, BLU/1/4/BU.1.

57 David Lloyd George to William George, 6 March 1916, William George Papers, 3054.

58 *Sunday Times*, 3 June 1917, quoted in Martin Gilbert, *Winston S. Churchill*, vol. IV: *1917–1922*, Heinemann, London, 1975, p. 23.

59 J. C. Smuts to David Lloyd George, 6 June 1917, CV IV, part 1, p. 69.

60 J. C. Smuts to WSC, 31 July 1917, ibid., p. 120.

61 Cornelia Wimborne to WSC, 18 July 1917, ibid., p. 101.

62 Walter Layton, 'Adventures in Peace and War' (unpublished memoirs), pp. 169–169A, Walter Layton Papers, Box 147.

63 WSC, preface to Jeremiah McVeagh, *Home Rule in a Nutshell* (n.d. but 1911), quoted in Paul Addison, 'Winston Churchill's Concept of "The

English-Speaking Peoples"', in Attila Pók (ed.), *The Fabric of Modern Europe: Essays in Honour of Éva Haraszti Taylor*, Nottingham, Astra Press, 1999, pp. 103–17, at 105.

64 Speech of 10 Dec. 1917.

65 J. M. McEwen, *The Riddell Diaries, 1908–1923*, Athlone Press, London and Atlantic Highlands, NJ, 1986, p. 267 (entry for 11 April 1919).

66 Speech of 4 Nov. 1920.

67 WSC to John Morley, 30 Nov. 1905, John Morley Papers, MS Eng. d. 3559, f. 22.

68 Speeches of 8 Feb. and 1 March 1912.

69 'Mr Churchill in Belfast', *The Times*, 9 Feb. 1912.

70 'The Home Rule Fight', *The Times*, 12 Aug. 1912.

71 WSC to John Redmond, 31 Aug. 1912, John Redmond Papers.

72 Speech of 14 March 1914.

73 Austen Chamberlain, 'Memo of Conversation with Winston Churchill. Nov. 27 1913', Austen Chamberlain Papers, AC 11/1/21.

74 Henry Wilson diary, 30 Aug. 1920, CV IV, part 2, p. 1195.

75 Speech of 16 Oct. 1920.

76 Keith Middlemas (ed.), *Thomas Jones, Whitehall Diary*, vol. III: *Ireland 1918–1925*, Oxford University Press, London, 1971, p. 85 (entry for 6 July 1921).

77 'Draft Reply Adopted at Gairloch', 21 Sept. 1921, ibid., p. 116.

78 See, for example, 'Mr Churchill's Speech: Sinn Fein's Answer', *Irish Times*, 29 Sept. 1921.

79 Collins's notes, quoted in Rex Taylor, *Michael Collins*, Hutchinson, London, 1958, pp. 154–5.

80 Erskine Childers diary, 5 Dec. 1921, copy in Eamon De Valera Papers, P150/1489.

81 James Mackay, *Michael Collins: A Life*, Mainstream Publishing, Edinburgh, 1996, p. 226.

82 Parliamentary Debates, House of Commons, 5th Series, vol. 149, 15 Dec. 1921, cols. 181–2.

83 Dáil Éireann Debates, vol. T, 19 Dec. 1921, 25.

84 Ibid., 3 Jan. 1922, 183.

85 Ibid., 19 Dec. 1921, 33.

86 Quoted in Gilbert, *Winston S. Churchill*, vol. IV, p. 894.

87 Kevin Matthews, *Fatal Influence: The Impact of Ireland on British Politics, 1920–1925*, University College Dublin Press, Dublin, 2004, p. 78.

88 Parliamentary Debates, House of Commons, 5th Series, vol. 149, 15 Dec. 1921, col. 182.

89 See, for example, Julian Amery diary, 28 Feb. 1951, Julian Amery Papers, 4/302.

90 WSC, minute of 18 June 1940, quoted in Martin Gilbert, *Winston S. Churchill*, vol. VI: *Finest Hour, 1939–1941*, Heinemann, London, 1983, p. 433.

91   Maurice Hankey diary, 8 Jan. 1921, Maurice Hankey Papers, 1/5.

92   Henry Wilson diary, 23 Jan. 1921, CV IV, part 2, p. 1319.

93   Clementine Churchill to WSC, 7 Feb. 1921, in Mary Soames, (ed.), *Speaking for Themselves: The Personal Letters of Winston and Clementine Churchill*, Doubleday, London, 1998, p. 226.

94   John Barnes and David Nicholson (eds.), *The Leo Amery Diaries*, vol. I: *1896–1929*, Hutchinson, London, 1980, p. 392 (entry for 21 Nov. 1924).

95   Ronald Hyam, 'Churchill and the British Empire', in Robert Blake and Wm. Roger Louis (eds.), *Churchill*, Oxford University Press, Oxford, 1993, pp. 167–85, at 178–9.

96   Lord Curzon to Lady (Grace) Curzon, 14 Feb. 1921, CV IV, part 2, p. 1349.

97   M. R. Lawrence (ed.), *The Home Letters of T. E. Lawrence and his Brothers*, Basil Blackwell, Oxford, 1954, p. 232.

98   WSC, *Great Contemporaries* [first published by Thornton Butterworth, London, 1937], CW, vol. XVI, p. 121. An insightful account of Churchill's view of Lawrence can be found in Paul K. Alkon, *Winston Churchill's Imagination*, Bucknell University Press, Lewisburg, 2006, ch. 1.

99   Gertrude Bell to Frank Balfour, 25 March 1921, Gertrude Bell online archive. For the complaints of others about Churchill, see Michael Makovsky, *Churchill's Promised Land: Zionism and Statecraft*, Yale University Press, New Haven, 2007, p. 112.

100 T. E. Lawrence to Robert Graves, quoted in Robert Graves, *Lawrence and the Arabs*, Jonathan Cape, London, 1927, pp. 396–7.

101 Gertrude Bell to Frank Balfour, 25 March 1921, Gertrude Bell online archive.

102 David Fromkin, *A Peace to End All Peace: The Fall of the Ottoman Empire and the Creation of the Modern Middle East*, Henry Holt & Co., New York, 1989, p. 25. See also, for example, Christopher Catherwood, *Winston's Folly: Imperialism and the Creation of Modern Iraq*, Constable, London, 2004.

103 Arthur Herman, *Gandhi & Churchill: The Epic Rivalry that Destroyed an Empire and Forged Our Age*, Bantam Books, New York, 2008, p. 272.

104 Lawrence James, *The Golden Warrior: The Life and Legend of Lawrence of Arabia*, revised edition, Abacus, London, 1995, pp. 384–5; Robert Olson, 'The Churchill–Cox Correspondence Regarding the Creation of the State of Iraq: Consequences for British Policy Towards the Nationalist Turkish Government, 1921–1923', *International Journal of Turkish Studies*, 5 (1991), pp. 121–36.

105 'Mesopotamia and Mr Churchill', *The Times*, 23 Feb. 1921.

106 Aylmer Haldane, *A Soldier's Saga*, William Blackwood & Sons, Edinburgh and London, 1948, pp. 371–2.

107 WSC to Lloyd George, 31 Aug. 1920 (unsent), CV IV, part 2, p. 1199.

108 WSC to Hugh Trenchard, 29 Aug. 1920, ibid., p. 1190. On the use of gas, see also Churchill's minute of 12 May 1919, CV IV, part 1, p. 649, and his note of 16 Dec. 1921, CV IV, part 3, p. 1695.

109 WSC to Hugh Trenchard, 22 July 1921, CV IV, part 3, p. 1561.

110 WSC, 'The Situation in Mesopotamia', 10 Dec. 1920, NA, CAB 14/116.

111 Cabinet minutes, 13 Dec. 1921 (two meetings), CC 69 (21) and CC 70 (21), NA, CAB 23/23; Parliamentary Debates, House of Commons, 5th Series, vol. 136, 15 Dec. 1920, col. 548.

112 Fromkin, *Peace to End All Peace*, p. 508.

113 WSC to Lloyd George, 1 Sept. 1922, CV IV, part 3, p. 1974.

114 WSC to J. C. Robertson, 27 Oct. 1922, ibid., p. 2094.

115 Henry Maxwell Coote diary, 24 March 1921, Henry Maxwell Coote Papers.

116 Coote diary, 29 March 1921, ibid.

117 WSC, memorandum, 25 Oct. 1919, CV IV, part 2, p. 938.

118 'Zionism versus Bolshevism', *Illustrated Sunday Herald*, 8 Feb. 1920, in *The Collected Essays of Sir Winston Churchill*, ed. Michael Wolff, 4 vols., Library of Imperial History, London, 1976, vol. IV, pp. 26–30, at 27, 29. In an editorial of 13 February 1920 the *Jewish Chronicle* criticized Churchill strongly for these views: Michael J. Cohen, *Churchill and the Jews*, 2nd edition, Frank Cass, London, 2003, p. 56. See also Norman Rose, 'Churchill and Zionism', in Robert Blake and Wm. Roger Louis (eds.), *Churchill*, Oxford University Press, Oxford, 1993, pp. 147–66, at 150–1, and Makovsky, *Churchill's Promised Land*, pp. 84–9.

119 Tom Segev, *One Palestine, Complete: Jews and Arabs under the British Mandate*, Little, Brown, London, 2000, pp. 38, 158.

120 Memorandum by the Palestinian Arab Congress, 14 March 1921, and the *Egyptian Gazette*, 30 March 1921, CV IV, part 2, pp. 1386–8, 1419–21.

121 A record of the meeting, which took place on 22 July 1921, can be found in CV IV, part 3, pp. 1558–61.

122 'Palestine: Correspondence with the Palestine Arab Delegation and the Zionist Organisation', Cmd. 1700, June 1922, pp. 18–19. Emphasis in original.

123 Rose, 'Churchill and Zionism', p. 157.

124 Parliamentary Debates, House of Commons, 5th Series, vol. 156, 4 July 1922, col. 355.

125 Malcolm MacDonald, *Titans & Others*, Collins, London, 1972, pp. 91–2.

126 See Michael Cohen's valuable article 'The Churchill–Gilbert Symbiosis: Myth and Reality', *Modern Judaism*, 28 (2008), pp. 204–28, which demolishes the case made in Martin Gilbert, *Churchill and the Jews*, Simon & Schuster, London, 2007.

127 WSC, memorandum, 25 Oct. 1919, CV IV, part 2, p. 938.

128 Ibid., p. 1260, n. 1.

129 WSC, memorandum, 25 Oct. 1919, ibid., p. 939.

130 'Empire Family Council', *The Times*, 14 Feb. 1921.

131 'Egyptian Independence Claim', *The Times*, 18 Feb. 1921. See also Lord Curzon to WSC, 13 June 1921, CV IV, part 3, p. 1503.

132 Curzon to Grace Curzon, 24 Oct. 1921, quoted in David Gilmour, *Curzon*, John Murray, London, 1994, p. 525.

133 Curzon to Lord Hardinge, 21 Oct. 1921, quoted ibid., p. 526.

134 'Report of the Committee appointed by the Government of India to investigate the disturbances in the Punjab, etc.', Cmd. 681, 1920, p. 29.

135 M. K. Gandhi, *An Autobiography, or, The Story of My Experiments with Truth*, Penguin, London, 1982 (first published 1927–9), p. 422.

136 H. H. Asquith to Venetia Stanley, 12 May 1915, in Michael and Eleanor Brock (eds.), *H. H. Asquith: Letters to Venetia Stanley*, Oxford University Press, Oxford, 1982, p. 593. Emphasis in original.

137 John Darwin, 'A Third British Empire? The Dominion Idea in Imperial Politics', in Judith M. Brown and Wm. Roger Louis (eds.), *The Oxford History of the British Empire: The Twentieth Century*, Oxford University Press, Oxford, 1999, pp. 64–87, at 78–9.

138 Alfred Draper, *The Amritsar Massacre: Twilight of the Raj*, Buchan & Enright, London, 1985, pp. 209–12.

139 'General Dyer's "Error"', *The Times*, 8 July 1920.

140 Parliamentary Debates, House of Commons, 5th Series, vol. 131, 8 July 1920, cols. 1707–8.

141 William Sutherland to David Lloyd George, 9 July 1920, CV IV, part 2, pp. 1140–1.

142 Austen Chamberlain to Ida Chamberlain, 11 July 1920, in Robert Self (ed.), *The Austen Chamberlain Diary Letters: The Correspondence of Sir Austen Chamberlain with his Sisters Hilda and Ida, 1916–1937*, Cambridge University Press for the Royal Historical Society, London, 1995, p. 138.

143 Parliamentary Debates, House of Commons, 5th Series, vol. 131, 8 July 1920, cols. 1719–33. For Churchill's struggles with the Army Council, see Nigel Collett, *The Butcher of Amritsar: General Reginald Dyer*, Hambledon, London, 2005, ch. 21.

144 The emphasis on the massacre's singularity was echoed by others. See Derek Sayer, 'British Reaction to the Amritsar Massacre, 1919–1920', *Past and Present*, 131 (1991), pp. 130–64.

145 'Punjab Press Abstract', 33, 29 (Lahore, 17 July 1920), pp. 283–4, IOR/L/R/5/202, quoting the Lahore *Tribune*, 13 July 1920.

146 Herman, *Gandhi & Churchill*, p. 258.

147 Elspeth Huxley, *White Man's Country: Lord Delamere and the Making of Kenya*, vol. II: *1914–1931*, Chatto & Windus, 1953 (first published 1935), p. 121.

148 WSC to Edwin Montagu, 8 Oct. 1921, CV IV, part 3, p. 1469.

149 Montagu to WSC 17 June 1921, ibid., pp. 1515–16.

150 'Proceedings of a Deputation', 9 Aug. 1921, NA, CO 533/270.

151 WSC to Montagu, 8 Oct. 1921, CV IV, part 3, pp. 1644–5.

152 Montagu to WSC, 12 Oct. 1921, ibid., p. 1649.

153 Huxley, *White Man's Country*, vol. II, pp. 126–7.

154 'Indians in East Africa', *The Times*, 28 Jan. 1922.

155 Montagu to WSC, 31 Jan. 1922, CV IV, part 3, p. 1747.

156 Conclusions of a Conference of Ministers held on 13 Feb. 1922, NA, CAB 23/39.

157 'Impressions and Views of Speeches', *East African Standard*, 4 Feb. 1922.

158 'Mr Churchill's Masters and Ours', *East African Standard* (weekly edition), 26 Aug. 1922.

159 'Mr Montagu's Reply', *The Times*, 13 March 1922.

160 'India and Mr Montagu', ibid.

161 Robert M. Maxon, 'The Devonshire Declaration: The Myth of Missionary Intervention', *History in Africa*, 18 (1991), pp. 259–70, at p. 262.

162 'A Dangerous Despatch', *East African Standard*, 19 Aug. 1922.

163 An unnamed Indian civil servant, quoted in Huxley, *White Man's Country*, vol. II, p. 135.

164 This was embodied in the so-called 'Devonshire Declaration', which gave the settlers what they wanted over the highlands and the question of voting, but not over segregation. The immigration issue was fudged. Cleverly, the declaration sidestepped the question of equality between Whites and Indians by stating that the welfare of Africans in the country was to be considered paramount and that, where there was a conflict of interest with those of 'the immigrant races', African interests were to prevail. In practice, however, the Whites remained dominant. 'Indians in Kenya', Cmd. 1922, July 1923, p. 10; Maxon, 'The Devonshire Declaration', p. 259.

165 WSC, despatch of 5 Sept. 1921, in the *Official Gazette of the Colony and Protectorate of Kenya*, 19 Oct. 1921.

166 H. R. Tate, Provincial Commissioner of Kenya Province, quoted in Bruce Berman, *Control and Crisis in Colonial Kenya: The Dialectic of Domination*, East African Educational Publishers, Nairobi, 1990, p. 153.

167 Harry Thuku, *An Autobiography*, Oxford University Press, Nairobi, 1970, pp. 32–3.

168 Anthony Clayton and Donald C. Savage, *Government and Labour in Kenya, 1895–1963*, Frank Cass, London, 1974, p. 121.

169 A. C. C. Parkinson, memorandum reviewing Thuku's case, 17 June 1929, NA, CO 533/388/9; Martin L. Kilson, Jr., 'Land and the Kikuyu: A Study of the Relationship between Land and Kikuyu Political Movements', *Journal of Negro History*, 40 (1955), pp. 103–53, n. 105.

170 'Papers relating to native disturbances in Kenya', March, 1922, Cmd. 1691, 1922.

171 Press communiqué, 16 Sept. 1922, CV IV, part 3, p. 1994.

172 W. M. Hughes, *The Splendid Adventure: A Review of Empire Relations Within and Without the Commonwealth of Britannic Nations*, Ernest Benn, London, 1929, p. 243; Freudenberg, *Churchill and Australia*, pp. 161–4.

173 'The Call to the Empire', *The Times*, 26 Sept. 1922.

174 J. C. Smuts to WSC, 13 Oct. 1922, CV IV, part 3, p. 2086.

175 W. L. Mackenzie King diary, 17 Sept. 1922.

176 Ibid., 4 Oct. 1922.

177 'The Spotlight: Winston Churchill', *Toronto Daily Star*, 22 Sept. 1922.
178 WSC to J. C. Robertson, 27 Oct. 1922, CV IV, part 3, p. 2095.
179 'The Near East: Pronouncement by Mr Bonar Law', *The Times*, 7 Oct. 1922.
180 WSC, *The Second World War*, vol. I: *The Gathering Storm* [first published by Cassell, London, 1948], CW, vol. XXII, p. 14.
181 Cecil Harmsworth diary, 19 Oct. 1922, Cecil Harmsworth Papers.
182 'Dominions and Elections', *The Times*, 20 Nov. 1922.
183 Mackenzie King diary, 19 Oct. 1922.
184 'Dominions and Elections', *The Times*, 20 Nov. 1922.
185 John Ramsden, *Man of the Century: Winston Churchill and His Legend since 1945*, HarperCollins, London, 2002, p. 438.
186 Mackenzie King diary, 26 Jan. 1923.
187 Quoted in Vaidehi Ramanathan, 'Gandhi, Non-Cooperation, and Socio-civic Education in Gujarat, India: Harnessing the Vernaculars', *Journal of Language, Identity & Education*, 5 (2006), pp. 229–50, at 237.
188 WSC to Curzon, note passed in Cabinet, 4 July 1921, CV IV, part 3, p. 1543.

6. Diehard

1 H. G. Wells, 'The Future of the British Empire', *Empire Review*, 38 (1923), pp. 1071–9. Quotation at p. 1078.
2 Winston Churchill, 'Mr H. G. Wells and the British Empire', *Empire Review*, 38 (1923), pp. 1217–23. Quotations at p. 1218.
3 H. G. Wells, 'Winston', 10 Nov. 1923, in *A Year of Prophesying* (T. Fisher Unwin, London, 1924), pp. 52–6. Quotation at p. 54. This article was originally published in the *Westminster Gazette*.
4 David C. Smith, 'Winston Churchill and H. G. Wells: Edwardians in the Twentieth Century', *Cahiers Victoriens et Edouardien*, 30 (1989), pp. 93–116, at 104.
5 H. G. Wells, 'An Open Letter to an Elector in N.W. Manchester', *Daily News*, 21 April 1908; WSC to H. G. Wells, 16 April 1908, H. G. Wells Papers, C-238–1.
6 WSC, 'Mr H. G. Wells and the British Empire', pp. 1218, 1221.
7 Wells, 'Winston', p. 54.
8 WSC, 'Mr H. G. Wells and the British Empire', p. 1223.
9 Lord Derby diary, 25 Oct. 1922 (copy), Randolph Churchill Papers, 3/6/1/5.
10 Speech of 16 Nov. 1923.
11 Speech of 17 Nov. 1923.
12 WSC to Stanley Baldwin, 7 March 1924, CV V, part 1, p. 119.
13 Speech of 18 March 1924, quoted in Martin Gilbert, *Winston S. Churchill*, vol. V: *1922–1939*, Heinemann, London, 1976, p. 36.

14 'Westminster Election News', 2 (March 1924), Edward Spears Papers, 1/76. This was a Labour Party publication.

15 W. L. Mackenzie King diary, 7 Nov. 1924.

16 Speech of 25 Sept. 1924.

17 Gertrude Bell to Hugh Bell, 8 April 1925, Gertrude Bell online archive.

18 John Barnes and David Nicholson (eds.), *The Leo Amery Diaries*, vol. I: *1896–1929*, Hutchinson, London, 1980, p. 423 (entry for 19 Oct. 1925).

19 See, for example, the letters in the Stanley Baldwin Papers from Amery to Baldwin of 28 Jan. 1926 (vol. 92, ff. 196–9), 27 Feb. 1926 (vol. 96, ff. 108–10), 29 March 1926 (vol. 93, ff. 244–5), 11 April 1927 (vol. 94, ff. 69–70) and 26 Nov. 1928 (vol. 97, ff. 19–20).

20 Leo Amery to Baldwin, 10 April 1927, Leo Amery Papers, 2/1/13.

21 WSC to Amery, 30 April 1927, CV V, part 1, p. 995.

22 Amery to J. C. Smuts, 26 June 1929, Leo Amery Papers, 2/2/24.

23 Churchill did, in fact, impose a range of new duties, bringing him criticism from free traders; but there was no general tariff, nor was there protection for the all-important iron and steel industry. See Paul Addison, *Churchill on the Home Front, 1900–1955*, Pimlico, London, 1993 (first published by Jonathan Cape, 1992), p. 274.

24 WSC to Worthington-Evans, 14 July 1928, Laming Worthington-Evans Papers, MSS. Eng. Hist. c.896, ff. 25–6.

25 Stephen Constantine, *The Making of British Colonial Development Policy, 1914–1940*, Frank Cass, London, 1984, pp. 138–58.

26 Speech of 28 April 1925.

27 Martin Daunton, *Just Taxes: The Politics of Taxation in Britain, 1914–1979*, Cambridge University Press, Cambridge, 2002, p. 135.

28 This assumption is questionable given, for example, the popularity of the British Empire Exhibition held at Wembley in 1924–5. See, however, Bernard Porter, *The Absent-Minded Imperialists: Empire, Society, and Culture in Britain*, Oxford University Press, Oxford, 2004, pp. 265–6.

29 'Imperial Conference, 1926: Summary of Proceedings', Cmd. 2768, 1926, p. 14.

30 Speech of 3 Jan. 1927.

31 Baldwin to Lord Irwin, 25 Feb. 1929, in Philip Williamson and Edward Baldwin (eds.), *Baldwin Papers: A Conservative Statesman, 1908–1947*, Cambridge University Press, Cambridge, 2004, p. 214.

32 Lord Irwin to Stanley Baldwin, 28 March 1929, CV V, part 2, p. 1452.

33 WSC, draft memoirs, CV V, part 1, p. 1431.

34 Amery to Neville Chamberlain, 4 May 1929, Leo Amery Papers, 2/3/6.

35 In the words of Clement Attlee (as recalled by Harold Wilson in 1983): 'Trouble with Winston: nails his trousers to the mast. Can't climb down.' Quoted in Matthew Parris and Phil Mason, *Read My Lips: A Treasury of Things Politicians Wish They Hadn't Said*, Penguin, Harmondsworth, 1997 (first published 1996), p. 13.

36 Speech of 26 July 1929.

37 WSC, draft memoirs, CV V, part 2, pp. 25–6.

38 Mackenzie King diary, 15 Aug. 1929.

39 'The Goal in India', *The Times*, 1 Nov. 1929.

40 Samuel Hoare to Irwin, 13 Nov. 1929, CV V part 2, p. 111.

41 'The Peril in India', *Daily Mail*, 16 Nov. 1929, reproduced with the title 'Dominion Status', in WSC, *India: Speeches and an Introduction*, Thornton Butterworth, London, 1931, pp. 29–35, quotations at 34–5.

42 'Joint Committee on Indian Constitutional Reform (Session 1932–33)', vol. I, HMSO, London, 1933, p. 1777.

43 Speech of 30 Jan. 1931.

44 Broadcast of 30 Jan. 1935, CV V, part 2, p. 1055.

45 Speech of 11 Dec. 1930.

46 WSC to Lord Linlithgow, 7 May 1933, CV V, part 2, pp. 595–6.

47 See, for example, Baldwin's remarks in Parliamentary Debates, House of Commons, 5th Series, vol. 249, 12 March 1931, cols. 1423–4.

48 WSC, *India*, p. 5.

49 Ibid., p. 7.

50 WSC to Edwin Montagu, 8 Oct. 1921, CV IV, part 3, p. 1644. In his reply of 12 October Montagu stated that the 'accepted policy of HM's Government is the achievement in due course by India of Dominion status, and I have never understood that you were an opponent of this'; on the contrary he had believed Churchill approved of it (ibid., p. 1650).

51 John Julius Norwich (ed.), *The Duff Cooper Diaries, 1915–1951*, Weidenfeld & Nicolson, London, 2005, p. 133 (entry for 4 Nov. 1920).

52 Minutes of a conference of ministers, 9 Feb. 1922, CV IV, part 3, p. 1763.

53 Churchill's speech of 15 June 1921 quoted by Irwin: 'India's Debt To Britain', *The Times*, 20 July 1931.

54 Neville Chamberlain to Hilda Chamberlain, 18 June 1921, in Robert Self (ed.), *The Neville Chamberlain Diary Letters*, vol. II: *The Reform Years, 1921–1927*, Ashgate, Aldershot, 2000, p. 65. Unfortunately, Chamberlain did not record Sastri's precise words.

55 WSC to Baldwin, 24 Sept. 1930, CV V, part 2, p. 186.

56 'Editor's introduction' in Mrinalini Sinha (ed.), *Katherine Mayo: Selections from 'Mother India'*, Kali for Women, New Delhi, 1998, pp. 1–64; Katherine Mayo, *Mother India*, Jonathan Cape, London, 1927, p. 38.

57 Victor Cazalet diary, 10 Aug. 1927, in Robert Rhodes James, *Victor Cazalet: A Portrait*, Hamish Hamilton, London, 1976, p. 120.

58 Roger Keyes to WSC, 23 March 1931 and WSC to Katherine Mayo, 9 March 1935, CV V, part 2, pp. 309, 1111.

59 Speech of 18 March 1931.

60 His most prominent Muslim supporter was Waris Ameer Ali, a former judge who lived in London after his retirement in 1929 and who served on the Council of the Indian Empire Society.

61 John Campbell, *F. E. Smith, First Earl of Birkenhead*, Jonathan Cape, London, 1983, p. 516.

62 Lord Birkenhead to Lord Reading, 5 March 1925, quoted ibid., p. 734.

63 WSC, draft memoirs, CV V, part 1, p. 1432.

64 WSC, *Great Contemporaries* [first published by Thornton Butterworth, London, 1937], CW, vol. XVI, p. 110.

65 WSC, 'The Palestine Crisis', *Sunday Times*, 22 Sept. 1929, in *The Collected Essays of Sir Winston Churchill*, ed. Michael Wolff, 4 vols., Library of Imperial History, London, 1976, vol. II, pp. 168–71, quotation at 169.

66 WSC, 'Will the British Empire Last?', *Answers*, 26 Oct. 1929, ibid., pp. 172–5, quotation at 175.

67 Kenneth Young (ed.), *The Diaries of Sir Bruce Lockhart*, vol I: *1915–1938*, Macmillan, London, 1973, p. 132 (entry for 23 Oct. 1930).

68 On the collapse of free trade culture in Britain at this time see Frank Trentmann, *Free Trade Nation: Commerce, Consumption, and Civil Society in Modern Britain*, Oxford University Press, Oxford, 2008, chs 4–7.

69 Baldwin to J. C. C. Davidson, 13 Nov. 1930, CV V, part 2, p. 222.

70 Speech of 11 Dec. 1930.

71 WSC to Abe Bailey, 19 Dec. 1930, Churchill Papers, CHAR 2/169/64.

72 John Barnes and David Nicholson (eds.), *The Empire at Bay: The Leo Amery Diaries, 1929–1945*, Hutchinson, London, 1988, p. 146 (entry for 30 Jan. 1931).

73 Speech of 23 Feb. 1931.

74 Speech of 18 March 1931.

75 Speech of 11 Dec. 1930.

76 MKG, 'The Loin-Cloth', *Young India*, 30 April 1931, in *Collected Works*, 100 vols., Government of India Publications Division, New Delhi, 1960–94, vol. XLVI, pp. 54–6.

77 WSC to Clementine Churchill, 26 Feb. 1931, in Mary Soames (ed.), *Speaking for Themselves: The Personal Letters of Winston and Clementine Churchill*, Doubleday, London, 1998, p. 354.

78 Lord Halifax, *Fulness of Days*, Collins, London, 1957, p. 151.

79 Austen Chamberlain to Hilda Chamberlain, 7 March 1931, in Robert Self (ed.), *The Correspondence of Sir Austen Chamberlain with His Sisters Hilda and Ida, 1916–1937*, Cambridge University Press for the Royal Historical Society, Cambridge, 1995, p. 365.

80 'Indian Affairs in London', *Statesman*, 20 March 1931.

81 Both quoted in 'Note on the Press: United Provinces of Agra and Oudh', 12 (of 1931: week ending 21 March), IOR/L/R/5/99.

82 'St George's for England', *Times of India*, 21 March 1931.

83 Harcourt Butler, *India Insistent*, London, Heinemann, 1931, p. vii.

84 Arnold Gyde to Harcourt Butler, 24 Aug. 1931, Harcourt Butler Papers, MS Eur. F116/86.

85 WSC, 'India Insistent', *Daily Mail*, 7 Sept. 1931, in *Collected Essays*, vol. II, pp. 228–32, quotation at 228.

86 Quoted in 'Note on the Press: United Provinces of Agra and Oudh', 36 (of 1931: week ending 5 September), IOR/L/R/5/99.

87 MKG, interview to Associated Press, 11 Sept. 1931, in *Collected Works*, vol. XLVII, p. 418.
88 MKG, interview to the press, 12 Sept. 1931, in *Collected Works*, vol. XLVIII, p. 7.
89 Parliamentary Debates, House of Commons, 5th Series, vol. 259, 20 Nov. 1931, col. 1198.
90 Ibid., vol. 260, 3 Dec. 1931, col. 1300.
91 Samuel Hoare to Lord Willingdon, 3 Dec. 1931, CV V, part 2, p. 381.
92 Speech of 25 May 1932, ibid., p. 435.
93 Speech of 29 Sept. 1931.
94 Barnes and Nicolson, *Empire at Bay*, p. 384 (entry for 19 July 1934); Addison, *Churchill on the Home Front*, p. 306.
95 Amery to Hoare, 1 June 1934, IOR/L/PO/11/14, f. 75.
96 David Reynolds, *In Command of History: Churchill Fighting and Writing the Second World War*, Allen Lane, London, 2004, p. 105.
97 'Proposals for Indian constitutional reform', Cmd. 4268, March 1933.
98 Ian St John, 'Writing to the Defence of Empire: Winston Churchill's Press Campaign against Constitutional Reform in India, 1929–35', in Chandrika Kaul (ed.), *Media and the British Empire*, Macmillan, Basingstoke, 2006, pp. 104–24.
99 D. J. Wenden, 'Churchill, Radio, and Cinema', in Robert Blake and Wm. Roger Louis (eds.), *Churchill*, Oxford University Press, Oxford, 1993, pp. 215–39, at 219.
100 Robert Rhodes James (ed.), *Memoirs of a Conservative: J. C. C. Davidson's Memoirs and Papers, 1910–37*, Weidenfeld & Nicolson, London, 1969, p. 384.
101 As related in J. H. Morgan to A. C. Murray, 4 Dec. 1949, quoted in Paul Addison, *Churchill: The Unexpected Hero*, Oxford University Press, Oxford, 2005, p. 134. Emphasis in original.
102 Lord Croft, *My Life of Strife*, Hutchinson, London, 1949, p. 224.
103 Lord Derby to Lord Lloyd, 18 June 1934, George Lloyd Papers, 19/5.
104 Rhodes James, *Memoirs of a Conservative*, p. 385.
105 Cazalet diary, 19 April 1933, in Rhodes James, *Victor Cazalet: A Portrait*, p. 154.
106 R. A. Butler to Lord Brabourne, 22 March, 1934, Brabourne Papers, MSS Eur. F97/20C, ff. 206–8.
107 Rhodes James, *Memoirs of a Conservative*, p. 385.
108 WSC to Hoare, 5 April 1933, CV V, part 2, p. 566.
109 Hoare to Willingdon, 6 April 1933, ibid., p. 567.
110 'Indian Constitutional Reform', *The Times*, 3 Nov. 1933.
111 'Joint Committee on Indian Constitutional Reform', p. 1810.
112 'Mr Churchill's Message', *The Times*, 28 Oct. 1922; G. D. Birla to MKG, 25 Aug. 1935, CV V, part 2, p. 1244.
113 'Joint Committee on Indian Constitutional Reform', p. 1776.
114 R. H. A. Carter, 'Note on some points in Mr Churchill's Memorandum', 21 Oct. 1933, IOR/L/PO/6/82.

115 Both quoted in 'Mr Churchill's Views on India', *The Times*, 28 Oct. 1933. Similarly, see 'Mr Churchill's "Four Conditions"', *Star of India*, 28 Oct. 1933.

116 'India in Our Politics', *The Times*, 30 Oct. 1933.

117 'Joint Committee on Indian Constitutional Reform', p. 1843.

118 Quoted in 'Mr Churchill's Views on India', *The Times*, 28 Oct. 1933.

119 'India in Our Politics', *The Times*, 30 Oct. 1933.

120 George Stanley to Lord Stonehaven, 9 Aug. 1933, Baldwin Papers, vol. 16, ff. 135–6.

121 Victor Cazalet to Baldwin, 30 Jan. 1934, CV V, part 2, p. 715. Emphasis in original.

122 Brabourne to Hoare, 30 April 1934, Templewood Papers, VII/4, f. 83.

123 Telegram from Delhi to London, 18 April 1934, enclosed with letter of the same date from Geoffrey Dawson to Hoare, IOR/L/PO/11/14, ff. 150–1.

124 Thomas Jones diary, 28 April 1934, Thomas Jones Papers, Class Z.

125 For the debate see Andrew Muldoon, '"An Unholy Row in Lancashire": The Textile Lobby, Conservative Politics, and Indian Policy, 1931–1935', *Twentieth Century British History*, 14 (2003), pp. 93–111, and Martin Pugh, 'Lancashire, Cotton, and Indian Reform: Conservative Controversies in the 1930s', *Twentieth Century British History*, 15 (2004), pp. 143–51.

126 'Report of the Committee of Privileges', 6 June 1934, HMSO, London, 1934.

127 Carl Bridge, 'Churchill, Hoare, Derby and the Committee of Privileges, April to June 1934', *Historical Journal*, 22 (1979), pp. 215–27.

128 See Marguerite Dupree (ed.), *Lancashire and Whitehall: The Diary of Raymond Streat*, vol. I: *1931–39*, Manchester University Press, Manchester, 1987, p. 329 (entry for 4 May 1934).

129 See WSC, 'My Fight For Lancashire', *Sunday Despatch*, 1 July 1934, in *Collected Essays*, vol. II, pp. 344–7.

130 Parliamentary Debates, House of Commons, 5th Series, vol. 290, 13 June 1934, col. 1738.

131 'The Privilege Report', *The Times*, 14 June 1934.

132 Randolph Churchill, address to the electors, 1 Feb. 1935, Randolph Churchill Papers 5/10.

133 Broadcast of 30 Jan. 1935, CV V, part 2, p. 1058 and n. 1 (see also n. 134); 'The India Bill: Mr Churchill's Criticism', *The Times*, 30 Jan. 1935.

134 Churchill's original typescript gave 'shams' but both the *Listener* and *The Times* reported 'shame'. For his avowal of what he had said, see Nicholas Mansergh, *The Commonwealth Experience*, Weidenfeld & Nicolson, London, 1969, p. 267n.

135 Robert Bernays to Lucy Brereton, 6 June 1935, in Nick Smart (ed.), *The Diaries and Letters of Robert Bernays, 1932–1939*, Edwin Mellen Press, Lewiston/Queenston/Lampeter, 1996, p. 201.

136 Speech of 5 June 1935.

137 'House of Commons', *The Times*, 6 June 1935.

138 Louis Fischer, *The Life of Mahatma Gandhi*, HarperCollins, London, 1997 (first published 1951), p. 466.

139 Birla to MKG, 25 Aug. 1935, CV V, part 2, pp. 1243–5.

140 Baldwin to William Bridgeman, 12 June 1935, in Williamson and Baldwin, *Baldwin Papers*, p. 333.

141 Interview to the press, 17 Nov. 1939, in *Selected Works of Jawaharlal Nehru*, first series, 15 vols., Orient Longman/B. R. Publishing Corporation, New Delhi, 1972–82, vol. IX, p. 203.

142 Jawaharlal Nehru, *The Discovery of India*, Meridian Books, London, 1946, p. 376.

143 Lord Tweedsmuir to Baldwin, 3 Feb. 1937, Baldwin Papers, vol. 97, f. 183.

144 '"Winnie" For Sea Lord', *Time*, 17 July 1939.

145 Roderick Macleod and Denis Kelly (eds.), *The Ironside Diaries, 1937–1940*, Constable, London, 1962, p. 42 (entry for 6 Dec. 1939).

146 Butler to Brabourne, 22 November 1937, Brabourne Papers, MSS Eur. F97/22B, f. 108.

147 Broadcast of 30 April 1937; 'Defence of the Empire' *The Times*, 1 May 1937.

148 Speech of 20 April 1939.

149 Paul Addison, 'Winston Churchill's Concept of "The English-Speaking Peoples"', in Attila Pók (ed.), *The Fabric of Modern Europe: Essays in Honour of Éva Haraszti Taylor*, Astra Press, Nottingham, 1999, pp. 103–17, at 105–6; Jason Tomes, *Balfour and Foreign Policy: The International Thought of a Conservative Statesman*, Cambridge, Cambridge University Press, 1997, esp. p. 190; Philip Williamson, 'The Doctrinal Politics of Stanley Baldwin', in Michael Bentley (ed.), *Public and Private Doctrine: Essays in British History Presented to Maurice Cowling*, Cambridge, Cambridge University Press, 1993, pp. 181–208, at 199.

150 Wendy Webster, *Englishness and Empire, 1939–1965*, Oxford University Press, Oxford, 2005, pp. 16–17.

151 Richard S. Grayson, 'Leo Amery's Imperialist Alternative to Appeasement in the 1930s', *Twentieth Century British History*, 17 (2006), pp. 489–515. For a trenchant statement by Churchill of his opposition to the return of colonies, see 'The Colony Racket', *Collier's*, 19 Nov. 1938, *Collected Essays*, vol. II, pp. 406–14.

152 Broadcast of 16 Nov. 1934.

153 WSC to Baldwin, 15 Dec. 1924, CV V, part 1, p. 306.

154 Naval Programme Committee (27), 6th meeting, 2 Feb. 1928, NA, CAB 27/355, quoted in Christopher M. Bell, 'Winston Churchill, Pacific Security, and the Limits of British Power, 1921–41', in John H. Maurer (ed.), *Churchill and Strategic Dilemmas before the World Wars*, Frank Cass, London, 2003, pp. 51–87, at 51.

155 Broadcast of 30 April 1937.

156 Mackenzie King diary, 1 July 1939.

157 Ibid., 15 Sept. 1939.
158 Menzies' 1935 diary, quoted in A. W. Martin and Patsy Hardy (eds.), *Dark and Hurrying Days: Menzies' 1941 Diary*, National Library of Australia, Canberra, 1993, p. 4. See also David Day, *Menzies & Churchill at War*, Oxford University Press, Oxford, 1993 (first published 1986), pp. 6–8.
159 WSC to J. C. Smuts, 7 Sept. 1939, in *Selections from the Smuts Papers*, vol. VI, *December 1934–August 1945*, ed. Jean van der Poel, Cambridge University Press, Cambridge, 1973, p. 191.
160 Mackenzie King diary, 28 Aug. 1939.
161 WSC, 'Will the British Empire Last?', *Answers*, 26 Oct. 1929, in *Collected Essays*, vol. II, pp. 172–5, at 175.

7. UNDISMAYED AGAINST DISASTER

 1 Lady Blood to WSC, 7 Sept. 1939, CWP, vol. I, p. 50. Emphasis in original.
 2 Speech to Lobby journalists, 29 Feb. 1940, CWP, vol. I, p. 832.
 3 Broadcast of 1 Oct. 1939.
 4 Charles Eade diary, n.d., describing a meeting on 6 Oct. 1939, Charles Eade Papers.
 5 Nigel Nicolson (ed.), *Harold Nicolson: Diaries and Letters 1939–1945*, Collins, London, p. 37 (entry for 26 Sept. 1939).
 6 WSC to Dudley Pound and others, 5 Sept. 1939, CWP, vol. I, pp. 28–9.
 7 WSC to Lord Halifax, 20 Oct. 1939, CWP, vol. I, p. 270.
 8 War Cabinet minutes, 24 Oct. 1939, WM (39) 58th, NA, CAB 65/1/58.
 9 Nigel West (ed.), *The Guy Liddell Diaries*, vol. I: *1939–1942: MI5's Director of Counter-Espionage in World War II*, Routledge, London, 2005, p. 41 (entry for 2 Nov. 1939).
10 John Harvey (ed.), *The Diplomatic Diaries of Oliver Harvey, 1937–1940*, Collins, London, 1970, p. 326 (entry for 30 Oct. 1939).
11 David Stafford, *Churchill and Secret Service*, Abacus, London, 2000 (first published 1997), pp. 189–90.
12 WSC to Dudley Pound and others, 24 Sept. 1939, CWP, vol. I, p. 143.
13 Harvey, *Diplomatic Diaries*, p. 326 (entry for 30 Oct. 1939).
14 WSC to Charles Little, 14 Oct. 1939, CWP, vol. I, p. 240.
15 John Barnes and David Nicholson (eds.), *The Empire at Bay: The Leo Amery Diaries, 1929–1945*, Hutchinson, London, 1988, p. 842 (entry for 12 Nov. 1942).
16 Congress resolution of 20 March 1940, in 'India and the War', Cmd. 6196, April 1940, p. 5.
17 'Note of an interview between His Excellency the Viceroy and Mr M. A. Jinnah, at the Viceroy's house, New Delhi, on 4th November 1939', Lord Linlithgow Papers, MSS Eur. F25/8.
18 War Cabinet minutes, 2 Feb. 1940, WM (40) 30th, NA, CAB 65/5/30.

19 Muslim League resolution, 24 March 1940, in 'India and the War', Cmd. 6196, April 1940, p. 7.

20 War Cabinet minutes, 12 April 1940, WM (40) 89th, NA, CAB 65/6/34.

21 John Colville, *The Fringes of Power: Downing Street Diaries, 1939–1955*, Hodder & Stoughton, London, 1985, p. 103 (entry for 12 April 1940).

22 Quoted in David Reynolds, *In Command of History: Churchill Fighting and Writing the Second World War*, Allen Lane, London, 2004, p. 126.

23 Barnes and Nicolson, *Empire at Bay*, p. 592 (entry for 7 May 1940); Parliamentary Debates, House of Commons, 5th Series, vol. 360, 7 May 1940, col. 1150.

24 WSC, *The Second World War*, vol. I: *The Gathering Storm* [first published by Cassell, London, 1948], CW, vol. XXII, p. 428.

25 War Cabinet minutes, 14 May, at 7 p.m., WM (40) 122nd, NA, CAB 65/7/17.

26 As recalled by Harold Macmillan, quoted in Betty D. Vernon, *Ellen Wilkinson*, Croom Helm, London, 1982, p. 184.

27 *Labour Party Annual Conference Report*, Labour Party, London, 1940, pp. 128–9.

28 'Empire Unity in the War', *The Times*, 17 May 1940.

29 W. L. Mackenzie King diary, 11 May 1940.

30 'We Shall Be Together', *Time*, 27 May 1940.

31 'New Premier', *Daily Gleaner*, 11 May 1940.

32 'New Pilot for the Storm', *Canberra Times*, 13 May 1940.

33 'The New Leader', *Palestine Post*, 13 May 1940.

34 'A Leader at Last', *Sunday Statesman*, 12 May 1940.

35 Nirad C. Chaudhuri, *Thy Hand, Great Anarch! India: 1921–1952*, Chatto & Windus, London, 1987, p. 566.

36 S. D. Jupp, 'Burma Press Abstract', 23 May 1940, IOR/L/R/5/207.

37 Jawaharlal Nehru, 'India, China and England', *National Herald*, 21 July 1940, in *Selected Works of Jawaharlal Nehru*, first series, 15 vols., Orient Longman/B. R. Publishing Corporation, New Delhi, 1972–82, vol. XI, pp. 83–6.

38 Nehru, speech of 27 July 1940, in *Selected Works*, vol. XI, pp. 87–8.

39 Deutschlandsender, in German for Germany, 13 May 1940, quoted in Daily Digest of Foreign Broadcasts, 13–14 May 1940, BBC Written Archives.

40 Speech of 13 May 1940.

41 Speech of 19 May 1940.

42 Speech of 4 June 1940.

43 German medium-wave broadcast, in English for England, 22.15 BST, 5 June 1940, in Daily Digest of Foreign Broadcasts, 6 June 1940, BBC Written Archives.

44 Speech of 18 June 1940.

45 Broadcast of 14 July 1940. For the reaction, see 'Australian Tribute' and 'Call to New Zealand', *Irish Times*, 16 July 1940.

46 Speech of 20 Aug. 1940.

47 Speech of 9 Oct. 1940.

48 Nelson Mandela, *Long Walk to Freedom*, Abacus, London, 1995 (first published 1994), p. 58.

49 Ashley Jackson, *The British Empire and the Second World War*, Hambledon Continuum, London, 2006, p. 26.

50 *Daily Telegraph*, 20 Oct. 1950, quoted in R. Palme Dutt, *The Crisis of Britain and the British Empire*, Lawrence & Wishart, London, 1957, pp. 35–6. A variant retelling can be found in Lord Halifax, *Fulness of Days*, Collins, London, 1957, p. 273.

51 WSC, note of 27 May 1940, CWP, vol. II, p. 162.

52 Reynolds, *In Command of History*, p. 189; WSC to Peter Fraser and Robert Menzies, 11 Aug. 1940, in WSC *The Second World War*, vol. II: *Their Finest Hour*, CW XXIII [first published by Cassell, London, 1949], p. 281; David Day, *The Politics of War*, HarperCollins, Sydney, 2003, pp. 71–4.

53 George Orwell, letter to *Partisan Review*, 3 Jan. 1943, in Sonia Orwell and Ian Angus (eds.), *The Collected Essays, Journalism and Letters of George Orwell*, vol. II: *My Country Right or Left, 1940–1943*, Secker & Warburg, London, 1968, p. 280.

54 'Hitler Re-Tells the Old Story', *The Times*, 20 July 1940.

55 'Demoralizing', *Time*, 8 July 1940.

56 Adolf Hitler, *Mein Kampf*, Hutchinson, London, 1969 (first published in English 1933), p. 601.

57 'Minutes of the Conference in the Reich Chancellery, Berlin, November 5, 1937' (the 'Hossbach Memorandum'), *Documents on German Foreign Policy 1918–1945*, Series D, vol. I: *From Neurath to Ribbentrop (September 1937–September 1938)*, HMSO, London, 1949, p. 33.

58 See Mark Mazower, *Hitler's Empire: Nazi Rule in Occupied Europe*, Allen Lane, London, 2008.

59 Parliamentary Debates, House of Commons, 5th Series, vol. 365, 5 Sept. 1940, col. 40.

60 WSC to W. L. Mackenzie King, 5 June 1940, CWP, vol. II, p. 255.

61 Speech of 20 Aug. 1940.

62 Richard B. Moore, 'The Passing of Churchill and Empire', *Liberator*, March 1965, in W. Burghardt Turner and Joyce Moore Turner (eds.), *Richard B. Moore, Caribbean Militant in Harlem: Collected Writings, 1920–1972*, Indiana University Press, Bloomington and Indianapolis, 1992, p. 247.

63 See WSC to FDR, 6 March 1941, in Warren F. Kimball (ed.), *Churchill & Roosevelt: The Complete Correspondence*, vol. I: *Alliance Emerging, October 1933–November 1942*, Princeton University Press, Princeton, NJ, 1984, p. 140.

64 War Cabinet minutes, 16 June 1940, at 10.15 a.m., WM (40) 168th, NA, CAB 65/7/63.

65 David Dilks (ed.), *The Diaries of Sir Alexander Cadogan O.M., 1938–1945*, Cassell, London, 1971, p. 305 (entry for 20 June 1940).

66 War Cabinet minutes, 20 June 1940, WM (40) 173rd, NA, CAB 65/7/68.

67 Brian Girvin, *The Emergency: Neutral Ireland, 1939–45*, Macmillan, 2006, pp. 133–5.
68 WSC to FDR, 5 July 1940 (unsent draft), in Kimball, *Complete Correspondence*, vol. I, p. 54.
69 Jim Phelan, *Churchill Can Unite Ireland*, Victor Gollancz, London, 1940.
70 John Maffey to Lord Caldecote, 16 July 1940, NA, DO 130/12.
71 Parliamentary Debates, House of Commons, 5th Series, vol. 365, 5 Nov. 1940, col. 1243.
72 'Extracts from the British press following Mr Churchill's reference to the Irish Ports on 5 November 1940', National Archives of Ireland, DFA 2002/19/527.
73 Edward Corse, 'British Propaganda in Neutral Eire after the Fall of France, 1940', *Contemporary British History*, 22 (2008), pp. 163–80, at 166–7; Girvin, *Emergency*, pp. 169–70.
74 Joseph Walshe to Eamon De Valera, 13 Nov. 1940, National Archives of Ireland, DFA A/82, quoted in Girvin, *Emergency*, p. 171.
75 WSC, *Gathering Storm*, p. 174.
76 'Conscription Issue', 22 May 1941, National Archives of Ireland, DFA P70.
77 Colville, *Fringes of Power*, p. 237 (entry for 1 Sept. 1940).
78 *Lustige Blätte*, 15 Nov. 1940, copy at http://www.calvin.edu/academic/cas/gpa/ (consulted 15 Aug. 2008).
79 A. W. Martin and Patsy Hardy (eds.), *Dark and Hurrying Days: Menzies' 1941 Diary*, National Library of Australia, Canberra, 1993, pp. 63–4 (entry for 22 Feb. 1941).
80 Andrew Stewart, *Empire Lost: Britain, the Dominions and the Second World War*, Continuum, London, 2008, pp. 44–5.
81 David Day, *Menzies & Churchill at War*, Oxford University Press, Oxford, 1993 (first published 1986), pp. 30–1; WSC to Lord Cranborne, 3 Jan. 1941, CWP, vol. III, p. 15; Menzies to S. M. Bruce, conveying message for WSC, 29 Sept. 1940, and note by Bruce of a conversation with WSC, 2 Oct. 1940, in DAFP, vol. IV, pp. 186, 198–200.
82 Robert Rhodes James (ed.), *'Chips': The Diaries of Sir Henry Channon*, Weidenfeld & Nicolson, London, 1993 (first published 1967), p. 290 (entry for 5 Feb. 1941).
83 Bruce to Menzies, 5 Jan. 1941, DAFP, vol. IV, p. 325.
84 Martin and Hardy, *Dark and Hurrying Days*, p. 64 (entry for 23 Feb. 1941).
85 Dilks, *Cadogan Diaries*, p. 358 (entry for 24 Feb. 1941).
86 Day, *Menzies & Churchill*, p. 84. WSC to Anthony Eden, 7 March 1941, in WSC, *The Second World War*, vol. III: *The Grand Alliance* [first published by Cassell, London, 1950], CW, vol. XXIV, p. 69; and generally, Sheila Lawlor, 'Greece, March 1941: The Politics of British Military Intervention', *Historical Journal*, 25 (1982), pp. 933–46.
87 Reynolds, *In Command of History*, p. 232.
88 Martin and Hardy, *Dark and Hurrying Days*, p. 83 (entry for 6 March 1941).

89 Day, *Menzies & Churchill*, p. 191.
90 Dilks, *Cadogan Diaries*, p. 358 (entry for 24 Feb. 1941).
91 Barnes and Nicholson, *Empire at Bay*, p. 684 (entry for 18 April 1941).
92 Menzies to A. W. Fadden, 4 March 1941, DAFP, vol. IV, p. 469.
93 Martin and Hardy, *Dark and Hurrying Days*, p. 112 (entry for 14 April 1941).
94 Ibid., pp. 118–19 (entry for 26 April 1941). Emphasis in original.
95 Advisory War Council minute, 28 May 1941, DAFP, vol. IV, p. 685.
96 Menzies to Bruce, 13 Aug. 1941, DAFP, vol. V, p. 71.
97 W. A. Riddell to Secretary of State for External Affairs, 21 Nov. 1941, in *Documents on Canadian External Relations, 1939–1941*, vol. VII, Department of External Affairs, Ottawa, 1974, p. 451.
98 Day, *Menzies & Churchill*, p. 151.
99 Mackenzie King diary, 23 Aug. 1941.
100 Francis Williams, *A Prime Minister Remembers: The War and Post-War Memoirs of Rt. Hon Earl Attlee*, London, Heinemann, 1961, p. 45.
101 Wm. Roger Louis, *Imperialism at Bay: The United States and the Decolonization of the British Empire, 1941–1945*, Oxford University Press, Oxford, 1977, pp. 121–2.
102 Reprinted in 'Declaration by United Nations', Cmd. 6388, London, 1942.
103 Robert E. Sherwood, *The White House Papers of Harry L. Hopkins*, vol. I: *September 1939–January 1942*, Eyre & Spottiswoode, London, 1948, p. 361.
104 Mackenzie King diary, 24 Aug. 1941.
105 See WSC to Clement Attlee, 11 Aug. 1941, CWP, vol. III, p. 1054. Beaverbrook's effort to take the credit does not seem convincing. For a different view, however, see Kenneth Young, *Churchill and Beaverbrook: A Study in Friendship and Politics*, Eyre & Spottiswoode, London, 1966, pp. 201–2.
106 Mackenzie King diary, 12 Aug. 1941.
107 Reprinted in 'Declaration by United Nations'.
108 Reginald Dorman-Smith to Leo Amery, 16 Aug. 1941, attached to Leo Amery, 'Interpretation of Point III of Atlantic Declaration in respect of the British Empire', WP (G) (41) 85, 29 Aug. 1941, NA, PREM 4/42/9.
109 Barnes and Nicholson, *Empire at Bay*, p. 710 (entry for 14 Aug. 1941).
110 Extract from 'West Africa', 23 Aug. 1941, NA, PREM 4/43A/3.
111 WSC to Amery, 20 Aug. 1941, CWP, vol. III, p. 1087.
112 War Cabinet minutes, 4 Sept. 1941, WM (41) 89th, NA, CAB 65/19/25.
113 Parliamentary Debates, House of Commons, 5th Series, vol. 374, 9 Sept. 1941, col. 69.
114 J. G. Winant to Cordell Hull, 4 Nov. 1941, FRUS, 1941, vol. III, pp. 181–4.
115 Louis, *Imperialism at Bay*, pp. 130–2. Quotation (from a minute by Macmillan of 1 Sept. 1942) at p. 132.
116 'Prime Minister's interview with U Saw and U Tin Tut, 18 October 1941', Leo Amery Papers, 2/3/20.
117 'Blunt Saw', *Time*, 17 Nov. 1941.

118 Wallace Murray, memorandum, 7 Nov. 1941, FRUS, 1941, vol. III, p. 185.

119 Robert H. Taylor, 'Politics in Late Colonial Burma: The Case of U Saw', *Modern Asian Studies*, 10 (1976), pp. 161–93, at 190–1; Christopher Bayly and Tim Harper, *Forgotten Armies: Britain's Asian Empire and the War with Japan*, Allen Lane, London, 2004, p. 104.

120 'Even Mr Churchill', *West African Pilot*, 5 Nov. 1941, quoted in Sam O. Idemili, 'What the *West African Pilot* Did in the Movement for Nigerian Nationalism between 1937 and 1957', *Black American Literature Forum*, 12 (1978), pp. 84–91, at 87.

121 Bernard Bourdillon to Lord Moyne, 15 Nov. 1941 and Moyne's reply of 25 Nov. 1941, NA, PREM 4/43A/3.

122 Idemili, 'What the *West African Pilot* Did', p. 87.

123 African National Congress, *Africans' Claims in South Africa*, African National Congress, Johannesburg, 1943 – text available at www.anc.org.za/ ancdocs/history/claims.html.

124 Ali A. Mazrui, *Power, Politics and the African Condition: Collected Essays*, vol. III, Africa World Press, Trenton, NJ, 2004, p. 316.

125 WSC to Eamon De Valera, 8 Dec. 1941, CWP, vol. III, p. 1579.

126 Eamon De Valera's contemporaneous note, quoted in the Earl of Longford and Thomas P. O'Neill, *Eamon De Valera*, Hutchinson, London, 1970, p. 393.

127 Ibid., p. 394.

128 Note by De Valera, 10 Dec. 1941, Eamon De Valera Papers, P150/2632.

129 FDR to WSC, 8 Dec. 1941, in Kimball, *Complete Correspondence*, vol. I, p. 282.

130 As Christopher Bell has shown, Churchill has been blamed too harshly for this calamity: 'The "Singapore Strategy" and the Deterrence of Japan: Winston Churchill, the Admiralty, and the Dispatch of Force Z', *English Historical Review*, 116 (2001), pp. 604–34.

131 Day, *Politics of War*, pp. 220–31.

132 Ian Jacob diary, [27 Dec. 1941], CWP, vol. III, p. 1698.

133 'Battle for the Pacific Comes First', *Canberra Times*, 29 Dec. 1941.

134 WSC to Clement Attlee, 29 Dec. 1941, in War Cabinet minutes, 29 Dec. 1941, WM (41) 137th, NA, CAB 65/20/29.

135 Mackenzie King diary, 29 Dec. 1941.

136 Lord Moran, *Winston Churchill: The Struggle for Survival, 1940–1965*, Constable, London, 1966, p. 19.

137 Malcolm MacDonald to Lord Cranborne, 1 Aug. 1941, quoted in David Dilks, *'The Great Dominion': Winston Churchill in Canada, 1900–1954*, Thomas Allen, Toronto, 2005, p. 152.

138 Speech of 30 Dec. 1941.

139 WSC's press conference at Government House, 31 Dec. 1941, in Dilks, *'The Great Dominion'*, p. 221.

140 WSC to Archibald Wavell, 10 Feb. 1942, in WSC, *The Second World War*,

vol. IV: *The Hinge of Fate* [first published by Cassell, London, 1951], CW, vol. XXV, p. 66.

141 Piers Brendon, *The Decline and Fall of the British Empire, 1781–1997*, Jonathan Cape, London, 2007, p. 422.

142 WSC, *Hinge of Fate*, p. 60.

143 Talk by William Joyce ('Lord Haw-Haw'), in English for England and North America, 16 Feb. 1942, quoted in Daily Digest of Foreign Broadcasts, 16–17 Feb. 1942, BBC Written Archives.

144 Vincent Sheean, *Between the Thunder and the Sun*, Random House, New York, 1943, p. 365.

145 'Feelings About the British Empire', Mass-Observation File Report 1158, March 1942, Mass-Observation Archive.

146 John Harvey (ed.), *The War Diaries of Oliver Harvey, 1941–1945*, Collins, London, 1978, p. 88 (entry for 25 Jan. 1942).

147 Lord Casey, *Personal Experience, 1939–1946*, Constable, London, 1962, p. 97.

148 H. V. Evatt to Bruce, 23 March 1942, DAFP, vol. V, p. 676.

149 Bruce, note of a conversation with WSC, 31 March 1942, ibid., p. 691.

150 Clem Lloyd and Richard Hall (eds.), *Backroom Briefings: John Curtin's War*, National Library of Australia, Canberra, 1997, p. 119 (briefing of 30 Dec. 1942).

151 Day, *Politics of War*, p. 5.

152 Moran, *Struggle for Survival*, p. 21.

153 John Ramsden, *Man of the Century: Winston Churchill and His Legend since 1945*, HarperCollins, London, 2002, esp. pp. 445–9.

154 Barnes and Nicholson, *Empire at Bay*, p. 617 (entry for 13 May 1940).

155 Maharaj Singh to the editor, *Sunday Statesman*, 19 May 1940.

156 Lord Linlithgow to Amery, 21 May 1940, Linlithgow Papers, MSS Eur. F125/8.

157 Wm. Roger Louis, *In the Name of God, Go! Leo Amery and the British Empire in the Age of Churchill*, W. W. Norton & Co., New York, 1992, pp. 130–3.

158 Barnes and Nicholson, *Empire at Bay*, p. 637 (entry for 26 July 1940).

159 Louis, *In the Name of God*, p. 135; Barnes and Nicholson, *Empire at Bay*, p. 637 (entry for 30 July 1940).

160 'Constitution Of India', *The Times*, 9 Aug. 1940.

161 Lawrence James, *Raj: The Making and Unmaking of British India*, Abacus, London, 1998 (first published 1997), p. 542.

162 Nehru to Josiah Wedgwood, 21 Nov. 1941, in *Selected Works*, vol. XI, pp. 741–2.

163 Reginald Coupland diary, MSS Brit. Emp. S15, 29 Jan. 1942.

164 Coupland diary, 22 Feb. 1942. However, according to one American observer, the prominence given to the Atlantic Charter issue in the US press was not matched in Indian newspapers: Thomas M. Wilson to Cordell Hull, 28 Nov. 1941, FRUS, 1941, vol. III, p. 188.

165 Peter Clarke, *The Cripps Version: The Life of Sir Stafford Cripps, 1889–1952*, Allen Lane, London, 2002, p. 277.

166 Tej Bahadur Sapru et al. to WSC, enclosure to Gilbert Laithwaite, 2 Jan. 1942, TOPI, vol. I, p. 4.

167 WSC to Attlee, 7 Jan. 1942, ibid., p. 14.

168 Amery to Linlithgow, 13 Jan. 1942, ibid., p. 22.

169 R. J. Moore, *Churchill, Cripps and India, 1939–1945*, Clarendon Press, Oxford, 1979, pp. 53–6.

170 WSC, *Hinge of Fate*, p. 137.

171 M. S. Venkataramani and B. K. Shrivastava, *Roosevelt, Gandhi, Churchill: America and the Last Phase of India's Freedom Struggle*, Sangam Books, London, 1997 (first published 1983), p. 23.

172 Amery to Linlithgow, 10 March 1942, TOPI, vol. I, p. 404. Emphasis in original.

173 Dilks, *Cadogan Diaries*, p. 440 (entry for 5 March 1942).

174 Peter Clarke and Richard Toye, 'Cripps, Sir (Richard) Stafford (1889–1952)', *Oxford Dictionary of National Biography*, Oxford University Press, Sept. 2004; online edition, Jan. 2008.

175 WSC to Mackenzie King, 18 March 1942, in TOPI, vol. I, p. 440.

176 WSC, *Hinge of Fate*, p. 140.

177 J. C. Smuts to WSC, 5 March 1942, John Curtin to WSC 6 March 1942, Mackenzie King to WSC, 6 March 1942, in TOPI, vol. I, pp. 327–8, 349–50.

178 Coupland diary, 14 March 1942. Emphasis in original.

179 'Indians and Sir S. Cripps', *The Times*, 24 March 1942.

180 Colville, *Fringes of Power*, p. 309 (entry for 12 Dec. 1940).

181 Geoffrey Wilson, 'My Working Life' (unpublished memoir), p. 16.

182 H. R. Trevor-Roper (ed.), *Hitler's Table Talk, 1941–1944: His Private Conversations*, Phoenix Press, London, 2000 (first published Weidenfeld & Nicolson, London, 1953; repr. 1973), p. 368 (27 March 1942).

183 Louis P. Lochner, *The Goebbels Diaries*, Hamish Hamilton, London, 1948, p. 109 (entry for 31 March 1942).

184 Clarke, *Cripps Version*, p. 305.

185 Robert Pearce (ed.), *Patrick Gordon Walker: Political Diaries, 1932–1971*, The Historians' Press, London, 1991, p. 110 (entry for 25 April 1942).

186 Coupland diary, 8 April 1942.

187 Speech of 21 May 1942, in Nehru, *Selected Works*, vol. XI, p. 324.

188 WSC, *Hinge of Fate*, p. 142.

189 Clarke, *Cripps Version*, p. 329.

190 Barnes and Nicolson, *Empire at Bay*, p. 786 (entry for 8 March 1942).

191 'A Vote of No-Confidence', *National Herald*, 3 July 1942, in Nehru, *Selected Works*, vol. XII, p. 381.

192 James, *Raj*, pp. 564–5.

193 Linlithgow to WSC, 31 August 1942, TOPI, vol. II, p. 853.

194 Subhas Chandra Bose, 'Guerrilla War and Plan of Action', 4 Sept. 1942, in W. J. West (ed.), *George Orwell: The War Commentaries*, Penguin, Harmondsworth, 1987 (first published 1985), pp. 230–1.

195 Brendon, *Decline and Fall*, p. 396; 'The Time is Now', *Time*, 5 Oct. 1942.

196 War Cabinet minutes, 31 Aug. 1942, WM (42) 119th, NA, CAB 195/1.

197 Amery to Linlithgow, 1 September 1942, in TOPI, vol. II, p. 875.

198 War Cabinet minutes, 31 Aug. 1942, WM (42) 119th, NA, CAB 195/1.

199 Amery to Linlithgow, 1 Sept. 1942, TOPI, vol. II, p. 875.

200 Amery to Stafford Cripps, 2 Oct. 1942, ibid., p. 71.

201 WSC, 'The Indian Representatives at the War Cabinet', 7 Sept. 1942, ibid., p. 920.

202 A. R. Mudaliar to G. Laithwaite, 21 Sept. 1942 and Amery to Linlithgow, 13 Nov. 1942, TOPI, vol. III, pp. 3, 251.

203 Barnes and Nicholson, *Empire at Bay*, p. 832 (entry for 9 Sept. 1942).

204 Parliamentary Debates, House of Commons, 5th Series, vol. 383, 10 Sept. 1942, cols. 302–5.

205 Barnes and Nicholson, *Empire at Bay*, p. 832 (entry for 10 Sept. 1942).

206 The Indian press reaction is summarized in 'A Chorus of Criticism', *The Times*, 14 Sept. 1942.

207 'Our Indian Observer', 'Political Comments', *Sunday Statesman*, 20 Sept. 1942.

208 India League, *The Prime Minister on India: An Examination of Mr Churchill's Statement on India in the House of Commons on the 10th September 1942*, India League, London, 1942, in Fabian Colonial Bureau Papers, Box 1/5, MSS Brit. Emp. S365. The speech also inspired another published attack on Churchill: Hira Seth Lal, *Churchill on India: Let His Past Records [sic] Speak*, First National Publishers, Lahore, 1942.

209 'Reports of a Press Conference held by Mr Jinnah', 13 Sept. 1942, TOPI, vol. II, p. 958.

210 Lord Halifax to Anthony Eden, 14 Sept. 1942, Lord Halifax Papers, HLFX 2.

211 Pearce, *Gordon Walker: Diaries*, p. 113 (entry for 1 Oct. 1942).

212 Rhodes James, *'Chips'*, p. 341 (entry for 21 Oct. 1942).

213 Nicolson, *Harold Nicolson: Diaries and Letters*, p. 251 (entry for 21 Oct. 1942); Barnes and Nicolson, *Empire at Bay*, p. 839 (entry for 21 Oct. 1942).

214 'General Smuts on Aims in War and Peace' *The Times*, 22 Oct. 1942.

215 R. A. C. Parker, *The Second World War: A Short History*, Oxford University Press, Oxford, 1997 (first published 1989), pp. 105–6.

216 Speech of 10 Nov. 1942.

217 Ibid.

218 '"Great Design" in Africa', *The Times*, 11 Nov. 1942.

219 Louis, *Imperialism at Bay*, p. 8.

220 'Commonwealth of the World', *The Times*, 28 Oct. 1942.

221 Speech of 10 Nov. 1942.

222 Martin Gilbert rightly notes that the sentence about democracy is rarely quoted, but he appears to take it as a simple statement of Churchill's (undoubted) commitment to majority rule in Britain: *Churchill's Political Philosophy*, Oxford University Press, Oxford, 1981, p. 88.

223 'Double Noncooperation', *Time*, 23 Nov. 1942.

224 Nehru diary, 13 Nov. 1942, in *Selected Works*, vol. XIII, p. 29.

225 '"Old Imperialistic Order"', *The Times*, 18 Nov. 1942; H. G. Nicholas (ed.), *Washington Despatches, 1941–45: Weekly Political Reports from the British Embassy*, University of Chicago Press, Chicago, 1981, p. 122 (report of 8 Dec. 1942).

226 'Episodes of the Month: Mr Churchill's Declaration', *National Review*, 119 (1942), pp. 462–3; 'Empire Union Chides Mr Spender', *Canberra Times*, 20 Nov. 1942.

227 Parliamentary Debates, House of Commons, 5th Series, vol. 385, 26 Nov. 1942, col. 938.

228 'Imperialist Order', *Washington Post*, 20 Nov. 1942.

229 Mackenzie King diary, 5 Dec. 1942. In 1944, FDR commented privately to a journalist that Churchill 'has that grandiose statement haunting him all the time – the one about not becoming the King's first Minister in order to preside over the liquidation of the "empah"'. Quoted in Auriol Weigold, *Churchill, Roosevelt and India: Propaganda During World War II*, Routledge, London, 2008, p. 95.

8. HANDS OFF THE BRITISH EMPIRE

1 Quoted in 'Britain "Tottering Colossus"', *Irish Times*, 17 Dec. 1943.

2 Axis broadcast, quoted in 'Battle of Babble', *Time*, 16 Feb. 1942.

3 John Charmley, *Churchill, The End of Glory: A Political Biography*, Hodder & Stoughton, London, 1993, p. 455.

4 War Cabinet minutes, 7 Jan. 1943, WM (43) 4th, NA, CAB 195/2.

5 WSC to Lord Linlithgow, 13 Feb. 1943, TOPI, vol. III, p. 659.

6 Linlithgow to WSC, 15 Feb. 1943, ibid., p. 669.

7 WSC to Harry Hopkins, 24 Feb. 1943, Churchill Papers, CHAR 20/107, f. 21.

8 WSC to J. C. Smuts, 26 Feb. 1943, TOPI, vol. III, p. 738.

9 Unused speech notes for WSC's broadcast of 21 March 1943, Churchill Papers, CHAR 9/193A, ff. 87–8.

10 Amartya Sen, *Poverty and Famines: An Essay on Entitlement and Deprivation*, Clarendon Press, Oxford, 1981, pp. 52–83.

11 Cormac Ó Gráda, 'The Ripple that Drowns? Twentieth-century Famines in China and India as Economic History', *Economic History Review*, 61 (2008), pp. 5–37.

12 Lance Brennan, 'Government Famine Relief in Bengal, 1943', *Journal of Asian Studies*, 47 (1988), pp. 541–66.

13 Penderel Moon (ed.), *Wavell: The Viceroy's Journal*, Oxford University Press, Karachi, 1997, p. 19 (entry for 24 Sept. 1943); John Barnes and David Nicholson (eds.), *The Empire at Bay: The Leo Amery Diaries, 1929–1945*, Hutchinson, London, 1988, p. 950 (entry for 10 Nov. 1943).

14 Lord Wavell to Amery, 9 Feb. 1944, TOPI, vol. IV, pp. 706–7.

15 Wavell to Amery, 25 Feb. 1944, ibid., p. 758.

16 Amery to Wavell, 27 April 1944, ibid., pp. 933–4.

17 Barnes and Nicholson, *Empire at Bay*, pp. 839, 848, 874 (entries for 14 Oct. and 30 Nov. 1942, 27 Feb. 1943).

18 Moon, *Viceroy's Journal*, p. 23 (entry for 8 Oct. 1943).

19 R. A. Butler, *The Art of the Possible*, Hamish Hamilton, London, 1971, p. 111.

20 William Phillips, *Ventures in Diplomacy*, John Murray, London, 1955, p. 253.

21 'Indian Leader Again Tells Britain to Quit', *Observer*, 25 Dec. 1943.

22 'Statistical Material presented during the Washington Negotiations', Cmd. 6707, Dec. 1945, p. 11, Table 7; B. R. Tomlinson, *The Political Economy of the Raj, 1914–1947: The Economics of Decolonization in India*, Macmillan, London, 1979, p. 140.

23 'Psywarrior', 'Axis Propaganda against Indian Troops', http://www.psywarrior.com/AxisPropIndia.html, accessed 17 June 2009.

24 Barnes and Nicholson, *Empire at Bay*, p. 836 (entry for 24 Sept. 1942).

25 Ibid., p. 901 (entry for 27 July 1943).

26 Moon, *Viceroy's Journal*, pp. 12–13 (entry for 27 July 1943).

27 'Agreement between the Governments of the United Kingdom and the United States of America on the principles applying to mutual aid', Cmd. 6341, 1942, p. 3.

28 FDR to WSC, 11 Feb. 1942, in Warren F. Kimball (ed.), *Churchill & Roosevelt: The Complete Correspondence*, vol. I: *Alliance Emerging, October 1933–November 1942*, Princeton University Press, Princeton, NJ, 1984, p. 357.

29 E. F. Penrose, *Economic Planning for the Peace*, Princeton University Press, Princeton NJ, 1953, p. 24.

30 Ben Pimlott (ed.), *The Second World War Diary of Hugh Dalton, 1940–45*, Jonathan Cape, London, 1986, pp. 710–11 (entry for 23 Feb. 1944).

31 Wm. Roger Louis, *In the Name of God, Go! Leo Amery and the British Empire in the Age of Churchill*, W. W. Norton & Co., New York, 1992, p. 147.

32 Donald Moggridge (ed.), *The Collected Writings of John Maynard Keynes*, vol. XXIV: *Activities, 1944–1946: The Transition to Peace*, Macmillan, London, 1979, pp. 302–3.

33 John Morton Blum (ed.), *From the Morgenthau Diaries: Years of War, 1941–1945*, Houghton Mifflin, Boston, 1967, p. 308 (entry for 19 Aug. 1944).

34 H. G. Nicholas (ed.), *Washington Despatches, 1941–45: Weekly Political Reports from the British Embassy*, University of Chicago Press, Chicago, 1981, p. 192 (24 May 1943).

35 Alan Watt to Colonel Hodgson, 24 May 1943, quoted in David Day, *The Politics of War*, HarperCollins, Sydney, 2003, p. 476.

36 WSC, *The Second World War*, vol. IV: *The Hinge of Fate* [first published by Cassell, London, 1951], CW, vol. XXV, p. 522.

37 John Morton Blum (ed.), *The Price of Vision: The Diary of Henry A. Wallace,*

1942–1946, Houghton Mifflin, Boston, 1973, p. 208 (entry for 22 May 1943).

38 Conversation recorded in W. L. Mackenzie King diary, 20 May 1943.

39 He used this phrase on a number of occasions, notably in his first broadcast as Prime Minister on 19 May 1940.

40 David Dilks, *'The Great Dominion': Winston Churchill in Canada, 1900–1954*, Thomas Allen, Toronto, 2005, p. 270.

41 Note by S. M. Bruce, 22 March 1943, quoted in Day, *Politics of War*, p. 455.

42 Speech of 30 June 1943.

43 Dilks, *'The Great Dominion'*, p. 236.

44 David Reynolds, *Rich Relations: The American Occupation of Britain, 1942–1945*, HarperCollins, London, 1996, pp. 127–40; Ashley Jackson, *The British Empire and the Second World War*, Hambledon Continuum, London, 2006, p. 66.

45 Dilks, *'The Great Dominion'*, pp. 239–41.

46 Alex Danchev and Daniel Todman (eds.), *War Diaries, 1939–1945: Field Marshal Lord Alanbrooke*, Weidenfeld & Nicolson, London, 2001, p. 432 (entry for 21 July 1943).

47 W. L. Mackenzie King to Lord Moran, 9 June 1950, quoted in Lord Moran, *Winston Churchill: The Struggle for Survival, 1940–1965*, Constable, London, 1966, p. 109n.

48 Mackenzie King diary, 10 Aug. 1943.

49 Dilks, *'The Great Dominion'*, p. 253.

50 Mackenzie King diary, 11 Aug. 1943.

51 Philip Ziegler, 'Mountbatten, Louis Francis Albert Victor Nicholas, first Earl Mountbatten of Burma (1900–1979)', *Oxford Dictionary of National Biography*, Oxford University Press, 2004; online edition, Jan. 2008.

52 Danchev and Todman, *War Diaries*, p. 451 (entry for 30 Aug. 1943).

53 Wm. Roger Louis, *Imperialism at Bay: The United States and the Decolonization of the British Empire, 1941–1945*, Oxford University Press, Oxford, 1977, pp. 281–2, 289–91, 307; Day, *Politics of War*, pp. 555–6.

54 Alexander Cadogan used this phrase about Stalin, Truman and Attlee at the close of the 1945 Potsdam conference, although this was presumably intended as a dig at the new Prime Minister: David Dilks (ed.), *The Diaries of Sir Alexander Cadogan O.M., 1938–1945*, Cassell, London, 1971, p. 778 (entry for 2 Aug. 1945).

55 W. Averell Harriman and Elie Abel, *Special Envoy to Churchill and Stalin. 1941–1946*, Random House, New York, 1975, p. 265.

56 'Bohlen minutes', 28 Nov. 1943, in FRUS, *The Conferences at Cairo and Tehran*, pp. 485–6.

57 Harriman and Abel, *Special Envoy*, p. 268.

58 'Bohlen minutes', 29 Nov. 1943, in FRUS, *Cairo and Tehran*, p. 554.

59 Martin Gilbert, *Winston S. Churchill*, vol. VII: *Road to Victory, 1941–1945*, Heinemann, London, 1986, p. 587.

60 Frances Perkins, *The Roosevelt I Knew*, HarperColophon, New York, 1964 (first published 1946), p. 84.

61 'Baroness Asquith of Yarnbury [Violet Bonham Carter] in conversation with Kenneth Harris', *Listener*, 17 Aug. 1967.

62 War Cabinet minutes, 7 Jan. 1943, WM (43) 4th, NA, CAB 195/2.

63 Louis, *Imperialism at Bay*, p. 310; WSC, *Hinge of Fate*, p. 520.

64 Charles W. Taussig memorandum, 16 Jan. 1945, quoted in Louis, *Imperialism at Bay*, pp. 437–8.

65 Ibid., pp. 348–9.

66 'Through German Eyes', *The Times*, 13 May 1944.

67 As Wavell noted: Moon, *Viceroy's Journal*, p. 79 (entry for 11 July 1944).

68 Day, *Politics of War*, pp. 586–7; Mackenzie King diary, 15 May 1944.

69 Mackenzie King diary, 11 May 1944.

70 Day, *Politics of War*, pp. 587–97, quoting (at p. 588) WSC to Hastings Ismay, 16 April 1944, NA, PREM 3/63/8.

71 Clem Lloyd and Richard Hall (eds.), *Backroom Briefings: John Curtin's War*, National Library of Australia, Canberra, 1997, pp. 210–11 (briefing of 3 July 1944).

72 'Conference Results for Australia', *Canberra Times*, 30 May 1944.

73 Day, *Politics of War*, pp. 594–5; Mackenzie King diary, 15 May 1944.

74 Reynolds, *Rich Relations*, pp. 218–19.

75 Ibid., p. 226; War Cabinet minutes, 13 Oct. 1942, WM (42) 140th, NA, CAB 195/2.

76 Dilks, *Cadogan Diaries*, p. 483 (entry for 13 Oct. 1942).

77 R. A. C. Parker, *The Second World War: A Short History*, Oxford University Press, Oxford, 1997 (first published 1989), p. 198.

78 Moran, *Struggle for Survival*, p. 206.

79 Danchev and Todman, *War Diaries*, p. 589 (entry for 8 Sept. 1944).

80 John Colville, *The Fringes of Power: Downing Street Diaries, 1939–1955*, Hodder & Stoughton, London, 1985, p. 510 (entry for 7 Sept. 1944).

81 Joan Bright Astley, *The Inner Circle: A View of War at the Top*, Hutchinson, London, 1971, p. 153.

82 Mackenzie King diary, 12 Sept. 1944.

83 Ibid., 13 Sept. 1944.

84 See Brooke's account of the conference in Danchev and Todman, *War Diaries*, esp. p. 592 (entry for 14 Sept. 1944).

85 Lord Ismay, *The Memoirs of Lord Ismay*, Heinemann, London, 1960, p. 375.

86 WSC to John Curtin, 15 Sept. 1944, in Dilks, *'The Great Dominion'*, p. 342.

87 Blum, *Morgenthau Diaries*, p. 309 (entry for 19 Aug. 1944).

88 Peter Clarke, *The Last Thousand Days of the British Empire*, Allen Lane, London, 2007, pp. 65–6.

89 Colville, *Fringes of Power*, p. 515 (entry for 14 Sept. 1944).

90 WSC to Smuts, 9 Oct. 1944, in WSC, *The Second World War*, vol. VI: *Triumph and Tragedy* [first published by Cassell, London, 1954], CW, vol. XXVII, p. 502.

91 Barnes and Nicholson, *Empire at Bay*, p. 1018 (entry for 6 Nov. 1944).

92 'Eden Statement on Moyne Murder', *Palestine Post*, 10 Nov. 1944.

93 Clarke, *Last Thousand Days*, p. 91.

94 Quoted in 'Yishuv Must Cast Out Pest', *Palestine Post*, 9 Nov. 1944.

95 Barnes and Nicholson, *Empire at Bay*, p. 1018 (entry for 6 Nov. 1944).

96 'Mr Churchill Eulogizes Old Friend', *Palestine Post*, 8 Nov. 1944.

97 Parliamentary Debates, House of Commons, 5th Series, vol. 404, 17 Nov. 1944, col. 2242.

98 Yehoshua Porath, 'Weizmann, Churchill and the "Philby Plan", 1937–1943', *Studies in Zionism*, 5 (1984), pp. 239–72.

99 War Cabinet minutes, 2 July 1943, WM (43) 92nd, NA, CAB 195/2.

100 Michael J. Cohen, *Churchill and the Jews*, 2nd edition, Frank Cass, London, 2003, pp. 255–60; Harold B. Hoskins to Paul Alling, 5 March 1945, FRUS, 1945, vol. VIII, p. 690.

101 WSC to Oliver Stanley and the Chiefs of Staff, 1 July 1945, in WSC, *Triumph and Tragedy*, p. 502.

102 Parliamentary Debates, House of Commons, 5th Series, vol. 404, 17 Nov. 1944, col. 2243.

103 Minute by WSC, 31 Dec. 1944, NA, PREM 4/31/4, quoted in Louis, *Imperialism at Bay*, p. 433.

104 The account here of the Yalta episode owes much to Louis, *Imperialism at Bay*, pp. 458–60.

105 Dennis Angelo Castillo, *The Maltese Cross: A Strategic History of Malta*, Praeger Security International, Westport, CT, 2006, pp. 213–14; Douglas Austin, *Churchill and Malta: A Special Relationship*, Spellmount, Stroud, 2006, pp. 160–4.

106 'Bohlen minutes', 9 Feb. 1945, in FRUS, *The Conferences at Malta and Yalta*, p. 844.

107 James F. Byrnes, *Speaking Frankly*, Harper & Brothers, New York, 1947, p. x.

108 Anthony Eden, *The Reckoning*, Cassell, London, 1965, p. 595.

109 Byrnes, *Speaking Frankly*, p. x.

110 Louis, *Imperialism at Bay*, p. 459.

111 War Cabinet minutes, 3 April 1945, WM (45) 38th, NA, CAB 195/2.

112 On the significance of UN pressure see Ronald Hyam, *Britain's Declining Empire: The Road to Decolonization, 1918–1968*, Cambridge University Press, Cambridge, 2006, esp. pp. 93, 304–8.

113 Trefor E. Evans (ed.), *The Killearn Diaries, 1934–1946*, Sidgwick & Jackson, London, 1972, p. 327 (entry for 17 Feb. 1945).

114 Ibn Saud's account of the meeting is paraphrased in William A. Eddy to Edward Stettinius, 22 Feb. 1945, FRUS, 1945, vol. VIII, pp. 689–90.

115 Evans, *Killearn Diaries*, pp. 329–30 (entry for 17 Feb. 1945).

116 WSC to Killearn, 28 Jan. 1945, quoted in Gilbert, *Road to Victory*, p. 1053.

117 Amery to WSC, 4 May 1944, TOPI, vol. IV, p. 950; Moon, *Viceroy's Journal*, p. 78 (entry for 5 June 1944).

118 The letter, of 17 July 1944, read: 'Dear Prime Minister, You are reported to have the desire to crush the simple "naked fakir" as you are said to have described me. I have been long trying to be a fakir and that naked – a more difficult task. I, therefore, regard the expression as a compliment though unintended. I approach you then as such, and ask you to trust and use me for the sake of your people and mine and through them those of the world. Your sincere friend, M. K. Gandhi' (MKG, *Collected Works*, 100 vols., Government of India Publications Division, New Delhi, 1960–94, vol. LXXVII, pp. 391–2). It initially miscarried and in September Gandhi asked that it be resent: 'Though the psychological moment has passed, I attach very great importance to my letter which was written in answer to deep heart-searching' (MKG to Evan M. Jenkins, 17 Sept. 1944, MKG, *Collected Works*, vol. LXXVIII, p. 109). Wavell wrote of the letter: 'I think it shows that Gandhi's mental powers are failing; and it will not improve the prospects of the P.M. approving any negotiations' (Moon, *Viceroy's Journal*, p. 91, entry for 21 Sept. 1944). He was certainly right about the latter point.

119 Barnes and Nicholson, *Empire at Bay*, pp. 993, 1018 (entries for 4 Aug. and 6 Nov. 1944).

120 WSC to Clementine Churchill, 1 Feb. 1945, in Mary Soames (ed.), *Speaking for Themselves: The Personal Letters of Winston and Clementine Churchill*, Doubleday, London, 1998, p. 512.

121 Walter Layton, 'Note of talk with Lord Wavell 19th April 1945', Walter Layton Papers, Box 104/126.

122 Moon, *Viceroy's Journal*, p. 120 (entry for 29 March 1945).

123 Ibid., p. 127 (entry for 26 April 1945).

124 Barnes and Nicholson, *Empire at Bay*, p. 1040 (entry for 30 April 1945).

125 Moon, *Viceroy's Journal*, p. 134 (entry for 30 May 1945).

126 Barnes and Nicholson, *Empire at Bay*, p. 1045n (note of 2 Dec. 1947).

127 WSC to FDR, 13 Nov. 1943, in Warren F. Kimball (ed.), *Churchill and Roosevelt: The Complete Correspondence*, vol. II: *Alliance Forged, November 1942– February 1944*, Princeton University Press, Princeton, NJ, 1984, p. 599.

128 He had earlier written that 'The removal of Spears at this juncture would destroy the confidence of the Syrians and Lebanese in our resolve to make good the pledges [about independence] into which we and the French jointly entered.' WSC to Duff Cooper, 17 Aug. 1944, Duff Cooper Papers, 4/3. See also Max Egremont, *Under Two Flags: The Life of Major-General Sir Edward Spears*, Weidenfeld & Nicolson, London, 1997, pp. 257–62.

129 François Kersaudy, *Churchill and de Gaulle*, Collins, London, 1981, pp. 402–9.

130 John Julius Norwich (ed.), *The Duff Cooper Diaries, 1915–1951*, Weidenfeld & Nicolson, London, 2005, p. 369 (entry for 26 May 1945).

131 'British Election', *Washington Post*, 23 May 1945, typed extract in Churchill Papers, CHAR 9/208C, f. 337.

132 Broadcast of 4 June 1945.

133 'Labour Case for Socialism', *The Times*, 6 June 1945.

134 Barnes and Nicholson, *Empire at Bay*, p. 1046 (entries for 4 and 5 June 1945).

135 See, for example, F. A. Cooper, 'Where Labour Has Ruled for 27 Years and They've Never Seen a Gestapo Man', *Reynolds News*, 24 June 1945. This article discussed Queensland, of which Cooper was Premier.

136 John Ramsden, *Man of the Century: Winston Churchill and His Legend since 1945*, HarperCollins, London, 2002, esp. pp. 446–7. However, Chifley's immediate reaction to the speech was a calm one. See 'Objects to Slur by Mr Churchill', *Canberra Times*, 6 June 1945.

137 Stuart Ball (ed.), *Parliament and Politics in the Age of Churchill and Attlee: The Headlam Diaries, 1935–1951*, Cambridge University Press for the Royal Historical Society, Cambridge, 1999, p. 466 (entry for 2 July 1945).

138 Broadcast of 13 June 1945. On pro-natalism during this period, see John Toye, *Keynes on Population*, Oxford University Press, Oxford, 2000, pp. 208–13.

139 F. W. S. Craig (ed.), *British General Election Manifestos, 1918–1966*, Political Reference Publications, Chichester, 1970, pp. 88, 105–6.

140 Susan Howson and Donald Moggridge (eds.), *The Collected Papers of James Meade*, vol. IV: *The Cabinet Office Diary, 1944–46*, London, Unwin Hyman, 1990, p. 98 (entry for 25 June 1945); R. F. Harrod, *The Prof: A Personal Memoir of Lord Cherwell*, London, Macmillan, 1959, p. 252.

141 Amery was probably referring here to Rajani Palme Dutt, who stood against him as a Communist, making India a key issue in his campaign. Dutt won fewer than 2,000 votes, not enough to affect the outcome. Amery to WSC, 14 Dec. 1944, IOR/L/PO/11/4, ff. 252–3; 'Verdict', *Statesman*, 27 July 1945.

142 'Empire Views on Election', *The Times*, 28 July 1945.

143 Mackenzie King diary, 26 July 1945.

144 'Discussion with Director of British Daily', *Harijan*, 10 Nov. 1946, in MKG, *Collected Works*, vol. LXXXVI, pp. 50–1.

145 'Expectations Roused in Political Circles', *Times of India*, 27 July 1945.

146 Nirad C. Chaudhuri, *Thy Hand, Great Anarch! India: 1921–1952*, Chatto & Windus, London, 1987, p. 755.

147 Nicholas, *Washington Despatches*, pp. 595–6 (28 July 1945).

148 'Young Bob Speaks', *Time*, 11 June 1945.

149 'Mr Morrison in New York', *The Times*, 12 Jan. 1946.

150 Charmley, *End of Glory*, p. 649.

151 Ashley Jackson, 'Tswana War Poetry: Part One', *Botswana Notes and Records*, 27 (1995), pp. 97–110. Quotation at 106. For examples of war poetry from the Gold Coast, including a paean to Churchill, see Ohenaba Sakyi Djan and Maurice S. Cockin, 'Drums and Victory: Africa's Call to the Empire', *Journal of the Royal African Society*, 41 (1942), pp. 29–41.

152 Jackson, *British Empire*, pp. 180, 187.

153 Kwame Nkrumah, *Neo-Colonialism: The Last Stage of Imperialism*, Thomas Nelson & Sons, London, 1965, p. 40.

9. ONCE MAGNIFICENT AND STILL CONSIDERABLE

1 'The Light of Llandudno', *Time*, 18 Oct. 1948.
2 Speech of 9 Oct. 1948.
3 'Conservative Conference', *The Times*, 9 Oct. 1948.
4 Klaus Larres, *Churchill's Cold War: The Politics of Personal Diplomacy*, Yale University Press, New Haven and London, 2002, p. 104.
5 Speech of 9 Oct. 1948.
6 'Mr Churchill at Llandudno' *The Times*, 11 Oct. 1948.
7 Alexander Cadogan diary, 20 Aug. 1945, Alexander Cadogan Papers, 1/15.
8 For a full discussion of this episode, see Richard Toye, 'Churchill and Britain's "Financial Dunkirk" ', *Twentieth Century British History*, 15 (2004), pp. 329–60.
9 Amery diary, 27 Aug. 1945, Leo Amery Papers, 7/39. Amery was alluding to the poem 'Say not the struggle naught availeth' by Arthur Hugh Clough (1819–61).
10 'Information and comments from London embassy on commercial policy discussions', 26 Sept. 1945, Frederick M. Vinson Papers, Box 166.
11 Amery diary 11 Sept. 1945, Leo Amery Papers, 7/39.
12 Ibid., 22 Nov. 1945.
13 'Mr John Amery', *Manchester Guardian*, 20 Nov. 1942.
14 David Faber, *Speaking for England: Leo, Julian and John Amery – The Tragedy of a Political Family*, The Free Press, London, 2005, p. 4. See also Wm. Roger Louis, 'Leo Amery and the Post-War World, 1945–55', *Journal of Imperial and Commonwealth History*, 30 (2002), pp. 71–90.
15 Harold Macmillan, *Tides of Fortune, 1945–1955*, London, Macmillan, 1969, p. 77.
16 Hugh Dalton diary, 14 Dec. 1945, Hugh Dalton Papers, I/33; see also Dalton, *High Tide and After: Memoirs, 1945–1960*, Frederick Muller, London, 1962, pp. 87–8.
17 'Tory Leadership and the Loan Vote', *Manchester Guardian*, 15 Dec. 1945.
18 Hugh Dalton diary, 14 Dec. 1945, Hugh Dalton Papers, I/33.
19 Harry Crookshank diary, MS Eng. Hist. d.361, entry for 13 Dec. 1945.
20 Amery diary, 14 Dec. 1945, Leo Amery Papers, 7/39.
21 'Bretton Woods Will Cause Fierce Lords Battle', *News Chronicle*, 15 Dec. 1945.
22 David Carlton, *Anthony Eden: A Biography*, Allen Lane, London, 1981, p. 259.
23 Speech of 5 March 1946; W. L. Mackenzie King diary, 1, 3 and 5 March 1946.
24 Walter Lippmann, 'Mr Churchill's Speech', *New York Herald Tribune*, 7 March 1946.
25 'Churchill Taken to Task', *New York Times*, 18 March 1946.

26 L. B. Pearson to W. L. Mackenzie King, 11 March 1946, *Documents on Canadian External Relations*, vol. XII: *1946*, Department of External Affairs, Ottawa, 1977, p. 2043.

27 'The Loan Hearings', *The Economist*, 23 March 1946, quoted in Richard N. Gardner, *Sterling-Dollar Diplomacy in Current Perspective: The Origins and Prospects of Our International Economic Order*, Columbia University Press, New York, 1980, p. 249n.

28 J. A. Hudson, 'Mr Churchill and the Loan', 14 March 1946, NA, PREM 8/197.

29 'Vandenberg Urges Full British Loan for "Self-Interest"', *New York Times*, 23 April 1946; Gardner, *Sterling-Dollar Diplomacy*, p. 250.

30 Frank Fellows to WSC, 1 April 1949, Churchill Papers, CHUR 2/162, f. 187.

31 This was the opinion of the Republican Senator William Langer, quoted in 'Churchill "is a Propagandist"', *Canberra Times*, 2 April 1949.

32 F. E. Evans, to A. R. K. Mackenzie, 21 March 1946, NA, FO 71/51624. The speech was given on 18 March.

33 L. S. Amery, *The Washington Loan Agreements: A Critical Study of American Economic Foreign Policy*, MacDonald, London, 1946, p. xi.

34 Amery diary, 26 Nov. 1946, Leo Amery Papers, 7/39.

35 See Richard Toye, 'The Attlee Government, the Imperial Preference System, and the Creation of the GATT', *English Historical Review*, 118 (2003), pp. 912–39.

36 Clement Davies to Archibald Sinclair, 30 May 1946, Thurso Papers, IV 1/10.

37 'Break-Up', *Time*, 3 June 1946.

38 Ronald Hyam, *Britain's Declining Empire: The Road to Decolonisation, 1918–1968*, Cambridge University Press, Cambridge, 2006, p. 221.

39 Amery diary, 8 Aug. 1946, Leo Amery Papers, 7/40.

40 Penderel Moon (ed.), *Wavell: The Viceroy's Journal*, Oxford University Press, Karachi, 1997, p. 168 (entry for 31 Aug. 1945).

41 Recollections of Harold C. Edwards, 1968, quoted in Martin Gilbert, *Winston S. Churchill*, vol. VIII: *'Never Despair', 1945–1965*, Heinemann, London, 1988, p. 141.

42 WSC to Amery, 14 May 1946, Leo Amery Papers, 2/2/4.

43 Parliamentary Debates, House of Commons, 5th Series, vol. 434, 6 March 1947, cols. 669, 671, 678.

44 Robert Cary to Leo Amery, 6 March [1947], Leo Amery Papers, 2/1/40.

45 Stuart Ball (ed.), *Parliament and Politics in the Age of Churchill and Attlee: The Headlam Diaries, 1935–1951*, Cambridge University Press for the Royal Historical Society, Cambridge, 1999, p. 492 (entry for 6 March 1947).

46 Amery diary, 2 April 1946, Leo Amery Papers, 7/40.

47 Peter Clarke, *The Last Thousand Days of the British Empire*, Allen Lane, London, 2007, p. 480.

48 WSC, memorandum on India, 20 Feb. 1947, quoted in Nicholas Owen,

'The Conservative Party and Indian Independence, 1945–1947', *Historical Journal*, 46 (2003), pp. 403–36, at 421.

49 Clarke, *Last Thousand Days*, p. 468.

50 Amery diary, 12 Dec. 1946, Leo Amery Papers, 7/40.

51 B. R. Ambedkar to WSC, 13 Nov. 1946, Churchill Papers, CHUR 2/52A/41.

52 Owen, 'Conservative Party', esp. p. 427.

53 Gilbert, *'Never Despair'*, p. 334.

54 Lawrence James, *Raj: The Making and Unmaking of British India*, Abacus, London, 1998 (first published 1997), pp. 635–6.

55 Speech of 6 Dec. 1947.

56 Parliamentary Debates, House of Commons, 5th Series, vol. 457, 28 Oct. 1948, col. 250.

57 'India and the Crown', *The Times*, 6 Oct. 1948.

58 It was the omission of word 'British' before 'Commonwealth' in the final communiqué of the meeting of Commonwealth Prime Ministers that attracted attention. Attlee claimed that this had been inadvertent, but, nonetheless, 'British' did drop from official usage the following year. Clement Attlee, 'Cabinet nomenclature', 30 Dec. 1948, in Ronald Hyam (ed.), *British Documents on the End of Empire*, Series A, vol. II, part 4, HMSO, London, 1992, p. 178.

59 Parliamentary Debates, House of Commons, 5th Series, vol. 457, 28 Oct. 1948, col. 246.

60 Mackenzie King diary, 30 Oct. 1948.

61 Note by Clement Attlee on a meeting with Opposition leaders, 16 Dec. 1948, in Hyam, *British Documents*, p. 177.

62 WSC to J. C. Smuts, 22 May 1949, in *Selections from the Smuts Papers*, vol. VII: *August 1945–October 1950*, ed. Jean van der Poel, Cambridge University Press, Cambridge, 1973, p. 298.

63 Julian Amery diary, 20 July 1952, Julian Amery Papers, 4/302.

64 Nehru diary, 17 Dec. 1943, in *Selected Works of Jawaharlal Nehru*, first series, 15 vols., Orient Longman/B. R. Publishing Corporation, New Delhi, 1972–82, vol. XIII, p. 311.

65 John Kenneth Galbraith, *Ambassador's Journal: A Personal Account of the Kennedy Years*, Hamish Hamilton, London, 1969 (entry for 23 April 1961).

66 David Reynolds, *In Command of History: Churchill Fighting and Writing the Second World War*, Allen Lane, London, 2004, pp. 355–6.

67 'Churchilliana', *Indian News Chronicle*, 27 Sept. 1951.

68 Amery diary, 7 Sept. 1951, Leo Amery Papers, 7/45.

69 See esp. Reynolds, *In Command of History*.

70 Amery to Reginald Dorman-Smith, 15 April 1943, in Hugh Tinker (ed.), *Burma: The Struggle for Independence, 1944–1948*, vol. I: *From Military Occupation to Civil Government, 1 January 1944 to 31 August 1946*, HMSO, London, 1983, p. 26.

71 WSC to James Stuart, 3 Dec. 1944, in Tinker, *Burma*, vol. I, p. 117.

72 John Barnes and David Nicholson (eds.), *The Empire at Bay: The Leo Amery Diaries, 1929–1945*, Hutchinson, London, 1988, p. 1040 (entry for 4 May 1945).

73 'Burma: Statement of Policy by His Majesty's Government', Cmd. 6635, May 1945, p. 9.

74 Speech of 20 Dec. 1946.

75 Hugh Tinker, 'Burma's Struggle for Independence: The Transfer of Power Thesis Re-Examined', *Modern Asian Studies*, 20 (1986), pp. 461–81, at 476.

76 Parliamentary Debates, House of Commons, 5th Series, vol. 443, 5 Nov. 1947, cols. 1846–8.

77 Ibid., col. 1859.

78 Gilbert Laithwaite to Hubert Rance, Gilbert Laithwaite Papers, MS Eur. F138/74.

79 Tinker, 'Burma's Struggle for Independence', p. 479.

80 Parliamentary Debates, House of Commons, 5th Series, vol. 426, 1 Aug. 1946, cols. 1254, 1257.

81 Amery diary, 8 Aug. 1946, Leo Amery Papers, 7/40.

82 Parliamentary Debates, House of Commons, 5th Series, vol. 434, 6 March 1947, col. 675.

83 Ibid., vol. 443, 5 Nov. 1947, col. 1846.

84 Clarke, *Last Thousand Days*, p. 484.

85 'Many Labour MPs Abstain in Palestine Division', *The Times*, 27 Jan. 1949.

86 Amery to Chaim Weizmann, 27 Jan. 1949, Leo Amery Papers, 2/2/28.

87 Henri Grimal, *Decolonization: The British, French, Dutch and Belgian Empires, 1919–1963*, Routledge & Kegan Paul, London, 1978, p. 135.

88 'Trends in Attitudes to Government Leaders', Mass Observation File Report 2476, April 1947, Mass-Observation Archive.

89 Clarke, *Last Thousand Days*, p. 506.

90 Broadcast of 17 Feb. 1950.

91 F. W. S. Craig (ed.), *British General Election Manifestos, 1918–1966*, Political Reference Publications, Chichester, 1970, p. 123.

92 'Labour Party "Falsehoods"', *The Times*, 9 Feb. 1950.

93 Speech of 28 Jan. 1950.

94 R. W. Ferrier, *The History of the British Petroleum Company*, vol. I: *The Developing Years, 1901–1932*, Cambridge University Press, Cambridge, 1982, pp. 194–7. By convention, the government did not interfere in the running of the company.

95 J. H. Bamberg, *The History of the British Petroleum Company*, vol. II: *The Anglo-Iranian Years, 1928–1954*, Cambridge University Press, Cambridge, 1994, p. 513.

96 Sue Onslow, ' "Battlelines for Suez": The Abadan Crisis of 1951 and the Formation of the Suez Group', *Contemporary British History*, 17 (2003), pp. 1–28, esp. 6–7.

97 D. E. Butler, *The British General Election of 1951*, Macmillan, London, 1952, pp. 86, 116.
98 Speech of 6 Oct. 1951.
99 Quoted in Butler, *British General Election of 1951*, p. 121.
100 Speech of 23 Oct. 1951.
101 Amery diary, 25 June 1945, Leo Amery Papers, 7/39.
102 Ibid., 28 Sept. 1951, Leo Amery Papers, 7/45.
103 'Labour's Defeat', *Manchester Guardian*, 26 Oct. 1951.
104 Speech of 12 Oct. 1951.
105 'Canada Has Doubts on Empire Policy', *Observer*, 28 Oct. 1951; 'Appeal to Mr Churchill to Be a National Leader', *Manchester Guardian*, 29 Oct. 1951.
106 'Churchill Called to Great Tasks', *Canberra Times*, 27 Oct. 1951.
107 'Tory Victory', *Hindustan Times Weekly*, 28 Oct. 1951.
108 Quoted in 'Lord Ismay's Appointment Reassures India', *Manchester Guardian*, 29 Oct. 1951. For Ismay's concern that Churchill would disapprove of his posting with Mountbatten, see *The Memoirs of Lord Ismay*, Heinemann, London, 1960, p. 410.
109 Letter of 1 Nov. 1951 in G. Parthasarathi (ed.), *Jawaharlal Nehru: Letters to Chief Ministers, 1947–1964*, vol. III: *1952–1954*, Jawaharlal Nehru Memorial Fund, New Delhi, 1987, pp. 527–8.
110 'The Tories' Return and West Africa', *West African Pilot*, 30 Oct. 1951.
111 Richard Koebner and Helmut Dan Schmidt, *Imperialism: The Story and Significance of a Political Word, 1840–1960*, Cambridge University Press, Cambridge, 1964, p. 306.
112 Broadcast of 7 Feb. 1952.
113 'The Queen's Congratulations to Everest Expedition', *Manchester Guardian*, 3 June 1953.
114 Cabinet Secretary's notebook, 20 Nov. 1951, CC (51) 9th, NA, CAB 195/10.
115 Parliamentary Debates, House of Commons, 5th Series, vol. 504, 30 July 1952, col. 1509.
116 John Cloake, *Templer, Tiger of Malaya: The Life of Field Marshal Sir Gerald Templer*, Harrap, London, 1985, p. 204.
117 Oscar Nemon, unpublished memoirs, p. 72, Oscar Nemon Papers, 3/1.
118 R. H. Ferrell (ed.), *The Eisenhower Diaries*, W. W. Norton & Co., New York, 1981, pp. 222–4 (entry for 6 Jan. 1953).
119 David Stafford, *Churchill and Secret Service*, Abacus, London, 2000 (first published 1997), pp. 390–6.
120 Kermit Roosevelt, *Countercoup: The Struggle for the Control of Iran*, McGraw-Hill, New York, 1979, p. 207.
121 Amery diary, 12 May 1953, Leo Amery Papers, 7/47. The 1925 Locarno Pact was a treaty of mutual guarantee between Germany, Belgium, France, Great Britain and Italy.
122 'Lord Swinton's Own Notes of the Commonwealth Prime Ministers' Meeting, June, 1953', Lord Swinton Papers, I/6.
123 Amery diary, 21 Sept. 1952, Leo Amery Papers, 7/47.

124 'The Men for Oldham', *Oldham Daily Standard*, 26 June 1899.

125 Evelyn Shuckburgh, *Descent to Suez: Diaries, 1951–56*, Weidenfeld & Nicolson, London, 1986, p. 75 (entry for 29 Jan. 1953).

126 Gilbert, *'Never Despair'*, pp. 797–9; Cabinet Secretary's notebook, 15 March 1954, CC (54) 18th, NA, CAB 195/12.

127 See Onslow, ' "Battlelines for Suez" '.

128 Interview with Julian Amery for the television series *Churchill*, c. 1991, Churchill Additional Papers, WCHL 15/2/51.

129 Carlton, *Anthony Eden*, p. 358.

130 See John Charmley, *Churchill's Grand Alliance: The Anglo-American Relationship, 1940–57*, Hodder & Stoughton, London, 1995, p. 278.

131 Interview with Julian Amery for *Churchill*.

132 'Leaving the Suez', *Time*, 26 July 1954.

133 'Decline of Empire', *Time*, 9 Aug. 1954; Parliamentary Debates, House of Commons, 5th Series, vol. 531, 28 July 1954, col. 499.

134 Parliamentary Debates, House of Commons, 5th Series, vol. 531, 29 July 1954, col. 750.

135 Lord Moran, *Winston Churchill: The Struggle for Survival, 1940–1965*, Constable, London, 1966, pp. 630–1.

136 John Ramsden, *Man of the Century: Winston Churchill and His Legend since 1945*, HarperCollins, London, 2002, pp. 493–504.

137 R. G. Menzies, 'Churchill and the Commonwealth', in James Marchant (ed.), *Winston Spencer Churchill: Servant of Crown and Commonwealth*, Cassell, London, 1954, pp. 91–9, at 94, 96.

138 Memorandum by Lester B. Pearson, 9 Dec. 1951, in David Dilks, *'The Great Dominion': Winston Churchill in Canada, 1900–1954*, Thomas Allen, Toronto, 2005, p. 376.

139 Broadcast of 13 May 1945.

140 The Earl of Longford and Thomas P. O'Neill, *Eamon De Valera*, Hutchinson, London, 1970, p. 443.

141 Ramsden, *Man of the Century*, p. 259.

142 Moran, *Struggle for Survival*, p. 473. De Valera appears to have extended an invitation to Churchill to visit Ireland. The latter 'spoke very appreciatively' of this offer, although he never took it up. Before returning to office, Churchill had thought of visiting Ireland in order to see Canyon Kid, a racehorse he owned, run in the Irish Derby, but the horse died of heart failure and the plan lapsed. Churchill told the Irish ambassador of his regrets: 'You know I have had many invitations to visit Ulster but I have refused them all. I don't want to go there at all, I would much rather go to Southern Ireland. Maybe I'll buy another horse with an entry in the Irish Derby.' (He never did.) Shane Leslie, undated note, Eamon De Valera Papers, P150/1507; F. H. Boland to the Secretary, Department of External Affairs, 9 May 1951, National Archives of Ireland, DFA P250.

143 This paragraph owes much to Andrew Roberts, *Eminent Churchillians*, Weidenfeld & Nicolson, London, 1994, ch. 4.

144 Moran, *Struggle for Survival*, pp. 651–2.
145 Cabinet Secretary's notebook, 3 Feb. 1954, CC (54) 7th, NA, CAB 195/11.
146 Peter Catterall (ed.), *The Macmillan Diaries: The Cabinet Years, 1950–1957*, Macmillan, London, 2003, p. 382 (entry for 20 Jan. 1955).
147 Ian Gilmour, *Inside Right: A Study of Conservatism*, Hutchinson, London, 1977, p. 134.
148 Winston James, 'The Black Experience in Twentieth Century Britain', in Philip D. Morgan and Sean Hawkins (eds.), *Black Experience and the Empire*, Oxford University Press, Oxford, 2004.
149 Zig Layton-Henry, *The Politics of Immigration: Immigration, 'Race' and 'Race' Relations in Post-war Britain*, Blackwell, Oxford, 1992, p. 31.
150 Hyam, *Britain's Declining Empire*, p. 217.
151 Quotations in Roberts, *Eminent Churchillians*, p. 214.
152 'Change in World Outlook', *The Times*, 22 April 1953; Cabinet Secretary's notebook, 28 April 1953, CC (53) 29th, NA, CAB 195/11.
153 WSC, 'Report on visit to Natal', 7 Oct. 1941, NA, PREM 4/44/1. Churchill's purpose in writing this note was to defend the British inhabitants of Natal against the aspersions he thought had been cast on them by Lord Harlech, the High Commissioner to South Africa, in a report on his visit to the territory. Harlech had criticized them for being indifferent to the need for cooperation between races.
154 Cabinet Secretary's notebook, 10 March 1954, CC (54) 17th, NA, CAB 195/12.
155 Parliamentary Debates, House of Commons, 5th Series, vol. 526, 13 April 1954, col. 966.
156 WSC, minute of 30 Aug. 1954, NA, PREM 11/1765.
157 Hyam, *Britain's Declining Empire*, p. 220.
158 See ibid., pp. 168–70, 217.
159 Kwame Nkrumah, *The Autobiography of Kwame Nkrumah*, Thomas Nelson & Sons, Edinburgh, 1957, p. 103.
160 Hyam, *Britain's Declining Empire*, p. 182.
161 Cabinet Secretary's notebook, 27 May 1953, CC (53) 34th, NA, CAB 195/11.
162 David Anderson, *Histories of the Hanged: Britain's Dirty War in Kenya and the End of Empire*, Weidenfeld & Nicolson, London, 2005, esp. pp. 1, 5, 7, 84, 152.
163 Philip Murphy, *Alan Lennox-Boyd: A Biography*, I. B. Tauris, London, 1999, p. 149.
164 'Irony of Churchill's Nobel Prize and Kenyans' Sufferings', *East African Standard*, 3 Feb. 2007.
165 Anderson, *Histories of the Hanged*, p. 62.
166 Lord Alexander to WSC, 30 Oct. 1952, NA, PREM 11/472.
167 WSC to Alexander and Oliver Lyttelton, 12 Nov. 1952, ibid.
168 WSC to Lyttelton, 26 Nov. 1952, ibid.

169 Churchill was properly sceptical of a news report, published within a few days of the massacre, which said that of a thousand people rounded up afterwards two or three hundred had been identified as perpetrators. How, he wondered, could they have been identified so quickly? See Anthony Montague Brown to P. J. Kitcatt, 29 March 1953, ibid.

170 WSC to Anthony Eden, 28 March 1953, ibid.

171 Anderson, *Histories of the Hanged*, p. 105.

172 WSC to Lord Swinton, 20 April 1953, NA, DO 35/5340, in David Goldsworthy (ed.), *The Conservative Government and the End of Empire, 1951–1957*, Series A, vol. III, part 1: *International Relations*, HMSO, London, 1994, p. 132.

173 Quoted in Caroline Elkins, *Britain's Gulag: The Brutal End of Empire in Kenya*, Jonathan Cape, London, 2005, p. 52.

174 Ibid., p. 53.

175 Paul Addison, *Churchill on the Home Front, 1900–1955*, Pimlico, London, 1993 (first published by Jonathan Cape, 1992), pp. 119–20.

176 Parliamentary Debates, House of Commons, 5th Series, vol. 434, 3 March 1947, col. 42.

177 For the details of the case see Richard Rathbone, 'A Murder in the Colonial Gold Coast: Law and Politics in the 1940s', *Journal of African History*, 30 (1989), pp. 445–61, and Stacey Hynd, 'Imperial Gallows: Capital Punishment, Violence and Colonial Rule in Britain's African Territories, c. 1903–68', unpublished D.Phil. thesis, University of Oxford, 2007, pp. 205–14.

178 Anderson, *Histories of the Hanged*, p. 154.

179 Cabinet minutes, 21 May 1953, CC (53) 33rd, NA, CAB 128/26.

180 Lyttelton to Evelyn Baring, 28 May 1953, NA, CO 822/702, quoted in Anderson, *Histories of the Hanged*, p. 154.

181 Anderson, *Histories of the Hanged*, p. 154.

182 Ibid., pp. 230–4.

183 Cabinet Secretary's notebook, 10 Feb. 1954, CC (54) 8th, NA, CAB 195/11.

184 Cabinet minutes, 10 Feb. 1954, CC (54) 8th, NA, CAB/128/27.

185 Cabinet Secretary's notebook, 10 Feb. 1954, CC (54) 8th, NA, CAB 195/11.

186 Telegram from Baring, 1 March 1954, NA, PREM 11/696.

187 Cabinet Secretary's notebook, 17 Feb. 1954, CC (54) 9th, NA, CAB 195/11.

188 Cabinet minutes, 1 March 1954, CC (54) 13th, NA, CAB 128/27.

189 Anderson, *Histories of the Hanged*, p. 234.

190 'Action in Kenya Criticized', *The Times*, 5 March 1954.

191 Anderson, *Histories of the Hanged*, pp. 275–6.

192 Michael Blundell, *A Love Affair with the Sun: A Memoir of Seventy Years in Kenya*, Kenway Publications, Nairobi, 1994, p. 109.

193 Elkins, *Britain's Gulag*, p. 280.

194 Cabinet Secretary's notebook, 13 Jan. 1955, CC (55) 3rd, and 13 Jan. 1955, CC (55) 4th, NA, CAB 195/13.

195 Quoted in D. J. Morgan, *The Official History of Colonial Development*, vol. V: *Guidance Towards Self-Government in British Colonies, 1941–1971*, Macmillan, London, 1980, p. 59.

196 K. P. S. Menon, *The Flying Troika*, Oxford University Press, London, 1963, p. 45 (entry for 16 May 1953).

197 Dwight Eisenhower to WSC, 22 July, 1954, in Peter G. Boyle (ed.), *The Churchill–Eisenhower Correspondence, 1953–1955*, University of North Carolina Press, Chapel Hill and London, 1990, p. 164.

198 WSC to Eisenhower, 8 Aug. 1954, ibid., p. 167.

199 Catterall, *Macmillan Diaries*, p. 338 (entry for 23 July 1954).

200 Nemon, unpublished memoirs, p. 72.

201 Nirad C. Chaudhuri, *Thy Hand, Great Anarch! India: 1921–1952*, Chatto & Windus, London, 1987, p. 757.

202 Amery diary, 5 April 1955, Leo Amery Papers, 7/49.

203 'Sir W. Churchill on "Great Patriot"', *The Times*, 17 Sept. 1955.

204 Quoted in Gilbert, *'Never Despair'*, p. 1121.

205 F. A. Ridley, 'The Last of the Victorians', *Socialist Leader*, 16 April 1955. The *Daily Worker* was also unaffected by the strike, as were local newspapers outside London.

206 'Churchill démissione', *l'Humanité*, 6 April 1955.

207 'Sir Anthony to Succeed Sir Winston', *Daily Graphic*, 7 April 1955.

EPILOGUE

1 Anita Leslie, *Cousin Clare: The Tempestuous Career of Clare Sheridan*, Hutchinson, London, 1976, p. 263. Emphasis in original.

2 John Colville, *The Fringes of Power: Downing Street Diaries, 1939–1955*, Hodder & Stoughton, London, 1985, p. 708.

3 *Daily Telegraph*, 3 Jan. 1956, quoted in D. R. Thorpe, *Eden: The Life and Times of Anthony Eden, First Earl of Avon, 1897–1977*, Chatto & Windus, London, 2003, p. 459.

4 WSC to Clementine Churchill, 3 Aug. 1956, in Mary Soames (ed.), *Speaking for Themselves: The Personal Letters of Winston and Clementine Churchill*, Doubleday, London, 1998, p. 610.

5 Peter Catterall (ed.), *The Macmillan Diaries: The Cabinet Years, 1950–1957*, Macmillan, London, 2003, p. 584 (entry for 6 Aug. 1956).

6 Clarissa Eden, *A Memoir: From Churchill to Eden*, Weidenfeld & Nicolson, London, 2007, p. 237.

7 Catterall, *Macmillan Diaries*, p. 585 (entry for 7 Aug. 1956).

8 Andrew J. Goodpaster, 'Memorandum of a Conference with the President, 30 Oct. 1956', FRUS, 1955–1957, vol. XVI, p. 853.

9 'Sir W. Churchill's Support', *The Times*, 5 Nov. 1956.

10 Colville, *Fringes of Power*, p. 721.
11 Mark Pottle (ed.), *Daring to Hope: The Diaries and Letters of Violet Bonham Carter, 1946–1969*, Weidenfeld & Nicolson, London, 2000, p. 185 (entry for 15 Jan. 1957). Emphasis in original.
12 Clementine Churchill to Harold Wilson, 15 Feb. 1965, quoted in Martin Gilbert, *Winston S. Churchill*, vol. VIII: *'Never Despair', 1945–1965*, Heinemann, London, 1988, p. 1225.
13 WSC to Lionel Curtis, 25 April 1933, Lionel Curtis Papers, MSS Curtis 9, f. 26.
14 Anthony Montague Browne, *Long Sunset: Memoirs of Winston Churchill's Last Private Secretary*, Cassell, London, 1995, pp. 191–2.
15 Statement of 9 April 1963.
16 WSC to Jack Churchill, 2 Dec. [1897], CV I, part 2, p. 836.
17 'Mr Macmillan's Appeal to South Africans', *The Times*, 4 Feb. 1960.
18 Norman Brook to Harold Macmillan, 3 March 1960, NA, PREM 11/3073.
19 Pottle, *Daring to Hope*, p. 224 (entry for 17 Feb. 1960).
20 WSC to Robert Menzies, 30 Oct. 1961, quoted in John Ramsden, *Man of the Century: Winston Churchill and His Legend since 1945*, HarperCollins, London, 2002, p. 500.
21 'Lord Montgomery Sees Sir Winston', *The Times*, 15 Aug. 1962.
22 Some of the details of this episode can be found in David Anderson, 'Mau Mau at the Movies: Contemporary Representations of an Anti-Colonial War', *South African Historical Journal*, 48 (2003), pp. 71–89, at 80–5.
23 Patrick McGilligan, *Backstory 2: Interviews with Screenwriters of the 1940s and 1950s*, University of California Press, Berkeley, 1991, pp. 54–6.
24 Ibid., p. 56.
25 The prologue was later restored to the VHS version, but was omitted from the recent DVD release.
26 *Al-Thawra al-Arabiyya*, 19 Jan. 1965, copy (with accompanying translation) in NA, FO 371/180673.
27 Quoted in Ramsden, *Man of the Century*, p. 262.
28 When criticized in the press, Lemass said, 'The arrangements made to associate this country with his [Churchill's] funeral were strictly in order, even if they did not represent the cap-in-hand attitude which these newspaper commentators seem to think is the appropriate posture for Irishmen in their relations with Britain.' Dáil Éireann Debates, vol. 214, 17 Feb. 1965, col. 585.
29 'Britain's Unique Honour for Great War Leader', *Irish Independent*, 1 Feb. 1965.
30 'Leader with Magic Personality' and 'Tributes from Many Lands', *The Times*, 25 Jan. 1965; Malcolm MacDonald, *Titans & Others*, Collins, London, 1972, pp. 124–6.
31 'Tributes to a Great Leader', *Daily Times*, 25 Jan. 1965.
32 Quoted in Wendy Webster, *Englishness and Empire, 1939–1965*, Oxford University Press, Oxford, 2005, p. 187.

33 Radio Talk for USA and Canada, 16 Jan. 1965, Harold Macmillan Papers, MS Dep. C. 535, ff. 42–5.

34 'Sir Robert Speaks of a Friend', *Guardian*, 1 Feb. 1965.

35 *National Geographic*, Aug. 1965, quoted in Webster, *Englishness and Empire*, p. 188.

36 *The State Funeral of Sir Winston Churchill*, quoted ibid., pp. 186–7.

37 Alan Megahey, *Humphrey Gibbs: Beleaguered Governor: Southern Rhodesia, 1929–69*, Macmillan, Basingstoke, 1998, p. 93.

38 *Sunday Times*, 6 Nov. 1966, quoted in Webster, *Englishness and Empire*, p. 185.

39 John Grigg, 'Churchill and After', *Guardian*, 25 Jan. 1965.

40 John Charmley, *Churchill, The End of Glory: A Political Biography*, Hodder & Stoughton, London, 1993.

41 'Churchill: Defender of Empire and Commonwealth', *Round Table*, 218 (March 1965), pp. 103–5, at 103.

42 Richard B. Moore, 'The Passing of Churchill and Empire', *Liberator*, March 1965, in W. Burghardt Turner and Joyce Moore Turner (eds.), *Richard B. Moore, Caribbean Militant in Harlem: Collected Writings, 1920–1972*, Indiana University Press, Bloomington and Indianapolis, 1992, pp. 245–6.

43 Speech of 16 July 2001, quoted in Richard Toye, 'The Churchill Syndrome: Reputational Entrepreneurship and the Rhetoric of Foreign Policy since 1945', *British Journal of Politics and International Relations*, 10 (2008), pp. 364–78, at 364.

44 Joe Klein, 'Even Churchill Couldn't Figure Out Iraq', *Time*, 30 July 2006.

45 Rory Carroll, 'Mbeki Attacks "Racist" Churchill', *Guardian*, 5 Jan. 2005.

46 Anonymous letter postmarked 27 Jan. 1990, Churchill Additional Papers, WCHL 2/9.

47 'Churchill Calls for Unity', *Canberra Times*, 30 April 1953.

48 Speech notes prepared for debate on India, 30 March 1943, Churchill Papers, CHAR 9/191A, ff. 3–10. Piers Brendon draws attention to this important document in *The Decline and Fall of the British Empire, 1781–1997*, Jonathan Cape, London, 2007, p. 397.

49 John Barnes and David Nicholson (eds.), *The Empire at Bay: The Leo Amery Diaries, 1929–1945*, Hutchinson, London, 1988, p. 879 (entry for 29 March 1945).

50 Charles de Gaulle, *Memoires de Guerre: Le Salut, 1944–1946* (1959), quoted in François Kersaudy, *Churchill and de Gaulle*, Collins, London, 1981, p. 382.

51 'Pater's Chats with the Boys', *Otago Witness*, 16 Aug. 1900.

52 Speech notes for debate on India, 30 March 1943, Churchill Papers, CHAR 9/191A, f. 10.

53 Nelson Mandela, *Long Walk to Freedom*, Abacus, London, 1995 (first published 1994), p. 110.

Bibliography

ARCHIVAL SOURCES

BBC Written Archives Centre, Caversham
Daily Digests of Foreign Broadcasts

Bodleian Library, Oxford
H. H. Asquith Papers
Violet Bonham Carter Papers
Harry Crookshank diary
Lionel Curtis Papers
Harcourt Papers
Harold Macmillan Papers
Alfred Milner Papers
John Morley Papers
Selborne Papers
Lord Southborough Papers
Laming Worthington-Evans Papers

British Library, London
C. P. Scott Papers
J. A. Spender Papers

British Library, Oriental and India Office Collections, London
Lord Brabourne Papers
Harcourt Butler Papers
Lord Curzon Papers
India Office Records
Gilbert Laithwaite Papers
Lord Linlithgow Papers
Lord Reading Papers

British Library of Political and Economic Science, London
Hugh Dalton Papers

Cambridge University Library
Stanley Baldwin Papers
Lord Randolph Churchill Papers
Templewood Papers

Churchill Archives Centre, Cambridge
Leo Amery Papers
Julian Amery Papers
Broadwater Collection (Churchill-related press cuttings)
Alexander Cadogan Papers
Winston Churchill Papers
Winston Churchill Additional Papers
Alfred Duff Cooper Papers
Charles Eade Papers
Lord Halifax Papers
Maurice Hankey Papers
George Lloyd Papers
Oscar Nemon Papers
Edward Spears Papers
Lord Swinton Papers
Thurso Papers

Fitzwilliam Museum, Cambridge
Wilfrid Scawen Blunt Papers

King's College, Cambridge
Oscar Browning Papers

King's College, London: Liddell Hart Centre
Henry Maxwell Coote Papers

Library of Congress, Washington DC
Marlborough Papers

The National Archives, Kew, London
Cabinet records
Colonial Office records
Dominions Office records
Foreign Office records
Prime Ministers' files

National Archives of Ireland, Dublin
Department of Foreign Affairs records

National Army Museum, London
William Birdwood Papers

National Library of Ireland, Dublin
John Redmond Papers

National Library of Wales, Aberystwyth
William George Papers
Thomas Jones Papers

Parliamentary Archives, London
Ralph David Blumenfeld Papers
John St Loe Strachey Papers

Rhodes House, Oxford
Reginald Coupland diary
Fabian Colonial Bureau Papers
Lugard Papers
Marjorie Perham Papers

Trinity College, Cambridge
Walter Layton Papers

Harry S. Truman Library, Independence, Missouri
Frederick M. Vinson Papers (consulted on microfilm)

University of Birmingham, Special Collections
Austen Chamberlain Papers

University College Dublin
Eamon De Valera Papers

University of Exeter
Cecil Harmsworth Papers

University of Illinois
H. G. Wells Papers

University of Sussex
Mass-Observation Archive

Official Sources

The Official Gazette of the Colony and Protectorate of Kenya
Parliamentary Debates (Hansard)

Published Document Series

Australia

W. J. Hudson and H. J. W. Stokes (eds.), *Documents on Australian Foreign Policy, 1937–49*, vol. IV: *July 1940–June 1941*, Australian Government Publishing Service, Canberra, 1980
——, *Documents on Australian Foreign Policy, 1937–49*, vol. V: *July 1941–June 1942*, Australian Government Publishing Service, Canberra, 1982

Burma

Tinker, Hugh (ed.), *Burma: The Struggle for Independence 1944–1948*, vol. I: *From Military Occupation to Civil Government, 1 January 1944 to 31 August 1946*, HMSO, London, 1983

Canada

Documents on Canadian External Relations vol. VII: *1939–1941*, Department of External Affairs, Ottawa, 1974
Documents on Canadian External Relations, vol. XII: *1946*, Department of External Affairs, Ottawa, 1977

Germany

Documents on German Foreign Policy, 1918–1945, Series D, vol. I: *From Neurath to Ribbentrop (September 1937– September 1938)*, HMSO, London, 1949

India

Nicholas Mansergh (ed.), *India: The Transfer of Power, 1942–7*, 12 vols., HMSO, London, 1970–83

United Kingdom

David Goldsworthy (ed.), *The Conservative Government and the End of Empire, 1951–1957*, Series A, vol. 3, part 1: *International Relations*, HMSO, London, 1994
Hyam, Ronald (ed.), *British Documents on the End of Empire*, Series A, vol. II, part 4, HMSO, London, 1992

United States

US Department of State, *Foreign Relations of the United States: Diplomatic Papers, 1941*, vol. III, US Government Printing Office, Washington, DC, 1959

——, *Foreign Relations of the United States: Diplomatic Papers, The Conferences at Cairo and Tehran, 1943*, US Government Printing Office, Washington, DC, 1961

——, *Foreign Relations of the United States: The Conferences at Malta and Yalta, 1945*, US Government Printing Office, Washington, DC,1955

——, *Foreign Relations of the United States: Diplomatic Papers, 1945*, vol. VIII, US Government Printing Office, Washington, DC, 1969

——, *Foreign Relations of the United States, 1955–1957*, vol. XVI, US Government Printing Office, Washington, DC, 1990

ELECTRONIC AND INTERNET RESOURCES

African National Congress, *Africans' Claims in South Africa*, African National Congress, Johannesburg, 1943, http://www.anc.org.za/ancdocs/history/claims.html

Gertrude Bell archive, http://www.gerty.ncl.ac.uk

Dáil Éireann debates, http://historical-debates.oireachtas.ie

German Propaganda Archive, http://www.calvin.edu/academic/cas/gpa/

House of Commons Parliamentary Papers database, Joint Information Systems Committee: Command Papers Cd. 6689 (1913), Cmd. 681, (1920), Cmd. 1474 (August 1921), Cmd. 1691 (1922), Cmd. 1700 (June 1922), Cmd. 1922 (July 1923), Cmd. 2768 (1926), Cmd. 4268 (March 1933), Cmd. 6196 (April 1940), Cmd. 6388 (1942), Cmd. 6341 (1942), Cmd 6635 (May 1945), Cmd. 6707 (Dec. 1945); 'Joint Committee on Indian Constitutional Reform (Session 1932–33)' (1933); 'Report of the Committee of Privileges' (6 June 1934)

W. L. Mackenzie King diary, http://www.collectionscanada.gc.ca

Oxford Dictionary of National Biography, online edition, http://www.oxforddnb.com

'Psywarrior', 'Axis propaganda against Indian troops', http://www.psywarrior.com/AxisPropIndia.html

R. E. van der Ross, *Say It Out Loud: The APO Presidential Addresses and other Major Political Speeches, 1906–1940, of Dr Abdullah Abdurahman*, Western Cape Institute for Historical Research, University of the Western Cape, Bellville, 1990, http://www.sahistory.org.za

NEWSPAPERS AND PERIODICALS

Birmingham Daily Post
Broad Arrow
*Canberra Times**
Critic
Daily Chronicle
Daily Gleaner (Jamaica)

Daily Graphic (Gold Coast/Ghana)
Daily Mail
*Daily News**
Daily Telegraph
Daily Times (Lagos)
East African Standard (Nairobi)
The Economist
Evening Post (Wellington, NZ)*
Freeman's Journal (Ireland)*
*Glasgow Herald**
Globe (Toronto)
*Guardian**
Harrovian
Hawera & Normanby Star (New Zealand)*
Hindustan Times Weekly
Indian News Chronicle
Irish Independent
*Irish Times**
*Jackson's Oxford Journal**
l'Humanité (France)
*Leeds Mercury**
Listener
Madras Weekly Mail
*Manchester Guardian**
Morning Post
National Review
New York Herald Tribune
*New York Times**
News Chronicle
*Northern Echo**
*Observer**
Oldham Daily Standard
Oldham Evening Chronicle
Otago Witness (New Zealand)*
Ottawa Free Press
*Palestine Post**
Pall Mall Gazette
Public Opinion
Punch
*Reynolds's Newspaper/Reynolds News**
Round Table
*Scotsman**
Socialist Leader
Spectator
Star of East Africa

Star of India
Statesman / Sunday Statesman (Calcutta)
Sunday Pictorial
Taranaki Herald (New Zealand)*
*Time**
*The Times**
Times of India
*Toronto Daily Star**
Transvaal Leader
Tuapeka Times (New Zealand)*
Wanganui Herald (New Zealand)*
Washington Post
West African Pilot
*Western Mail**
Westminster Gazette
*consulted wholly or partly in electronic form

BOOKS AND ARTICLES

Official Biography of Winston Churchill

Churchill, Randolph S., *Winston S. Churchill*, vol. I: *Youth, 1874–1900*, Heinemann, London, 1966
——, *Winston S. Churchill*, vol. II: *Young Statesman, 1901–1914*, Heinemann, London, 1967
Gilbert, Martin, *Winston S. Churchill*, vol. III: *1914–1916*, Heinemann, London, 1971
——, *Winston S. Churchill*, vol. IV: *1917–1922*, Heinemann, London, 1975
——, *Winston S. Churchill*, vol. V: *1922–1939*, Heinemann, London, 1976
——, *Winston S. Churchill*, vol. VI: *Finest Hour, 1939–1941*, Heinemann, London, 1983
——, *Winston S. Churchill*, vol. VII: *Road to Victory, 1941–1945*, Heinemann, London, 1986
——, *Winston S. Churchill*, vol. VIII: *'Never Despair', 1945–1965*, Heinemann, London, 1988

Companion Volumes to the Official Biography

Churchill, Randolph S. (ed.), *Companion Volume I*, parts 1 and 2, Heinemann, London, 1967
——, *Companion Volume II*, parts 1, 2 and 3, Heinemann, London, 1969
Gilbert, Martin (ed.), *Companion Volume III*, parts 1 and 2, Heinemann, London, 1972
——, *Companion Volume IV*, parts 1, 2 and 3, Heinemann, London, 1977
——, *Companion Volume V*, parts 1, 2 and 3, Heinemann, London, 1979

——, *The Churchill War Papers*, vol. I: *At the Admiralty: September 1939–May 1940*, W.W. Norton & Co., New York, 1993

——, *The Churchill War Papers*, vol. II: *Never Surrender: May 1940–December 1940*, W.W. Norton & Co., New York, 1994

——, *The Churchill War Papers*, vol. III: *The Ever Widening War: 1941*, W.W. Norton & Co., New York, 2000

Other Sources

Aberigh-Mackay, George R., *Twenty-One Days in India or The Tour of Sir Ali Baba K.C.B.*, W. Thacker & Co., London, 1910 (first published 1880)

Addison, Paul, *Churchill on the Home Front, 1900–1955*, Pimlico, London, 1993 (first published by Jonathan Cape, 1992)

——, *Churchill: The Unexpected Hero*, Oxford University Press, Oxford, 2005

Alkon, Paul K., *Winston Churchill's Imagination*, Bucknell University Press, Lewisburg, 2006

Amery, L. S., *Days of Fresh Air*, Jarrolds, London, 1939

——, *My Political Life*, vol. I: *England before the Storm, 1896–1914*, Hutchinson, London, 1953

——, *The Washington Loan Agreements: A Critical Study of American Economic Foreign Policy*, MacDonald, London, 1946

Anderson, David, *Histories of the Hanged: Britain's Dirty War in Kenya and the End of Empire*, Weidenfeld & Nicolson, London, 2005

——, 'Mau Mau at the Movies: Contemporary Representations of an Anti-Colonial War', *South African Historical Journal*, 48 (2003), pp. 71–89

Asher, Michael, *Khartoum: The Ultimate Imperial Adventure*, Penguin, London, 2006 (first published 2005)

Astley, Joan Bright, *The Inner Circle: A View of War at the Top*, Hutchinson, London, 1971

Atkins, John Black, *The Relief of Ladysmith*, Methuen & Co., London, 1900

Austin, Douglas, *Churchill and Malta: A Special Relationship*, Spellmount, Stroud, 2006

Avon, Earl of, *The Eden Memoirs: The Reckoning*, Cassell, London, 1965

Baijnath, Lala, *England and India*, Jehangir B. Karani & Co., Bombay, 1893

Ball, Stuart (ed.), *Parliament and Politics in the Age of Churchill and Attlee: The Headlam Diaries, 1935–1951*, Cambridge University Press for the Royal Historical Society, Cambridge, 1999

Bamberg, J. H., *The History of the British Petroleum Company*, vol. II: *The Anglo-Iranian Years, 1928–1954*, Cambridge University Press, Cambridge, 1994

Barnes, John and Nicholson, David (eds.), *The Empire at Bay: The Leo Amery Diaries, 1929–1945*, Hutchinson, London, 1988

——, *The Leo Amery Diaries*, vol. I: *1896–1929*, Hutchinson, London, 1980

Bayly, Christopher and Harper, Tim, *Forgotten Armies: Britain's Asian Empire and the War with Japan*, Allen Lane, London, 2004

Bell, Christopher, 'The "Singapore Strategy" and the Deterrence of Japan: Winston Churchill, the Admiralty, and the Dispatch of Force Z', *English Historical Review*, 116 (2001), pp. 604–34

Bell, Hesketh, *Glimpses of a Governor's Life*, Sampson, Low, Marston & Co., London, n.d.

Bellamy, Frank and Makins, Clifford, *The Happy Warrior*, Hulton Press, London, 1958

Bennett, Ernest N., 'After Omdurman', *Contemporary Review*, 75 (1899), pp. 18–33

——, *The Downfall of the Dervishes, or, The Avenging of Gordon: Being a Personal Narrative of the Final Soudan Campaign of 1898*, Negro Universities Press, New York, 1969 (first published 1898)

Bentley, Michael (ed.), *Public and Private Doctrine: Essays in British History Presented to Maurice Cowling*, Cambridge, Cambridge University Press, 1993

Beresford, Lord Charles, 'The Naval Outlook: Mr Churchill's Promises and Performances', *Empire Review*, 26, 154 (Nov. 1913), pp. 217–24

Berman, Bruce, *Control and Crisis in Colonial Kenya: The Dialectic of Domination*, East African Educational Publishers, Nairobi, 1990

Best, Geoffrey, *Churchill: A Study in Greatness*, Penguin, London, 2002 (first published by Hambledon, London, 2001)

——, *Churchill and War*, Hambledon, London, 2005

Blake, Robert and Louis, Wm. Roger (eds.), *Churchill*, Oxford University Press, Oxford, 1993

Blum, John Morton (ed.), *From the Morgenthau Diaries: Years of War, 1941–1945*, Houghton Mifflin, Boston, 1967

——, *The Price of Vision: The Diary of Henry A. Wallace, 1942–1946*, Houghton Mifflin, Boston, 1973

Blundell, Michael, *A Love Affair with the Sun: A Memoir of Seventy Years in Kenya*, Kenway Publications, Nairobi, 1994

——, *So Rough a Wind*, Weidenfeld & Nicolson, London, 1964

Blunt, Wilfrid Scawen, *My Diaries: Being a Personal Narrative of Events, 1888–1914: Part Two* [1900–1914], Martin Secker, London, n.d

——, *The Poetical Works of Wilfrid Scawen Blunt: A Complete Edition*, vol. II, Macmillan, London, 1914

——, 'Randolph Churchill: A Personal Recollection', *Nineteenth Century and After*, 59 (1906), pp. 401–15

Bonham Carter, Violet, *Winston Churchill as I Knew Him*, Reprint Society, London, 1966 (originally published by Eyre & Spottiswoode, 1965)

Boyce, D. George (ed.), *The Crisis of British Power: The Imperial and Naval Papers of the Second Earl of Selborne, 1895–1910*, The Historians' Press, London, 1990

Boyle, Peter G. (ed.), *The Churchill–Eisenhower Correspondence, 1953–1955*, University of North Carolina Press, Chapel Hill and London, 1990

Brendon, Piers, *The Decline and Fall of the British Empire, 1781–1997*, Jonathan Cape, London, 2007

Brennan, Lance, 'Government Famine Relief in Bengal, 1943', *Journal of Asian Studies*, 47 (1988), pp. 541–66

Bridge, Carl, 'Churchill, Hoare, Derby and the Committee of Privileges, April to June 1934', *Historical Journal*, 22 (1979), pp. 215–27

Broad, Lewis, *Winston Churchill, 1874–1951*, Hutchinson, London, 1951

Brock, Michael and Brock, Eleanor (eds.), *H. H. Asquith: Letters to Venetia Stanley*, Oxford University Press, Oxford, 1982

Brown, Judith M. and Louis, Wm. Roger (eds.), *The Oxford History of the British Empire: The Twentieth Century*, Oxford University Press, Oxford, 1999

Browne, Anthony Montague, *Long Sunset: Memoirs of Winston Churchill's Last Private Secretary*, Cassell, London, 1995

Butler, D. E., *The British General Election of 1951*, Macmillan, London, 1952

Butler, Harcourt, *India Insistent*, London, Heinemann, 1931

Butler, Josephine, *Native Races and the War*, Gay & Bird, London, 1900

Butler, R. A., *The Art of the Possible*, Hamish Hamilton, London, 1971

Byrnes, James F., *Speaking Frankly*, Harper & Brothers, New York, 1947

Callahan, Raymond A., *Churchill: Retreat from Empire*, Scholarly Resources Inc., Wilmington, DE, 1984

Campbell, John, *F. E. Smith: First Earl of Birkenhead*, Jonathan Cape, London, 1983

Carlton, David, *Anthony Eden: A Biography*, Allen Lane, London, 1981

Casey, Lord, *Personal Experience, 1939–1946*, Constable, London, 1962

Castillo, Dennis Angelo, *The Maltese Cross: A Strategic History of Malta*, Praeger Security International, Westport, CT, 2006

Catherwood, Christopher, *Winston's Folly: Imperialism and the Creation of Modern Iraq*, Constable, London, 2004

Catterall, Peter (ed.), *The Macmillan Diaries: The Cabinet Years, 1950–1957*, Macmillan, London, 2003

Chaplin, E. D. W. (ed.), *Winston Churchill and Harrow*, Harrow School Book Shop, Harrow-on-the-Hill, 1941

Charmley, John, *Churchill, The End of Glory: A Political Biography*, Hodder & Stoughton, London, 1993

——, *Churchill's Grand Alliance: The Anglo-American Relationship, 1940–57*, Hodder & Stoughton, London, 1995

Chaudhuri, Nirad C., *Thy Hand, Great Anarch! India: 1921–1952*, Chatto & Windus, London, 1987

Chesney, George, *Indian Polity: A View of the System of Administration in India*, Longmans, Green & Co., London, 1868

Chiozza, Leone George, *British Trade and the Zollverein Issue*, The Commercial Intelligence Publishing Co., London, 1902

Churchill, Lord Randolph, *Men, Mines and Animals in South Africa*, Sampson, Low, Marston & Co., London, 1893

Churchill, Winston, 'The British Officer', *Pall Mall Magazine*, 23 (1901), pp. 66–75

——, *The Collected Essays of Sir Winston Churchill*, ed. Michael Wolff, 4 vols., Library of Imperial History, London, 1976

——, *The Collected Works of Sir Winston Churchill*, 34 vols., Library of Imperial History/Hamlyn, London, 1973–6

——, 'Mr H. G. Wells and the British Empire', *Empire Review*, 38 (1923), pp. 1217–23

——, *India: Speeches and an Introduction*, Thornton Butterworth, London, 1931

——, *The River War: An Historical Account of the Reconquest of the Sudan*, 2 vols, Longmans, Green & Co., London, 1899

——, *The River War*, Sceptre, London, 1987

Clarke, Peter, *The Cripps Version: The Life of Sir Stafford Cripps, 1889–1952*, Allen Lane, London, 2002

——, *Lancashire and the New Liberalism*, Cambridge University Press, London, 1971

——, *The Last Thousand Days of the British Empire*, Allen Lane, London, 2007

Clayton, Anthony and Savage, Donald C., *Government and Labour in Kenya, 1895–1963*, Frank Cass, London, 1974

Cloake, John, *Templer, Tiger of Malaya: The Life of Field Marshal Sir Gerald Templer*, Harrap, London, 1985

Cohen, Michael J., *Churchill and the Jews*, 2nd edition, Frank Cass, London, 2003

——, 'The Churchill–Gilbert Symbiosis: Myth and Reality', *Modern Judaism*, 28 (2008), pp. 204–28

Collett, Nigel, *The Butcher of Amritsar: General Reginald Dyer*, Hambledon, London, 2005

Colville, John, *The Fringes of Power: Downing Street Diaries, 1939–1955*, Hodder & Stoughton, London, 1985

Constantine, Stephen, *The Making of British Colonial Development Policy, 1914–1940*, Frank Cass, London, 1984

Corse, Edward, 'British Propaganda in Neutral Eire after the Fall of France, 1940', *Contemporary British History*, 22 (2008), pp. 163–80

Craig, F. W. S. (ed.), *British General Election Manifestos, 1918–1966*, Political Reference Publications, Chichester, 1970

Croft, Lord, *My Life of Strife*, Hutchinson, London, 1949

Dalton, Hugh, *High Tide and After: Memoirs, 1945–1960*, Frederick Muller, London, 1962

Danchev, Alex and Todman, Daniel (eds.), *War Diaries, 1939–1945: Field Marshal Lord Alanbrooke*, Weidenfeld & Nicolson, London, 2001

Daunton, Martin, *Just Taxes: The Politics of Taxation in Britain, 1914–1979*, Cambridge University Press, Cambridge, 2002

David, Edward (ed.), *Inside Asquith's Cabinet: From the Diaries of Charles Hobhouse*, John Murray, London, 1977

Day, David, *Menzies & Churchill at War*, Oxford University Press, Oxford, 1993 (first published 1986)

——, *The Politics of War*, HarperCollins, Sydney, 2003

De Mendelssohn, Peter, *The Age of Churchill: Heritage and Adventure, 1874–1911*, Thames & Hudson, London, 1961

Dilks, David, *'The Great Dominion': Winston Churchill in Canada, 1900–1954*, Thomas Allen, Toronto, 2005

Dilks, David (ed.), *The Diaries of Sir Alexander Cadogan O.M., 1938–1945*, Cassell, London, 1971

Djan, Ohenaba Sakyi and Cockin, Maurice S., 'Drums and Victory: Africa's Call to the Empire', *Journal of the Royal African Society*, 41 (1942), pp. 29–41

Dockter, Warren, 'Winston Churchill and the Islamic World: Early Encounters', *The Historian*, 101 (spring 2009), pp. 19–21

Draper, Alfred, *The Amritsar Massacre: Twilight of the Raj*, Buchan & Enright, London, 1985

Dubow, Saul, 'Smuts, the United Nations and the Rhetoric of Race and Rights', *Journal of Contemporary History*, 43 (2008), pp. 45–73

Dupree, Marguerite (ed.), *Lancashire and Whitehall: The Diary of Raymond Streat*, vol. I: *1931–39*, Manchester University Press, Manchester, 1987

Dutt, R. Palme, *The Crisis of Britain and the British Empire*, Lawrence & Wishart, London, 1957

Eade, Charles (ed.), *Churchill, By His Contemporaries*, Reprint Society, London, 1955 (first published 1953)

Eden, Anthony, *The Reckoning*, Cassell, London, 1965

Eden, Clarissa, *A Memoir: From Churchill to Eden*, Weidenfeld & Nicolson, London, 2007

Egremont, Max, *Under Two Flags: The Life of Major-General Sir Edward Spears*, Weidenfeld & Nicolson, London, 1997

Elkins, Caroline, *Britain's Gulag: The Brutal End of Empire in Kenya*, Jonathan Cape, London, 2005

Emmert, Kirk, *Winston S. Churchill on Empire*, Carolina Academic Press, Durham, NC, 1989

Erickson, Edward J., 'Strength against Weakness: Ottoman Military Effectiveness at Gallipoli, 1915', *Journal of Military History*, 65 (2001), pp. 981–1011

Evans, Trefor E. (ed.), *The Killearn Diaries 1934–1946*, Sidgwick & Jackson, London, 1972

'Eyewitness', 'The Tirah Campaign', *Fortnightly Review*, 375 (1 March 1898), pp. 390–400

Faber, David, *Speaking for England: Leo, Julian and John Amery – The Tragedy of a Political Family*, The Free Press, London, 2005

Ferrell, R. H. (ed.), *The Eisenhower Diaries*, W. W. Norton & Co., New York, 1981

Ferrier, R. W., *The History of the British Petroleum Company*, vol. I: *The Developing Years, 1901–1932*, Cambridge University Press, Cambridge, 1982

Fincastle, Viscount and Eliott-Lockhart, P. C., *A Frontier Campaign: A Narrative of the Malakand and Buner Field Forces, 1897–8*, R. J. Leach & Co., London, 1990 (first published 1898)

Fischer, Louis, *The Life of Mahatma Gandhi*, HarperCollins, London, 1997 (first published 1952)

Foster, Roy, *Lord Randolph Churchill: A Political Life*, Clarendon Press, Oxford, 1981

Fox Bourne, H. R., *Blacks and Whites in South Africa: An Account of the Past Treatment and Present Condition of South African Natives under British and Boer Control*, 2nd edition, P. S. King & Son, London, 1900

Freudenberg, Graham, *Churchill and Australia*, Macmillan, Sydney, 2008

Fromkin, David, *A Peace to End All Peace: The Fall of the Ottoman Empire and the Creation of the Modern Middle East*, Henry Holt & Co., New York, 1989

Galbraith, John Kenneth, *Ambassador's Journal: A Personal Account of the Kennedy Years*, Hamish Hamilton, London, 1969

Gandhi, Mohandas K., *An Autobiography, or, The Story of My Experiments with Truth*, Penguin, London, 1982 (first published 1927–9)

——, *Collected Works*, 100 vols., Government of India Publications Division, New Delhi, 1960–94

Gardner, Richard N., *Sterling-Dollar Diplomacy in Current Perspective: The Origins and Prospects of Our International Economic Order*, Columbia University Press, New York, 1980

Gilbert, Martin, *Churchill and the Jews*, Simon & Schuster, London, 2007

——, *Churchill: A Life*, Heinemann, London, 1991

——, *Churchill's Political Philosophy*, Oxford University Press, Oxford, 1981

Gilmour, David, *Curzon*, John Murray, London, 1994

Gilmour, Ian, *Inside Right: A Study of Conservatism*, Hutchinson, London, 1977

Girvin, Brian, *The Emergency: Neutral Ireland, 1939–45*, Macmillan, 2006

Golland, Jim, *Not Winston, Just William? Winston Churchill at Harrow School*, The Herga Press, Harrow, 1988

Gooch, John (ed.), *The Boer War: Direction, Experience and Image*, Frank Cass, London, 2000

Gordon, Donald C., 'The Admiralty and Dominion Navies, 1902–1914', *Journal of Modern History*, 33 (1961), pp. 407–22

Graves, Robert, *Lawrence and the Arabs*, Jonathan Cape, London, 1927

Grayson, Richard S., 'Leo Amery's Imperialist Alternative to Appeasement in the 1930s', *Twentieth Century British History*, 17 (2006), pp. 489–515

Grimal, Henri, *Decolonization: The British, French, Dutch and Belgian Empires, 1919–1963*, Routledge & Kegan Paul, London, 1978

Haldane, Aylmer, *How We Escaped from Pretoria*, William Blackwood & Sons, Edinburgh and London, 1901

——, *A Soldier's Saga*, William Blackwood & Sons, Edinburgh and London, 1948

Halifax, Lord, *Fulness of Days*, Collins, London, 1957

Hamilton, Ian, *Listening for the Drums*, Faber & Faber, London, 1944

Hamilton, Ian B. M., *The Happy Warrior: A Life of General Sir Ian Hamilton*, Cassell, London, 1966

Harnetty, P., 'The Indian Cotton Duties Controversy, 1894–1896', *English Historical Review*, 77 (1962), pp. 684–702

Harriman, W. Averell and Abel, Elie, *Special Envoy to Churchill and Stalin, 1941–1946*, Random House, New York, 1975

Harrod, R. F., *The Prof: A Personal Memoir of Lord Cherwell*, London, Macmillan, 1959

Harvey, John (ed.), *The Diplomatic Diaries of Oliver Harvey, 1937–1940*, Collins, London, 1978

——, *The War Diaries of Oliver Harvey 1941–1945*, Collins, London, 1978

Hassall, Christopher, *Edward Marsh: Patron of the Arts: A Biography*, Longman's, London, 1959

Herman, Arthur, *Gandhi & Churchill: The Epic Rivalry that Destroyed an Empire and Forged Our Age*, Bantam Books, New York, 2008

Hitler, Adolf, *Mein Kampf*, Hutchinson, London, 1969 (first published in English 1933)

Howson, Susan and Moggridge, Donald (eds.), *The Collected Papers of James Meade*, vol. IV: *The Cabinet Office Diary, 1944–46*, Unwin Hyman, London, 1990

Hughes, W. M., *The Splendid Adventure: A Review of Empire Relations Within and Without the Commonwealth of Britannic Nations*, Ernest Benn, London, 1929

Hulme, John, 'Winston Churchill, MP: A Study and . . . a Story', *Temple Magazine*, 5 (Jan. 1901), pp. 291–6

Huxley, Elspeth, *White Man's Country: Lord Delamere and the Making of Kenya*, vol. I: *1870–1914* and vol. II: *1914–1931*, Chatto & Windus, London, 1953 (first published 1935)

Hyam, Ronald, *Britain's Declining Empire: The Road to Decolonisation, 1918–1968*, Cambridge University Press, Cambridge, 2006

——, *Elgin and Churchill at the Colonial Office, 1905–1908: The Watershed of the Empire-Commonwealth*, Macmillan, London, 1968

——, 'Winston Churchill before 1914', *Historical Journal*, 12 (1969), pp. 164–73

Hyam, Ronald and Henshaw, Peter, *The Lion and the Springbok: Britain and South Africa since the Boer War*, Cambridge University Press, Cambridge, 2003

Hynd, Stacey, 'Imperial Gallows: Capital Punishment, Violence and Colonial Rule in Britain's African Territories, c. 1903–68', unpublished D.Phil. thesis, University of Oxford, 2007

Idemili, Sam O., 'What the *West African Pilot* Did in the Movement for Nigerian Nationalism between 1937 and 1957', *Black American Literature Forum*, 12 (1978), pp. 84–91

Ismay, Lord, *The Memoirs of Lord Ismay*, Heinemann, London, 1960

Jablonsky, David, 'Churchill's Initial Experience with the British Conduct of Small Wars: India and the Sudan, 1897–98', *Small Wars and Insurgencies*, 11 (2000), pp. 1–25

Jackson, Ashley, *The British Empire and the Second World War*, Hambledon Continuum, London, 2006

——, 'Tswana War Poetry: Part One', *Botswana Notes and Records*, 27 (1995), pp. 97–110

James, Lawrence, *The Golden Warrior: The Life and Legend of Lawrence of Arabia*, revised edition, Abacus, London, 1995

——, *Raj: The Making and Unmaking of British India*, Abacus, London, 1998 (first published 1997)

Jenkins, Roy, *Churchill*, Macmillan, London, 2001

Kapuscinski, Ryszard *The Shadow of the Sun: My African Life*, Penguin, London, 2002 (first published 2001)

Kaul, Chandrika (ed.), *Media and the British Empire*, Macmillan, Basingstoke, 2006

Kennedy, Greg and Neilson, Keith (eds.), *Far-Flung Lines: Essays on Imperial Defence*, Frank Cass, London, 1997

Kersaudy, François, *Churchill and de Gaulle*, Collins, London, 1981

Kilson, Martin L., Jr., 'Land and the Kikuyu: A Study of the Relationship between Land and Kikuyu Political Movements', *Journal of Negro History*, 40 (1955), pp. 103–53

Kimball, Warren F. (ed.), *Churchill & Roosevelt: The Complete Correspondence*, vol. I: *Alliance Emerging, October 1933–November 1942*, Princeton University Press, Princeton, NJ, 1984

——, *Churchill and Roosevelt: The Complete Correspondence*, vol. II: *Alliance Forged, November 1942–February 1944*, Princeton University Press, Princeton, NJ, 1984

Koebner, Richard and Schmidt, Helmut Dan, *Imperialism: The Story and Significance of a Political Word, 1840–1960*, Cambridge University Press, Cambridge, 1964

Labour Party Annual Conference Report, Labour Party, London, 1940

Lal, Hira Seth, *Churchill on India: Let His Past Records Speak*, First National Publishers, Lahore, 1942

Larres, Klaus, *Churchill's Cold War: The Politics of Personal Diplomacy*, Yale University Press, New Haven and London, 2002

Lawlor, Sheila, 'Greece, March 1941: The Politics of British Military Intervention', *Historical Journal*, 25 (1982), pp. 933–46

Lawrence, M. R. (ed.), *The Home Letters of T. E. Lawrence and his Brothers*, Basil Blackwell, Oxford, 1954

Layton-Henry, Zig, *The Politics of Immigration: Immigration, 'Race' and 'Race' Relations in Post-war Britain*, Blackwell, Oxford, 1992

Leslie, Anita, *Cousin Clare: The Tempestuous Career of Clare Sheridan*, Hutchinson, London, 1976

Lloyd, Clem and Hall, Richard (eds.), *Backroom Briefings: John Curtin's War*, National Library of Australia, Canberra, 1997

Lochner, Louis P., *The Goebbels Diaries*, Hamish Hamilton, London, 1948

Longford, Earl of, and O'Neill, Thomas P., *Eamon De Valera*, Hutchinson, London, 1970

Louis, Wm. Roger, *Imperialism at Bay: The United States and the Decolonization of the British Empire, 1941–1945*, Oxford University Press, Oxford, 1977

——, 'Leo Amery and the Post-War World, 1945–55', *Journal of Imperial and Commonwealth History*, 30 (2002), pp. 71–90

——, *In the Name of God, Go! Leo Amery and the British Empire in the Age of Churchill*, W. W. Norton & Co., New York, 1992

Macaulay, Lord, *Critical and Historical Essays*, vol. II, Longmans, Green & Co., London, 1866

MacDonald, Malcolm, *Titans & Others*, Collins, London, 1972

Mackay, James, *Michael Collins: A Life*, Mainstream Publishing, Edinburgh, 1996

MacKenzie, John (ed.), *Imperialism and Popular Culture*, Manchester University Press, Manchester, 1986

Macleod, Roderick and Kelly, Denis (eds.), *The Ironside Diaries, 1937–1940*, Constable, London, 1962

Macmillan, Harold, *Tides of Fortune, 1945–1955*, London, Macmillan, 1969

Makovsky, Michael, *Churchill's Promised Land: Zionism and Statecraft*, Yale University Press, New Haven, 2007

Mandela, Nelson, *Long Walk to Freedom*, Abacus, London, 1995 (first published 1994)

Mangan, J. A. *'Benefits Bestowed': Education and British Imperialism*, Manchester University Press, Manchester, 1988

Mansergh, Nicholas, *The Commonwealth Experience*, Weidenfeld & Nicolson, London, 1969

Marchant, James (ed.), *Winston Spencer Churchill: Servant of Crown and Commonwealth*, Cassell, London, 1954

Marks, Shula, 'White Masculinity: Jan Smuts, Race and the South African War', *Proceedings of the British Academy*, 111 (2001), pp. 199–223

Marsh, Edward, *A Number of People: A Book of Reminiscences*, William Heinemann, London, 1939

Marsh, John, *The Young Winston Churchill*, Evans Brothers Ltd, 1955

Marsh, Peter T., *Joseph Chamberlain: Entrepreneur in Politics*, Yale University Press, New Haven and London, 1994

Martin, A. W. and Hardy, Patsy (eds.), *Dark and Hurrying Days: Menzies' 1941 Diary*, National Library of Australia, Canberra, 1993

Matthews, Joseph J., 'Heralds of the Imperialistic Wars', *Military Affairs*, 19 (1955), pp. 145–55

Matthews, Kevin, *Fatal Influence: The Impact of Ireland on British Politics, 1920–1925*, University College Dublin Press, Dublin, 2004

Maurer, John H. (ed.), *Churchill and Strategic Dilemmas before the World Wars*, Frank Cass, London, 2003

Maurice, F. and Arthur, George, *The Life of Lord Wolseley*, Doubleday, Page & Co., New York, 1924

Maxon, Robert M., 'The Devonshire Declaration: The Myth of Missionary Intervention', *History in Africa*, 18 (1991), pp. 259–70

Maxse, F. I., 'Inaccurate History', *National Review*, 35 (1900), pp. 262–75

Mayo, Katherine, *Mother India*, Jonathan Cape, London, 1927

Mazower, Mark, *Hitler's Empire: Nazi Rule in Occupied Europe*, Allen Lane, London, 2008

Mazrui, Ali A., *Power, Politics and the African Condition: Collected Essays*, vol. III, Africa World Press, Trenton, NJ, 2004

McDevitt, Patrick F., *May the Best Man Win: Sport, Masculinity, and Nationalism in Great Britain and the Empire, 1880–1935*, Macmillan, New York, 2004

McEwen, J. M., *The Riddell Diaries, 1908–1923*, Athlone Press, London and
   Atlantic Highlands, NJ, 1986

McGilligan, Patrick, *Backstory 2: Interviews with Screenwriters of the 1940s and 1950s*,
   University of California Press, Berkeley, 1991

McKitterick, R. and Quinault, R. (eds.), *Edward Gibbon and Empire*, Cambridge
   University Press, Cambridge, 1997

McMenamin, Michael and Zoller, Curt J., *Becoming Winston Churchill: The Untold
   Story of Young Winston and His American Mentor*, Greenwood World Publishing,
   Oxford/Westport CT, 2007

Megahey, Alan, *Humphrey Gibbs: Beleaguered Governor: Southern Rhodesia, 1929–69*,
   Macmillan, Basingstoke, 1998

Menon, K. P. S., *The Flying Troika*, Oxford University Press, London, 1963

Middlemas, Keith (ed.), *Thomas Jones, Whitehall Diary*, vol. III: *Ireland 1918–1925*,
   Oxford University Press, London, 1971

Moggridge, Donald (ed.), *The Collected Writings of John Maynard Keynes*, vol. XXIV:
   Activities, 1944–1946: The Transition to Peace, Macmillan, London, 1979

Montague Browne, Anthony, *Long Sunset: Memoirs of Winston Churchill's Last Private
   - Secretary*, Cassell, London, 1995

Moon, Penderel (ed.), *Wavell: The Viceroy's Journal*, Oxford University Press,
   Karachi, 1997

Moore, R. J., *Churchill, Cripps and India, 1939–1945*, Clarendon Press, Oxford, 1979

Moran, Lord, *Winston Churchill: The Struggle for Survival, 1940–1965*, Constable,
   London, 1966

Morgan, D. J., *The Official History of Colonial Development*, vol. V: *Guidance Towards
   Self-Government in British Colonies, 1941–1971*, Macmillan, London, 1980

Morgan, Philip D. and Hawkins, Sean (eds.), *Black Experience and the Empire*,
   Oxford University Press, Oxford, 2004

Morgan, Ted, *Churchill: Young Man in a Hurry, 1874–1915*, Simon & Schuster,
   New York, 1982

Muldoon, Andrew ' "An Unholy Row in Lancashire": The Textile Lobby,
   Conservative Politics, and Indian Policy, 1931–1935', *Twentieth Century British
   History*, 14 (2003), pp. 93–111

Murphy, Philip, *Alan Lennox-Boyd: A Biography*, I. B. Tauris, London, 1999

Nehru, Jawaharlal, *The Discovery of India*, Meridian Books, London, 1946

——, *Selected Works of Jawaharlal Nehru*, first series, 15 vols., Orient Longman/B.
   R. Publishing Corporation, New Delhi, 1972–82

Nevinson, Henry W., *Last Changes, Last Chances*, Nisbet & Co. Ltd, London, 1928

Nicholas, H. G. (ed.), *Washington Despatches, 1941–45: Weekly Political Reports from
   the British Embassy*, University of Chicago Press, Chicago, 1981

Nicolson, Nigel (ed.), *Harold Nicolson: Diaries and Letters, 1930–1939*, Collins,
   London, 1966

——, *Harold Nicolson: Diaries and Letters 1939–1945*, Collins, London

Nkrumah, Kwame, *The Autobiography of Kwame Nkrumah*, Thomas Nelson & Sons,
   Edinburgh, 1957

——, *Neo-Colonialism: The Last Stage of Imperialism*, Thomas Nelson & Sons, London, 1965

Norwich, John Julius (ed.), *The Duff Cooper Diaries, 1915–1951*, Weidenfeld & Nicolson, London, 2005

Ó Gráda, Cormac, 'The Ripple that Drowns? Twentieth-century Famines in China and India as Economic History', *Economic History Review*, 61 (2008), pp. 5–37

Ohlinger, Gustav, 'Winston Spencer Churchill: A Midnight Interview', *Michigan Quarterly Review*, 5 (1966), pp. 75–9

Olson, Robert, 'The Churchill–Cox Correspondence Regarding the Creation of the State of Iraq: Consequences for British Policy Towards the Nationalist Turkish Government, 1921–1923', *International Journal of Turkish Studies*, 5 (1991), pp. 121–36

Onslow, Sue, ' "Battlelines for Suez": The Abadan Crisis of 1951 and the Formation of the Suez Group', *Contemporary British History*, 17 (2003), pp. 1–28

Orwell, Sonia and Angus, Ian (eds.), *The Collected Essays, Journalism and Letters of George Orwell*, vol. II: *My Country Right or Left, 1940–1943*, Secker & Warburg, London, 1968

Owen, Nicholas, 'The Conservative Party and Indian Independence, 1945–1947', *Historical Journal*, 46 (2003), pp. 403–36

Pakenham, Thomas, *The Boer War*, Weidenfeld & Nicolson, London, 1979

Palmer, Alan, *Dictionary of the British Empire and Commonwealth*, John Murray, London, 1996

Parker, R. A. C., *The Second World War: A Short History*, Oxford University Press, Oxford, 1997 (first published 1989)

Parris, Matthew and Mason, Phil, *Read My Lips: A Treasury of Things Politicians Wish They Hadn't Said*, Penguin, Harmondsworth, 1997 (first published 1996)

Parthasarathi, G. (ed.), *Jawaharlal Nehru: Letters to Chief Ministers, 1947–1964*, vol. III: *1952–1954*, Jawaharlal Nehru Memorial Fund, New Delhi, 1987

Pearce, Robert (ed.), *Patrick Gordon Walker: Political Diaries, 1932–1971*, The Historians' Press, London, 1991

Pelling, Henry, *Winston Churchill*, Macmillan, London, 1974

Penrose, E. F., *Economic Planning for the Peace*, Princeton University Press, Princeton NJ, 1953

Perham, Margery, *Lugard: The Years of Authority, 1898–1945*, Collins, London, 1960

Perkins, Frances, *The Roosevelt I Knew*, HarperColophon, New York, 1964 (first published 1946)

Phelan, Jim, *Churchill Can Unite Ireland*, Victor Gollancz, London, 1940

Phillips, William, *Ventures in Diplomacy*, John Murray, London, 1955

Pimlott, Ben (ed.), *The Second World War Diary of Hugh Dalton, 1940–45*, Jonathan Cape, London, 1986

Pinney, Thomas (ed.), *The Letters of Rudyard Kipling*, vol. IV: *1911–19*, Macmillan,

Basingstoke, 1999; vol. V: *1920–30*, Macmillan, Basingstoke, 2004; vol. VI: *1931–36*, Macmillan, Basingstoke, 2004

Pók, Attila (ed.), *The Fabric of Modern Europe: Essays in Honour of Éva Haraszti Taylor*, Astra Press, Nottingham, 1999

Pollock, John, *Kitchener*, Constable, London, 1998

Ponting, Clive, *Churchill*, Sinclair-Stevenson, London, 1994

Porath, Yehoshua,'Weizmann, Churchill and the "Philby Plan", 1937–1943', *Studies in Zionism*, 5 (1984), pp. 239–72

Porter, Bernard, *The Absent-Minded Imperialists: Empire, Society, and Culture in Britain*, Oxford University Press, Oxford, 2004

Pottle, Mark (ed.), *Champion Redoubtable: The Diaries and Letters of Violet Bonham Carter, 1914–1945*, Weidenfeld & Nicolson, London, 1998

——, *Daring to Hope: The Diaries and Letters of Violet Bonham Carter, 1946–1969*, Weidenfeld & Nicolson, London, 2000

Price, M. Philips, *My Three Revolutions*, George Allen & Unwin, 1969

Pugh, Martin, 'Lancashire, Cotton, and Indian Reform: Conservative Controversies in the 1930s', *Twentieth Century British History*, 15 (2004), pp. 143–51

Quinault, Roland, 'Churchill and Black Africa', *History Today*, June 2005, pp. 31–6

Ramanathan, Vaidehi, 'Gandhi, Non-Cooperation, and Socio-civic Education in Gujarat, India: Harnessing the Vernaculars', *Journal of Language, Identity & Education*, 5 (2006), pp. 229–50

Ramsden, John, *Man of the Century: Winston Churchill and His Legend since 1945*, HarperCollins, London, 2002

Rathbone, Richard, 'A Murder in the Colonial Gold Coast: Law and Politics in the 1940s', *Journal of African History*, 30 (1989), pp. 445–61

Reade, Winwood, *The Martyrdom of Man*, Watts & Co., London, 1934 (first published 1872)

Readman, Paul, 'The Conservative Party, Patriotism, and British Politics: The Case of the General Election of 1900', *Journal of British Studies*, 40 (2001), pp. 107–45

Reynolds, David, *In Command of History: Churchill Fighting and Writing the Second World War*, Allen Lane, London, 2004

——, *Rich Relations: The American Occupation of Britain, 1942–1945*, HarperCollins, London, 1996

Rhodes James, Robert, *Victor Cazalet: A Portrait*, Hamish Hamilton, London, 1976

Rhodes James, Robert (ed.), *'Chips': The Diaries of Sir Henry Channon*, Weidenfeld & Nicolson, London, 1993 (first published 1967)

——, *Memoirs of a Conservative: J. C. C. Davidson's Memoirs and Papers, 1910–37*, Weidenfeld & Nicolson, London, 1969

——, *Winston S. Churchill: His Complete Speeches, 1897–1963*, 8 vols., Chelsea House, New York, 1974

Roberts, Andrew, *Eminent Churchillians*, Weidenfeld & Nicolson, London, 1994

Roberts, Brian, *Churchills in Africa*, Hamish Hamilton, London, 1970

Roosevelt, Kermit, *Countercoup: The Struggle for the Control of Iran*, McGraw-Hill, New York, 1979

Rose, Norman, *Churchill: An Unruly Life*, Simon & Schuster, London, 1994

Rosebery, Earl of, *Lord Randolph Churchill*, Arthur L. Humphreys, London, 1906

Rubinstein, William D.,'The Secret of Leopold Amery', *Historical Research*, 73 (2000), pp. 175–96

Russell, Douglas S., *Winston Churchill: Soldier*, Conway, London, 2006 (first published 2005),

Sandys, Celia, *Churchill Wanted Dead or Alive*, HarperCollins, London, 1999

Satre, Lowell J., 'St John Brodrick and Army Reform, 1901–1903', *Journal of British Studies*, 15 (1976), pp. 117–39

Sayer, Derek, 'British Reaction to the Amritsar Massacre, 1919–1920', *Past and Present*, 131 (1991), pp. 130–64

Segev, Tom, *One Palestine, Complete: Jews and Arabs under the British Mandate*, Little, Brown, London, 2000

Self, Robert (ed.), *The Correspondence of Sir Austen Chamberlain with His Sisters Hilda and Ida, 1916–1937*, Cambridge University Press for the Royal Historical Society, Cambridge, 1995

——, *The Neville Chamberlain Diary Letters*, vol. II: *The Reform Years, 1921–1927*, Ashgate, Aldershot, 2000,

Sen, Amartya, *Poverty and Famines: An Essay on Entitlement and Deprivation*, Clarendon Press, Oxford, 1981

Sheean, Vincent, *Between the Thunder and the Sun*, Random House, New York, 1943

Sherwood, Robert E., *The White House Papers of Harry L. Hopkins*, vol. I: *September 1939–January 1942*, Eyre & Spottiswoode, London, 1948

Shuckburgh, Evelyn, *Descent to Suez: Diaries, 1951–56*, Weidenfeld & Nicolson, London, 1986

Sinha, Mrinalini (ed.), *Katherine Mayo: Selections from 'Mother India'*, Kali for Women, New Delhi, 1998

Smart, Nick (ed.), *The Diaries and Letters of Robert Bernays, 1932–1939*, Edwin Mellen Press, Lewiston/Queenston/Lampeter, 1996

Smith, David C., *H. G. Wells: Desperately Mortal: A Biography*, Yale University Press, New Haven and London, 1986

——, 'Winston Churchill and H. G. Wells: Edwardians in the Twentieth Century', *Cahiers Victoriens et Edouardien*, 30 (1989), pp. 93–116

Smuts, Jan, *Selections from the Smuts Papers*, vol. I: *June 1886–May 1902*, ed. W. K. Hancock and Jean van der Poel, Cambridge University Press, Cambridge, 1966

——, *Selections from the Smuts Papers*, vol. II: *June 1902–May 1910*, ed. W. K. Hancock and Jean van der Poel, Cambridge University Press, Cambridge, 1966

——, *Selections from the Smuts Papers*, vol. VI: *December 1934–August 1945*, ed. Jean van der Poel, Cambridge University Press, Cambridge, 1973

——, *Selections from the Smuts Papers*, vol. VII: *August 1945–October 1950*, ed. Jean van der Poel, Cambridge University Press, Cambridge, 1973

Soames, Mary (ed.), *Speaking for Themselves: The Personal Letters of Winston and Clementine Churchill*, Doubleday, London, 1998

Somervell, Robert, *Chapters of Autobiography*, Faber & Faber, London, 1935

Spiers, Edward M. (ed.), *Sudan: The Reconquest Reappraised*, Frank Cass, London, 1998

Stafford, David, *Churchill and Secret Service*, Abacus, London, 2000 (first published 1997)

Stearn, Roger T., 'G. W. Steevens and the Message of Empire', *Journal of Imperial and Commonwealth History*, 17 (1989), pp. 210–31

Steevens, G. W., 'From the New Gibbon', *Blackwood's Edinburgh Magazine*, 165 (1899), pp. 241–9

——, *With Kitchener to Khartum*, Thomas Nelson & Sons, London, n.d. (first published 1898)

Stewart, Andrew, *Empire Lost: Britain, the Dominions and the Second World War*, Continuum, London, 2008

Surridge, Keith, *Managing the South African War, 1899–1902: Politicians v. Generals*, Royal Historical Society, London, 1998

Taylor, Fred (ed.), *The Goebbels Diaries, 1939–1941*, Hamish Hamilton, London, 1982

Taylor, Rex, *Michael Collins*, Hutchinson, London, 1958

Taylor, Robert H., 'Politics in Late Colonial Burma: The Case of U Saw', *Modern Asian Studies*, 10 (1976), pp. 161–93

Thompson, Andrew S., *Imperial Britain: The Empire in British Politics, c. 1880–1932*, Longman, Harlow, 2000

Thorpe, D. R., *Eden: The Life and Times of Anthony Eden, First Earl of Avon, 1897–1977*, Chatto & Windus, London, 2003

Thuku, Harry, *An Autobiography*, Oxford University Press, Nairobi, 1970

Tidrick, Kathryn, *Gandhi: A Political and Spiritual Life*, I. B. Tauris, London and New York, 2006

Tinker, Hugh, 'Burma's Struggle for Independence: The Transfer of Power Thesis Re-Examined', *Modern Asian Studies*, 20 (1986), pp. 461–81

Tomes, Jason, *Balfour and Foreign Policy: The International Thought of a Conservative Statesman*, Cambridge, Cambridge University Press, 1997

Tomlinson, B. R., *The Political Economy of the Raj, 1914–1947: The Economics of Decolonization in India*, Macmillan, London, 1979

Toye, John, *Keynes on Population*, Oxford University Press, Oxford, 2000

Toye, Richard, 'The Attlee Government, the Imperial Preference System, and the Creation of the GATT', *English Historical Review*, 118 (2003), pp. 912–39

——, 'Churchill and Britain's "Financial Dunkirk"', *Twentieth Century British History*, 15 (2004), pp. 329–60

——, 'The Churchill Syndrome: Reputational Entrepreneurship and the Rhetoric of Foreign Policy since 1945', *British Journal of Politics and International Relations*, 10 (2008), pp. 364–78

——, *Lloyd George and Churchill: Rivals for Greatness*, Macmillan, London, 2007

Trapido, Stanley, 'African Divisional Politics in the Cape Colony, 1884 to 1910', *Journal of African History*, 9 (1968), pp. 79–98

Trentmann, Frank, *Free Trade Nation: Commerce, Consumption, and Civil Society in Modern Britain*, Oxford University Press, Oxford, 2008

Trevor-Roper, H. R. (ed.), *Hitler's Table Talk, 1941–1944: His Private Conversations*, Phoenix Press, London, 2000 (first published Weidenfeld & Nicolson, London, 1953; repr. 1973)

Turner, W. Burghardt and Turner, Joyce Moore (eds.), *Richard B. Moore, Caribbean Militant in Harlem: Collected Writings, 1920–1972*, Indiana University Press, Bloomington and Indianapolis, 1992

Tvedt, Terje, *The River Nile in the Age of the British: Political Ecology and the Quest for Economic Power*, I. B. Tauris, London, 2004

Venkataramani, M. S. and Shrivastava, B. K., *Roosevelt, Gandhi, Churchill: America and the Last Phase of India's Freedom Struggle*, Sangam Books, London, 1997 (first published 1983)

Vernon, Betty D., *Ellen Wilkinson*, Croom Helm, London, 1982

Warwick, Peter, *Black People and the South African War, 1899–1902*, Cambridge University Press, Cambridge, 1983

Webster, Wendy, *Englishness and Empire, 1939–1965*, Oxford University Press, Oxford, 2005

Weigold, Auriol, *Churchill, Roosevelt and India: Propaganda During World War II*, Routledge, London, 2008

Welldon, J. E. C., *Forty Years On: Light and Shadows (A Bishop's Reflections on Life)*, Ivor Nicolson & Watson, London, 1935

——, 'The Imperial Aspects of Education', *Proceedings of the Royal Colonial Institute*, 26 (1894–5), pp. 322–39

——, *Recollections and Reflections*, Cassell, London, 1915

Wells, H. G., 'The Future of the British Empire', *Empire Review*, 38 (1923), pp. 1071–9

——, *A Year of Prophesying*, T. Fisher Unwin, London, 1924

West, Nigel (ed.), *The Guy Liddell Diaries*, vol. I: *1939–1942: MI5's Director of Counter-Espionage in World War II*, Routledge, London, 2005

West, W. J. (ed.), *George Orwell: The War Commentaries*, Penguin, Harmondsworth, 1987 (first published 1985)

Williams, Francis, *Nothing So Strange: An Autobiography*, Cassell, London, 1970

——, *A Prime Minister Remembers: The War and Post-War Memoirs of Rt. Hon Earl Attlee*, London, Heinemann, 1961

Williamson, Philip, 'Christian conservatives and the totalitarian challenge, 1933–40', *English Historical Review*, 115 (2000), pp. 607–42

Williamson, Philip and Baldwin, Edward (eds.), *Baldwin Papers: A Conservative Statesman, 1908–1947*, Cambridge University Press, Cambridge, 2004

Wilson, Geoffrey, *My Working Life* (unpublished memoirs)

Woods, Frederick (ed.), *Young Winston's Wars: The Original Despatches of Winston S. Churchill, War Correspondent, 1897–1900*, Leo Cooper, London, 1972

Young, Kenneth, *Churchill and Beaverbrook: A Study in Friendship and Politics*, Eyre & Spottiswoode, London, 1966

—— (ed.), *The Diaries of Sir Bruce Lockhart*, vol. I: *1915–1938*, Macmillan, London, 1973

Zulfo, 'Ismat Hasan, *Karari: The Sudanese Account of the Battle of Omdurman*, Frederick Warne, London, 1980

Index

Picture Acknowledgements

Getty: 1, 7, 12, 13, 14, 19–22, 29, 34–36

Mary Evans Picture Library: 2, 3, 4, 6, 8, 10, 11, 17,

National Portrait Gallery, London: 5

Private Collection: 9

Illustrated London News Ltd/Mary Evans Picture Library: 15

Gertrude Bell Archive: 16

Solo Syndication/Associated Newspapers Ltd: 18, 33

Australian War Memorial: 23 (negative number: 006414),
24 (Unknown 'Let us go forward together', c.1940,
photolithograph, 76.4 x 51.8 cm, negative number: ARTV02119),
25 (negative number: 013354), 26 (negative number: PO2366_002),
28 (negative number: 128501), 30 (negative number: MED2037)

Kind permission of the John Curtin Prime Ministerial Library
and the Curtin Family: 27, 31

Science Museum/SSPL: 32, 37